Exam Ref 70-341
Core Solutions of
Microsoft Exchange
Server 2013

Paul Robichaux
Bhargav Shukla

PUBLISHED BY
Microsoft Press
A Division of Microsoft Corporation
One Microsoft Way
Redmond, Washington 98052-6399

Library of Congress Control Number: 2014951861
ISBN: 978-0-7356-9724-9

Printed and bound in the United States of America.

First Printing

Microsoft Press books are available through booksellers and distributors worldwide. If you need support related to this book, email Microsoft Press Book Support at mspinput@microsoft.com. Please tell us what you think of this book at *http://aka.ms/tellpress*.

Acquisitions Editor: Karen Szall
Developmental Editor: Karen Szall
Editorial Production: Troy Mott, Ellie Volckhausen
Technical Reviewers: Charlie Russel; Technical Review services provided
by Content Master, a member of CM Group, Ltd.
Copyeditor: Marcia Baker
Indexer: Julie Grady
Cover: Twist Creative • Seattle

Contents at a glance

Contents

What do you think of this book? We want to hear from you!

Microsoft is interested in hearing your feedback so we can continually improve our
books and learning resources for you. To participate in a brief online survey, please visit:

www.microsoft.com/learning/booksurvey/

What do you think of this book? We want to hear from you!

Microsoft is interested in hearing your feedback so we can continually improve our
books and learning resources for you. To participate in a brief online survey, please visit:

www.microsoft.com/learning/booksurvey/

Introduction

This book is written for IT Professionals who want to earn MCSE: Messaging certification. This certification includes four exams:

- 70-341 Core Solutions of Microsoft Exchange Server 2013
- 70-342 Advanced Solutions of Microsoft Exchange Server 2013
- 70-346 Managing Office 365 Identities and Requirements
- 70-347 Enabling Office 365 Services

Exam 70-341, the focus of this book, is intended for IT Professionals who have experience managing Exchange Server 2013 environment. This book covers all four exam domains and all related objectives for each domain. The domains and objectives measure the core knowledge needed to administer an Exchange Server 2013 infrastructure.

While the book covers details of each exam domain and objective, it does not intend to teach its readers Exchange Server 2013 from scratch. The book assumes that the reader is an experienced Exchange 2013 administrator who is looking to enhance their understanding of Exchange Server 2013 and prepare for exam 70-341.

This book covers every exam objective, but it does not cover every exam question. Only the Microsoft exam team has access to the exam questions themselves and Microsoft regularly adds new questions to the exam, making it impossible to cover specific questions. You should consider this book a supplement to your relevant real-world experience and other study materials. If you encounter a topic in this book that you do not feel completely comfortable with, use the links you'll find in text to find more information and take the time to research and study the topic. Great information is available on MSDN, TechNet, and in blogs and forums.

Microsoft certifications

Microsoft certifications distinguish you by proving your command of a broad set of skills and experience with current Microsoft products and technologies. The exams and corresponding certifications are developed to validate your mastery of critical competencies as you design and develop, or implement and support, solutions with Microsoft products and technologies both on-premises and in the cloud. Certification brings a variety of benefits to the individual and to employers and organizations.

> **MORE INFO**   **ALL MICROSOFT CERTIFICATIONS**
>
> For information about Microsoft certifications, including a full list of available certifications, go to *http://www.microsoft.com/learning/en/us/certification/cert-default.aspx*.

Acknowledgments

Bhargav Shukla   As any author can attest, turning their knowledge and writing into a published book is never a task a single person can take on. I'd like to start with my sincere thanks to Karen Szall and team at Microsoft Press who kept us honest, provided valuable guidelines, constant feedback and important edits that can turn our technical mumblings into something a bit more consumable for the readers. I'd also like to thank my mentors and friends who have never ceased to amaze me with their deep knowledge of Exchange server. Over past 20 years, I have only learnt more every day. I could never be an Exchange expert without their help and willingness to share. Huge thanks to all of you who I have learnt from over the years! And for my ability to write this book, it took some determination and commitment. Nights, weekends and holidays were a blur and spending time with me was luxury at times for my family. Without their support, understanding and encouragement, I could have never finished writing this book on time! My sincere thanks to them!

Paul Robichaux   All the books I've worked on during my career have shared similarities, but each one is unique too. I share Bhargav's appreciation for the large number of people who have mentored and taught me over the years. Karen Szall ably guided the Microsoft Press team into taking our text and turning it into a polished finished product, and we benefited greatly from the expert technical review of Microsoft certification guru Charlie Russel.

Free ebooks from Microsoft Press

From technical overviews to in-depth information on special topics, the free ebooks from Microsoft Press cover a wide range of topics. These ebooks are available in PDF, EPUB, and Mobi for Kindle formats, ready for you to download at:

http://aka.ms/mspressfree

Check back often to see what is new!

Errata, updates, & book support

We've made every effort to ensure the accuracy of this book and its companion content. You can access updates to this book—in the form of a list of submitted errata and their related corrections—at:

http://aka.ms/ER341/errata

If you discover an error that is not already listed, please submit it to us at the same page.

If you need additional support, email Microsoft Press Book Support at *mspinput@microsoft.com.*

Please note that product support for Microsoft software and hardware is not offered through the previous addresses. For help with Microsoft software or hardware, go to *http://support.microsoft.com.*

We want to hear from you

At Microsoft Press, your satisfaction is our top priority, and your feedback our most valuable asset. Please tell us what you think of this book at:

http://aka.ms/tellpress

The survey is short, and we read every one of your comments and ideas. Thanks in advance for your input!

Stay in touch

Let's keep the conversation going! We're on Twitter: *http://twitter.com/MicrosoftPress.*

Preparing for the exam

Microsoft certification exams are a great way to build your resume and let the world know about your level of expertise. Certification exams validate your on-the-job experience and product knowledge. Although there is no substitute for on-the-job experience, preparation through study and hands-on practice can help you prepare for the exam. We recommend that you augment your exam preparation plan by using a combination of available study materials and courses. For example, you might use the Exam ref and another study guide for your "at home" preparation, and take a Microsoft Official Curriculum course for the classroom experience. Choose the combination that you think works best for you.

Note that this Exam Ref is based on publicly available information about the exam and the author's experience. To safeguard the integrity of the exam, authors do not have access to the live exam.

CHAPTER 1

Install, configure, and manage the mailbox role

The mailbox server role in Exchange 2013 hosts mailbox databases and other items, such as Client Access protocols, Transport service and Unified Messaging. All processing of a specific mailbox takes place on the Mailbox server hosting an active copy of the mailbox. Client connectivity is handled by the Client Access role, which can be co-located on the same server. But it only proxies the connections to Mailbox server components for further processing and rendering of the mailbox data being requested.

The Mailbox role is also expanded in Exchange 2013 to include Public Folders. Public Folders do not use dedicated public folder databases and are now stored in specially designed mailboxes store both public folder hierarchy and public folder content. This allows for public folders to take advantage of the existing high availability and storage technologies in use by mailbox databases.

> **IMPORTANT**
> **Have you read page xvii?**
> It contains valuable information regarding the skills you need to pass the exam.

With Exchange 2013, there is higher focus on service availability, easier management, and reduced costs. To achieve such goals, managed availability is introduced to provide internal monitoring. The *internal monitoring* of components is aimed at preventing failures, proactively restoring services, and initiating server failovers automatically or alerting administrators to take action. Automation, coupled with managed availability, is driven by the focus on measuring quality and the continuous availability of service to end users, instead of focusing on the uptime of individual components.

Simplification and automation have also been integrated in other database functions. When using JBOD configuration to achieve cost efficiency, disk failures in previous versions meant manual intervention to maintain healthy copies of mailbox databases. Automatic reseed functionality allows for automatic database reseeding on a spare disk on the same server. Failures affecting resiliency or redundancy, such as long I/O times or excessive memory consumption by replication processes, are addressed by automatically rebooting the server. While this might sound like a drastic measure, it doesn't affect service availability because the assumption is that redundancy is provided using Database Availability Groups (DAGs) and other high availability features provided by Exchange 2013.

The network configuration of DAGs has also been simplified by automatically configuring DAG networks. DAGs can also distinguish between the Messaging Application Programming

Interface (MAPI) and Replication networks, configuring them automatically. This greatly simplifies the setup, thus protecting against errors when configuring DAG networks manually.

> *NOTE* **MANUAL VS. AUTOMATIC CONFIGURATION OF DAG NETWORKS**
>
> While Exchange 2013 functionality makes setup easier by configuring DAG networks automatically, in complex networks you might need to configure DAG networks manually. You might also need to troubleshoot DAG networks if errors are encountered and if replication or MAPI traffic is affected. It is important for you to pay attention to cmdlets and parameters that enable you to configure DAG networks manually.

Objectives in this chapter:

- Objective 1.1: Plan the mailbox role
- Objective 1.2: Configure and manage the mailbox role
- Objective 1.3: Deploy and manage high availability solutions for the mailbox role
- Objective 1.4: Monitor and troubleshoot the mailbox role
- Objective 1.5: Develop backup and recovery solutions for the mailbox role and public folders
- Objective 1.6: Create and configure mail-enabled objects
- Objective 1.7: Manage mail-enabled object permissions

Objective 1.1: Plan the mailbox role

Deploying the mailbox role requires the careful planning of mailbox role components. Despite advancements in storage technologies and improved I/O characteristics, it's detrimental to deploy mailbox storage without considering storage characteristics, such as disk latency. Capacity planning is also just as important. With 16 terabytes as the supported maximum database size, it could be tempting to maximize database size with larger Serial ATA (SATA) disks. When considering such extremes, it's important to consider other dependencies, such as time to reseed after a disk failure, time to restore from backups when multiple copies of the database are neither deployed nor available, the ability to meet recovery time objectives in case of an outage or a disaster, and so on.

> **This objective covers how to:**
>
> - Plan for storage requirements
> - Plan mailbox role capacity and placement
> - Plan for virtualization
> - Design public folder placement strategy
> - Validate storage by running Jetstress

Planning for storage requirements

Exchange 2013 supports multiple storage architectures and physical disk types. Each feature offers different performance characteristics and has its benefits. Direct attached storage, for example, has no dependency on an external data network used by Internet Small Computer System Interface (iSCSI) or a dedicated storage network used by Fibre-Channel storage. Similarly, Solid State Disk (SSD) drives offer fast data transfers at a cost of much smaller storage capacities per drive. In general, Exchange 2013 is designed to achieve efficiencies by reducing costs, and the goal is achieved by shifting balance in code, reducing I/O footprint, and optimizing reads and writes, so multiple databases can be placed on the same physical drive. Using bigger SATA drives allows for such efficiencies to materialize.

Anyone with a few years of experience deploying Microsoft Exchange environments can attest that no single solution meets customer requirements, since every customer is unique and so are their design requirements. The Microsoft guidance on Exchange 2013 storage design aims to address most common configurations by providing best practices guidance. For example, single copy databases may be best protected by using a redundant array of independent disks (RAID) configuration, while JBOD might provide best efficiencies when at least three copies of a database exist in a DAG.

EXAM TIP

It is important for you to be able to differentiate which configuration serves a proposed design the best. It is also important to understand the caveats spelled out in exam questions such as, "What is the supported configuration that is most cost effective?" Sometimes the requirements might seem to conflict, but paying close attention to details will help identify possible answers and rule out distractors.

When configuring disks, it is important for you to understand how to create a supported layout. When configuring disk sector size, you must pay attention to nuances such as a 512-byte sector that is supported on Exchange 2013, while 4 kilobyte sector disks aren't supported on any version of Microsoft Exchange server.

EXAM TIP

If a question in the exam has a possibility of producing a different answer based on a different version of Exchange server (that is, RTM vs SP1), exam questions will clearly spell out which version of Exchange Server is applicable for a given question.

The placement of database and related files is another important consideration for a Mailbox server. Best practices suggest that the operating system, and the pagefile should be a RAID-protected volume separate from any Exchange data logical unit numbers (LUNs).The placement of the database and log files is also an important consideration. If you're deploying a stand-alone mailbox database and protecting it with traditional backup systems, whether to separate database and log files on their own separate volumes depends on the backup methodology in use. Placing database and log files on the same volume is supported. Best practices, however, suggest that database files and log files should be located on separate volumes backed by separate physical discs in stand-alone configurations. When multiple copies of a database are deployed in a DAG configuration, the requirement changes to a single database and a log per volume.

When determining the disk size, the size of the database being hosted becomes one of many factors to consider. You'll find that the Exchange Role Requirements Calculator accounts for other items, such as impact of content index, which now equals roughly 20 percent of the size of the database file. An additional requirement for space is used by the master merge process. You can benefit from a reduction in space required for the master merge if you choose to place multiple databases per volume. No restriction exists on the placement of an active copy of a database or on the same volume as a replica of a different database.

While considering all of these factors for a database or a set of databases that are going to reside on a given disk, it not only becomes important to stay within supportability guidance, but you must also stay within the design requirements laid out for a given environment. Factors such as the time required to recover a database in case of a disaster, can affect your ability to benefit from large supported database sizes. The best practice guidance from Microsoft also differentiates between stand-alone database configurations and a database protected by multiple copies in a DAG. For example, the recommendation is not to exceed 200 gigabytes for a database if it's in a stand-alone configuration. But if you plan to setup multiple copies for a database, best practices accommodates up to 2 terabytes for any given database.

EXAM TIP

Pay attention to exam questions that differentiate between supported vs. best practices recommendations. Microsoft documents both scenarios clearly, and, for a given configuration, the difference between the supported configuration and best practices can be significant.

The transaction logs required to recover from a catastrophe also differ from one configuration to another. A stand-alone database configuration protected by traditional backups requires backups to protect transaction logs. Using circular logging doesn't provide the capability to revert to a given point in time before data loss. In contrast, if multiple copies of a database are deployed in a DAG configuration, circular logging is the recommended best practice in the light of complementary functionality, such as lagged copy and single item recovery. Depending on how you choose to truncate logs has a direct impact on how much disk space you need to allocate for a given configuration.

Other important considerations for disk configuration are: partition type GUID Partition Table (GPT) vs. Master Boot Record (MBR), volume type (simple vs. dynamic), and File System—easy to remember because only the NTFS file system is supported for compression—which isn't supported for Exchange database and log files. The other two features relate to the security of data on the disk. How should you secure database and log files from prying eyes in a highly secure environment? Two possibilities are Encrypting File System (EFS) and BitLocker. EFS isn't supported for Exchange database and log files, while BitLocker is fully supported. The last feature to consider is file share support. NFS file systems are unsupported and shouldn't be deployed to host database and log files. The Server Message Block (SMB) 3.0, introduced with Windows Server 2012, is supported only when configured in a virtualized environment. This configuration assumes SMB 3.0 file share is presented to a hypervisor host and a VHD disk is created on a given SMB volume. The VHD disk is attached to a virtualized Exchange server, and the disk is presented as block storage. It isn't supported to present the SMB 3.0 share directly to an Exchange server, and host database and log files on it.

Planning mailbox role capacity and placement

Planning for the capacity of a mailbox role involves the consideration of a number of factors. These factors include the understanding of an existing messaging deployment if the planned deployment is a migration from a previous version, the understanding of user messaging profiles, and the desired mailbox size. The other factors to consider are desired resiliency and disaster recovery objectives, compliance and data retention requirements, data recovery objectives, Service Level Agreements (SLAs), organizational growth plans, and the use of third-party applications.

All of these factors help you determine the number of servers, server hardware utilization, server placement, and environmental dependencies, such as domain controller configuration and placement.

> **REAL WORLD** **DOMAIN CONTROLLER PLACEMENT**
>
> When planning for an Exchange deployment, I learned that the customer environment consisted of an empty domain root and two child domains: Domain A and Domain B. Users of both domains were hosted on Exchange servers located in Domain A. Typically, you deploy a set of domain controllers in the same Active Directory site as Exchange servers for a given Active Directory domain, which is Domain A in this example. However, in this case, we needed to account for additional domain controllers to contain the Global Catalog of users from Domain B to provide the best possible user experience and resiliency. Without such a configuration, any time a user from Domain B logged in to their mailboxes, the Exchange servers would have to reach out to domain controllers located in a different site that belonged to Domain B and was connected through WAN links. As you'll notice, the centralized Exchange server design had an impact on hardware and software requirements for the additional domain controllers.

The user profile is one of the most important factors when determining compute resources required by a mailbox server. A software development firm with a staff of developers and support professionals located in a different geographic region might depend more heavily on an email system than a company developing locomotives where design professionals might frequently communicate via email, while production and factory workers might need limited access to emails. How many emails are sent on average by a given user category is as important as how big an average email is for any given category. This helps you determine processing, storage, and network resources required by a given mailbox server.

Determining a user profile when migrating from an earlier version of Exchange server is relatively easy, because you can use Exchange Profile Analyzer if you're migrating from Exchange 2007. You can leverage performance counters if you're migrating from Exchange 2010 to obtain detailed per-user statistics.

Another important factor is mailbox database size. How big of a mailbox is desired for a given user profile? Each job profile may have different capacity requirements. Compliance requirements can change these requirements drastically, however, challenging your storage requirements assumptions.

REAL WORLD **IMPACT OF LEGAL HOLD ON MAILBOX STORAGE SIZING**

An organization had strict mailbox size requirements, deploying the smallest possible number of mailboxes for any given job profile. Storage design accounted for storage overhead for content indexing, as well as 20 percent free space for buffering. They had a requirement that when any person is involved in a legal action, the mailbox must be placed on indefinite legal hold and all data must be retained in the mailbox including deletions. The legal hold was removed from the mailbox only when legal action had concluded and the legal requirements no longer applied to the mailbox. This requirement meant a design consideration for a mailbox server with additional storage to accommodate for additional data when a mailbox is placed on legal hold and a business-process automation script. This script automatically moved mailboxes on legal hold from their mailbox server to a server designated for litigation; this server contained other similar mailboxes and had the additional storage required for such mailboxes.

Another important consideration in mailbox server design is high availability and site resiliency requirements. For example, you might be required to provide all users with uninterrupted mailbox access despite the failure of a single mailbox server. This requirement means accounting for additional mailbox servers hosting mailbox database copies of all users. You also have to reduce the usable capacity of a given server to account for failover capacity. In a two server configuration, this could mean up to 50 percent of capacity needs to be reserved to help mailbox failovers. Similarly, in a three mailbox server configuration with each server hosting active mailboxes, the minimum reserved capacity can be as much as 33 percent.

If a requirement dictates that all mailboxes must be available in case of disaster at the primary site where all active mailboxes are located, you need to create a DAG that spans multiple sites, and place a mailbox server containing copies of mailbox databases at a secondary site. This impacts the requirement of additional hardware, an additional datacenter location and space considerations, and network requirements to accommodate database replication traffic. Other requirements include active user traffic in case of a failover, or activation in case of a disaster or outage at the primary site.

What if existing IT standards or procurement contracts with the vendor dictate using specific server hardware profile for mailbox servers? This might mean you need to scale out by deploying more servers if the given hardware profile can't accommodate all of the planned mailbox resources.

Should you migrate or deploy Public Folder databases? This might impact storage capacity planning and the location of mailbox servers in a distributed environment to account for resiliency and user experience.

When determining the scale out vs. the scale up model, you need to account for the number of database copies, resiliency requirements, and tolerance to failure domains. In a scale up configuration, you are planning to have more mailboxes per server, which means bigger servers with more processing power and storage capacity, as well as a higher number of mailboxes impacted during failures. The scale-out model requires the same account of total resources divided into smaller chunks, resulting in a larger number of smaller servers deployed to the account for the given environment. This increases the numbers of servers, but reduces the impact on the number of mailboxes affected for given failure. The cost for smaller servers can also provide a cost advantage. Conversely, a larger number of servers in the scale out model also means more management overhead for IT to license, install, monitor, and maintain a higher number of servers. The datacenter footprint is also affected directly by your choice of the scale up vs. the scale out model.

No single design can accommodate all of the possible variations and different require-ments for an Exchange deployment. This is why every successful Exchange deployment considers each of these unique factors based on the given requirements to select the most effective model for deployment.

When designing for storage capacity, the size of the mailboxes is only one of many factors. You need to account for the space required for a mailbox for its given capacity, including the database whitespace, a recoverable items folder size, content indexing, log space (if logs are stored on the same disk as the database), and an additional—usually about 20 percent—buf-fer, because you can't fill the disk at 100 percent capacity and expect the system to function with no triggered alerts.

Disk I/O is another important consideration. While the Exchange 2013 code improvements have reduced I/O requirements significantly, you still need to account for proper I/O calcula-tions to ensure the given disk not only has sufficient capacity to host the planned number of mailboxes, but also that the I/O for the given disk is sufficient to address all read-and-write requirements for mailbox data and related tasks, such as content indexing.

When using external storage such as iSCSI or Fibre-Channel storage, plan for aggregate I/O capacity of each storage channel. When using iSCSI, network bandwidth consideration is crucial. Fibre-Channel SAN is limited by capacity of underlying Fibre-Channel fabric. And, don't forget transport storage, because transport components are now part of the Mailbox role. Transport capacity planning needs to account for queuing for active emails, shadow queues, and a Safety Net. To account for failures, you have to account for poison queue messages, messages queued for delivery to unreachable targets (failed database copy or an inability to reach the Internet destination for outbound messages), and messages stored as part of the Safety Net mechanism for transporting high availability.

Planning for memory requirements includes accounting for database cache, which makes up for a significant portion of server memory, content indexing, and other exchange processes that provide vital functions, such as background maintenance, managed availability, and other agents. If you deploy multi-role servers, you must also account for the additional memory required for Front-End server role components also sharing resources on the same server hardware.

To perform actual calculations for a given mailbox profile and other factors, Microsoft has documented formulas that can be used if you want to size the mailbox role manually. For more information about those published formulas, see: *http://blogs.technet.com/b/exchange/archive/2013/05/06/ask-the-perf-guy-sizing-exchange-2013-deployments.aspx*. Using the Exchange 2013 role requirements calculator is recommended, in order to avoid errors and calculate for all scenarios based on the provided input.

Planning for virtualization

In today's IT environments, it's difficult to imagine a datacenter with no virtualization in use, no matter at how large or small a scale. Some environments use virtualization for some workloads, and physical servers for another. Then, there are environments that deploy virtualized workloads for nearly anything that can be virtualized!

When planning for an Exchange 2013 deployment, you'll most likely face a question of whether the Exchange 2013 servers can be virtualized. That question has no simple answer. Look at the many variables that affect the decision to virtualize Exchange 2013 servers.

Because Exchange 2013 supports virtualizing all server roles, you don't need to determine whether a given server role is supported when virtualized.

Exchange 2013 is supported on any version of Windows Server with Hyper-V technology, or a Hyper-V Server. It's also fully supported to virtualize Exchange 2013 servers using any third-party hypervisor validated under Windows Server Virtualization Validation Program (SVVP). Some well-known virtualization platforms found on the SVVP validated list include VMware's vSphere and ESX platforms, Citrix XenServer, and Oracle VM.

> *IMPORTANT* **MICROSOFT AZURE AND EXCHANGE 2013**
>
> While it's possible to virtualize Exchange 2013 server roles using Microsoft Azure VMs, the deployment of production Exchange servers on Microsoft Azure VMs is not supported. See *http://support2.microsoft.com/kb/2721672* for a list of supported server software and roles on Azure VMs.

After determining the supported platform, the design discussions usually turn to features of the given virtualization platform to determine which features can be used in conjunction with Exchange server functionality to get the most out of the technology and platforms features being deployed.

The Live Migration of a virtual machine (VM) is a popular feature that every virtualization administrator wants to deploy and know if Exchange supports it. Live Migration enables administrators to move VMs from one hypervisor host to another to achieve better resource utilization and perform scheduled software or hardware maintenance. Exchange 2013 supports such functionality with Microsoft Hyper-V and other hypervisors.

The key to being supported when deploying such migration functionality is to ensure that the migration process for a VM doesn't deploy snapshot-type functionality where a VM is saved to the disk and restored from it. The VM must remain online during the migration process, or the VM must shut down and perform a cold boot.

Another popular feature is snapshot functionality. Think of *snapshot functionality* as a point-in-time backup of your VM. For example, let's say you're planning to make significant changes to your environment and want to be able to revert to the current stable configuration in case of a failure. Your virtualization administrator may be happy to point out the ability to take snapshots and revert to them if needed. The virtualization administrator may not know the application specifics and complexities of using snapshots with Exchange. Exchange components, such as log shipping for database replication which are dependent on accurate time keeping and when the snapshot feature is used. The introduced time travel to the time passed by reverting to an older snapshot has undesired and unpleasant side effects. This can help understand why the snapshot feature isn't supported for use with Exchange VMs. Using snapshots on Exchange VMs has some unexpected and most commonly undesired consequences. In most circumstances, these consequences can't be undone, leaving you to deal with bigger issues than you bargained for.

While they aren't a variation of the snapshot feature, differencing disks are a similarly interesting feature that promises to reduce disk space usage by creating a master or parent disk that contains common shared data, primarily the VMs operating system. By creating differencing disks, all changes are written to a differencing disk, which has its own issues. Take dependency on the parent disk, for an example. Even an accidental change to the parent disk invalidates the differencing disks that depend upon the parent disk. In the case of a change to the parent disk, you end up with Exchange servers that can't boot anymore. While data might not be lost, the service to end users is certainly affected, at the very least. As you probably guessed by now, the snapshot feature is not supported with Exchange VMs.

Another great feature many modern hypervisors offer is guest replication. This feature replicates VMs to another host, local or remote, to provide the capability to start up replica VM if the hypervisor host with a primary VM copy fails. For Exchange 2013 VMs, the recommendation is to use DAG functionality, as well as other availability and disaster recovery features provided by Exchange server. Using hypervisor-based replication functionality with Exchange 2013 isn't supported.

Maximizing resource usage with virtualization is a natural tendency. It often results in the oversubscription of processors, as well as memory overcommit using dynamic memory mechanisms. While modern hypervisors are continuously improving to provide better resource sharing, it cannot protect against intentional overcommit. When you have critical workloads, such as Exchange server roles in a VM, oversubscription usually has negative effects on such workloads. Unexpected behavior of Exchange server services is often observed when resource oversubscription is deployed.

> **REAL WORLD** **IMPACT OF DYNAMIC MEMORY ON EXCHANGE VM**
>
> While testing Exchange 2013 features in my lab environment, I was unable to perform the expected functions, and the errors weren't descriptive enough to determine what the problem was. As I started looking into the issue, I noticed that some of the Exchange services were stopped. After spending many hours troubleshooting the issue, I noticed that default configuration was using dynamic memory when creating the VM. Like most personal labs, my hypervisor host was oversubscribed and, when multiple VMs ramped up resource demand, it started affecting resource availability to VMs. When the Exchange server lost some of its allocated memory, which is an expected behavior when dynamic memory is configured, the services using the memory crashed due to the loss of the resource they were depending on. The issue was fixed by setting the memory on Exchange VM to a static amount, which is a change that requires VM to be shut down and restarted.

Exchange 2013 code is optimized to strike a balance between the efficient use of memory and reducing the I/O footprint. To achieve these efficiencies, Exchange relies on a calculated cache for each database being hosted on the server, as well as the memory reserved for Exchange subsystems. When dynamic memory is in use, this can result in incorrect memory calculations and it can cause Exchange to start with less memory than is available. Not surprisingly, Microsoft doesn't support the use of dynamic memory with Exchange VMs.

Processor oversubscription is supported, but the recommended ratio is 1:1, with a supported ratio of 2:1 over the subscription maximum. This means that for every physical processor core on a hypervisor host, no more than two virtual processors should be assigned to VMs running on the given host. This isn't only limited to Exchange VMs running on the host, but it does include processors assigned to all VMs.

Hyperthreading is another advanced feature that can improve performance. An example of *hyperthreading*, as you can see in Figure 1–1, is when your system detects four logical processors when the system is configured with only one physical socket and two physical cores.

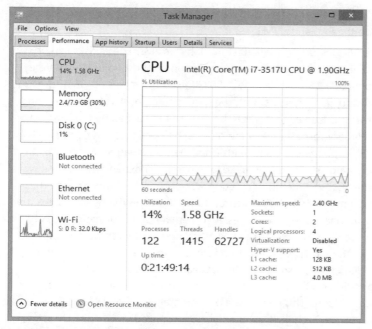

FIGURE 1-1 An example of a system with hyperthreading enabled

Hyperthreading is great for managing multiple workloads with the parallel execution of threads, but it isn't designed to provide you more processing capacity than the system has. For example, the system referred to in Figure 1-1 has a CPU with a maximum speed of 2.4 GHz. The system has one socket, with two CPU cores and four logical processors. How much processing capacity does the system have? 2.4 GHz? 4.8 GHz or 9.6 GHz? The correct answer is 4.8 GHz, because the system has two physical cores, each capable of running at a maximum of 2.4 GHz. Four logical cores is an indication that hyperthreading is enabled on the system. This might allow four parallel threads to execute instead of two, making the system more efficient. But, as discussed earlier, it can't provide more than 4.8GHz of maximum processing power.

When configuring processing capacity for virtualization environment and virtualizing Exchange servers, it's supported to have hyperthreading enabled on the virtualization host. But, when sizing Exchange servers for your environment, you need to consider the actual processor cores available to the system and not the logical processor count.

When considering storage for VMs, the virtualization administrator has many options at their disposal to deploy appropriate storage for given VMs. Options include local storage, DAS, iSCSI storage, Fibre-Channel storage, NFS shares, and, beginning with Windows Server 2012, SMB 3.0 shares.

For Exchange VMs to be supported, the disks assigned to Exchange VMs must be a block storage. This means, you can't map the NFS or SMB share to Exchange VM and store database and log files on it. The disk where Exchange related files are stored must be available to VM as a block-level storage disk. These disks must be visible through the disk management console or when you run Diskpart on the Exchange VM.

Hypervisors use different virtual disk formats to store data for VMs. These disks can be configured as fixed disks, taking up all of the allocated space on the host volume when they are created. For example, on a 500 GB host volume, a 50 GB fixed disk takes 50 GB of space on a host volume upon creation, leaving 450 GB of free space on the host volume, assuming nothing else is stored on it. This is true even though the disk isn't initialized by the VM and no data is stored on it yet. Hypervisors also allow the disks to be configured as dynamically expanding disks. *Dynamically expanding disks* take little space upon creation and only expand in proportion to the actual data being stored on it. So, a dynamically expanding disk may only take 1 MB or less on the host volume upon creation. When the VM stores data on the disk, it expands to accommodate the data being written to it. While this might sound like the most efficient way to use disk space on host volumes, it comes with a performance penalty. When VM needs to store more data to a dynamically expanding disk, hypervisor needs to expand the virtual disk file as the data is being written to it, causing delays in responding to I/O calls from VM. The delays may be small and unnoticeable, or they can amount to noticeable thresholds, depending on the underlying storage architecture and the parallel I/O activity on the same host volume. This can have a detrimental effect on Exchange performance and is undesirable, so Exchange 2013 only supports fixed virtual disks.

Where you store these virtual disks it is also important for your deployment of Exchange servers to be supported. Virtualized Exchange 2013 supports virtual disks stored in the following scenarios:

- Local or directly attached storage
- Fibre-Channel storage presented as block-level volumes to the virtualization host
- iSCSI storage presented as block-level storage to the virtualization host
- iSCSI storage presented as block-level storage to the Exchange VM
- SMB 3.0 share mappe to virtualization host

The virtual disks must be fixed virtual disks. When using SMB 3.0 share, it is not supported to map the share to Exchange 2013 VM and store database and log files directly to it.

Hypervisors such as VMware also support NFS shares to store virtual disks attached to VMs. But it isn't supported to store virtual disks attached to an Exchange VM on NFS storage. While this might be a point of contention between Exchange administrators and virtualization administrators, it helps you understand why Exchange doesn't support such storage.

Exchange requires various guarantees, such as Forced Unit Access, Write-Through, Write Ordering, and so on from storage, to maintain data integrity and system reliability. When storage is unable to provide such guarantees, the critical Exchange system and user data are at risk, which isn't acceptable or desirable to any system administrator supporting such complex systems. NFS storage implementations, historically, haven't met these guarantees, so it isn't a supported solution for Exchange deployments.

The sum of all individual components makes up for a fully functioning system, but it doesn't end there. What if the hypervisor host your Exchange VM is running on fails? The answer might sound as easy as deploying multiple instances of mailbox servers and creating DAG with each database having two or three replicas, providing there's enough protection from failures. But, it's just as important to account for all of the possible failure domains. Are your hypervisor hosts configured to have separate failure domains, so a failed router in one rack doesn't affect a replica of your database? Are they in separate racks? Are they using separate phases of power, so a failure on one power line doesn't affect all replicas at the same time? Are all disks used for all replicas separated, so single SAN failure doesn't affect all the replicas of a given database? All these questions lead to one goal: failures are a fact of any IT infrastructure. Failures will happen, so account for all possible failure domains. Determine the cost of deploying a solution that can account for mitigating all possible failure domains, while staying within your design and budget guidelines. Strike the best possible balance to achieve highest possible availability by eliminating ill effects of single failures on your Exchange environment.

> **MORE INFO   VIRTUALIZING EXCHANGE 2013**
>
> You can find current information and guidance for virtualizing Exchange 2013 here: *https://technet.microsoft.com/en-us/library/jj619301.*

Designing public folder placement strategy

In Exchange 2013, public folders were given special treatment. Instead of using dedicated public folder databases in previous versions, *public folders* are now hosted on regular mailbox databases. By moving public folders to mailbox database, Exchange can now provide better resiliency by leveraging the same DAG architecture that regular mailboxes have enjoyed since Exchange 2010.

Public folders still maintain a hierarchy, however, the hierarchy isn't stored in a public folder mailbox, known as the Primary hierarchy mailbox. Primary Hierarchy Mailbox is the only writable copy of the public folder hierarchy in the entire Exchange organization. An Exchange administrator can create additional public folder mailboxes, and each of these secondary hierarchy mailboxes contains a read-only copy of the public folder hierarchy. Both Primary and Secondary hierarchy mailboxes can contain public folder content.

Creating new public folder mailboxes is a function now moved to New-Mailbox cmdlet. When creating a new public folder mailbox, use the PublicFolder parameter. This is different from creating a new public folder. Once a mailbox to host public folders is created, you can create a new public folder by using the New-PublicFolder cmdlet.

When you create multiple public folder mailboxes, Exchange server automatically distributes users equally across public folder mailboxes for load-balancing purposes. In large environments, restricting the new public folder from the serving hierarchy is important because when users access a new public folder mailbox, which isn't excluded from serving hierarchy, they might only see an incomplete public folder structure until the hierarchy synchronization is complete. Use the IsExcludedFromServingHeirarchy parameter when creating a new public folder mailbox to exclude it from serving an incomplete hierarchy to its users.

When hierarchy synchronization completes, the value of the IsHeirarchyReady parameter on public-folder mailbox properties is set to $true. This helps the administrator determine when an exclusion set on the public folder can be removed. While users can access public folder hierarchy from any public folder mailbox, because only one writeable copy of hierarchy exists, any new public folder creation or deletion request is proxied to the primary hierarchy mailbox.

Unlike regular mailboxes, the *public folder mailbox* is a shared resource accessed by multiple users simultaneously. Activity on a public folder has a direct impact on the server where the public folder mailbox is located. To avoid client connectivity issues, consider having multiple public folder mailboxes in the environment. If a certain public folder in hierarchy is heavily used, create or move the public folder to a dedicated public folder mailbox. Also consider restricting a heavily used public folder mailbox from the serving hierarchy.

In a geographically dispersed environment, create public folder databases in the location nearest to the user that access the public folder contents stored in them. This reduces round trips to remote locations that might be connected with slower wide area network (WAN) links and can introduce excessive delays, resulting in a poor Outlook client behavior and user experience. When deploying public folder mailboxes in close proximity to user locations, also consider changing the DefaultPublicFolderMailbox property on user mailboxes, so users can use their closest public folder mailbox to retrieve the public folder hierarchy.

When deploying public folders on Exchange 2013 servers, it's important to understand that because Exchange 2013 servers don't support legacy public-folder databases, there's no co-existence. When migrating from Exchange 2010 or Exchange 2007, the recommendation is not to create any modern public folder mailboxes on Exchange 2013 until after all the user mailboxes are migrated to Exchange 2013.

Migration from older versions of Exchange server to new public folder mailboxes is a one-way process in the sense that you can roll back to legacy public folders by deleting all public folder mailboxes on Exchange 2013, setting the PublicFolderMigrationComplete parameter to false on a previous version of Exchange server. But, any data changed or added to the new public folder mailboxes doesn't synchronize with legacy public folders and is lost when public folder mailboxes on Exchange 2013 are deleted during the roll-back process. This is an important consideration during the migration planning process from legacy public folders to new public folder mailboxes on Exchange 2013.

With new public-folder mailbox functionality, you can easily move a rapidly growing public folder and its contents to a different public folder mailbox. Because of the separation that can happen from using different mailboxes for different public folders, it becomes complex to account for all of the subfolders that belong to the public folder being moved. If you need to keep the data of all subfolders with the parent public folder being moved, you need to use the Move-PublicFolderBranch.ps1 script, provided with the Exchange 2013 server installation.

With a new mailbox architecture, the public folder mailboxes now automatically inherit the size limits from the mailbox database that they belong to. You must carefully evaluate mailbox sizes, including warning, send, and receive quotas that a public folder mailbox might inherit and change it for a public folder mailbox, if necessary. When changing public-folder mailbox quotas from database defaults, it's important that the underlying storage has enough capacity to account for those exceptions and additional storage that public folder mailboxes might consume because of non-default quotas configured on them.

Because modern public folders are now similar in architecture as mailboxes and use the same underlying mailbox databases, it's natural to think mechanisms, such as mailbox audit logs that work with regular mailboxes, would also work with public folder mailboxes. But, currently, mailbox audit logs don't work on public folder mailboxes. This is important when you define goals for meeting auditing requirements for each of the messaging components being deployed.

It is also important to distinguish mailbox audit logging from public-folder access permissions auditing. Assigning permissions is an administrative action that moved to role based access control (RBAC) in Exchange 2013. This allows for auditing administrative actions when permissions on public folders are changed.

Validating storage by running Jetstress

Even though the I/O requirements were significantly reduced in Exchange 2013 when compared to previous versions, performing validation using proper testing tools is still as important to ensure the success of any Exchange 2013 deployment. *Jetstress* is used to validate all of the hardware and software I/O components, including storage drivers, disk firmware, and many other storage-related components. While Jetstress doesn't actually verify details, such as whether a particular firmware version is present for a given disk, a successful Jetstress result validates the storage stack that is configured optimally to meet your design requirements. While it might be obvious, it's important to point out that as any other tool, Jetstress is going to test what it's asked to test for. If the provided user profile information and other test parameters are incorrect, the passing result might not be an accurate reflection of your production requirements and a failing result might not mean much in reality.

The installation of Jetstress is dependent on ESE libraries that are going to be used on production Exchange 2013 server. Also, Jetstress is run before Exchange server is installed on the server to be tested. This means, required ESE libraries must be obtained manually from installation media of Exchange 2013 server version that are going to be used to install Exchange 2013 on a given server. Jetstress should never be run on a server that has Exchange 2013 already installed.

When validating storage using Jetstress, all of the factors affecting the given storage should be considered. If shared storage, such as SAN, is planned, all concurrent I/O profiles on shared storage should be tested or simulated to achieve accurate pass/fail results. Testing single LUN on new SAN with no load may pass the test with flying colors, but it doesn't accurately reflect the reality under which the shared storage is performing when in production. If multiple databases are planned to be located on the same volume, the test should account for it. If shared workloads other than exchange are expected to have I/O impact on the same volume, expected I/O from other applications should also be simulated during Jetstress testing. Freely available tools, such as Iometer, can be leveraged to test shared I/O on the volume, if needed.

When testing RAID subsystems, accounting for disk failures is also important. When a disk in a RAID array fails, access to the data stored on the array is uninterrupted. Performance of the RAID array is degraded until the failed disk is replaced and rebuild process is complete. Jetstress tests should account for both healthy operation and performance degradation during the rebuild operation.

While required storage performance characteristics don't change when Exchange 2013 servers are virtualized, the factors that can affect storage performance certainly do! Virtualized environments might mean a shared logical unit number (LUN) hosting virtual disks for many VMs. Each VM have its own I/O requirements. During peak usage periods, this can result in concentrated I/O causing degradation in storage performance. When host-based failovers are configured, a failed host might mean additional resource usage on surviving hosts due to additional VMs now running on it. This also requires additional I/O on shared spindles. When testing virtualized Exchange servers for storage system performance with Jetstress, accounting for these additional factors is important.

When running Jetstress, how much time you allocate for testing is an important factor to ensure that test results are accurate. The tuning of test parameters might be required before running extended tests, so the recommendation is to run initial short 15-minute tests to determine the number of simultaneous threads an underlying storage system can support. Once the appropriate level of disk latency and IOPs are achieved using tuned parameters in short tests, longer tests should be carried out. Strict mode tests should be carried out for durations from up to six hours, and lenient mode tests should be carried out for durations greater than six hours. The strict mode tests storage for stricter maximum read and write latencies of 100ms. The lenient mode, in contrast, tests the storage against the maximum read and write latency target of 200ms.

Before performing any testing, you should also ensure that the test systems are configured optimally for an underlying storage subsystem. Factors such as server BIOS, storage controller firmware and driver levels, and hard disk firmware have a direct impact on the outcome of Jetstress and should be at manufacture-recommended and -supported levels. When SAN- based storage is planned, the same considerations apply to Fibre-Channel HBA drivers, Fibre-Channel switch firmware, and SAN controller operating-system levels.

When Jetstress tests result in a failure, it usually means one of two factors. A natural tendency is to look at a storage subsystem and tune or reconfigure it to ensure the tests pass. But it might also be the result of misconfiguration of Jetstress test parameters. Starting with the validation of test parameters and storage driver/firmware levels is the best first step toward remediation. If further tests still fail, this almost always means the storage has failed to meet the test requirements and must be remediated. Putting the solution in production is detrimental, assuming the failure is of the tool testing the storage, because Jetstress is a simple tool that directly relies on the test parameters and the storage subsystem being tested.

For the test to be successful, all three criteria being evaluated must pass. The three criteria are database IOPS target, I/O database read averaged latency, and I/O log write averaged latency. Database I/O target is derived by using IOPS requirements calculated per storage-sizing guidance.

Thought experiment
Exchange 2013 design considerations

In this thought experiment, apply what you have learned about this objective. You can find answers to these questions in the "Answers" section at the end of this chapter.

You are an Exchange administrator for Contoso, Ltd. Contoso doesn't have a messaging system and plans to deploy Exchange 2013. Contoso currently uses Microsoft Hyper-V as its virtualization platform. The Hyper-V administrator recommends use of dynamic VHDX files located on the SAN volume for virtual machines for Exchange 2013 server roles. The Virtualization administrator states his goal of achieving a consolidation ratio of 100 VMs per virtualization host. The Storage administrator prefers to create large RAID arrays consisting of multiple disks and creates multiple volumes from the existing array as needed.

Contoso also plans to deploy public folders for collaboration. Contoso has multiple locations connected with slower WAN links and wants to ensure the best possible user experience when accessing public folder content.

1. What would be your recommendations for virtualization platform configuration to ensure Exchange 2013 deployment is supported?

2. Do you agree with the proposed storage configuration? Do you have any concerns to discuss?

3. How would you plan public folder deployment to address the requirement?

Objective summary

- Exchange 2013 storage doesn't require fast disks. Optimal storage design for Exchange 2013 requires striking a careful balance of price, performance, and capacity.
- Deploying newer functionality can replace traditional practices, such as deploying lagged copies of database along with single item recovery, which can address backup requirements of an organization replacing traditional backups.
- What Exchange 2013 considers supported configuration may differ from what the vendor is willing to support. This applies to storage, as well as virtualization.
- Placement of Exchange 2013 server roles isn't always a strictly technical decision. Centralized deployments may work for a small company with a highly mobile workforce, but it might not be the best option for a large company with multiple international locations, each governed by different rules and compliance requirements.

- While supported, not every environment can benefit from the high availability and resource management functionality modern virtualization platforms provide. Exchange 2013, when using database replicas, can ensure the integrity of data that HA provided by virtualization platform can't due to lack of application awareness.

Objective review

Answer the following questions to test your knowledge of the information in this objective. You can find the answers to these questions, and explanations of why each answer choice is correct or incorrect, in the "Answers" section at the end of this chapter.

1. Select supported disk configuration for Exchange 2013 deployment. The deployment must provide the best possible cost benefits for design consisting of large mailboxes for every user. The planned minimum mailbox size is 5 GB per user.

   A. Dedicated RAID5 configuration of 10 SSD disks per server.

   B. VHD files stored on 7,200 RPM 4 TB SATA disks, served by NFS storage array using dedicated 10 Gbps network.

   C. Dedicated RAID5 volume consisting of 15,000 RPM 1 TB SCSI disks on fiber channel SAN storage array.

   D. Dedicated RAID10 volume consisting of 15,000 RPM 1 TB SCSI disks on Direct Attached Storage.

2. You need to determine the user profile for the existing Exchange 2010 environment that will be used to determine server and storage sizing for planned Exchange 2013 deployment. Which tool should you use to minimize administrative effort and meet the requirement?

   A. Exchange Profile Analyzer

   B. Performance Counters

   C. Transaction Log Files

   D. Exchange Log Analyzer

3. You plan to create a new public folder mailbox on an Exchange 2013 server located at a remote site that's connected to the main site using slower WAN links. You want to ensure users don't get incomplete folder hierarchy. What should you do?

   A. Create a new public folder mailbox using the New-Mailbox cmdlet. Exclude the new public folder from the serving hierarchy using the IsExcludedFromServingHeirarchy parameter.

   B. Create a new public folder mailbox using the New-Mailbox cmdlet. Set the IsHierarchyReady parameter to $false to exclude the new public folder from the serving hierarchy.

   C. Create a new public folder mailbox using the New-Publicfolder cmdlet. Set the IsHierarchyReady parameter to $false to exclude the new public folder from the serving hierarchy.

Objective 1.2: Configure and manage the mailbox role

Exchange 2013 setup is now greatly simplified, and it also accounts for installing operating system component prerequisites as a part of the setup, if selected. But this simplification doesn't prevent the need to carefully plan the deployment of the mailbox server roles, taking into account the unique qualities of the environment where Exchange 2013 is being deployed. In this section, you learn the details of how to configure and manage mailbox role and related components.

> **This objective covers how to:**
> - Deploy mailbox server roles
> - Create and configure Offline Address Book (OAB)
> - Design and create hierarchical address lists
> - Create and configure public folders

Deploying mailbox server roles

The first step to successfully deploy a mailbox server is to ensure that all of the prerequisites are met. Starting with authentication provider, you must be certain that at least one writeable domain controller exists in each Active Directory site where you plan to deploy an Exchange 2013 server. The supported operating system running on the Active Directory controller is Windows Server 2003 or later. Referencing mail-enabled objects is critical for Exchange server roles. For Exchange server to function properly, you must deploy at least one global catalog server in each Active Directory site where you plan to deploy an Exchange 2013 server.

The network infrastructure using the IPv6 protocol is supported only when IPv4 is also installed and enabled.

In small environments, it's tempting to collocate Exchange 2013 server on a server that's also a domain controller to reduce the number of servers required. While it is a supported to install Exchange 2013 on a domain controller, for security and performance reasons, the recommendation is to install Exchange 2013 server on a member server in a domain. If you choose to collocate an Exchange server with a domain controller, the server can't later be demoted to a member server or promoted to a domain controller from a member server after Exchange server is installed.

Since the Resilient File System (ReFS) was introduced in Windows Server 2012, it hasn't shared much of the limelight, despite the new features that offer a better integrity of data. Exchange 2013 supports storing database files, transaction log files, and content index files on partitions formatted with ReFS. But partitions storing Exchange binary files and diagnostics logging data generated by Exchange server must be formatted using the NTFS file system.

Windows Server Core installations reduce the management overhead and increase the security profile of the server by reducing the attack surface. Core installations, however, aren't supported for Exchange 2013 server installations. If you have Windows Server 2012 or Windows Server 2012 R2, it's possible to convert from a Core installation to a Full installation of the server. But if you have a Windows 2008 R2 Core installation, you must reinstall the operating system using the Full installation option. Windows Server 2012 R2 is only supported with Exchange 2013 Service Pack 1 or later.

Preparing the organization is one of the first steps that needs to be run before installing any Exchange 2013 server roles. In an environment where role separation is required, the Exchange administrator might not have the ability to modify the Active Directory schema. In such cases, the Active Directory administrator with Schema Admins and Enterprise Admins privileges needs to run the preparation steps before the Exchange administrator can install Exchange 2013 servers. In Active Directory forests with multiple domains, it's also important to run Active Directory preparation steps from a computer in the same domain and site as the domain controller that is a Schema Master.

Because this first step requires access to Active Directory, tools that enable you to administer Active Directory are required on the server where the setup is being run. Remote Tools Administration Pack (RSAT) includes all of the required tools and must be installed if the computer is not a domain controller; it can be installed via server manager interface or by using PowerShell. If the server is running Windows Server 2008 R2, you can use the command line Add-WindowsFeature RSAT-ADDS. On Windows Server 2012 or later, run Install-WindowsFeature RSAT-ADDS instead. While the difference is subtle, note the cmdlet, which is different between the two versions, while the component being installed is the same.

When using setup.exe in unattended mode, which can also be used for unattended setup, you must also use the /IAcceptExchangeServerLicenseTerms switch for setup to succeed. No abbreviated aliases exist for the switch.

When preparing a schema, you must allow for the replication to complete from a schema master to all of the domain controllers in all of the domains of the forest. You need to do this before you can proceed to the next steps of preparing Active Directory and preparing domains where Exchange servers and Exchange server users are to be located. In an Active Directory forest with multiple domains, you must prepare every domain where Exchange server users reside, even if an Exchange server won't be installed in that domain.

When extending the Active Directory schema, Exchange server setup adds and updates classes, attributes, and other items. In simple terms, this is how Active Directory is made aware of what Exchange objects are going to be made up of.

When preparing Active Directory, in new environments, an Exchange Organization is created using the name provided by the administrator. In existing environments, an existing Exchange organization is updated to include Exchange containers, objects, and attributes. When an Exchange server is installed, you'll find that the corresponding Exchange server object is created within the Exchange organization container in Active Directory.

The last step in preparation of Active Directory is the preparation of domains. During this step, Exchange-related containers and security groups are created. Setup also assigns permissions to the containers, so the Exchange server can access them.

If the Exchange administrator also has required Active Directory permissions, the Exchange Setup Wizard can run all three Active Directory preparation steps automatically.

After the successful installation of Exchange servers, Exchange administrators with permissions to create objects can create new security principals, such as a user in Active Directory, before creating an Exchange mailbox if needed. This model of security might not be preferred in organizations with strict role separation requirements. In such environments, Active Directory administrators are unable to manage Exchange objects, such as mailbox creation, distribution group creation, and so on. Likewise, an Exchange administrator isn't permitted to create a new user in Active Directory. To achieve such role separation, Exchange setup provides the capability to create Active Directory split permissions. This can be achieved during the setup or after Exchange servers are set up, by running setup.exe with the /ActiveDirectorySplitPermissions switch set to True.

When using the Setup Wizard, the Apply Active Directory split permission security model to the Exchange organization option is only available if you are setting up the first Exchange server in a new organization. In an existing organization, you must use setup.exe in unattended mode with the previously mentioned switch to change the existing permission model.

EXAM TIP

It's possible to change the Exchange server security model from Active Directory split permissions to shared permissions and vice versa. An Exchange administrator with the proper Active Directory permissions can run setup.exe with the /ActiveDirectorySplitPermissions switch set to true or false to implement or remove Active Directory split permissions, respectively.

When permissions are involved, larger environments tend to have separation of roles and duties that extend beyond just separation between Exchange and Active Directory administrators. For example, you can have an Exchange architect who is responsible for setting objectives for the Exchange server design and deployment. They might also serve as a subject matter expert and a point of escalation when needed. Daily management tasks might be further delegated to other Exchange administrators. Similarly, an organization might hire temporary staff to assist with time-bound, short-term needs where hiring a new person might not be warranted or possible.

Exchange setup accounts for such requirements where the person setting up an Exchange server might not be responsible for managing an entire Exchange organization and might only need limited permissions that enable them to successfully install new Exchange server roles.

For delegated setup to work, you must have at least one Exchange server installed in the organization. Next, the organization administrator must provision a new Exchange server in Active Directory. This can be achieved by running setup.exe from the command line and using the /NewProvisionedServer switch. If you're provisioning a new server using a different computer to run the setup, you must also include the computer name of the server being provisioned with the /NewProvisionedServer switch. After provisioning a new server, the user who is performing an installation of Exchange server needs to be added to the Delegated Setup role group.

Creating and configuring Offline Address Book

Address books are part of the functionality Exchange server offers to enable users to find other users easily. Address books are created and maintained by mailbox servers. The *Offline Address Book* (OAB) enables users to use Address Book functionality when they aren't connected to Exchange server.

Address lists are a building block of OAB. Address lists represent a collection of recipients and other mail-enabled objects, such as contacts, groups, and room/equipment resources. When Exchange 2013 is installed, it automatically creates multiple default address lists that contain contacts, distribution lists, rooms, users, and public folders. The default Global Address List (GAL), which contains all mailbox-enabled or mail-enabled objects from the Active Directory forest where Exchange is installed, is also created.

You can also create custom address lists to contain mail-enabled objects from certain departments, geography, or any other organizational entity that can help users identify which address list is most likely to contain a user they want to find. Custom address lists tend to be a subset of objects contained in a global address list. New address lists can be created using the New-AddressList cmdlet or by using the Exchange Admin Center (EAC).

When creating a new address list, you can restrict which recipients should be included in the new address list by using built-in filter parameters, such as the ConditionalDepartment. This only selects users with a department attribute that matches a defined value of the parameter. Here's an example of creating a new address list named Finance that includes all users with a department attribute set to Finance.

Create new address list

```
New-AddressList –Name Finance –IncludedRecipients AllRecipients –ConditionalDepartment Finance
```

The same can be achieved using the Exchange Admin Center, as you can see in Figure 1–2.

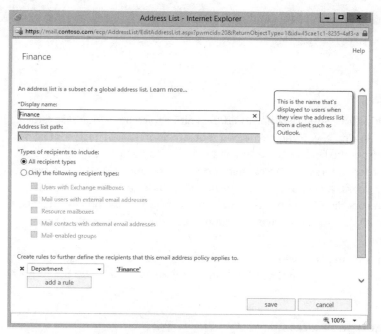

FIGURE 1-2 Create a new address list using Exchange Admin Center

When built-in filter parameters might not be sufficient to create a custom address list, you can create recipient filters using the OPATH filtering syntax. To create a custom address list using the recipientfilter parameter, you can't use the Exchange Admin Center (EAC) and you must use the Shell. In the following example, let's create a custom address list to include all users with a mailbox from finance or the sales department, based on their department attribute value.

Create new address list using recipient filter

```
New-AddressList –Name ""Finance-Sales"" –RecipientFilter {((RecipientType -eq
'UserMailbox') -and ((Department -eq 'Finance') -or (Department -eq 'Sales')))}
```

For the list of filterable properties that can be used with a recipient filter, see the article Filterable properties for the RecipientFilter parameter at *http://technet.microsoft.com/en-us/library/bb738157(v=exchg.150).aspx*.

While default GAL contains all objects, when an organization is required to provide separation between different departments to achieve compliance or other business reasons, a single default GAL doesn't serve the purpose. To address the requirement, you need to create additional global address lists and provide separation using Address Book policies. The process is also referred to as Global Address List (GAL) segmentation.

Each Address Book policy consists of four components:

- Address Lists
- Room Address List
- Global Address List
- Offline Address Book

When you create address lists, you use recipient address filters to create a logical separation between entities. For example, you can create two separate address lists, each containing employees and contacts from the Finance department and the Sales department, respectively. You also create separate room address lists to contain rooms and resources that should only be available to one department. A new GAL is then created to include custom address and room lists, as well as corresponding OAB objects containing their corresponding GAL objects. When this procedure is complete, you will have two Address Book policies separating two department Address Books.

The logical separation still isn't achieved since user mailboxes need to be configured to start using their corresponding GALs and OABs. You can configure user mailboxes to use new GALs and OABs by using the Set-Mailbox cmdlet.

> **NOTE CREATE GAL AND OAB OBJECTS**
>
> Currently, EAC doesn't provide an interface to create new GAL or OAB objects. You must use Shell to create GAL and OAB objects.
>
> When creating Address Book Policies (ABPs), a room address list is required, even if you don't have any room objects or shared resources to include in the list. In the following example, we create an empty room list to meet the requirement. The example assumes that no conference room mailboxes exist in the environment.

Let's walk through this process.

GAL segmentation walk-through

```
#Create address lists for each department
New-AddressList -Name "Finance AL" -IncludedRecipients AllRecipients
-ConditionalDepartment Finance
New-AddressList -Name "Sales AL" -IncludedRecipients AllRecipients
-ConditionalDepartment Sales


#Create room address lists for each department
New-AddressList -Name "Finance Room AL" -RecipientFilter {(RecipientDisplayType
-eq 'ConferenceRoomMailbox')}
New-AddressList -Name "Sales Room AL" -RecipientFilter {(RecipientDisplayType
-eq 'ConferenceRoomMailbox')}


#Create Global Address Lists for each department
New-GlobalAddressList -Name "Finance Global Address List" -IncludedRecipients
MailboxUsers -ConditionalDepartment Finance
New-GlobalAddressList -Name "Sales Global Address List" -IncludedRecipients MailboxUsers
-ConditionalDepartment Sales
```

```
#Create Offline Address book objects for each department
New-OfflineAddressBook -Name "Finance OAB" -AddressLists "\Finance Global Address List"
-VirtualDirectories "SERVER01\OAB (Default Web Site)"
New-OfflineAddressBook -Name "Sales OAB" -AddressLists "\Sales Global Address List"
-VirtualDirectories "SERVER01\OAB (Default Web Site)"

#Create Address Book Policies (ABPs) for each department
New-AddressBookPolicy -Name "Finance ABP" -AddressLists "Finance AL" -OfflineAddressBook
"\Finance OAB" -GlobalAddressList "\Finance Global Address List" -RoomList "\Finance
Room AL"
New-AddressBookPolicy -Name "Sales ABP" -AddressLists "Sales AL" -OfflineAddressBook "\
Sales OAB" -GlobalAddressList "\Sales Global Address List" -RoomList "\Sales Room AL"

#Assign the ABPs for each mailbox
Set-Mailbox "FinUser1" -AddressBookPolicy "Finance ABP"
Set-Mailbox "SalesUser1" -AddressBookPolicy "Sales ABP"
```

So far, we've followed all of the logical steps to provide a separation between two departments. Notice how we only changed one mailbox for each department in the previous example.
Obviously, in the real world, you have to change all of the mailboxes of each department to
apply the correct ABPs to each.

Here's one more item not covered yet: name resolution. When a user from Outlook types
a name in the address bar, Outlook provides the capability to resolve the name from GAL.
Despite the separation created using ABPs, name resolution continues to work across logical
boundaries created by ABPs. This is because *name resolution* is an organizational function
and, despite logical separation, the objects from both departments continue to exist in a
single Exchange organization. To address this problem, two departments, when using ABPs,
must be considered external to each other. The Address Book Policy routing agent provides
this function.

The ABP routing agent must be manually installed and enabled to provide name resolution separation. Take a look at the process.

Install and enable ABP routing agent

```
#Install ABP routing agent
Install-TransportAgent -Name "ABP Routing Agent" -TransportAgentFactory
"Microsoft.Exchange.Transport.Agent.AddressBookPolicyRoutingAgent.
AddressBookPolicyRoutingAgentFactory" -AssemblyPath $env:ExchangeInstallPath\
TransportRoles\agents\AddressBookPolicyRoutingAgent\Microsoft.Exchange.Transport.Agent.
AddressBookPolicyRoutingAgent.dll

#Enable transport agent
Enable-TransportAgent "ABP Routing Agent"

#Restart transport service
Restart-Service MSExchangeTransport

#Enable ABP routing agent
Set-TransportConfig -AddressBookPolicyRoutingEnabled $true
```

After following these steps, name resolution across departments shouldn't work and, along with configured Address Book policies, it provides the desired separation between two departments.

Figure 1–3 provides an example of a Sales user trying to resolve the display name of a Finance user (finuser1) while ABP separation is in place and the ABP routing agent is configured.

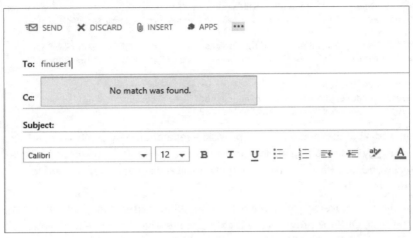

FIGURE 1-3 ABP routing agent blocking name resolution across ABP boundaries

Now let's look at more details of Offline Address Books. Because OABs are offline copies of address lists associated with an OAB, the files corresponding to the OABs need to be generated on Exchange servers. On Exchange 2013 servers, this is the function of the Microsoft Exchange OABGen service. The Microsoft Exchange OABGen service isn't a schedule-based function. Instead, based on server resource availability, it's throttled or paused as needed.

Exchange 2013 supports and produces OAB v4 files only. OAB v4 was introduced with the release of Exchange 2003 Service Pack 2 and is supported by Outlook 2007 and later. OAB v4 Unicode format allows client computers to receive differential updates, instead of full OAB downloads, as well as a reduction in file size.

Exchange 2013 uses web-based distribution, which Outlook clients use to download OAB files. In contrast to public folder-based distribution in previous versions, web-based distribution provides distinct advantages, such as the ability to support more concurrent clients for OAB distribution, a reduction in bandwidth usage, and more control over the distribution end point. Clients use Autodiscover to locate the OAB distribution point they should connect to, which, in turn, can be load-balanced end points providing better resiliency.

Another change in Exchange 2013 regarding OAB is generation. OAB generation is
no longer associated with a particular mailbox server like in previous versions. When we
created an example OAB in the previous ABP exercise, you may have noticed we didn't specify
a generation server. The OAB generation functionality is now associated with a specialized
mailbox called the *arbitration mailbox*. When Exchange server is installed, multiple arbitration
mailboxes are automatically created and are associated with different persisted capabilities,
which define the purpose and function of an arbitration mailbox. An arbitration mailbox with
persisted capability OrganizationCapabilityOABGen is responsible for OAB generation. The
new functionality can now benefit from higher availability provided by a DAG when a mailbox
is located on a database protected by DAG.

Because no generation server exists, changing the OAB generation server simply means
moving the arbitration mailbox to a different database on a different server if the database
isn't protected by DAG. If a mailbox is located on a database copy protected by DAG, you can
simply activate a different copy of the database on a different server to move the arbitration
mailbox to a different server.

To provide close proximity to an OAB generation mailbox in a distributed environment, you
can create additional arbitration mailboxes as needed. When creating an arbitration mailbox,
specify the Arbitration parameter to the New-Mailbox cmdlet. After creating an arbitration
mailbox in the desired location, enable OAB generation by using the –OABGen $True param-
eter with the Set-Mailbox cmdlet.

When an OAB download request is received by a client access server, it proxies the request
to the mailbox server hosting an active arbitration mailbox in the same Active Directory site. If
more than one mailbox server contains an active arbitration mailbox with an OAB generation
capability, the client access server sends the requests using round-robin distribution. This could
result in the frequent full download of OABs by the client and isn't recommended.

The OAB generation schedule configuration has also been changed in Exchange 2013. Schedule property on the OAB object is no longer affected when the OAB is generated. The OAB generation is now controlled based on the configuration of the OABGeneratorWorkCycle and the OABGeneratorWorkCycleCheckpoint properties of a mailbox server. The default values of these attributes are set to one day, resulting in the OAB generation taking place once every day. Values of these parameters can be changed using the Set-MailboxServer cmdlet.

If you need to manually force the generation of a particular OAB, you can use the Update-OfflineAddressBook cmdlet. You can also restart the mailbox assistant service, but it's more impactful on the server resources and it isn't the best or most preferred option when a better option exists.

Designing and creating hierarchical address lists

While GAL provides the ability to easily find recipients from an organization, it doesn't reflect management or seniority relationships within recipients of the organization. The hierarchical address book (HAB) enables end users to look for recipients using an organizational hierarchy, thus providing an efficient method for locating internal recipients.

The HAB is enabled at the organization level by using the Set-OrganizationConfig cmdlet. When enabling HAB, you need to provide a distribution group to use as the root of HAB. You can create a separate organizational unit (OU) to store all HAB-related distribution groups or use an existing OU in Active Directory.

You also need to create more distribution groups, each corresponding to the hierarchy of the company. For example, HQ, designating company headquarters, locations, and departments.

The hierarchy is created by using a distribution group nesting. You need to add subordinate distribution groups to their parents as a member. For example, distribution group HQ is added to the root distribution group, and department distribution groups HR and Accounting are added to the distribution group HQ to represent a hierarchy.

Individual recipients show up in the HAB based on their distribution group membership. For example, the CEO of the company might be a member of distribution group HQ, whereas the Director of Human Resources might be added to the HR distribution group, and so on.

Once the distribution group for the HAB root is created and the HAB is enabled at the organization level, set the value of the IsHierarchicalGroup property on the distribution group to $true. You also need to repeat this step for all of the distribution groups that are members of the HAB.

When you have multiple members for a given location, such as HQ, in the HAB display, they are organized alphabetically in ascending order. It might be more desirable to show the members based on their seniority. HAB enables you to achieve that by setting the value of the SeniorityIndex attribute on the recipient or the distribution group. In HAB, objects are organized based on seniority index values from higher to lower.

Let's take a look at the process of creating the HAB root distribution group and enabling HAB for Contoso, Ltd.

Enable Hierarchical Address Book

```
#Add OU for Hierarchical Address Book
dsadd ou "OU=HAB,DC=Contoso,DC=com"

#Create root Distribution group
New-DistributionGroup -Name "Contoso,Ltd" -DisplayName "Contoso,Ltd" -Alias
"ContosoRoot" -OrganizationalUnit "Contoso.com/HAB" -SamAccountName "ContosoRoot" -Type
"Distribution"

#Enable HAB using Contoso Distribution Group created for HAB root
Set-OrganizationConfig -HierarchicalAddressBookRoot "Contoso,Ltd"

#Designate distribution group as member of HAB
Set-Group -Identity "Contoso,Ltd" -IsHierarchicalGroup $true
```

At this point, you have an empty HAB, which would look similar to Figure 1–4 when using the Outlook client.

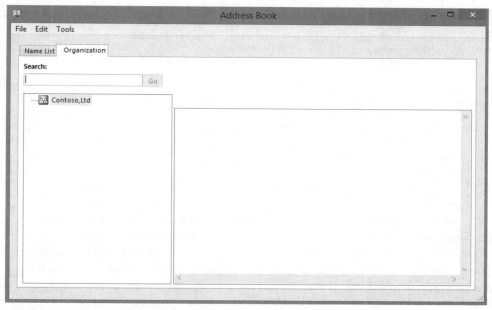

FIGURE 1-4 Hierarchical Address Book with no members

Now let's create subordinate distribution groups HQ, New York, and London, and then add them to their relevant parent distribution groups. HQ also has HR and Accounting sub groups. We also set the seniority index of a few recipients and add them to the appropriate distribution groups in the hierarchy.

Create subordinate groups and configure hierarchy

```
#Create subordinate distribution groups
New-DistributionGroup -Name "HQ" -DisplayName "HQ" -Alias "HQ" -OrganizationalUnit
"Contoso.com/HAB" -SamAccountName "HQ" -Type "Distribution"
New-DistributionGroup -Name "HR" -DisplayName "HR" -Alias "HR" -OrganizationalUnit
"Contoso.com/HAB" -SamAccountName "HR" -Type "Distribution"
New-DistributionGroup -Name "Accounting" -DisplayName "Accounting" -Alias "Accounting"
-OrganizationalUnit "Contoso.com/HAB" -SamAccountName "Accounting" -Type "Distribution"
New-DistributionGroup -Name "New York" -DisplayName "New York" -Alias "New York"
-OrganizationalUnit "Contoso.com/HAB" -SamAccountName "NY" -Type "Distribution"
New-DistributionGroup -Name "London" -DisplayName "London" -Alias "London"
-OrganizationalUnit "Contoso.com/HAB" -SamAccountName "London" -Type "Distribution"

#Designate distribution groups as member of HAB
Set-Group -Identity "HQ" -IsHierarchicalGroup $true
Set-Group -Identity "HR" -IsHierarchicalGroup $true
Set-Group -Identity "Accounting" -IsHierarchicalGroup $true
Set-Group -Identity "New York" -IsHierarchicalGroup $true
Set-Group -Identity "London" -IsHierarchicalGroup $true

#Add distribution groups to appropriate parent
Add-DistributionGroupMember -Identity "ContosoRoot" -Member "HQ"
Add-DistributionGroupMember -Identity "ContosoRoot" -Member "New York"
Add-DistributionGroupMember -Identity "ContosoRoot" -Member "London"
Add-DistributionGroupMember -Identity "HQ" -Member "HR"
Add-DistributionGroupMember -Identity "HQ" -Member "Accounting"

#Add members to appropriate distribution groups
Add-DistributionGroupMember -Identity "HQ" -Member "Ray"
Add-DistributionGroupMember -Identity "HQ" -Member "Peter"
Add-DistributionGroupMember -Identity "HR" -Member "Mary"

#Assign appropriate seniority index to members
Set-Group -Identity "HR" -SeniorityIndex 100
Set-User -Identity "Ray" -SeniorityIndex 100
Set-User -Identity "Peter" -SeniorityIndex 99
```

After the completion of the previous steps, we now have an example HAB, complete with subordinate groups and their members. Because we also assigned seniority to Ray, he is displayed before Peter in the list, overriding the default alphabetical ordering. The same also applies to the HR department, which displays before Accounting in the hierarchy. Figure 1–5 represents the example HAB.

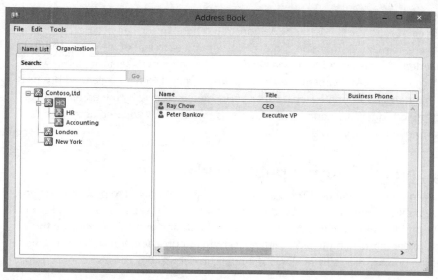

FIGURE 1-5 Hierarchical Address Book with members

Notice how London is listed after HQ and before New York. Because we chose not to assign any seniority index to the locations, they're displayed using default alphabetical display order. However, Ray is displayed before Peter and HQ is displayed before Accounting as defined by the seniority index.

The Name List tab still provides you with a nonhierarchical reference to all recipient objects, as shown in Figure 1–6.

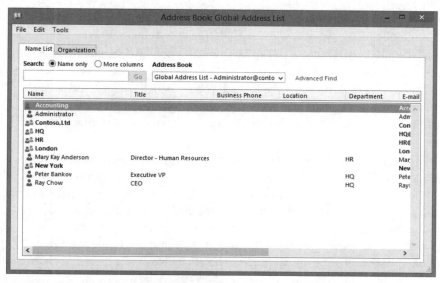

FIGURE 1-6 Name List view of the Address Book

It's important for you to understand that the effort involved in a large environment to enable HAB goes beyond the simple steps demonstrated here. In such an organization, you might need to create many distribution groups representing each leaf of hierarchy and then add DLs as needed. You also need to define each individual member's seniority index where necessary, which in large environments can be daunting. It's best to have a defined business process that mandates appropriate steps, either performed manually by the administrative staff or by scripting triggered on appropriate intervals to keep HAB updated according to changes occurring in the environment.

Creating and configuring public folders

Creating public folders in Exchange 2013 is a different process compared to previous versions. This is because public folders are now stored in public folder mailboxes. In a new installation where no public folders exist, the first step is to create a public folder mailbox. Because this is the first public folder mailbox in the organization, it contains public folder hierarchy information and becomes the primary hierarchy mailbox. The public folder mailbox can also contain public folder content.

The primary hierarchy mailbox is the only writeable copy of the hierarchy in the organization. All other public folder mailboxes created contain a read-only copy of the public folder hierarchy.

You can create a public folder mailbox using EAC or the Shell. Similar to any other mailbox, the cmdlet you use to create the public folder mailbox is New-Mailbox. To designate a mailbox as a public folder mailbox, use the PublicFolder parameter. There is no difference in the syntax for creating the first public folder mailbox containing the primary public folder hierarchy and secondary public folder mailboxes. Exchange server automatically creates the public folder with an appropriate copy of the hierarchy. To verify which mailbox contains the primary writeable copy of the public folder hierarchy, you can issue Get-OrganizationConfig | Format-List RootPublicFolderMailbox at the Shell.

After creating a public folder mailbox, you can now create a public folder that users see in the hierarchy and can store content in. To create a public folder, you can use New-PublicFolder cmdlet or EAC. You can specify a name for the folder being created, the path in the hierarchy where the folder is created and, optionally, the public folder mailbox where the content for the folder is stored. You don't need to define the path if you're creating a public folder in the root of the hierarchy.

When you create a public folder, it inherits the settings of its parent folder, which includes the permissions assigned to the parent public folder. To assign permissions to a public folder, you can use EAC or use the Add-PublicFolderClientPermission cmdlet. You can either choose to assign permissions such as ability to read, create or delete items, or assign a role, such as owner, editor, or author. Each role represents a combination of permissions on the public folder. For example, the Reviewer role enables the assignee permissions to see the public folder and its contents, but it has no ability to edit or delete them.

Public folders also allow the ability to submit content via email. To do so, you must mail-enable a public folder. Similar to other public folder-related procedures, you can use EAC to mail-enable a public folder, or you can use the Enable-MailPublicFolder cmdlet. When mail-enabling a public folder, you don't need to provide an email address for the folder. You can, however, change the primary email address or assign additional email addresses to a mail-enabled public folder, if needed. If you use the Shell, you can use the Set-MailPublicFolder cmdlet to update an email address and other mailbox properties, such as the mailbox quota.

Another important consideration for when you mail-enable a public folder mailbox, is to ensure that only authorized users can submit content via email. You can choose to accept emails from individual recipients or members of a distribution group. Use the Set-MailPublicFolder cmdlet with the AcceptMessagesOnlyFrom, AcceptMessagesOnlyFromDLMembers, or AcceptMessagesOnlyFromSendersOrMembers parameters to assign appropriate sender restrictions.

Now that only one writeable copy of the public folder hierarchy exists, it's critical that the public folder mailbox containing a writeable copy of the hierarchy is highly available. Ensure that the public folder mailbox is located on a database copy protected by DAG and has multiple database copies located in appropriate locations to provide protection against local and site failures. The same protection should also be applied to all public folder mailboxes that store critical public folder content.

If public folders are accessed by users located across multiple locations and regions connected via WAN or slower network links, you can improve the user experience when accessing a public folder hierarchy. You can also provide uninterrupted access in case of network failures between a client location and other sites. You do this by creating a public folder mailbox in close proximity to the client location where network connectivity between client and Exchange server is robust. After creating a public folder mailbox in such a location, you need to change all user mailboxes for a given office or regions to use the new public folder mailbox as their default access location for the public folder hierarchy. You can do so by using the Set-Mailbox cmdlet with the DefaultPublicFolderMailbox parameter.

While this provides users with uninterrupted access to the public folder hierarchy, uninterrupted access to the content can only be guaranteed if the public folder content is also stored on public folder mailboxes that are locally accessible. That is why locating public folder content requires careful planning and an understanding of the usage of public folders and the factors affecting it, such as a public folder containing regional data or a public folder containing company data that might be applicable to all public folder users.

Moving a public folder mailbox may be necessary due to organizational or infrastructure changes. If you need to move a public folder mailbox, you can do so by issuing a mailbox move request, similar to moving a regular mailbox. This enables you to move the public folder mailbox, including all of its content, including the primary or read-only copy of a public folder hierarchy, to a different database located on the same or a different server, which may or may not be a part of DAG. When you need to provide high availability to a public folder mailbox, you should move it to a database configured with multiple copies protected by DAG. If you're using the Shell, you can use the New-MoveRequest cmdlet to move a public folder server.

When the organization grows, you might need to change where the public folders are stored. You might need to move a public folder to a different public folder mailbox to provide close proximity access to its primary user base. Or, you might need to move a public folder that exceeds the assigned mailbox storage quota. Moving a single public folder is as simple as issuing the New-PublicFolderMoveRequest cmdlet.

> *NOTE* **PUBLIC FOLDER MOVE REQUESTS**
>
> You can perform only one public folder move request at a time. Before creating another public folder move request, you must remove the completed public folder move requests, using the Remove-PublicFolderMoveRequest cmdlet.

If you need to move a public folder, including all of the public folders within its branch, you can't use the New-PublicFolderMoveRequest cmdlet. While the cmdlet enables you to move multiple individual public folders to a different mailbox, it doesn't move an entire branch of a selected public folder. To move the entire branch of a public folder, you must use the Move-PublicFolderBranch.ps1 script, which is included with an Exchange server installation.

The process of creating public folders in a new environment might seem relatively simple. Migrating public folders from a previous version of Exchange servers requires careful planning. This is because when the public folder data is migrated to Exchange 2013 servers, it doesn't synchronize with a previous version of public folders.

Migrating from a previous version of public folders is a multi-step process. The supported version of Exchange servers for such a migration is Exchange Server 2007 SP3 RU10 and Exchange Server 2010 SP3 or later.

The first step in the migration process is to use public-folder migration scripts to create the public folder name to size mapping and the public folder to the proposed new public-folder mailbox mapping. The collection of statistics enables you to understand the impact on new Exchange 2013 servers. It also enables you to create the required public folder mailboxes according to the appropriate folder size mapping created by the scripts.

Before you proceed with migration, ensure that no public folder mailboxes exist on Exchange 2013 and that no public folder migration requests exist. You can verify any existing public-folder migration requests by running the Get-PublicFolderMigrationRequest cmdlet. If a migration request exists, you need to make sure no migration is in progress or you risk losing data when you remove the migration request to start the new migration.

After ensuring that starting a new public folder migration is appropriate, start the process by creating public folder mailboxes. When you create the first public folder mailbox, set the property of the HoldForMigration parameter to $true. Use the csv file created by the migration script PublicFoldertoMAilboxMapGenerator.ps1 to create additional public folder mailboxes.

After the successful creation of all required public folder mailboxes, you can start the migration request by using the New-PublicFolderMigrationRequest cmdlet. The time it takes to migrate the public folder data depends on the amount of data being migrated, the load on the source and destination servers, and other environmental factors, such as the network infrastructure.

When the migration is started, Exchange servers synchronize public folder data from a previous version of Exchange servers to the new public folder mailboxes created earlier. However, during the initial data synchronization process, users can continue using legacy public folders and make changes.

When the migration process reaches the status of autosuspended, you can lock the public folders on a legacy exchange server for final migration. To verify the status of the migration process, run the Get-PublicFolderMigrationRequest cmdlet. To lock down the legacy public folders for final migration, run Set-OrganizationConfig -PublicFoldersLockedForMigration:$true. After performing this step, users won't be able to access public folders or make any changes. If public folder databases are distributed across multiple locations, it might take several hours for the change to converge. You can verify the status of public folder databases by verifying the PublicFoldersLockedForMigration flag.

Once all of the legacy public folders are locked for migration, you can set the PreventCompletion property on the public folder migration request to $false. This action allows the final synchronization of public folder data to take place. You also need to resume the public folder migration request by issuing the Resume-PublicFolderMigrationRequest cmdlet. The amount of time required for the final synchronization depends on the amount of changes made by users to the public folder data after the migration process reaches the autosuspended status, and before the legacy public folders are locked for migration.

Before you can enable public folders on Exchange 2013, you need to ensure that the migration is complete, which you can verify by running the Get-PublicFolderMigrationRequest cmdlet and ensuring that the status is Completed. Once complete, you can allow user access to migrated public folders on Exchange 2013 servers by setting the IsExcludedFromServingHierarchy property on the public folder mailboxes to $false. You also need to set the organization configuration property PublicFolderMigrationComplete to $true on legacy Exchange servers, and then set the PublicFoldersEnabled property of the organization configuration on Exchange 2013 servers to Local.

Users can access data from migrated public folders on Exchange 2013 after the successful completion of the previously shown process. But there might be times when a migration doesn't complete successfully and you need to roll back the migration, so users can continue to access public folders from legacy exchange servers. To roll back the migration, you need to set the organization property PublicFoldersLockedForMigration on legacy Exchange servers to $false, remove all of the public folder mailboxes created on Exchange 2013 servers, and set the PublicFolderMigrationComplete flag on the organization property to $false from legacy Exchange servers.

Once the new public folders are deployed on the Exchange 2013 mailbox, you might need to address such issues as accidental deletions of a public folder or the deletion of a public folder mailbox. This can happen because of a user action, a failed public folder, or a public folder mailbox move. Because the public folder mailboxes are now similar to user mailboxes, restoring a deleted public folder mailbox is similar to restoring a deleted mailbox. Use the New-MailboxRestoreRequest cmdlet and provide the appropriate values for SourceStoreMailbox, SourceDatabase and TargetMailbox. If the public folder mailbox is intact, but a public folder is deleted instead, you can restore the public folder by using a similar process to the one previously mentioned. You also need to include the IncludeFolders parameter with the public folder path of the folder that needs restoring.

The process gets more involved when a deleted public folder or the public folder mailbox is past its retention period as defined on the mailbox and mailbox database properties.

The process to restore a public folder mailbox and public folders past their retention period requires recovering data using a recovery database. For more information on this topic, see Develop backup and recovery solutions for the mailbox role and public folders in Objective 1.5 later in this chapter, which covers this topic in detail. The process applies to both regular and public folder mailboxes. At a high level, the process involves creating a recovery database, restoring data from backups, mounting restored databases, and extracting the data from the recovery database. Extracted data can then be exported to a folder or merged into an existing mailbox.

Thought experiment
Public Folders and GAL considerations

In this Thought experiment, apply what you learned about this objective. You can find answers to these questions in the "Answers" section at the end of this chapter.

You are an Exchange administrator for Litware, Inc. Litware is migrating from Exchange 2010 and has deployed Exchange 2013 servers. Litware frequently acquires small companies that complement its products. It requires acquired companies to migrate to Litware's existing Exchange platform.

Litware requires that each acquired company have a limited view of the Address Book and it shouldn't be able to look up other units through GAL.

Litware also requires that public folders be available during single server failures. The company requires that users can browse the public folder structure without lengthy delays, regardless of their location and their connectivity to the centralized datacenter where all Exchange 2013 servers are located.

1. Recommend a solution to meet Litware's goals to provide Address Book lookups.

2. What is the impact of public folder requirements proposed by Litware?

Objective summary

- Schema updates are required anytime you install an Exchange 2013 server, including when you apply updates. Plan for schema update dependencies, including OS components required, such as the Remote Tools Administration Toolkit to make schema updates.

- If you're using the Setup Wizard and have appropriate permissions to make schema and domain changes, you don't need to perform schema updates separately before running setup.

- When using the command line setup, if you run Prepare Domain before applying schema updates and before preparing Active Directory, setup tries to perform those steps automatically and it will succeed if the account running setup has required permissions.

- Address book segmentation allows logical separation between business units or different companies hosted on the same Exchange organization.

- HABs provides an organizational hierarchy view, making navigation and search of recipient easier compared to flat address-book structure provided by the default address-book view.

- Public folder migration requires that careful planning and downtime is required. Rollback is possible, but it might involve data loss because no backward synchronization exists from Exchange 2013 public folders to legacy public folders.

Objective review

Answer the following questions to test your knowledge of the information in this objective. You can find the answers to these questions and explanations of why each answer choice is correct or incorrect in the "Answers" section at the end of this chapter.

1. Contoso, Ltd. has deployed an Exchange 2013 environment in the child domain ny.contoso.com. The empty forest root domain is called consoto.com. Contoso, Ltd. later introduces a new domain, London.contoso.com. What should you do before enabling recipient objects in the domain London.contoso.com?

   A. Run setup.exe /prepareschema.

   B. Run setup.exe /preparead.

   C. Run setup.exe /preparedomain.

2. When an Exchange server crashed, users complained their Address Books didn't include recent new hires. You need to move the OAB generation to a different server. What should you do?

   A. Run Move-OfflineAddressBook cmdlet.

   B. Run Set-OfflineAddressBook cmdlet.

   C. Run Move-Mailbox cmdlet.

   D. Run Update-OfflineAddressBook cmdlet

3. Contoso, Ltd. has implemented a hierarchical address book (HAB). You need to ensure the company's CEO is listed before other employees, regardless of the alphabetical order of names. What should you do?

   A. Run Set-Mailbox cmdlet to change CEO's mailbox.

   B. Run Set-DistributionGroup to change the seniority index.

   C. Run Set-OrganizationConfig –OrganizationSummary $true.

   D. Run Set-AddressList cmdlet.

Objective 1.3: Deploy and manage high availability solutions for the mailbox role

When deploying a critical platform such as messaging, the assumption is that such systems are going to be available without interruptions. Maintaining such complex systems without any downtime is a real challenge, especially if the platform doesn't provide native functionality to address maintenance and unexpected downtime scenarios. Exchange 2013 not only continues to provide native functionality, but it also has improved features providing high availability for the mailbox role. Improvements such as support for multiple databases per disk provide for better utilization of disk space, as well as disk IOPS by allowing to store active, passive, and lagged copies of different databases on the same disk. Enhancements, such as automatic log replay, ensure data integrity by allowing page patching on lagged copies.

This objective covers how to:
- Create and configure a Database Availability Group (DAG)
- Identify failure domains
- Manage DAG networks
- Manage mailbox database copies

Creating and configuring a Database Availability Group

In Exchange 2013, DAG is an integral component for both high availability and site resilience. DAG is a group of up to 16 mailbox servers that hosts mailbox database copies and provides automatic database level recovery from failures.

You can host a mailbox database copy on any mailbox server that's a member of DAG. You must ensure that at least two copies of a database are hosted on separate DAG members to provide high availability. DAG is a boundary for mailbox database replication. So, you can't create a copy of mailbox database on a mailbox that's a member of a different DAG.

Exchange 2013 makes deploying DAG easy because it leverages the concept of incremental deployment. The *incremental deployment process* enables you to install a mailbox server role without requiring a complex cluster setup. You can create DAG with a single Exchange server, and then add more Exchange servers when they are provisioned at a later date. While single server can't provide high availability, it makes the process of building DAG easier by staging the DAG object and configuration in the environment.

A DAG is created by using the New-DatabaseAvailabilityGroup cmdlet. When creating a DAG, you're required to provide the DAG name and, optionally, the witness server name and the location of the witness directory where the file share witness data is stored. DAG is created as an empty Active Directory object. When the first mailbox server is added as a DAG member, the directory object is used to store server membership information and DAG configuration settings.

While an administrator isn't required to create and configure a cluster setup, Exchange 2013 DAG relies on failover clustering components and creates a failover cluster automatically when adding the first server to the DAG. The Cluster Network Object (CNO) is also created in the Active Directory. The CNO is identified with the same name as the name of the DAG you're creating.

EXAM TIP

If DAG members are running Windows Server 2012 or Windows Server 2012 R2, prestaging the CNO is required. Pre-staging the CNO isn't required when creating DAG without a cluster administrative access point, as the following discusses.

If you need to pre-state a CNO for creating a new DAG, the process requires permissions in Active Directory to be able to create a computer object and assign necessary permissions to it. First, you must create a computer in Active Directory. Next, when you create the computer object, ensure the object name is the name of the DAG you plan to create. Then, for additional security, the recommendation is that you disable the CNO computer object. Finally, after you create the CNO, assign Full Control permissions to Exchange Trusted Subsystem on the CNO. Or, you can assign Full Control permissions only to the first node to be added to the DAG.

After the DAG is created, it's given a network name and an IP address. The failover cluster-core resource group contains an IP address resource and a network name resource in the cluster core group. The name of the DAG is registered in DNS and is resolvable on the network.

With changes to the failover cluster in Windows Server 2012 R2 and Exchange 2013 Service Pack 1, DAG can be created without an administrative access point. When you create a DAG without an administrative access point, an IP address and a network name aren't assigned to the cluster. The cluster-core resource group doesn't contain an IP address and network name resource. A CNO isn't created in Active Directory and the name of the cluster/DAG isn't registered in DNS. You can't use failover cluster administration tools to connect and manage the failover cluster, and you must use the Shell to manage a DAG without an administrative access point.

When creating a DAG with an administrative access point, if the DAG member servers are to be located across different IP subnets within an Active Directory site, or if the members are to be located across different Active Directory and physical sites for site resiliency, then you must provide multiple IP addresses for DAG configuration. You must provide one IP from each subnet the DAG members will be connected to. This allows for DAG to be managed, regardless of which DAG member owns the cluster-core resource group.

When creating a DAG, one of the design considerations is the configuration of a witness server. When using failover cluster, the decision of when to consider a node of cluster out of service relies on the number of votes. Each member of the DAG is considered one vote. When you have a DAG with an even number of nodes, this creates the possibility of a split number of votes, where half the DAG members might vote a node to be out of service and the other half might vote for it to be in service. This can happen when network connectivity between locations is affected and nodes are located across the affected link evenly. In such situations, a tie-breaker mechanism becomes essential. File witness provides that mechanism. When the vote achieves the majority among all failover cluster members, then it's considered to have reached a quorum.

When a DAG is created, a file witness is required. The file witness might not be required when the DAG has an odd number of members, but failover clustering and DAG failover decision-making automatically accounts for the file witness when it's necessary. If a file witness isn't specified, the task of creating a DAG searches for a Client Access server in the local Active Directory site that doesn't have a mailbox role installed. If one is found, it automatically creates a default directory and shares on that server to be used as a witness file share.

If you specify a witness server and the directory, the task tries to create a specified directory and share automatically. This can succeed if the server is Exchange 2013 server because the Exchange Trusted Subsystem object has required permission to create the directory and share on the server. If the witness server isn't an Exchange 2013 server, you must add the Exchange Trusted Subsystem group to the local Administrators group on the witness server. If the witness server is the Active Directory domain controller, the Administrators group permissions equate to permissions assigned to domain administrators. To provide required functionality, while assigning the least privilege necessary to do so, it isn't advisable to co-locate the file witness on the Active Directory domain controller. It is, however, a supported configuration.

The witness server can't be a server that's also a member of the same DAG. The witness server is required to be a Windows Server running any version of Windows Server 2003 or later. Using a single witness server for multiple DAGs is possible, but the witness directory must be unique for each DAG.

File witness location also plays an important role in ensuring availability of DAG members. In a single-site DAG configured to provide high availability to all users hosted on database copies protected by a given DAG, the file witness needs to be located into the same physical site location and Active Directory site.

When a DAG is designed to provide site resiliency in a configuration where all active users are located in a primary location, the file witness should be located at the primary site. This ensures that the majority is maintained at a primary site, even when the network link fails between primary and secondary sites.

If you have more than two locations available, Exchange 2013 also supports a locating file witness in a third location. This enables DAG members located in primary and secondary sites to participate in quorum, even when they're unable to communicate to each other between a primary and secondary site. This design can only work if network links provide robust connectivity between primary/secondary sites to the site where the file witness is located.

EXAM TIP

With Microsoft Azure Infrastructure as a Service offering, there's a lot of interest in using a file server located in Azure as a file share witness. Even with VPN links from each datacenter to Azure, this configuration is currently not supported by Exchange 2013.

When extending DAG across multiple datacenters, you must account for outages and its effect on active users. Exchange administrators often prefer to optimize the use of compute resources available to them. They consider hosting active users from two separate locations on mailbox servers that are part of same DAG. The problem with this design is it can't provide high availability to all users. When a network outage occurs between two locations, mailbox servers in only one of the two datacenters can achieve quorum. This means the active databases in the datacenter with lost quorum are dismounted and users experience service interruption. Overall design considerations, such as file share witness in the third datacenter, can affect the outcome as well. Without use of the third site for file share witness, it's better to deploy two separate DAGs with the majority of mailbox servers for each DAG located where the majority of active users are located. This can ensure that a lost quorum at any site affects the least possible users.

Once the DAG is created, the next step is to add a server to the DAG. You can add a server to the DAG using EAC or by running the Add-DatabaseAvailabilityGroupServer cmdlet. When you add the first server to the DAG, the CNO computer account for DAG is automatically enabled.

Existing databases aren't highly available until additional copies of the databases are created manually. You can use the EAC or run the Add-MailboxDatabaseCopy cmdlet to add copies to a database. A new database copy can be created on any mailbox server within the same DAG. A mailbox server can host only one active or passive copy of a database. Circular logging must be disabled before creating the first copy of the database. You can enable circular logging after adding the first copy of the database. Circular logging doesn't need to be disabled when adding additional copies of the database.

Identifying failure domains

Any solution is as strong as its weakest component. To provide the best possible availability using DAG, you must account for all the components that affect it and how to remove the points of failure by providing redundancy. Another factor to consider when designing such highly available solutions is the cost. As you add more components and more redundancy to account for the failure of each component, the cost of the solution increases. Good designs always account for striking an optimal balance between availability and cost based on the available budget. Discussions of the cost benefit of a design is beyond the scope of this book. This section covers each failure domain and its impact on the high availability of Exchange 2013.

When looking at possible failures, you need to look at software, hardware, and environmental factors that can affect the operations of a component and the service itself. For example, the failure of a disk might affect only a database, while Exchange 2013 continues to function. Whereas, the failure of the Top of the Rack (ToR) router might affect more than one server in a given rack.

Starting at server level failures, the server hardware, such as the power supply, network, and disk, are the most common factors. Most of the modern server class hardware now supports and commonly ships with redundant power supplies and network cards. But they still need to be configured properly to provide resiliency against failures. If a power supply fails on a server equipped with two power supplies, the server continues to function. But what if both power supplies were connected to the same power feed? What if the feed itself fails?

The same concept applies to the network and disks. If your network adapters are teamed, you need to make sure they're connected to separate switches and that the switches are configured properly. For storage, a common practice is to protect against disk failures by using different RAID levels.

As you might have noticed, to protect against failures, adding more components to provide redundancy also raises the cost of the solution.

Exchange 2013 is designed to provide the best cost efficiencies, while reducing the cost where possible. When DAG is configured and databases have multiple copies configured appropriately, a single power supply failure or a network card failure would affect the given server, but not the service to the user. This provides the administrator with the flexibility to fix the failed component, while the end user is provided with uninterrupted service.

With the use of spare disks and auto-reseed functionality, Exchange 2013 automates the process that the administrator would have to manually perform otherwise. When combined with at least three copies of a database, Exchange 2013 supports JBOD configuration, eliminating the need for RAID and extra disks needed for the RAID configuration, reducing the cost of the required hardware and providing automation with the automatic reseed functionality.

For a single datacenter deployment, it's best to ensure that servers from the same DAG are located in different racks, have connectivity to different network switches, and are connected to a separate power feed. This ensures that any power, network or other rack-level failures, or human errors won't affect the entire DAG and surviving components are sufficient to provide uninterrupted service to end users.

Another benefit of such a design is that, with proper capacity planning, Exchange administrators can remove a mailbox server from a service to perform required maintenance without interrupting service.

You also need to account for other external dependencies, such as file share witness. While it's possible to configure alternate witness server and alternate witness directory, if witness server fails, DAG doesn't automatically use alternate witness server and directory. Alternat the witness server and directory, if preconfigured, can only help speed site failovers, but not without manual intervention.

While a Distributed File System (DFS) might seem like a good solution to provide redundancy, it's possible that the replication of the latest data hasn't completed to the file-share witness copy that Exchange server might connect to. So, it isn't supported to use DFS to host the file-share witness directory.

Managing DAG networks

In Exchange 2010, when you create a DAG, the initial DAG networks were created automatically based on the subnets enumerated by the cluster service. For environments where the interfaces for a specified network (MAPI or Replication network), were on multiple subnets, multiple redundant DAG networks were created and the administrator had to perform the procedure manually to collapse the networks into their appropriate function, such as MAPI or Replication network. The process was many times overlooked, resulting in unexpected DAG behavior, such as incorrect network being used for replication.

In Exchange 2013, network management is automated. For automatic DAG network configuration to work correctly, MAPI networks must be registered in DNS and, in a routed network with multiple subnets, must also have a default gateway assigned. Replication networks must not be registered in DNS and they must not have a default gateway assigned to the interface. If these prerequisites are met, DAG network configuration is performed automatically and collapsing DAG networks is no longer necessary.

DAG network management is also automatic in Exchange 2013 by default. DAG networks aren't visible in EAC and can only be viewed using Shell. To view, edit, and otherwise manually manage DAG networks, you must configure DAG for manual network configuration. You can do so by checking the Configure Database Availability Group Networks Manually check box on the DAG object using EAC, or you can run the Set-DatabaseAvailabilityGroup cmdlet with the ManualDagNetworkConfiguration parameter set to $true.

Be default, DAG can use MAPI networks, not only for service client traffic, but also for replication traffic, if needed. If you create a dedicated replication network and want to force all of the replication to take place on a dedicated network when the link is operational, you can run the Set-DatabaseAvailabilityGroupNetwork cmdlet and set the value of the ReplicationEnabled parameter to $false on the MAPI network. This enables you to force replication traffic over a dedicated replication network, but this setting is ignored if DAG can't replicate data over replication networks, and the only available replication path is the MAPI network.

When using a dedicated iSCSI networks for data storage, it is important to segregate the iSCSI traffic from MAPI and replication traffic. After a manual network configuration is enabled on DAG, you can set the IgnoreNetwork parameter to $true.

Managing mailbox database copies

After creating a DAG, the first step to provide high availability for a database is to add the passive copy of an existing database. For any given database, you can have up to 15 maximum passive copies due to the maximum of 16 servers limit per DAG.

After adding a database copy, DAG starts the initial copy of the database from the active copy. This process is known as *seeding*. While this automated process works for most environments, you might want the seeding process not to start automatically. When creating a database copy, you can set the value of the SeedingPostponed parameter to $true. This suspends the seeding operation on the creation of the database copy and you must explicitly seed the database copy.

EXAM TIP

When creating a database copy, the mailbox server must not only be a member of the same DAG, but the database path used by the specified database must also match on the server where the copy is hosted. The creation of the database copy fails if the path to the directory or mount point where the original database is located isn't available on the mailbox server where the copy is being created.

A database on DAG might have more than one copy. When a passive copy of the database needs to be activated, many factors are taken into account by the best copy selection (BCS) process. One of the factors is the activation preference parameter, which can be set by the administrator. You can set the value of the ActivationPreference parameter on a database copy with the value of 1 or higher. The value of this parameter can't be more than the number of database copies of a given database.

While the activation preference helps define in which order a database copy is to be selected for activation, it's by no means a binding order for the BCS process of Exchange 2013. BCS takes into account multiple factors, such as the replay queue length and protocol health to ensure that not only is the selected database copy healthy, but that the server where the database copy is hosted is also healthy to ensure that a failover operation doesn't cause service interruption.

When creating a database copy, you can also opt to create a lagged copy of the database. A lag is defined by the ReplayLagTime and TruncationLagTime parameters. The maximum allowed lag time is 14 days. A lagged copy can be used as a backup. An administrator can roll back to a point in time within the configured lag window by manipulating log files that haven't been played back into the lagged database copy.

Exchange 2013 also introduces logic to improve service availability. If the database has a bad page, Exchange 2013 plays forward the lagged database copy over the risk of losing data. The play forward logic also applies to copies of the database, which might not have enough space to keep all the logs or be the only database copy available for activation.

When a database without an additional copy is using circular logging, it uses JET circular logging. When a database with multiple copies on the DAG uses circular logging, it uses the *continuous replication circular logging* (CRCL) instead of JET circular logging. To account for this difference in the circular logging method, circular logging must be disabled on the database before creating another copy of the database. After creating a second copy of the database, circular logging can be enabled, which then uses CRCL. When you create subsequent copies of the database, you don't need to disable circular logging because it's already configured to use CRCL, not JET circular logging.

After a database copy is created, over its lifecycle, it can have one of many states. The Get-MailboxDatabaseCopyStatus cmdlet enables you to view whether the database copy is healthy and what state it's in. For example, a newly created database copy can be in the Initializing state. While in this state, the system is verifying the database and log stream are in a consistent state. A database can also be in this state during the transition from one state to another.

EXAM TIP

The healthy state of a database copy can sometimes be confused with the mounted state. Only an active copy of the database can have a copy status of Mounted. All other database copies, when they aren't affected by failures or other conditions, have a copy status of Healthy.

When a database copy fails to activate, Exchange 2013 provides the ability to test the replication health for the given database by running the Test-ReplicationHealth cmdlet. This cmdlet performs tests against many components that can affect database replication health such as cluster service, replay service, and active manage. The Test-ReplicationHealth cmdlet is an important tool in an Exchange administrator's troubleshooting toolbox.

Let's take a look at some important mailbox database copy maintenance tasks.

Activate a mailbox database copy

When you're performing maintenance on a server hosting an active copy of a database, you can initiate a switchover of the active database to another server by activating a passive copy. The database switchover process dismounts the current active database and mounts the database copy on the specified server. The operation succeeds if the database copy on the selected server is healthy and current. The following example moves the active database named DB1 to server Server2.

Activating database DB1 on Server2

```
Move-ActiveMailboxDatabase DB1 –ActivateOnServer Server2
```

Besides simply activating a database copy on a different server, the Move-ActiveMailboxDatabase cmdlet also enables you to override the AutoDatabaseMountDial setting, as well as skip one of the many health check requirements. These parameters allow the administrator to provide service at a degraded level, instead of taking the database offline if the requirements, the health checks, or the database mount dial aren't met.

Activate a lagged mailbox database copy

Activating a lagged copy can be an operation preferred during times when a lagged copy is the only copy available, or a lagged copy can be activated when a point in time recovery is needed when other database copies are affected by database corruption.

If you want to activate a lagged copy simply to make it current, and activate it when all other database copies are unavailable, the operation is a simple process of replaying all the log files to make the database copy current. One important factor that must be considered for this operation is the time it takes to replay all of the log files into the database before the copy can be activated. The number of log files depends on the configured lag for the copy. If the database copy is configured for a 14-day lag, it can have up to 14 days of logs for a given database that must be replayed before the copy can be activated. The log replay rate is dependent on the storage architecture and the server resource configuration.

The process of activating a lagged copy and replaying all of the logs requires you to carry out the following steps.

- Suspend replication for the lagged copy being activated:

```
Suspend-MailboxDatabaseCopy DB1\Server3 -SuspendComment "Activate lagged copy of
DB1 on Server3" -Confirm:$false
```

- Make a copy of the database copy and log files. While this is an optional step, it's a highly recommended best practice because it protects you from losing the only lagged copy that might be needed if the next step of replaying log files fails.

- Activate lagged copy and replay all log files:

```
Move-ActiveMailboxDatabase DB1 -ActivateOnServer Server3 -SkipLagChecks
```

If a lagged copy needs to be activated for recovery to a certain point in time, the process is a bit different than activating copy to make it current. For example, a database copy is configured for a 14-day lag. For example, active copy of the database is found to be corrupt and it's determined that the corruption caused data loss 10 days ago. In this case, the lagged copy only needs to account for four days of logs that need to be replayed.

The process of activating lagged copy to a specific point in time requires you to carry out the following steps.

1. Suspend replication for the lagged copy being activated:

```
Suspend-MailboxDatabaseCopy DB1\Server3 -SuspendComment "Activate lagged copy of
DB1 on Server3" -Confirm:$false
```

2. Make a copy of the database copy and log files. While this is an optional step, it's a highly recommended best practice because it protects you from losing the only lagged copy that might be needed if the next step of replaying log files fails.

3. Remove all log files past the determined point of recovery (all log files past the first four days in the previous example).

4. Delete the checkpoint file for the database.

5. Perform the recovery using eseutil. This process replays the log files into the database and can take a considerable amount of time. Many factors affect how long the process can take, such as the number of log files to be replayed, the hardware configuration of the server performing the replay operation, and the disk configuration, which can determine the speed at which the logs can be replayed. In the following example, eXX should be replaced with the actual log generation prefix, such as E00.

   ```
   Eseutil /r eXX /a
   ```

6. After the log replay finishes successfully, the database is in a clean shutdown state, and it can be copied and used for a recovery purpose. The best practice for the recovery of lost data is to mount the database files in a recovery database created for the recovery purpose. You can create a recovery database using the New-MailboxDatabase cmdlet with the Recovery parameter.

7. You can extract recovered data by mounting the recovery database and using the mailbox restore request to export the data to a PST or merge into an existing mailbox.

8. After the recovery process is complete, resume replication for the database:

   ```
   Resume-MailboxDatabaseCopy DB1\Server3
   ```

Instances might occur when you need to activate a lagged database copy and request redelivery of missing emails from SafetyNet. This is similar—but improved—to the transport dumpster feature in Exchange 2013. By default, SafetyNet stores copies of the successfully processed messages for two days.

While the majority of steps to activate a lagged copy and request redelivery of messages from SafetyNet are similar to the previously mentioned process for point-in- time recovery, the following mentions certain differences.

- After suspending the lagged copy, you need to determine the logs required to bring the database to a clean shutdown state. You can determine these required logs by running eseutil and by inspecting the database header:

  ```
  Eseutil /mh <DBPath> | findstr /c:"Log Required"
  ```

- Note HighGeneration number from the output. The HighGeneration number indicates the last log file required. Move all log files with a generation number higher than High-Generation to a different location, so they're not played back in the database when it's activated.

- On the server hosting the active copy of the database, stop the Microsoft Exchange Replication service, so the logs don't continue replicating to the lagged copy.
- Perform the database switchover and activate the lagged copy:

```
Move-ActiveMailboxDatabase DB1 -ActivateOnServer Server3 -MountDialOverride
BestEffort -SkipActiveCopyChecks -SkipClientExperienceChecks -SkipHealthChecks
-SkipLagChecks
```

- After activation, the database automatically requests redelivery of the missing messages from SafetyNet.

Move the mailbox database path

After a database is created, if you need to move the database files from their current location to a new location, the actual steps might seem as simple as editing the database path using EAC or the Move-DatabasePath cmdlet.

But this is both a disruptive and a time-consuming operation. It's disruptive because when the database path is changed, the database is automatically dismounted for the move operation and it's mounted after files are copied to new location. The database is unavailable for the duration of the operation and users can't connect to their mailboxes. You can't change the database path on a replicated database. To move the database path of a replicated database, you must first remove all copies of the database, essentially bringing the database down to a single copy, then perform the move operation, and then add copies of the database.

For database copies, you need to create a new folder structure in the same path as the primary database's new location and manually copy all the files from the old location to the new location before adding the database copies again. This saves time and effort because seeding isn't required again. Only log files generated after removing the database copies need to be replicated.

EXAM TIP

You can't move a database path if circular logging is enabled on a database. You must first disable circular logging before moving the database path.

Update a mailbox database copy

Updating a mailbox database copy is essentially a seeding operation. The seeding process creates a baseline copy of the active database, which then continues replication of additional logs as they're generated. When creating a database copy, you can suspend the initial seeding operation. This creates a database copy, but it doesn't actually copy any data to create the baseline copy. A database copy that had its seeding suspended is eventually required to be updated before it can be considered a healthy copy that can be used as a switchover or failover target.

Updating to a database copy is also required when a database copy becomes diverged or is unrecoverable. Disk failure hosting a database copy is one such example where the database is unrecoverable and must be updated to create database baseline and resume replication. Other events requiring seeding of a database copy are corrupt log file that can't be replayed into the passive database copy and when offline defragmentation is performed on any copy of the database, after the log generation sequence of database is reset back to 1.

Before you can update a database copy, you must suspend it. When starting an update, you can select which database copy should be used as a source. This is helpful in situations where a passive database copy is local to the copy being updated and might be a better option than seeding from the active copy, which could be hosted in a different datacenter. While passive copy can be used for seeding, after an update is complete, log replication always uses active copy as its source. It's also possible to select which network should be used for seeding.

Here's an example where a database copy for database DB3 needs to be updated. If you use Server3, which has a healthy copy of the database as a source, the command to update the database copy is as follows.

```
Update-MailboxDatabaseCopy -Identity DB3\Server2 -SourceServer Server2
```

While using EAC or the previously mentioned cmdlet enables you to update a database copy online, you can also opt for an offline copy process to update a mailbox database copy. When you manually copy the offline database, you first need to dismount the copy of the active database. This results for in-service interruption for users hosted on the database. The process for the manual copy method is as follows:

- After you dismount the active copy of the database, copy the database and log files to a shared network location or an external drive.
- Mount the database to restore service to users.
- On the server that will host database copy, copy the database files from the shared network location or external drive to the same database path as the active database copy.
- Add the database copy with the SeedingPostponed parameter.

NOTE **CIRCULAR LOGGING**

When using the manual copy process, you must ensure that the database isn't configured for circular logging.

Objective summary

- DAG provides high availability when multiple database copies are created for the database the mailbox is hosted on. Creating a DAG and adding a mailbox server to DAG doesn't automatically provide redundancy to the databases located on the mailbox servers.

- Failovers or switchovers can cause resource overconsumption if the number of failures in a DAG aren't accounted for in the design. For example, if a mailbox server is designed for 5,000 active users and two servers in the DAG fail, resulting in two databases from other servers, each containing 3,000 users, can result in the mailbox server going over its designed limit of resource usage. This can have adverse effects on the service levels from degraded performance and slow response times or worse.

- When a DAG is designed to stretch across multiple sites, the file-share witness location is critical to ensuring high availability. The best practice is to locate the majority of the mailbox servers on the primary site. If users are located across multiple sites evenly, you should separate DAGs for each major site.

Objective review

Answer the following questions to test your knowledge of the information in this objective. You can find the answers to these questions and explanations of why each answer choice is correct or incorrect in the "Answers" section at the end of this chapter.

1. You are an Exchange administrator for Contoso, Ltd. You need to deploy a DAG without an administrative access point. What should you do?

    A. Deploy mailbox servers on Windows Server 2008 R2.

    B. Deploy mailbox servers on Windows Server 2012 R2.

    C. Deploy mailbox servers on Windows Server 2012.

2. You are an Exchange administrator for Contoso, Ltd. You need to move databases from the system drive to a new data drive. Select the required steps to complete the task successfully.

    A. Enable circular logging on the database.

    B. Disable circular logging on the database.

    C. Run Dismount-Database cmdlet.

    D. Run Move-DatabasePath cmdlet.

3. You are an Exchange administrator for Contoso, Ltd. You need to configure DAG networks to exclude SCSI network from replication. Which steps must you take? Select all that apply.

    A. Run Set-DatabaseAvailabilityGroup and set ManualDagNetworkConfiguration to $false

    B. Run Set-DatabaseAvailabilityGroup and set ManualDagNetworkConfiguration to $true

    C. Set-DatabaseAvailabilityGroupNetwork cmdlet and set IgnoreNetwork to $true

    D. Set-DatabaseAvailabilityGroupNetwork cmdlet and set IgnoreNetwork to $false

Objective 1.4: Monitor and troubleshoot the mailbox role

Maintaining a healthy and highly available Exchange 2013 environment requires monitoring the environment for issues affecting database replication, database copy activation, and mailbox role performance. Managed availability provides the monitoring and remediation of known issues when possible. But, that shouldn't replace monitoring of the environment for misconfigurations or other environmental health issues, which can potentially result in larger unplanned outages if not addressed early.

Troubleshooting database replication and replay

In a normal operation, transaction logs are replicated to database copies, inspected for errors, and, if no errors are encountered, they're replayed into the database copy. In case of lagged copy of a database, the logs are inspected, but not replayed until the lagged copy meets the lag time requirements. Log truncation also occurs on the active copy of the database when the truncation criteria is met and the process requires all of the copies to be healthy. All of the database copies must have replayed the log file to be truncated. In the case of lagged copies, the logs must have been inspected successfully. If one of the database copies doesn't meet this criteria, log truncation can't occur, even if circular logging is configured or the database backup has successfully completed.

If a database copy is offline or unreachable, it can cause a problem in log replication and truncation. This is because an active copy won't truncate any logs until all of the copies are verified. When the logs aren't truncated, all of the database copies, including the active ones, keep accumulating logs. This creates the potential of running out of disk space if the faulty database copy isn't remediated or removed to allow the truncation process to resume.

When planned maintenance takes an extended amount of time, and unplanned outages make database copies unavailable, both developments affect database copies and the log truncation process.

You can identify a copy with problems by running the Get-MailboxDatabaseCopyStatus cmdlet. Any copies with a copy queue length greater than zero, replay queue length greater than zero, or a failed or suspended state need to be investigated for cause and must be remediated.

When you have a database with a copy queue length greater than zero, the replication service is unable to replicate the required log files from the active database copy to the given replica. If the problem is on the source server, all of the passive copies of the database will have a copy queue length greater than zero. This usually occurs when a required log file is missing. This could be the result of a misbehaving or misconfigured anti-virus, or even an accidental delete by an administrator. In such instances, restoring the missing file becomes necessary before the replication can resume.

Once the missing log file is restored, run the Resume-MailboxDatabaseCopy cmdlet to resume the replication of log files to the passive database copies.

If mailbox servers hosting passive database are configured with a different disk layout and capacity, or if the disk hosting replica is shared with another application for storage, it may run out of disk space before the expected log truncation can occur. In this case, the affected database copy will have the copy queue length greater than zero. To resume log file copy from active database, address the disk space issue on the target server.

When you have a database with a replay queue length greater than zero, the replication service is unable to replay the received log files into the database copy.

In addition to the previously mentioned disk space and file level permission issues, this can also be caused by log file inspection failing to successfully inspect the received log files. Corruption of a received log file or file level anti-virus scanners are the common culprits, but they aren't the only ones.

When the database copy status is FailedandSuspended, the replication to the database is suspended and it is going to impact the log truncation process, as previously discussed. When a database copy is in this state, the detection of a failure requires manual intervention.

A common cause for this error is when the server is unable to mount the database for the replay of log files, or the database has diverged from the active mailbox database to the point where it must be updated manually using the Update-MailboxDatabaseCopy cmdlet. As discussed in the previous section, Managing mailbox database copies, you can specify which database copy should be used as a source if the target server is in a remote site and you need to avoid replication over WAN links.

The incremental resync feature included in Exchange 2013 is designed to automatically correct a divergence between database copies. When the incremental resync detects divergence, it searches a log file stream to locate a point of divergence, locates changed database pages, and then requests them from active copy. The changes are applied to the diverged database copy to bring it back in sync with the primary copy. Important to note is that when a database has reached failed and suspended status, the divergence can't be repaired by the incremental resync process and manual intervention becomes a necessity.

The database replication process also includes a content index catalog. The content index catalog is one of the components included in health checks, which is used by the BCS process. When a content index is corrupt, the Get-MailboxDatabaseCopyStatus shows the index state as FailedAndSuspended. Similar to the failed and suspended state of a mailbox database, the content index can be fixed by running the Update-MailboxDatabaseCopy cmdlet with the parameter CatalogOnly.

Troubleshooting database copy activation

For DAG to provide protection from failures and provide the ability to perform scheduled maintenance without affecting users, the passive copy of the database must be healthy and be able to mount as active copy when needed.

Activating a database copy is a complex operation involving many components, such as Active Manager, cluster service, and quorum and network components. Not only does a database need to be healthy, but the underlying components must also be healthy and functional.

When a database copy fails to mount, troubleshooting depends on symptoms and a combination of other factors. A methodical approach to troubleshooting yields the best results. Exchange 2013 also provides numerous events and tools that can be used to determine the status and possibly cause of the problem you're trying to troubleshoot. The proactive use of such tools can help prevent an unexpected outage.

One such tool is the Test-ReplicationHealth cmdlet. This cmdlet is designed to provide on demand an inspection of continuous replication, an availability of the Active Manager, the health and status of cluster service, and the quorum and network components. The cmdlet can be run locally on a mailbox server or remotely against a mailbox server that's a member of a DAG. The following is a sample output of the Test-ReplicationHealth cmdlet.

Sample output from Test-ReplicationHealth cmdlet

```
[PS] C:\>Test-ReplicationHealth

Server          Check                   Result      Error
------          -----                   ------      -----
Server1         ReplayService           Passed
Server1         ActiveManager           Passed
Server1         TasksRpcListener        Passed
Server1         DatabaseRedundancy      *FAILED*    There were database...
Server1         DatabaseAvailability    *FAILED*    There were database...
```

Each check against the given server checks the individual component or criteria for success or failure. You might have noticed that Server1 in the previous example has passed three checks and failed two. The first three checks are to ensure replication service is running, Active Manager is running and has a valid Primary Active Manager or Secondary Active Manager role, and the tasks listener is running and listening for remote requests.

The database redundancy and availability checks ensure that you have more than one copy of the database configured and that those copies are healthy.

When the first three checks fail, you need to ensure that the relevant services are running and, in case of Active Manager, the cluster service is functioning and Active Manager can communicate with other DAG members to achieve quorum.

If the database redundancy and availability checks fail, first you need to make sure the database in error is configured to have more than one copy. And for the databases with multiple copies, check the reason of failure by checking the detail status of each component provided by the cmdlet.

The replication issues previously discussed can also be a contributing factor to the redundancy and availability check failures. Be sure to perform the necessary troubleshooting, as discussed earlier.

Besides replication and copy configuration issues, database copy activation is also affected by configuration, which might not necessarily be a misconfiguration.

For example, a mailbox server can be configured to block database activation on a given server. This is usually the case when an administrator wants to perform maintenance on the server and has configured the server to avoid the activation of databases during the maintenance window. It is also possible to configure the DatabaseCopyAutoActivationPolicy parameter of the Set-MailboxServer cmdlet to the value IntrasiteOnly. This configuration enables an administrator to restrict the activation of the databases to the same site as the server where the database is currently active. This prevents cross-site failover and activation. While this isn't a misconfiguration, it can certainly block the activation of a database copy on a given server.

Other configuration parameters that can affect database activation on a server are MaximumActiveDatabases and MaximumPreferredActiveDatabases. These parameters are designed to provide a mechanism that can help address design requirements.

For example, if a mailbox server is designed to host 10 active databases with 5,000 users each, the server can still host more than 10 active database copies. This creates a potential of degraded server performance when more databases on the server are activated than the server is designed to handle. The MaximumActiveDatabases and MaximumPreferredActiveDatabases are designed to protect against such degradation by enabling administrators to configure preferred active database value. Limiting maximum number of active and preferred databases can help optimize server performance by hosting only the number of databases the server is designed to handle.. While it might seem that two parameters have the potential of conflict, MaximumPreferredActiveDatabases is only honored during the best copy and server selection, the database and server switchovers, and when rebalancing the DAG. So, preferred active database limit is a soft limit that should be configured for lower optimum active number of databases, whereas, the maximum active databases should be a number higher than the preferred active database number and should match the designed mailbox server capacity for maximum active databases.

When a database fails to mount, ensure you're not only checking for errors or database copy, Active Manager, cluster, network and server health conditions, but are also accounting for configuration parameters that might block activation of a database copy on a given server.

> **NOTE** **BEST COPY SELECTION PROCESS**
>
> While it isn't covered here, it's important to understand how the best copy selection (BCS) process finds a database that may best meet availability needs while minimizing potential of service interruption and data loss. More information about BCS can be found in this TechNet article at *http://technet.microsoft.com/en-us/library/dd776123(v=exchg.150).aspx*.

Troubleshooting mailbox role performance

When a server is unavailable, redundancy features for transport and high availability features for a mailbox role continue to provide service to end users. But what happens when a server is functional, but its performance is severely degraded?

Exchange 2013 has numerous workloads, each with its defined function. Replication service, for example, is responsible for the replication of log files to database copies, among other functions, and transport component is responsible for the routing of messages. Each resource consumes system resources, such as CPU, memory, and network resources.

Each user connecting to the Exchange 2013 servers also consumes resources. The client application or mobile devices they use can have a direct impact on how many resources are consumed by a user. Actions taken by a user, such as changing a view in Outlook or performing a long-running search query against an archive mailbox, can also have an impact on the mailbox server resources. Third-party applications connecting to Exchange using one of many protocols also have an impact on resource consumption on mailbox servers.

Exchange 2010 provided user-throttling functionality, which allowed controlling how resources are consumed by individual users. This capability is available and is expanded for Exchange 2013.

When released, Exchange 2013 also offers system workload management, which applies to system components and their impact on resource usage. The cmdlets enabling you to manage system workloads have been deprecated. The deprecated cmdlets include *-ResourcePolicy, *-WorkloadManagementPolicy, and *-WorkloadPolicy system workload management cmdlets.

New features in Exchange 2013 enable users to increase resource consumption for short periods without experiencing throttling or complete lockout. While lockout can still occur if users consume large amounts of resources, the lockout is temporary and the user is unblocked automatically as soon as usage budgets are recharged. You can set the rate at which users' resource budgets are recharged. Exchange 2013 also uses burst allowances to let users consume a higher amount of resources for short periods of time without any throttling, while implementing traffic shaping to introduce small delays, before user activity causes a significant impact on the server. Introducing small delays reduces the request rate from the user, but it's mostly unnoticeable by the user. This mechanism also helps prevent or reduce user lockouts.

Throttling policies in Exchange 2013 are managed by scopes. The built-in throttling policy has Global scope. This policy applies to all users in your organization, but it shouldn't be confused with the policy that has an Organization scope. The purpose of the organization policy is to allow customization of throttling parameters, which has different values from the defined default values in global policy. If you need to customize any of the built-in throttling parameter values, you shouldn't modify global policy, since it might be overwritten by future updates. Instead, you should create an organization policy and include only parameters that have a different value from global policy. This policy applies to all users.

You can also create a policy with the throttling scope as Regular. These policies can be applied to individual users, instead of the Global scope of the abovementioned policies. The Regular scope policies are quite useful when you need to change throttling behavior for only a small subset of users or applications.

To manage throttling configuration, use the *-ThrottlingPolicy cmdlets. For example, you can use the New-ThrottlingPolicy cmdlet to create a new throttling policy with the Regular-throttling policy scope. After customizing the required parameters, you can assign this policy to individual user mailboxes as needed, using the Set-ThrottlingPolicyAssociation cmdlet. Or, you can also configure throttling policy assigned to a user using set-Mailbox cmdlet. Many resources can be applied to a policy. You can refer to the individual parameters in this TechNet article at *http://technet.microsoft.com/en-us/library/dd351045(v=exchg.150).aspx*.

Monitoring database replication

Exchange 2013 provides built-in mechanisms to monitor database replication and database failovers.

Mailbox database copy status provides vital information about given database copies. Although you read about this earlier, let's look at some of the status information the mailbox database copy returns and what it means.

- **Failed**   When a database is in a failed state, the copy is unable to copy and replay log files, and it isn't suspended by administrative action. Because the copy isn't suspended, the system retries the failed operation periodically. If the system succeeds (for example, when the transient issue is resolved), the copy is marked as healthy.

- **Suspended**   The database copy state changes to suspended when administrative action, such as running the Suspend-MailboxDatabaseCopy cmdlet, suspends the database copy. This isn't an error state because it's the direct result of an administrative action.

- **Healthy**   The database copy is copying and replaying log files successfully.

- **ServiceDown**   When the Microsoft Exchange Replication Service isn't reachable or isn't running on the server that hosts the database copy, this state is reported. Manual intervention to remediate the faulty service is required.

- **Resynchronizing**   The mailbox database copy is suspected to have diverged from the active database. The system compares a diverged database copy with an active copy and tries to detect and resolve a divergence. The database copy returns to a healthy state if the divergence is resolved. If the error can't be addressed, the copy is transitioned to a FailedAndSuspended state.

- **DisconnectedAndHealthy**   This state is an indication that the database copy was in a healthy state before the loss of connectivity between an active database copy and the database copy reporting this state. Investigate network communication to remediate.

- **FailedAndSuspended**   When a database copy is in this state, it requires manual intervention to remediate the underlying issue that caused the copy to fail. Unlike the Failed state, the system won't retry the failed operation periodically.

Because of the verbosity and variety of status reported, the Get-MAilboxDatabaseCopyStatus can serve as a great monitoring and troubleshooting tool for database copies.

The Test-ReplicationHealth cmdlet is another such tool that can provide great insight into the replication of health of database copies, as previously discussed.

Another great source of information regarding high-availability system state and mailbox database failures is crimson channel event logs. In addition to the well-known Application, Security, and System event logs provided by Windows, a new event channel was introduced in Windows Server. *Crimson channel event logs* store events from a single application or a component, making it easier for the administrator to find relevant events.

Exchange 2013 logs events to crimson channels HighAvailability and MailboxDatabase FailureItems for DAG and database copies. The HighAvailability channel contains events related to startup and shutdown of the replication service. The HighAvailability channel is also used by Active Manager to log events related to Active Manager role monitoring and database action events, such as database mount operations and log truncation.

The MailboxDatabaseFailureItems channel is used to log events associated with any database copy failures.

When the database copies failover without administrative action, it might be important to find out what caused the database copy to failover, whether it was an administrative action, and why a passive copy was selected for activation. While this information is logged in the crimson event channels mentioned earlier, a correlation of multiple related events may be time-consuming. Exchange 2013 includes a script called CollectOverMetrics.ps1, which reads DAG member event logs and gathers information about database operations over a specified time period. The result of running this script can provide insight into information, such as the time at which switchover/failover operation started and ended, the server on which the database was mounted, the reason for operation such as administrative action or a failure, and if the operation completed successfully or failed to complete. The output is written to a CSV file and an HTML summary report can also be generated.

CollectReplicationMetrics.ps1 is another such script that collects metric in real time. The script collects data from performance counters related to database replication. The script can collect performance counter data from multiple mailbox servers, write the data to a CSV file, and report various statistics.

Thought experiment

Database failovers

In this Thought experiment, apply what you learned about this objective. You can find answers to these questions in the "Answers" section at the end of this chapter.

You are a consultant helping Contoso, Ltd. troubleshoot its Exchange 2013 environment. The manager states that the databases frequently fail over to different servers and don't always honor their activation preference. Many times, the databases failover to a third server located in a remote site, which results in slow response times. Contoso wants you to recommend how to determine the cause of the failovers and how to prevent databases from failing over to a remote site.

What would you recommend to address the stated concerns?

Objective summary

- The mailbox role performance is actively managed and internal processes are automatically throttled when the system is under stress and required resources could be scarce. Exchange 2013 allowed for the configuration of system workload policies on release, but an improper configuration might cause adverse effects, hence, the *-WorkLoadPolicy cmdlets have since been deprecated.

- User actions could have an adverse impact on server performance. Exchange 2013 includes a default Global throttling policy to prevent a user or a third-party application from monopolizing resources on the server. If a change to the built-in throttling parameters is required, the best practice is to create a new Organization throttling policy and include parameters that differ from the built-in policy. A throttling policy with Regular scope can also be created if changes only need to apply to a single user or a subset of users.

- Database replication, replay, and copy activation functionality is dependent on many environmental health and configuration factors. Anything from disk space issues to network connectivity can affect availability of a database copy or failure to replicate data from active copy to other copies. Built-in Exchange cmdlets and event logs provide important insight into what could be a potential cause and understanding status codes can help reduce the time to resolve the issue by methodically approaching the troubleshooting and remediation.

Objective review

Answer the following questions to test your knowledge of the information in this objective. You can find the answers to these questions and explanations of why each answer choice is correct or incorrect in the "Answers" section at the end of this chapter.

1. When a mailbox database copy is activated on a different mailbox server, you're asked to determine whether the copy failed as the result of an error on the active copy or because of an administrative action. Which of the following tools would you use? Choose all that apply.

   A. CollectOverMetrics.ps1.

   B. Crimson event logs.

   C. Search-AdminAuditLog.

   D. Get-DatabaseAvailabilityGroup

2. When troubleshooting replication errors for a database copy, you notice all the copies of the database have a copy queue length greater than zero. You verified that all servers hosting passive database copies are able to communicate to the server hosting active copy. Which of the following has the potential to cause this issue?

   A. Low disk space on servers hosting replica database copies.

   B. The required log file is missing on the server hosting the primary copy.

    C. A network issue resulting in the transmission failure of required log files.

    D. TCP chimney offload configuration is incorrect on nerwork adapter.

3. When troubleshooting a DAG, you noticed that performance on a Mailbox server is degraded. You noticed that it has more active mailbox databases than the server is designed to host. Which action can help ensure only defined number of mailbox databases can be active at a time?

    A. Run Set-MailboxServer cmdlet.

    B. Run Update-MailboxDatabaseCopy cmdlet.

    C. Run Set-DatabaseAvailabilityGroup cmdlet.

    D. Run Add-ServerMonitoringOverride cmdlet.

Objective 1.5: Develop backup and recovery solutions for the mailbox role and public folders

Objectives that define what's expected are as important as capabilities of a backup and recovery solution. Time required to recover data, also known as Recovery Time Objective (RTO), and the point to which the data must be restored, also known as Recovery Point Objective (RPO), are two of the most important design objectives for any backup and recovery solution. Without defined RPO and RTO objectives, a backup and recovery solution can only be as good as the guesswork of IT departments of what users expect of the system. Even though designing a backup and recovery solution is beyond the scope for this book, understanding what defined RPO and RTO mean to Exchange 2013 is important. You learn about the features and functionality of Exchange 2013 that can help with the restoration of data and meet RPO/RTO objectives when data loss has occurred.

> **This objective covers how to:**
> - Manage lagged copies
> - Determine most appropriate backup solution/strategy
> - Perform a dial tone restore
> - Perform item-level recovery
> - Recover the public folder hierarchy
> - Recover a mailbox server role

Managing lagged copies

Lagged copies are database copies configured to lag the log replay into the passive copy of the database. Exchange 2013 allows for a maximum of 14 days of lag. Unlike regular database copies that are designed to provide high availability, lagged copies are designed to provide protection against logical corruption. *Logical corruption* can occur when the data is expected to be written to disk, but despite an acknowledgement, the disk subsystem fails to write data to the disk. This is also known as a *lost flush*. Another possibility is that an application can add or update mailbox data in a way that isn't expected by the user. Unexpected malformed data is a valid MAPI operation for Exchange server, known as a *store logical corruption*.

While Exchange server has a built-in detection mechanism that detects and tries to correct lost flush occurrences, operations that cause store logical corruption are valid MAPI operations. Such corruptions require external backup mechanisms, such as a lagged database copy to prevent data loss.

The time it takes to recover data using a lagged copy depends on the configured lagged time for the lagged copy, the amount of logs that needs to be replayed to get to the point before corruption, and the speed at which the underlying hardware can replay the logs into the copy used for recovery.

Creating a lagged database copy is as simple an operation as creating a regular database copy. When creating a lagged copy, you need to run the Add-MailboxDatabaseCopy cmdlet with the ReplayLagTime parameter, configured with lag time span in dd:hh:mm:ss format. The TruncationLagTime parameter provides the ability to delay the truncation of logs that have been replayed into the database. You can set the truncation lag to the maximum of 14 days, which is similar to the replay lag time, but it shouldn't be used on its own to provide protection against corruption. The important difference is the status of the database. Replay lag time prevents logs from updating the database copy by stopping the log replay up to the configured lag time. This provides you with the ability to replay only the logs required before the time of corruption. Truncation lag preserves the logs, but only after it has been replayed in the database.

If a lagged copy is an important aspect of your data recovery strategy, you also need to make sure a single-lagged copy isn't susceptible to corruption itself. Storing lagged copy data on a RAID array, or having multiple lagged database copies is ideal, so a disk failure or corruption doesn't invalidate your lagged copy.

When configuring lagged copies, you also need to account for the additional disk space required to store additional logs that would otherwise be truncated. The importance of required disk space is worth stressing because for a very active user profile, the amount of daily mail storage can be high. Now add many active users to make up a database and you might account for more than a few gigabytes of space daily. If the database copy is lagged to a maximum of 14 days, it can easily balloon to a considerable log storage.

When you configure a lagged copy, it's also important to configure SafetyNet hold time to be equal to or more than lag time. This allows a lagged copy to request missing emails from SafetyNet successfully when activated. Increasing SafetyNet hold time has a direct impact on the disk space required to store emails protected by SafetyNet.

If SafetyNet is configured to exceed the lag time of a lagged database copy, the lagged copy can be activated without replaying the pending log files. This is because the activated copy requests the missing emails from SafetyNet, and SafetyNet can provide emails from the configured lagged time window.

When a database copy is created in DAG, the BCS process can select lagged copy for activation if it's the only copy available for activation when the active copy of the database fails. You can exclude a lagged database copy from the BCS process by suspending a database copy with the ActivationOnly parameter. This only excludes the database copy from activation, while allowing the logs to be replayed up to the configured lag time.

When activating a lagged copy, the best practice is to make a copy of the lagged database and log files first. This provides you with an additional copy in cases where an activated lagged copy may be determined not to provide all of the data expected, and you might need relay additional logs or fewer logs than originally determined.

Objective 1.3, previously discussed, covers the process of activating a lagged mailbox database copy.

Determining the most appropriate backup solution/strategy

When considering appropriate backup solutions, understanding the impact of defined SLAs, such as RPO and RTO, is critical. For example, if the requirement dictates that the backup solution must be able to protect the environment from database corruption for up to 30 days, lagged copies can't help protect the data due to its maximum configurable lag of 14 days.

If a requirement dictates that the time to restore data after data loss is reported must be less than 24 hours, you must account for the time it takes for offsite tapes to arrive, the time it takes to restore data from the tapes to the disk, the time it takes to replay restored logs and bring the database to its consistent state, and the time it takes to extract data from the recovery database into a PST file or a target mailbox.

DAGs provide the ability to recover not only from the disk, server, and other local failures, but also from disaster scenarios when DAG is spanned across sites, providing site resiliency and disaster recovery capabilities.

Exchange 2013 also provides the ability to recover accidentally deleted items using its single-item recovery features. When combined with an appropriate retention policy, this provides a vast improvement over using tape-based backup and restore strategy, which takes considerable time to restore a few items from the backup. Compliance and data loss prevention features of Exchange 2013 reduce the time to recover deleted items, while reducing administrative overhead associated with the restore process.

Even when using lagged database copies for recovery, the size of individual mailboxes and the size of the database on disk are the factors that greatly impact your ability to restore data while meeting RPO and RTO requirements. Exchange 2013 supports large mailboxes and databases that can be larger than 2 terabytes (TB). When recovering such mailboxes, it takes time to extract data from a lagged copy to the recovery database, and then onto the target mailbox or PST). As the mailbox size grows, so does its time to recover. While restoring data from tape eliminates time, lagged copies still need a replay of logs required to reach the determined point in time for successful recovery. The larger the database, the greater the amount of stored logs that need to be replayed into the lagged copy, directly impacting the time it can take to recover the data.

When selecting backup technologies for Exchange, you also need to ensure the selected backup technology is supported by Exchange 2013. Exchange server currently supports only Volume Shadow Copy Service (VSS)-based applications that support VSS writer for Exchange 2013. This requirement ensures that Exchange is made aware of the backup process start and completion times, as well as other important information that helps Exchange determine the state of backup and, upon successful completion, Exchange can truncate log files appropriately. The VSS writer functionality that was part of the Microsoft Exchange Information Store service was moved to the Microsoft Exchange Replication service. This new writer, named Microsoft Exchange Writer, is now used by Exchange aware VSS based applications, allowing them to backup from active or passive database copies.

Providing protection against the deletion of an entire mailbox is also built-in to Exchange 2013. When configuring a mailbox database, you have the ability to specify two retention- related parameters. While the DeletedItemRetention parameter doesn't provide the retention of an entire deleted mailbox, it enables you to configure the amount of time individual items deleted from a mailbox are retained and can be recovered. By default, this retention period is 14 days. This retention attribute applies to all mailboxes that don't have their unique deleted item retention value defined. MailboxRetention is the attribute that provides the ability to configure the retention period for a mailbox that was deleted. The database cleanup process won't delete the deleted mailbox permanently until after the configured mailbox retention time requirements are met. If the deleted mailbox needs to be restored within the mailbox retention period, the administrator doesn't need to rely on any lagged copies or other backup/restore applications. You can configure deleted item retention and mailbox retention parameters using the Set-MailboxDatabase cmdlet.

With the ability to integrate a Lync 2013 server with an Exchange 2013 server, administrators can choose to store user's Lync contact information in the Unified Contact Store, which is located in the user's mailbox. If a backup being restored exists before the time the Unified Contact Store integration was enabled, the restored data won't contain the user's Lync contacts. This results in the loss of Lync-related data while restoring the requested mailbox data. If the backup doesn't contain the user's Lync contacts, then it's important to determine the status of the Unified Contact Store and to move the user's contacts to the Lync server before performing the restore. The other important consideration is the time passed between the backup and the restore request. The user might have added more contacts since the last backup that contains their Unified Contact Store data. Restoring such backup results in losing the contacts added after the backup was performed. This can be prevented by moving a users' contacts back to the Lync server.

Performing a dial tone restore

Dial tone recovery allows the restoration of service to be separated from the restoration of data. In case of a data loss due to server or site failure, where restoring data from backup is the only option, you might want to provide users with the ability to continue sending and receiving emails while the lost data is being recovered. Using dial ti recovery, you can create an empty database on the same server in case of the loss of database or, on an alternate mailbox server, in case of a server failure. Users can continue using their mailbox to send and receive emails while the data is being restored. Once data is restored successfully, the administrator can merge the data, completely restoring the user's mailbox.

If the database has failed, but the server-hosting original database is still functional, you can choose to create a dial tone database on the same server. This eliminates the need to reconfigure client profiles that were configured manually.

If the server hosting the original mailbox database suffers hardware failures, you can create a dial tone database on a different server. Clients using Autodiscover are automatically updated to a new server. Clients configured manually might need to be updated to connect to a new server before they can connect to the dial tone database.

The process of performing dial tone recovery is mostly similar in both cases, with minor differences. Additional steps, which are listed here, are required when using a different server for dial tone recovery.

1. **Create an empty dial tone database to replace the failed database.**

   Creating the empty dial tone database is no different than creating a new mailbox database using the New-MailboxDatabase cmdlet. But you might want to make sure that any existing files of the database being recovered are preserved. This can be helpful if the files are needed for recovery operations.

   Create the dial tone database using the New-MailboxDatabase cmdlet.

   After creating the new database, all of the users from the failed database need to be homed to the newly created dial tone database. Use the Set-Mailbox cmdlet to rehome all of the affected mailboxes to the new dial tone database.

   Mount the dial tone database to allow client computers to connect and start using the new empty mailbox. For computers using Autodiscover, the configuration should be automatic. For clients with manually configured profiles, manual configuration needs to be updated before clients can connect to the dial tone database.

2. **Restore the old database.**

   Restoring the old database depends on your backup method. If you're relying on a lagged copy, determine the point in time to which you need to restore. Replay the required logs into a copy of the lagged database to bring the database to a consistent state.

   If you're using VSS-based backups using Windows Backup or third-party backup software, restore the database using its respective restore mechanism.

When using third-party software, most software also includes an option to mount the database after restore. While this might sound like a good option, it's important to understand what happens when mounting a restored database. When you mount a restored database, Exchange replays the required logs before mounting the database when it determines the database is in Dirty Shutdown state. Unless you dismount the database for each backup, every backed up database will be in Dirty Shutdown state, which is expected.

While backup software attempting to mount the database and replaying the log files automatically might seem less administrative effort, when the mount process fails for one reason or another, the impact is apparent. It takes much more time to restore data from tape than to copy it from one disk to another. If you have the capacity on the server, it's better to restore the data, but not to mount the database automatically; make a copy of the restored data; and then use eseutil to bring the restored database to a consistent Clean Shutdown state. If eseutil fails to bring the database to the consistent state, you can use the second copy on disk instead of reverting to tape for the restore.

If the failure doesn't require you to revert to a specific point in time, you can copy the logs from the point of backup to the current time if they're available from the failed copy. This lets you roll the database forward to the point of failure. This preserves all possible data up to the point of failure.

Use eseutil to replay the log files and bring the database to a consistent Clean Shutdown state. While this isn't required, it provides better control over a recovery process and enables you to address any failures more interactively than mounting the database and allowing it to replay the logs.

Create a recovery database. If you used eseutil, the recovery database won't be used for the log replay process. If you didn't use eseutil to bring the database to a consistent state, copy the recovered database and all of the required log files to the recovery database location. Mount the recovery database to force log replay and bring the recovered database to a consistent state. Dismount the recovery database after it mounts successfully, and then copy the recovered database files to a safe location.

3. **Swap the dial tone database with the restored database.**

At this point, your users are using a dial tone database and you have recovered the failed database. Now you need to swap the database files, so the dial tone database files are replaced with the recovered database. The dial tone database is smaller compared to the recovered database, so it's easier to take dial-tone database files, mount them in a recovery database, and merge the dial tone data with the recovered data, while users connect to their recovered mailbox and continue to use the service. This process involves downtime and, until the dial tone data is merged with the recovered database to which users are connected after the swap, users won't be able to access their newly created data.

To swap the database, dismount the dial tone database and copy the dial tone data-base files containing newly generated user data to the recovery database file location. Ensure you have preserved and moved the recovered database to a safe location to avoid the risk of overwriting recovered data in the recovery database location.

Now, copy the recovered database from the safe location to the dial-tone database file location, and mount the dial tone database. As discussed earlier, users can connect to their mailboxes containing recovered data, but they won't have access to their newly created data.

Mount the recovery database, which now contains the new dial tone data generated by users after the creation of the dial tone database and before the swap with the recovered data.

4. **Merge the data from recovery database to the dial tone database.**

At this point, you can issue New-MailboxRestoreRequest against each mailbox from the dial tone database. Use the recovery database as the source, and the mailbox on the dial tone database as a target, merge the dial tone data from the recovery data-base to the dial tone database. Once complete, users have access to both recovered and dial tone data. The recovery process is complete and the recovery database can now be removed.

Performing item-level recovery

When a user deletes items from their mailbox and the restoration of the items is required at a later date, either for legal discovery or because the user needs access to the accidentally deleted data, compliance and retention features of Exchange 2013 provide administrators with the flexibility to perform such recovery without requiring a lengthy recovery process of restoring from backups. This certainly impacts the online storage capacity and database size, and it must be carefully balanced not to impact one aspect of the system while addressing another.

The recoverable items folder provides the ability to retain the deleted items when the user accidentally deletes the mailbox items, or the items are deleted on purpose including purging, where the user is intent on permanently removing items from their mailbox. When the user empties the deleted items folder or uses hard delete, folders within the recoverable items folder, which are only accessible by the administrator, allow for the recovery of such items to meet recovery and compliance needs of the organization.

When a litigation hold or a single item recovery is enabled for a mailbox, the items that are hard deleted or removed from the deleted items folder are stored in the Purges folder in the user's mailbox. This folder isn't accessible to the user. Enabling a single item recovery is a simple operation of setting the SingleItemRecoveryEnabled parameter to $true using the Set-Mailbox cmdlet.

Recovering messages using single item recovery is a two-step process. The search performed to find deleted messages recovers found items from the user's mailbox to a defined mailbox, which can be any other mailbox except the source from which the messages are being recovered. While this isn't a requirement, the discovery mailbox is typically an ideal target for such operations.

After the data is recovered into the target mailbox, the next step is to restore the recovered items to the source mailbox or to a PST file if needed.

To perform the search, issue the Search-Mailbox cmdlet with the SearchQuery parameter. Search query uses Keyword Query Language (KQL) syntax. *KQL* includes search elements such as subject, sender, and other email properties or free-form test search looking for specific content within a message. You also need to specify the mailbox where items found by search query are stored.

Once the items are found and recovered to a specified mailbox, the next step is to run the same Search-Mailbox query on the mailbox where the items are recovered, and use the user mailbox as a target. This copies the recovered items from the mailbox used as a target in the first step to the user's mailbox. You can also use the DeleteContent parameter in this step to delete the recovered items from the source mailbox after the content is restored to the user's mailbox.

If these steps are used for legal discovery process, the final target mailbox might not be the user's mailbox and you could need to adjust the second step of the process accordingly.

If you need to export recovered data from the first step of the single item recovery process to a PST file, you can use the New-MailboxExportRequest cmdlet to extract data from the mailbox where it's stored after running the Search-Mailbox cmdlet in the first step. You also need to specify a file share location that Exchange server has permission to, ideally an Exchange server, in order to avoid permission issues. This location is then used to store the exported PST file.

While not directly a backup or restore requirement, you might have instances where a user reports corruption on their mailbox items, such as folders reporting on an incorrect item count or search folders not functioning as expected. This isn't a data loss, but a corruption of items that exist in the mailbox database.

Exchange 2013 provides the ability to address such corruption using the New-MailboxRepair-Request cmdlet. When you issue the cmdlet, you can specify a mailbox to run the repair request against a mailbox database if you believe corruption is affecting more than one mailbox in a given database.

The operation of running a repair request is disruptive and the mailbox being repaired is unavailable for the duration of the repair operation. Because of the disruption potential and performance impact on the server, only one repair request can be active for a given database and only 100 repair requests can be active for a mailbox-level repair per server.

Recovering the public folder hierarchy

Recovering public folder data historically has been a difficult request. Because public folders are now located on a mailbox database and use similar mailbox architecture, the recovery of data follows a similar logic as discussed in previous topics. Depending on whether or not the deleted items are within the retention window, you need to restore data either by using Outlook, by using the Recover Deleted Items option, or by using the recovery database if data needs to be restored from earlier backups.

However, the mailbox containing the public folder hierarchy plays a vital role for the public folder infrastructure. The loss of a primary or secondary hierarchy mailbox requires a restoration process that's different for a primary and a secondary hierarchy mailbox.

The impact of losing a secondary hierarchy mailbox means user mailboxes configured to use that mailbox for a hierarchy might connect to other hierarchy mailboxes in the environment, which might not be optimal, depending on the user location. Most commonly, the public folder account hosting the secondary public folder hierarchy is also used to store the public folder content. When such a public folder mailbox is accidentally deleted, users are unable to access data contained in the deleted public folder mailbox.

When a secondary hierarchy mailbox is accidentally deleted, if it's within the database retention period, it can simply be restored using the same steps as a user mailbox. You can simply connect the public folder mailbox back to the related Active Directory user account, which is created and disabled automatically when a public folder mailbox is created. If the Active Directory account deletion is the cause of the public folder mailbox being deleted, you can simply create a new user, disable it, and connect the recovered public folder mailbox to it. Use the Connect-Mailbox cmdlet to connect the disabled public folder mailbox to the related Active Directory user.

If the deleted mailbox is beyond the retention period, you need to recover the mailbox using the backup and recovery database. The process is similar to recovering a user mailbox.

If the deleted public folder mailbox contains public folder data as well, you must also point the public folders hosted on the deleted mailbox to an existing public folder mailbox or a newly created public folder mailbox. Use the Set-PublicFolder cmdlet with the OverrideContentmailbox parameter to point the public folder to an existing public folder mailbox. If you need to also restore the data from the deleted public folder, include the IncludeFolders switch.

When a primary public folder hierarchy mailbox is deleted, the impact on the public folder environment is bigger. This is because the primary hierarchy mailbox is the only mailbox in the environment that hosts writable copy of the hierarchy. When the only writable copy of the hierarchy is missing, you can't create new public folders. When using EAC, administrators are able to see the list of public folders in the environment.

While the restore process of the public folder mailbox with the primary copy of hierarchy is similar to other mailboxes, the restoration of the mailbox immediately initiates the full hierarchy sync with all the secondary hierarchy mailboxes. All of the changes made to the hierarchy between the time the primary hierarchy mailbox was last backed up and when it was deleted are lost. This includes newly created public folders and any updates to permissions on public folders.

This is also why it's critical to protect public folder mailboxes hosting primary hierarchy using multiple database copies on DAG, as well as to review backup procedures to ensure appropriate coverage exists to reduce exposure to data loss affecting the hierarchy and public folder permissions and content. The public folder account in Active Directory can be protected by enabling the feature Protect object from accidental deletion on the Active Directory container where the account is located.

Recovering a mailbox server role

When you lose a mailbox server due to a hardware issue or another event affecting the mailbox server, your mailboxes might survive the event if the server was a member of a DAG and if databases were configured with additional copies. If the server wasn't a member of a DAG or the affected databases weren't replicated, you can use concepts discussed earlier in this chapter to restore databases on different hardware, if available.

Recovering a mailbox server from failure requires the replacement hardware to have similar performance characteristics, have the same operating system version, and have the same drive letters and/or mount point configuration. You also need to determine the installation path if Exchange 2013 was installed in a nonstandard location. Because every Exchange server object is stored in the Active Directory, you can retrieve the install path from the Active Directory object using ADSIEdit or LDP.exe, if necessary. You can do so by inspecting the msExchInstallPath attribute on the Exchange server object located in the Configuration partition of Active Directory.

Once required information is available, reset the Active Directory account of the failed mailbox server. For recovery to succeed, you need to install the same operating system on the replacement server and name the new server with the same name of the failed server. The recovery will fail if the same name isn't used on the replacement server. Join the server to the Active Directory domain. This step will fail if you didn't reset the Active Directory account of the failed server because you're trying to join the new server to the domain using the same name. After successfully joining the domain and installing the required prerequisites for Exchange 2013, you can start the Exchange 2013 setup using a command-line setup with switch /m:RecoverServer. You must also use the /TargetDir switch if Exchange was installed in a nonstandard location on the server. After the setup is complete, you might need to restore any custom settings applied to the failed server.

If the failed server was a member of a DAG and contained replicated database copies, the process looks slightly different. Before you start with any of the previous recovery steps, you need to remove any existing mailbox database copies from the failed server. This is a configuration change only because the server doesn't exist anymore. Use the Remove-MailboxDatabaseCopy cmdlet to do so. Similarly, you also need to remove the failed server's configuration from the DAG by using the Remove-DatabaseAvailabilityGroupServer cmdlet. You might even need to use the ConfigurationOnly switch if the failed server isn't reachable on the network. You also need to evict the failed server node from the cluster using the Remove-ClusterNode cmdlet with the Force switch.

After performing these steps, perform the server recovery process mentioned earlier. Because the server was part of a DAG, after recovery you need to add the server back to the DAG using the Add-DatabaseAvailabilityGroupServer cmdlet. Add the mailbox database copies that existed on the server before the failure using the Add-MailboxDatabaseCopy cmdlet. Ensure that lag configuration is accurate for the lagged copies that might have existed on the server before the failure.

Thought experiment
Legal hold

In this Thought experiment, apply what you learned about this objective. You can find answers to these questions in the "Answers" section at the end of this chapter.

You are a consultant, who is engaged by Contoso, Ltd. to assist with the planning and deployment of appropriate data protection strategies for its Exchange 2013 environment. This company is often a target of lawsuits and must retain email records for the executives who could be involved in a litigation process. The emails must be retained, even if the user intentionally deletes them. The emails must be available as long as the litigation process requires and a litigation process averages six months.

The solution must require the least amount of administrative effort to produce emails required by the litigation team.

Can you use lagged copies to achieve the stated goals? Why?

Objective summary

- When configuring lagged copies, the impact on storage is higher because you are required to store larger amount of logs that can't be truncated like normal database copies. You should also account for additional storage space when a lagged copy needs to be used for the recovery process, because it's ideal to preserve an extra copy before replaying logs into lagged copy during the recovery process.

- If relying on SafetyNet when activating a lagged copy for recovery, the SafetyNet configuration must match or exceed the lag time configured on lagged copy to be effective during the recovery operation.

- Dial tone recovery is a fine balance between service availability and data availability. If data must be available when the user is accessing their mailbox, using dial tone might not be an effective strategy. In such cases, users could be without email access until the required data is restored.

- When using dial tone recovery, downtime can't be completely eliminated. When data is restored from backup, swapping the recovery database with the dial tone database involves downtime. To eliminate downtime, you can merge data from the recovered database to the dial tone database. But the time it might take to completely restore all of the data depends on the amount of data that needs to be merged from the restored database. This is always higher than the data contained in the dial tone database for each user.

- Single item recovery reduces administrative overhead and provides protection, both accidental and intentional deletions by the users, but the feature isn't enabled by default. Single item recovery and litigation hold can provide the ultimate protection against data loss, but at an additional cost for storage and other resources.

- While recovery of public folder hierarchy is significantly simplified compared to previous versions of Exchange server, careful planning is still required to prevent the loss of the primary hierarchy mailbox. Because public folder mailboxes can be hosted on regular mailbox databases and can be protected by a DAG, it's highly recommended to configure multiple database copies and include site resilience in the architecture where feasible.

Objective review

Answer the following questions to test your knowledge of the information in this objective. You can find the answers to these questions and explanations of why each answer choice is correct or incorrect in the "Answers" section at the end of this chapter.

1. An Exchange administrator reports that a lagged copy was activated during an outage at a primary datacenter. The administrator has since reconfigured the lagged copy, but wants to prevent it from being activated in the future without manual intervention. What must you do to configure the lagged copy to meet the stated requirements?

   A. Suspend lagged copy.

   B. Suspend lagged copy for activation only.

   C. Remove permissions assigned to the Exchange Trusted Subsystem on the lagged copy folder.

2. You have received reports of corrupt search folders from 50 users. You notice all of the users are on the same mailbox database. You want to fix the corruption in the shortest amount of time. What must you do?

   A. Issue New-MailboxRepairRequest against the mailbox database.

   B. Issue New-MailboxRepairRequest against the individual mailboxes.

   C. Distribute users to multiple databases and run New-MailboxRepairRequest on their mailboxes.

   D. Perform offline repair of database.

3. When applying new Exchange cumulative update on one of the Mailbox servers, the update failed. You need to fix the issue. What must you do? Choose all that apply. Restart the server and apply the update again.

   A. Restart the server and uninstall the failed update.

   B. Run setup.exe from commandline with /recoverserver switch

   C. Restart the server using last known good configuration option. Reinstall the update.

Objective 1.6: Create and configure mail-enabled objects

Recipients and mail-enabled objects are the core of the Exchange environment. A *mail-enabled object* is an object, such as a user mailbox, to which Microsoft Exchange can deliver or route messages. Exchange 2013 supports multiple different types of mail-enabled objects enabling various collaboration scenarios.

> **This objective covers how to:**
> - Configure resource mailboxes and scheduling
> - Configure team mailboxes
> - Configure distribution lists
> - Configure moderation
> - Configure a linked mailbox

Configuring resource mailboxes and scheduling

Resource mailboxes are mailboxes that represent a location based, or a nonlocation-based, resource, such as a meeting room or a projection system. For these shared resources, resource mailboxes provide the ability to send requests that allow the requestor to reserve the resource. The scheduling can be automated, if desired, in which case, the Exchange assistant processes automatically accept or decline the requests based on the defined time and availability restrictions. You also have an option to configure such resources to be managed by a delegate. In such cases, the delegate is responsible for manually accepting and rejecting the resource scheduling requests based on business processes or other approval criteria.

Location based resources are addressed in Exchange 2013 as room resources. When you create a meeting request, Outlook client automatically shows you the Room Finder with all of the available rooms. You can then select an appropriate room for your meeting and reserve it if it's available for the scheduled meeting time. Recurring requests can also be sent to the room resources and, if automatic processing is configured, acceptance depends on the configured criteria.

To create a room resource, you can use the New-Mailbox cmdlet with the Room parameter. You can also create a room resource from EAC. Let's create a room resource for a room called New York Executive Briefing Room using EAC.

To create a room mailbox, select the Resources tab from the recipients section, and then click + and, from the resulting drop-down menu, select the Room Mailbox option, as you can see in Figure 1–7.

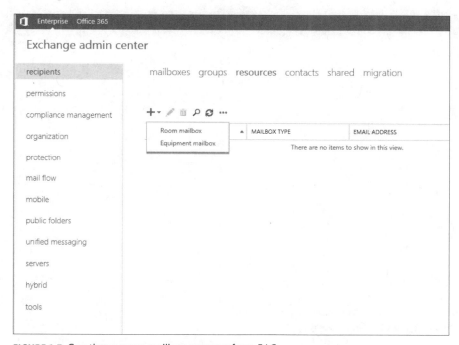

FIGURE 1-7 Creating a room mailbox resource from EAC

The resulting dialog box in Figure 1–8 enables you to provide the required details, such as display name, alias, room capacity, and location.

FIGURE 1-8 Room Mailbox details dialog box

You can also provide an organization unit (OU) if you need to store the resource mailbox you're creating in a specific OU. Creating the same resource mailbox using the Shell would look like the following.

Creating a room resource mailbox using the Shell

```
New-Mailbox `
-Name 'New York Executive Briefing Room' `
-DisplayName 'New York Executive Briefing Room' `
-ResourceCapacity '10' `
-Alias 'NYEBR' -Office 'New York City Office' `
-Room:$true
```

When creating the resource mailbox using EAC, you might notice it applies additional defaults to the room mailbox, such as the automatic acceptance of meeting requests.

Once created, room resources can be configured to set the meeting length and recurrence limits, assign a delegate, and auto reply to senders. Let's configure the room resource just created to limit the meeting duration to two hours and a recurrence limit of no more than three months from the request date. Using Shell, you need to use the Set-Mailbox cmdlet as follows.

Configuring room resource parameters

```
Get-Mailbox NYEBR | Set-CalendarProcessing -MaximumDurationInMinutes 120
-BookingWindowInDays 90
```

When using Outlook to create a meeting request, the newly created room is now visible in Room Finder. In large organizations with many locations and rooms, organizing rooms by location becomes critical to enable users to efficiently locate room resources without sifting through a long list of room resources. Exchange 2013 allows creating room lists, which enables you to organize room resources by location.

Essentially, room lists are distribution groups with RoomList designation. Once you create a room list, you can add rooms that belong to the location the room list represents. Let's create a room list for the New York City location and add the room resource created earlier to the room list.

Creating room list and adding room resource to the room list

```
New-DistributionGroup -Name "New York City Conference Rooms" -RoomList
Add-DistributionGroupMember -Identity "New York City Conference Rooms" -Member NYEBR
```

Figure 1-9 shows an example of a new meeting dialog box, which shows both the room list and the room created earlier in the Room Finder.

FIGURE 1-9 Outlook Room Finder

EXAM TIP

Familiarize yourself with a variety of scheduling and configuration parameters associated with room and equipment resources.

As mentioned, Exchange 2013 also enables you to create nonlocation-specific resource mailboxes, such as shared equipment. While most of the cmdlets and parameters are the same, the difference is, when creating an equipment resource, you issue the New-Mailbox cmdlet with –Equipment:$true, instead of –Room:$true used in the earlier example. Also note, you can't create special equipment distribution lists as you can with room lists.

Configuring team mailboxes

A *shared mailbox* is a resource created when multiple users need to access common information. This could be a mailbox receiving support queries from customers or a shared calendar for a team working on a project. This shared resource isn't a user mailbox and it doesn't have its own username and password. Instead, users logon to their own mailboxes, and then connect to the shared mailbox to access shared information.

You can create a shared mailbox using the New-Mailbox cmdlet with the Shared parameter. Once created, you can assign specific permissions to the team members or a distribution group to access the mailbox, and to be able to send as, or on behalf of, the shared mailbox. The three permissions need to be assigned using three unique methods. To assign full permissions to the mailbox so a user can manage the mailbox content, including editing and deleting mailbox items, you need to use the Add-MailboxPermission cmdlet with the FullAccess parameter.

EXAM TIP

The full access permission doesn't allow the user to send an email as, or on behalf of, the shared mailbox.

To assign the send on behalf of permission, you need to use the Set-Mailbox cmdlet with the GrantSendOnBehalfTo permission. To assign the send as permission, you need to use the Add-ADPermission cmdlet.

When a user is assigned full permission on the shared mailbox, the Exchange automapping process includes the mailbox in an Autodiscover response. If the user's Outlook client is configured using Autodiscover, the shared mailbox is automatically connected to the user's profile and becomes visible in the navigation pane, as you can see in Figure 1–10.

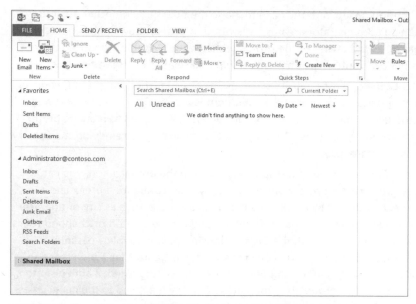

FIGURE 1-10 Shared mailbox displayed in Outlook navigation pane

While auto-mapping can help a user eliminate manual steps required to connect to a shared mailbox, if a user has permissions on multiple shared mailboxes, connecting all of them to the Outlook client automatically might become unnecessary.

Exchange 2013 provides an administrator with the ability to turn off auto-mapping for a given mailbox. The administrator can simply disable auto-mapping by setting the Automapping parameter value to $false when assigning permissions to the user using the Add-MailboxPermission cmdlet. If you want to disable auto-mapping after assigning the permissions, you must first remove the permissions, then assign them again with the Automapping parameter set to $false.

Configuring distribution lists

Distribution lists provide an important collaboration capability by allowing a sender to reach a group of recipients by sending an email to a group object, instead of sending it to each recipient individually.

When you create a new distribution group, Exchange creates a universal distribution group object in Active Directory. To mail enable an existing group in Active Directory, it must be a universal distribution group. But if you migrated from a previous version of Exchange server, it's possible you have distribution groups that are security groups, domain local groups, and global distribution groups in Active Directory.

By default, Exchange 2013 enables not only administrators, but also users to create distribution groups. When a user creates a distribution group, the user is the designated owner of the distribution group, and they can manage membership and other attributes of the group. When an administrator creates a distribution group, they can designate an appropriate individual as the owner of the group, which in turn, enables the designated owner to manage the distribution group membership and related configuration.

If you want to block the end users' ability to create their own distribution groups, you can use RBAC assignment policies to change the default permissions assigned to the users and block their ability to create a distribution group. You can also allow users to manage group members for the groups for which they're the designated owners, while removing their ability to create new distribution groups.

To provide the consistent naming of distribution groups in the organization, you can create a distribution groupnaming policy, which enables you to configure a prefix and a suffix based on predefined text or by using the value of an attribute, such as city or title. The group naming policy is stored at the organization level and can be created or changed using the Set-OrganizationConfig cmdlet with the DistributionGroupNamingPolicy parameter. You can only have a single group naming policy for an entire organization. When creating distribution groups using EAC, group naming policy is automatically ignored. If administrators use Shell to create a distribution group, the group naming policy is applied to the name unless the administrator uses the IgnoreNamingPolicy parameter.

Because distribution groups contain multiple users from a specific department or an entire organization, depending on the purpose of the distribution group, it's important to manage whether distribution groups accept email from outside senders or only from senders within the organization. By default, newly created distribution groups only accept emails sent by senders from the same organization. An administrator can configure a distribution group to accept messages from outside senders, if desired.

Along with simple email sender restrictions, distribution groups also allow for moderation capabilities. When enabled, a moderator or a group of moderators, must be assigned, so when a message is sent to the distribution group, it can be approved or rejected. It is also possible to create exceptions, so certain senders don't require approval by moderators to send messages to the distribution group.

Configuring moderation

As described in an earlier section, you can set moderation on distribution lists. But moderation is a transport function and it can also be applied to individual user mailboxes, if needed. To apply moderation to a distribution group, updating moderation properties of the distribution group is a relatively simple task. But, if you want to apply moderation to a user mailbox, you must create a transport rule that uses the Forward the message for approval action when an email is sent to a designated mailbox. In both cases, you can create exceptions, so designated senders can bypass the moderation process. The moderators always bypass the moderation process when they send an email to the distribution group or the mailbox they're required to moderate.

When a mailbox or distribution group configured for moderation receives a message, the message is forwarded to the moderators. Moderators can approve the message, in which case, the message is delivered to the intended recipients. The moderators can reject the message and, optionally, choose to provide a reason for the rejection, which is then visible to the sender without revealing the identity of the moderator; or the moderator can ignore the message, which eventually times out and the sender is notified that no action was taken by the moderator.

Because moderation is a transport function, it's important to understand that when co-existing with Exchange 2007, the moderation might not work when the message is routed through an Exchange 2007 hub transport server.

When a message is sent to multiple recipients and only a subset of the recipients are moderated, the messages is bifurcated. One message is sent to the recipients who don't require moderation and that message is delivered immediately. The other message is sent to the moderator, who must take the appropriate action. The message is then sent to the recipient or back to the sender, based on the moderator's action.

When a distribution group is moderated and it contains recipients who are also moderated, moderation must take place for each moderated recipient individually, even after the message is approved by the moderator of the distribution group. This might not be a desired behavior in certain environments. Distribution groups allow the moderator-accepted message to bypass further moderation when the BypassNestedModerationEnabled attribute is configured.

When more than one moderator is assigned to a distribution group or a recipient for moderation, what happens when one moderator approves the message while another rejects it? The moderation process ignores the subsequent moderator actions once it receives the first moderator's response. Whatever action the first moderator decides to take remains valid and the message is processed accordingly. If one moderator approves the message and other moderators are away, the message is deleted from their mailboxes by the moderation process because the message no longer needs a moderator's decision.

Configuring a linked mailbox

A *linked mailbox* is a mailbox accessed by a user who is in a separate trusted forest. Most common Exchange 2013 deployments are single forest deployments. But deployment requirements might exist where account forests that host user accounts are separated from resource forests that serve resources, such as Exchange mailboxes. In such a case, the two separate forests require a trust configured to allow the use of resources by the users from the separate forest. The trust must be set up, so the resource forest trusts the account forest.

While the one-way outgoing trust is sufficient to create linked mailboxes, the administrator is required to provider administrator credentials of the account forest every time a linked mailbox is created. This behavior can be avoided if a one-way outgoing trust is also established from the account forest trusting the resource forest, which is hosting the linked mailboxes.

Before you can create a linked mailbox, the user account, also known as *master linked account*, must exist in the account forest. To create a linked mailbox, use the New-Mailbox cmdlet. You need to provide a linked domain controller name and a linked master account name. The linked domain controller represents a domain controller in the account forest where the user account resides. The linked master account represents the user who is connected to linked mailbox. You also need to provide the administrator credentials of the account forest if the account forest doesn't trust the resource forest.

The following example shows how to create a linked mailbox in the resource forest Contoso for Ayla Kol, whose user account resides in the Fabrikam forest.

```
New-Mailbox `
-Name "Ayla Kol" `
-LinkedDomainController "DC1_FABRIKAM" `
-LinkedMasterAccount "FABRIKAM\aylak" `
-OrganizationalUnit Users `
-UserPrincipalName aylak@contoso.com `
-LinkedCredential:(Get-Credential FABRIKAM\administrator)
```

If required, you can change the master account linked to the linked mailbox using the Set-Mailbox cmdlet with the LinkedMasterAccount parameter.

Thought experiment
Moderation

In this Thought experiment, apply what you learned about this objective. You can find answers to these questions in the "Answers" section at the end of this chapter.

Contoso, Ltd. has deployed Exchange 2013 servers. You are tasked to deploy a strategy to address the following scenarios:

- Stop mail storms caused by the use of "reply all" to a distribution group.
- Stop the data leak of sensitive information by requiring manager approval.

Can you use moderation to address the requirements?

Objective summary

- Shared resources, such as Equipment and Room resources, can be managed in Exchange using special mailbox types. You can't convert an existing user mailbox into a resource mailbox. You must create a new resource mailbox.
- Moderation is a transport function, and it can be applied to both distribution groups and individual users. It can also be applied to create multiple layers of moderation, if needed.

■ Linked mailboxes requires the resource forest to trust the account forest. A trust from the account forest to the resource forest is optional.

Objective review

Answer the following questions to test your knowledge of the information in this objective. You can find the answers to these questions and explanations of why each answer choice is correct or incorrect in the "Answers" section at the end of this chapter.

1. You configured a shared mailbox and assigned full permissions to users. One of the users mentioned they already have multiple mailboxes connected to their Outlook and they don't want to connect to a shared mailbox automatically. What must you do?

   A. Run Set-ADPermission cmdlet.

   B. Run Set-Mailbox cmdlet.

   C. Remove mailbox permissions for the user, and then add it again.

   D. Run Set-CASMailbox cmdlet.

2. You deployed Exchange 2013 in a resource forest. You can configure required trust with the account forest. An administrator mentions they are prompted for the administrator account and password from the account domain every time they create a linked mailbox. What must you do to stop the credential prompts?

   A. Add an administrator's account to the Domain Admins group in the resource forest.

   B. Add an administrator's account to the Domain Admins group in the account forest.

   C. Add an administrator's account to the Enterprise Admins group in the account forest.

   D. Create a one-way trust from the account forest to the resource forest.

3. You recently created a new distribution group with default settings. The distribution group must be able to receive emails from external senders. Which of the following meets the requirement?

   A. No further action is needed. Default settings of new distribution group allows external senders to send email to members of the distribution group.

   B. Configure AccessMessagesOnlyFrom parameter on the distribution group.

   C. Configure BypassModerationFromSendersOrMembers parameter on the distribution group.

   D. Configure RequireSenderAuthenticationEnabled parameter on the distribution group.

Objective 1.7: Manage mail-enabled object permissions

In a collaborative environment, enabling users to be able to delegate permissions or use shared resources effectively requires permission manipulation on mail-enabled objects. Some permissions are manageable by users, while others could require administrative action.

> **This objective covers how to:**
> - Configure mailbox permissions
> - Set up room mailbox delegates
> - Set up auto-mapping

Configuring mailbox permissions

In scenarios such as a manager and their assistants, tasks are delegated to assistants when needed. These tasks might include responding to emails, accepting or rejecting meeting requests, and other organizational tasks.

To address such scenarios, Exchange allows the setting up of permissions on the mailbox. Users also have the ability to set up permissions using Outlook to delegate tasks by assigning appropriate permissions.

As an administrator, you can use EAC or Shell to assign permissions to delegates, as needed. Permissions can be assigned, so users have access to the mailbox, have the ability to send on behalf of, or to send as, a recipient. The permissions can also be assigned to distribution groups.

Earlier, in the section Configure Team Mailboxes, you learned about using the Add-MailboxPermission cmdlet to assign permissions. When a permission is assigned by an administrator to a mailbox using Shell or EAC, the change isn't visible to the user whose mailbox the permissions are assigned to. By default, Exchange Trusted Subsystem and Exchange Servers groups have full access on all mailboxes in the environment. This is required for the system to take necessary mailbox-related actions.

When assigning the permissions using Add-MailboxPermission, use of the InheritanceType parameter enables the administrator to specify whether or not all of the subfolders inherit the assigned permissions. To provide an inheritance on all subfolders of a mailbox when assigning the permissions, set the InheritanceType parameter to All.

Setting up room mailbox delegates

A room mailbox was created earlier in the section, Configure resource mailboxes and scheduling. In the example, room was configured to accept or decline booking requests automatically. You can configure room mailbox delegates to manage bookings manually instead.

To assign delegates, using EAC, edit the room mailbox, select the Booking Delegates option, and then click Select Delegates Who Can Accept Or Decline Booking Requests. Once selected, you need to add the delegates who can manage resource scheduling for the room mailbox. Figure 1–11 provides an example.

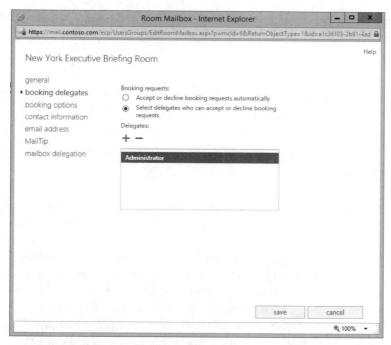

FIGURE 1-11 Configure delegates for room mailbox

You can also perform the same task using Shell, using the following cmdlet:

```
Set-CalendarProcessing -Identity 'New York Executive Briefing Room' -ResourceDelegates @
('Administrator')
```

In this example, an administrator was assigned as a delegate to the room mailbox. Figure 1-12 displays a resource booking request sent to the room being forwarded to the administrator for processing.

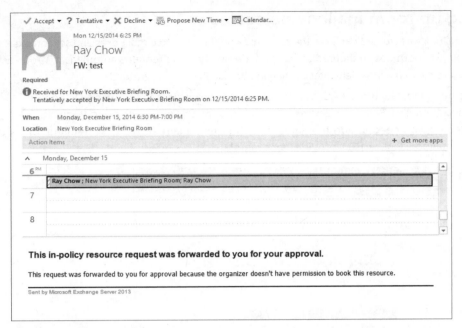

FIGURE 1-12 Resource booking request forwarded to administrator for processing

You can also decide whether the resource mailbox should automatically process the requests and other parameters, discussed earlier in the section Configure resource mailboxes and scheduling. And you can granularly control which users can request to book the resource automatically if the resource is available, and which users must require approval before they can schedule the resource. From EAC, select your Administrator Account drop-down menu located in the upper-right corner of EAC and select Another User. Select the room resource you want to configure. A new window opens, displaying the room resource's Options window. Select Settings and the Resource tab. Here you can configure scheduling permissions as needed. Figure 1-13 shows an example configuration, where user Ray Chow is allowed to schedule the resource automatically if the resource is available. The same can also be configured from Shell, using the Set-CalendarProcessing cmdlet.

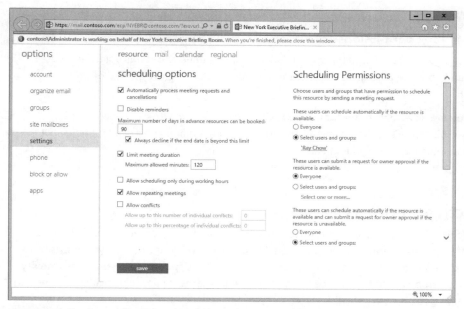

FIGURE 1-13 Configure scheduling permissions on a room mailbox

Setting up auto-mapping

When a user is assigned full permissions on a mailbox, the mailbox is automatically mapped to the user's profile. If the user is using an Outlook client that's configured to use the Auto-discover process, the auto-mapped mailbox is visible in the user's Outlook profile without any user intervention.

While this auto-mapping process eliminated manual configuration by the user, the user might have access to multiple mailboxes and might not like to have all of the mailboxes automatically mapped to their profile.

You can configure the auto-mapping feature only when assigning the permissions. The following example assigns user Ray Chow full access permissions to the shared mailbox and disables auto-mapping.

```
Add-MailboxPermission -Identity "Shared Mailbox" -User "Ray Chow" -AccessRights
FullAccess -InheritanceType All -AutoMapping $false
```

Auto-mapping can only be configured when assigning the permissions, and it can't be changed after the assignment. If you need to change the auto-mapping permissions, you can do so by removing the user's permissions and reassigning permissions with the desired auto-mapping configuration.

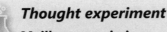
Objective summary

- While schedule processing for room mailboxes can be delegated to a user or a group of users, exceptions can be configured to allow in-policy or out-policy requests to be handled in an automated way for certain users. This depends on resource availability. This can be helpful to reduce the burden on delegates, while still providing the necessary controls.

- Auto mapping can be helpful to eliminate the manual steps required by the user to connect to other mailboxes they have permissions to. But, it's possible for the administrator to disable auto-mapping when configuring permissions on the mailbox object.

Objective review

Answer the following questions to test your knowledge of the information in this objective. You can find the answers to these questions and explanations of why each answer choice is correct or incorrect in the "Answers" section at the end of this chapter.

1. You have configured a shared mailbox and delegated approval tasks to a user. You need to allow CEO of the company to be able to request the room resource regardless of room scheduling restrictions. What must you do?

   A. Run Set-CalendarProcessing cmdlet with AllBookInPolicy parameter

   B. Run Set-CalendarProcessing cmdlet with AllRequestInPolicy parameter

   C. Run Set-CalendarProcessing cmdlet with AllRequestOutOfPolicy parameter

   D. Run Set-CalendarProcessing cmdlet with RequestOutOfPolicy parameter

2. You would like the room resource mailbox to stop from automatically accepting scheduling requests tentatively. What must you do?

   A. Configure AddNewRequestsTentatively parameter

   B. Configure AutomateProcessing parameter

   C. Configure Confirm parameter

   D. Configure ScheduleOnlyDuringWorkHours parameter

3. You have configured a shared mailbox and assigned full permissions to a user. The user reports that he is unable to send email as the shared mailbox. What must you do to fix the issue?

   A. Run Set-Mailbox cmdlet

   B. Run Add-ADPermission cmdlet

   C. Run Set-CASMailbox cmdlet

   D. Run Set-SharingPolicy cmdlet

Answers

This section contains the solutions to the Thought experiments and answers to the objective review questions in this chapter.

Objective 1.1: Thought experiment

1. The Hyper-V administrator recommends using dynamic VHDX files located on the SAN volume for virtual machines for the Exchange 2013 server roles. While the recommendation by itself might not be an issue, the administrator also stated his goal of achieving consolidation ratio of 100 VMs per virtualization host. This could mean the storage volume might be shared with multiple VMs. When sharing single volume with multiple VMs, I/O characteristics of the volume needs to be able to sustain a peak load of all VMs, while meeting storage I/O and latency requirements of virtualized Exchange server roles.

   The stated goal of achieving the consolidation ratio of 100 VMs per virtualization host is a concern. If more than two virtual CPUs are allocated per physical CPU core, the virtualized Exchange server role configuration will be unsupported.

2. The storage administrator prefers to create large RAID arrays consisting of multiple disks and creates multiple volumes from the existing array, as needed. The concern with this idea is, as more volumes are created, despite the ability to spread I/O from multiple workloads to multiple underlying spindles, the possibility of competing I/O is higher. This situation becomes more pronounced during peak usage periods. While the proposed solution might not be an issue, the concern should be discussed and a solution should be tested using Jetstress with load simulation that represents an expected concurrent I/O from all applications that will share the array.

3. To provide the best possible user experience in remote locations when connectivity is provided by slower WAN links, it's ideal to locate public folder mailboxes that host content frequently accessed by users in the datacenters that provide fast and robust connectivity to such locations. Careful planning of a public folder hierarchy is required, because only one writable copy can exist for any given public folder active at a time.

Objective 1.1: Review

1. **Correct answer:** C

   A. **Incorrect:** While both RAID5 and SSD disks are supported for use with Exchange 2013 mailbox server roles, it fails to meet the stated goal of achieving the best possible cost benefits for large mailboxes allocated to each user. SSD disks are fast, but they don't provide a large capacity at a low cost.

   B. **Incorrect:** NFS storage isn't supported for use by physical or virtualized Exchange 2013 roles.

C. **Correct:** While 15,000 RPM SCSI disks on Fibre-Channel SAN might not be the cheapest option, it is the only supported configuration that is cheaper of the two valid options, making it the only correct choice for the given objective.

D. **Incorrect:** Even though DAS deployments might be cheaper, when combined with RAID10 configuration, the number of disks required will increase the cost of overall solution.

2. **Correct answer:** B

A. **Incorrect:** Exchange Profile Analyzer is designed for Exchange 2007 and doesn't work with Exchange 2010 servers.

B. **Correct:** Performance counters from Exchange 2010 servers contain information required to determine the user profiles for a given environment.

C. **Incorrect:** Transaction log files might seem like a legitimate choice to determine user profile data, but they aren't human readable text files that can be parsed to obtain user profile information.

D. **Incorrect:** Exchange Log Analyzer is a tool to analyze message tracking logs. However, it can't provide required profile analysis per user.

3. **Correct answer:** A

A. **Correct:** New-Mailbox is the cmdlet used to create a new public folder mailbox in Exchange 2013. The IsExcludedFromServingHeirarchy parameter prevents Exchange from serving the public folder hierarchy to its user.

B. **Incorrect:** New-Mailbox is the correct cmdlet, but IsHeirarchyReady is a parameter managed by Exchange server. Its value is automatically changed to true by Exchange server when the hierarchy synchronization is complete.

C. **Incorrect:** The New-PublicFolder cmdlet is used to create a folder in the hierarchy after the public folder mailbox is created using the New-Mailbox cmdlet. The IsHierarchyReady parameter is irrelevant due to the wrong cmdlet usage.

Objective 1.2: Thought experiment

1. Because Litware requires the ability to limit the Address Book views to the Address Book, segmentation should be deployed. Creating separate address lists for each acquired company and assigning appropriate Address Book policies can provide required segmentation. The Address Book policy-routing transport agent should also be installed and enabled to block name resolution across logical boundaries created by ABPs.

2. An existing stated environment implies centralized design. Proposed public folder goals require installation of an Exchange server hosting public folder mailboxes in remote locations to avoid latency and poor performance. Availability requirements also implies that DAG should be deployed. The impact of these design changes require that Exchange servers be deployed in remote locations, departing from current centralized deployment, which has all Exchange servers deployed in a central location.

Objective 1.2: Review

1. **Correct answer:** C

    A. **Incorrect:** Preparing a schema is required only once per organization during setup or when applying updates.

    B. **Incorrect:** Preparing Active Directory is required only once per organization during setup or when applying updates.

    C. **Correct:** Preparing a domain is required once per domain that will host recipient objects or Exchange servers. In this example, a new domain is introduced after a deployment of Exchange servers was made in a different domain. Because the new domain was never prepared for Exchange server objects and is to be host recipients, it needs to be prepared.

2. **Correct answer:** C

    A. **Incorrect:** The Move-OfflineAddressBook cmdlet is used to set the OAB generation server in Exchange 2010.

    B. **Incorrect:** The Set-OfflineAddressBook cmdlet doesn't have parameters to move OAB generation to a different server.

    C. **Correct:** In Exchange 2013, OAB generation is moved to an arbitration mailbox. To move OAB generation to a different server, you must move the arbitration mailbox with OAB generation capabilities to a mailbox database hosted on the desired server.

    D. **Incorrect:** Update-OfflineAddressBook cmdlet forces an update to generate updated OAB files downloaded by users. It does not move generation to different server.

3. **Correct answer:** A

    A. **Correct:** To change the display order of the CEO's mailbox, the seniority index must be set on the mailbox object.

    B. **Incorrect:** Changing the seniority index on the distribution group changes the display order of the group object, but not of its member recipient objects.

    C. **Incorrect:** Set-OrganizationConfig has no impact on the display order of recipients in the HAB.

    D. **Incorrect**: Set-AddressList cmdlet does not change seniority property for a mailbox.

Objective 1.3: Thought experiment

1. The DAG design needs to account for a 60/40 split of users between two datacenters. A single DAG stretching two datacenters can provide service to all users during normal operation. But when connectivity between datacenters is lost, depending on the location of file share witness, only one of the two datacenters can obtain a majority and continue servicing users. Affecting 40 percent of users due to network outage isn't a desirable outcome. Creating two DAGs stretching across sites can provide users from each datacenter with uninterrupted service even during the outage of a network link between sites because each DAG can maintain the majority for its location. This design also has a higher cost impact. Because site resiliency is not a stated requirement, a single DAG for each location can provide the same level of availability, while saving money.

2. If a single DAG is deployed per location with no mailbox servers located across the sites, a file share witness should be located in the same site as the mailbox servers for DAG. If one stretched DAG per site is deployed, the file share witness should be located at the primary site being served by the DAG. A third site for a file share witness can't be recommended because there's no mention of availability of a third site, planned or existing. Also, network link quality and redundancy is an unknown. Locating a file share witness in a third site requires robust and redundant network links from each site to a third site where the file share witness is to be located.

Objective 1.3: Review

1. **Correct answer:** B

    A. **Incorrect:** Failover Cluster functionality required to create a cluster without an administrative point doesn't exist in Windows Server 2008 R2.

    B. **Correct:** Failover Cluster functionality required to create a cluster without an administrative point was introduced in Windows Server 2012 R2.

    C. **Incorrect:** Failover Cluster functionality required to create a cluster without an administrative point doesn't exist in Windows Server 2012.

2. **Correct answers:** B and D

    A. **Incorrect:** Database files of a database with circular logging can't be moved to a different location.

    B. **Correct:** Circular logging is required to be disabled before moving a database file to a different location.

    C. **Incorrect:** Database doesn't need to be dismounted before moving database files to a different path. The Move-DatabasePath cmdlet automatically dismounts the database and mounts it again. If a database is manually dismounted before running the Move-DatabasePath cmdlet, the cmdlet won't automatically mount the database after moving the database file to a new location.

    D. **Correct:** The Move-DatabasePath cmdlet dismounts the database, moves the database file to new path, and mounts the database.

3. **Correct answers:** B and C

   A. **Incorrect:** By default, DAG manages networks automatically Setting ManualDagNetworkConfiguration to $false is similar to automatic management of networks. The required goal is opposite.

   B. **Correct:** By setting ManualDagNetworkConfiguration to $true, you are enabling ability to manage DAG networks manually. This is required to achieve stated goal.

   C. **Correct:** to remove SCSI network from DAG networks, you need to set IgnoreNetwork to $true.

   D. **Incorrect:** Until IgnoreNetwork is congifured to $true, DAG automatically uses all networks. Setting IgnoreNetwork to $false does not help achieve the stated objective.

Objective 1.4: Thought experiment

You need to address two primary concerns. One is frequent failovers of the databases. It is important to find out why the failovers are occurring in the first place. Using CollectOverMetrics. ps1 is the best way to collect data from all servers in the DAG and correlate the events that could be causing the databases to fail over. This could also help prevent the failovers from happening if the root cause can be remediated. The concern about activation preference can be addressed by explaining the process of BCS, which uses an activation preference as one of many factors of determining which copy is the best copy for activation, given its health and the possibility of data loss or performance degradation. Along with a review of data collected by script, as previously discussed, it can be determined why the preferred copy wasn't selected. Lastly, as discussed in the section, Troubleshooting database copy activation, you can force activation of local copies only by configuring intrasite only property on the mailbox server configuration.

Objective 1.4: Review

1. **Correct answers:** A, B, and C

   A. **Correct:** CollectOverMetrics.ps1 can collect logs from a specified mailbox server or from all servers in the DAG. The CSV file and HTML report can help determine if the copy failed over due to an error or as the result of an administrative action.

   B. **Correct:** While not as efficient as CollectOverMetrics.ps1, crimson event logs can help determine if the copy failed over due to an error or as the result of an administrative action. This process requires more work because the administrator must manually collect all events from all servers and correlate the events manually.

C. **Correct:** Searching admin audit logs can help determine what actions the administrator performed and if an action could have affected the active database copy, resulting in a switchover or a failover of the database. If the database failed over due to an error on the server, and not as an administrative action, searching the administrative log isn't effective and can only partially address the concern.

D. **Inorrect:** Get-DatabaseAvailabilityGroup only returns database availability group properties and does not help achieve stated goal

2. **Correct answers:** A and B

A. **Correct:** Low disk space can prevent logs from being copied over to database copies.

B. **Correct:** A missing or corrupt log file required for database copies to be consistent can cause copy queue length greater than zero as the system can't replicate required data until the missing or corrupt log file is restored.

C. **Incorrect:** Because it's stated that all the servers are able to communicate to the server hosting active database copy, a network issue causing transmission failure was ruled out.

D. **Incorrect:** TCP chimney offload helps improve processing of network data.

3. **Correct answer:** A

A. **Correct:** Configuring MaximumActiveDatabases parameter using Set-MailboxServer cmdlet defines how many databases can be active on a mailbox server at a time.

B. **Incorrect:** Update-MailboxDatabaseCopy cmdlet does not have option to configure maximum databases per server.

C. **Incorrect:** Set-DatabaseAvailabilityGroup cmdlet allows configuration of DAG but can't set maximum databases per server.

D. **Incorrect:** Add-ServerMonitoringOverride cmdlet allows override of managed availability probes, monitors and responders.

Objective 1.5: Thought experiment

While it might seem that a 14-day maximum limit on lagged copies might not be able to meet the requirements of a litigation hold, which could be up to six months on average, the retention of deleted data is provided by a single item retention and legal hold features. These features store deleted data in folders hidden from a user, but they are part of the user's mailbox. The discovery and restoration of deleted data can be performed using a single-item recovery process and rarely requires the use of lagged copy. Lagged copies have the required data if the single item recovery and legal hold limits are configured appropriately. Lagged copies are merely holding the same data already protected by retention settings.

Objective 1.5: Review

1. **Correct answer:** B
    A. **Incorrect:** Suspending a lagged copy suspends all operations including a copy of the log files from the active copy of the database and replay of the log files that meet the lag requirements. This doesn't meet the stated goal.
    B. **Correct:** Only suspending a lagged copy for activation doesn't completely suspend the database copy. It only suspends the activation of the lagged copy by removing it from the BCS process. This allows a lagged copy to receive log files and replays them if the lagged configuration requirements are met. Because activation is blocked, manual intervention is required if the copy must be activated.
    C. **Incorrect:** Removing permissions assigned to Exchange Trusted Subsystem (ETS) on an Exchange server should never be recommended. It has undesired and unexpected consequences because Exchange server relies on the permissions to carry out required tasks on the server.
    D. **Incorrect:** Removing permissions assigned to Exchange Trusted Subsystem (ETS) on an Exchange server should never be recommended. It has undesired and unexpected consequences because Exchange server relies on the permissions to carry out required tasks on the server.

2. **Correct answer:** C
    A. **Incorrect:** Only one repair request can run against a mailbox database at any given time.
    B. **Incorrect:** While up to 100 active mailbox repair requests can be active on a server, only one request can be active against a given database.
    C. **Correct:** Distributing mailboxes to multiple databases allows multiple repair requests to run against mailboxes simultaneously. While this requires moving mailboxes, it's the only option that meets the stated goal of fixing corruption on all mailboxes in the shortest amount of time.
    D. **Incorrect:** performing offline repair on the database does not achieve stated goal.

3. **Correct answer:** C
    A. **Incorrect:** cumulative updates are full Exchange installs. If a CU fails, simply trying a reinstall does not fix the issue.
    B. **Incorrect:** cumulative update uninstalls Exchange before installing new updates. You can't uninstall a CU after it is installed.
    C. **Correct:** you must recover Exchange server using setup if CU fails to install, since CU install uninstalls Exchange from the server first before installing updated version of Exchange server.
    D. **Incorrect:** you can't recover a failed CU install by using last known good configuration option

Objective 1.6: Thought experiment

Mail storms caused by Reply All from multiple recipients on the distribution groups can be addressed by moderating the distribution group. Moderators can reject all unnecessary replies, or simply ignore them and only approve valid responses.

A data leak of sensitive information might be seen as best addressed by DLP features of Exchange 2013. But, at the core of the requirement, you're required to configure approval when certain content is detected in a message. Because moderation is a transport function, you can meet the stated requirement with moderation.

Objective 1.6: Review

1. **Correct answer:** C

    A. **Incorrect:** The Set-ADPermission cmdlet enables you to configure Send As permissions on a mailbox. It doesn't address a stated requirement.

    B. **Incorrect:** The Set-Mailbox cmdlet doesn't have the capability to configure auto-mapping properties on a shared mailbox.

    C. **Correct:** Auto-mapping properties can only be configured when assigning permissions using the Add-MailboxPermission cmdlet. If already assigned, you must remove the permissions to change the property of auto-mapping behavior.

    D. **Incorrect:** Set-CASMailbox cmdlet can't be used to configure auto mapping properties of a mailbox.

2. **Correct answer:** D

    A. **Incorrect:** Adding an administrator account to the Domain Admins group in resource forest provides access to domain administration functions in resource forest only.

    B. **Incorrect:** Adding an administrator account to the Domain Admins group in account forest provides access to domain administration functions in account forest only.

    C. **Incorrect**: Adding an administrator account to the Enterprise Admins group in account forest provides access to enterprise administration functions in account forest only.

    D. **Correct:** When an account forest trusts a resource forest, adding a linked mailbox can proceed without requiring an administrator to provide credentials due to an existing trust.

3. **Correct answer:** D

    A. **Incorrect:** Default configuration of a new distribution group only allows internal users to submit messages.

    B. **Incorrect:** AcceptMessagesOnlyFrom parameter allows you to configure recipients who can send messages to the distribution group. It is not practical for external senders who may not be known.

    C. **Incorrect:** BypassModerationFromSendersOrMembers parameter is used for moderation of a group. It does not allow external senders to submit messages to a distribution group.

    D. **Correct:** for external senders to be able to send messages to a distribution group, you must allow unauthenticated sender to submit messages. RequireSenderAuthenticationEnabled parameter allows you to do that.

Objective 1.7: Thought experiment

When using Add-MailboxPermission or EAC to assign delegate permissions on the mailbox, you need to account for few important aspects. One is the type of permissions you can assign to the mailbox. Most commonly discussed permissions are full access to the mailbox, but it may not be desired in all instances. Exchange allows you to assign other permissions such as read only, change permission and change if the delegate created the item.

Inheritance is another consideration. When permissions are assigned, you can configure the permission to apply to all folders within the mailbox. Again, this may not be desired and in such instances, do not set InheritanceType parameter to All.

When users have full or other limited access to another mailbox, chances are, they would also like to send email on behalf of the user or as the user if necessary. For an example, a support desk analyst may not want to be identified individually when responding to a support request. In such instance, you would need to assign send as permissions on the mailbox.

Objective 1.7: Review

1. **Correct answer:** D

    A. **Incorrect:** AllBookInPolicy applies to all users who can schedule the resource if their request is within defined policy requirements.

    B. **Incorrect:** AllRequestInPolicy applies to all users who are allowed to request scheduling of resource when their request is within defined policy requirements.

    C. **Incorrect:** AllRequestOutOfPolicy applies to all users. Users are allowed to request scheduling of resource if request is out of policy.

    D. **Correct:** RequestOutOfPolicy allows specified user to request resource scheduling even if the request is out of policy parameters configured for given resource mailbox.

2. **Correct answer:** A

   A. **Correct:** when AddNewRequestTentatively parameter is set to $false, the resource mailbox stops adding in-policy scheduling requests to be added to the resource calendar tentatively while awaiting approval from delegate.

   B. **Incorrect:** AutomateProcessing parameter allows you to configure calendar processing on the resource mailbox. This parameter affects all requests and isn't designed to handle tentative processing only.

   C. **Incorrect:** Confirm parameter applies to all PowerShell cmdlets and is used to stop processing when a confirmation from administrator is needed. It does not help achieve stated objective.

   D. **Inorrect:** ScheduleOnlyDuringWorkHours parameter allows you to control whether the resource mailbox should accept meeting requests outside of configured working hours of the resource mailbox. It does not help address stated requirement.

3. **Correct answer:** B

   A. **Incorrect:** Set-Mailbox cmdlet allows you to modify settings of an existing mailbox. It can't be used to configure send as permissions.

   B. **Correct:** Add-ADPermission cmdlet allows you to configure send as permissions on a mailbox using impersonation.

   C. **Incorrect:** Set-CASMailbox cmdlet is used to configure client access settings of a mailbox.

   D. **Incorrect:** Set-SharingPolicy cmdlet is used to modify free/busy sharing with users outside the organization.

CHAPTER 2

Plan, install, configure, and manage client access

The Client Access server (CAS) role in Exchange 2013 has evolved to account for changes in newer hardware, such as cheaper and more powerful central processing units (CPUs). The CAS role in Exchange 2013 is designed for simplicity of scale. Unlike previous versions of Exchange server, Client Access in Exchange 2013 is loosely coupled, meaning it's no longer responsible for rendering mailbox data. All processing and activity for a given mailbox occurs on the Mailbox server that holds the active copy of the mailbox. Because all of the data processing is carried out by the Mailbox server role, it eliminates concerns of version compatibility between the CAS and the Mailbox server.

Because of these changes, CAS is now a thin and stateless server. It provides authentication, redirection, and proxy services. Clients connect to CAS using Hypertext Transfer Protocol (HTTP), Post Office Protocol (POP), Internet Message Access Protocol (IMAP), or Single Mail Transfer Protocol (SMTP) and CAS redirects or proxies as necessary. Client Access does not queue or store anything on behalf of a Mailbox server.

EXAM TIP

Because of the loosely coupled architecture and the fact that Client Access is a stateless proxy, you must install the Exchange 2013 Mailbox server role before you install Exchange 2013 CAS. If you install CAS first, you will not be able to connect to the Exchange Management Shell because an Exchange 2013 Mailbox server does not exist and a connection to the virtual directory for the Shell can't be made successfully.

With new architecture in Exchange 2013 and a redefined Client Access role, you benefit from version upgrade flexibility, session indifference, and deployment simplicity. You are no longer required to upgrade CAS roles to a newer version before you can upgrade the Mailbox server role. The ability to independently upgrade the roles is a welcome development for many organizations.

Compared to Exchange 2013, where session affinity to the CAS was required, Exchange 2013 Client Access eliminates a session affinity requirement because it's a stateless proxy. This, in turn, simplifies the configuration of load balancers, reducing the administrative overhead and improving cost efficiencies.

The namespace requirements in Exchange 2013 are also less demanding. If you are coexisting with Exchange 2010, you need only two namespaces: one for client protocols and one for Autodiscover. If you are using SRV records or HTTP redirection, you can even use a single namespace for both client protocols and Autodiscover. When coexisting with Exchange 2007, an additional legacy namespace is also required.

Because of the architectural changes, clients can no longer use the RPC protocol to connect. All Outlook clients must connect using a remote procedure call (RPC) over HTTP, including internal clients. This change removes the need of RPC CAS on CASs, resulting in a reduction of namespaces that would be required when deployment spans more than one site.

The connection endpoint that an Outlook client uses to connect has also changed from the server Fully Qualified Domain Name (FQDN) used in previous versions of Exchange to the mailbox GUID@SMTP domain of the primary email address of the user. Combined with the removal of Client Access Array, this change enables users to connect to any of the CASs without getting prompted to restart the Outlook client. Figure 2-1 shows an example of a user profile.

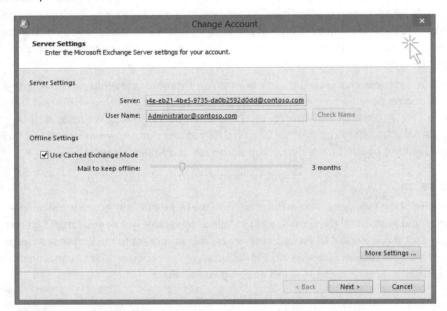

FIGURE 2-1 Example of a user profile connected to Exchange 2013

Certificate management is also simplified in Exchange 2013. Because the CAS role is a stateless proxy, it must connect to the Mailbox server role. You need a certificate on CAS, which is used by Outlook and other clients, and a certificate on Mailbox server, which is used by CAS. While the client facing certificate must be from a certificate authority trusted by clients, the certificate on the Mailbox server can be a self-signed certificate. This is because CAS automatically trusts the self-signed certificate on the Mailbox server. Exchange 2013 also makes it easier to see certificates nearing expiration with notification in EAC, as well as email notification if the administrator opts for it.

Objectives in this chapter:

- Objective 2.1: Plan, deploy, and manage a Client Access Server (CAS)
- Objective 2.2: Plan and configure namespaces and client services
- Objective 2.3: Deploy and manage mobility solutions
- Objective 2.4: Implement load balancing
- Objective 2.5 Troubleshoot client connectivObjective 2.1 Plan, deploy, and manage a Client Access Server (CAS)

Objective 2.1: Plan, deploy, and manage a Client Access Server (CAS)

Because of the architectural changes in the CAS role in Exchange 2013, you benefit from the simplified stateless connection requirements and a higher scalability of the Client Access tier. Because session affinity is no longer a requirement, it does not matter which CAS in an array of CAS servers receives each individual client request. In Exchange 2010, you needed to define a Client Access array per each Active Directory site. This was, in turn, tied to a unique namespace that Outlook clients connected to. No such requirement exists for CAS servers in Exchange 2013.

When CAS servers connect to a Mailbox server, a machine account used to authenticate is a privileged account that is a member of the Exchange Servers group. This allows CAS servers to pool connections to Mailbox servers from multiple clients. This results in fewer connections used to proxy the requests to the Mailbox servers, improving processing efficiency and end-to-end latency.

> **This objective covers how to:**
> - Design to account for differences between legacy CAS and Exchange 2013 CAS
> - Configure Office Web Apps server

Designing to account for differences between legacy CAS and Exchange 2013 CAS

When a client application makes a connection to Exchange 2013 Client Access, CAS authenticates the user, locates the mailbox and the server where the mailbox is active, and either proxies the connection to the Mailbox server or redirects it, where appropriate. When coexisting with older versions of Exchange server, Exchange 2013 CAS acts differently, based on the client application or protocol in use and the destination server version where the client mailbox is located. It's important to understand how Exchange 2013 CAS reacts to different scenarios, when it proxies the connection, and when the connection is redirected.

Coexistence with Exchange 2007

When you deploy Exchange 2013 in coexistence with Exchange 2007 servers, you must configure a legacy host name in DNS and change Exchange 2007 servers to use the legacy name as the ExternalURL. When Exchange 2013 Client Access is deployed, you need to associate an existing namespace, for example, mail.contoso.com, to newly deployed Exchange 2013 CAS servers. When this switch is complete, users will not need to use a legacy host name. The legacy host name is used by the Autodiscover and Client Access servers when redirecting users hosted on Exchange 2007 to the appropriate server.

When users whose mailboxes are hosted on Exchange 2007 connect using Outlook Anywhere or ActiveSync, Exchange 2013 proxies their connections to Exchange 2007. For Outlook clients, the transition becomes easier if all clients are configured to use Autodiscover and Outlook Anywhere is enabled and configured on the Exchange 2007 server.

When an Outlook client connects to Exchange 2013, but the user mailbox is located on Exchange 2007, Exchange 2013 CAS proxies the connection to Exchange 2007 CAS. For the proxy process to work, Outlook Anywhere must be enabled on Exchange 2007 CAS servers. You must also ensure that client authentication on all CAS servers, including Exchange 2013 and Exchange 2007, is set to Basic and the Internet Information Services (IIS) authentication method includes NTLM. NTLM is required on IIS because the Exchange 2013 CAS uses Windows authentication to authenticate to Exchange 2007 servers.

In Exchange 2007, for deployments with multiple sites where you have an Internet facing site and another site with no Internet connectivity, you can configure Outlook Anywhere only on the site with Internet connectivity. However, during coexistence with Exchange 2013, you must also enable Outlook Anywhere on all Exchange 2007 servers, regardless of their location and whether the site they're located on has Internet connectivity.

EXAM TIP

You might wonder what the Outlook Anywhere host name should be when configuring Outlook Anywhere on Exchange 2007 servers on non-Internet facing site. You must use the same host name as the one assigned to servers in the Internet facing site. This name is different from the legacy host name and it usually resolves to Exchange 2013 CAS servers in DNS.

Outlook Web App (OWA) connections are redirected to Exchange 2007 using the legacy host name configured on Exchange 2007 servers using the ExternalURL parameter. For this reason, you must maintain at least one Exchange 2007 server with the ExternalURL parameter configured to use the legacy host name until all users are migrated from Exchange 2007 servers.

When a user logs on to Exchange 2013 OWA using Forms Based Authentication (FBA), which is the default, Exchange 2013 CAS then determines the user mailbox being located on Exchange 2007. It sends a redirect to the legacy namespace it determined using Autodiscover and ExternalURL configured on Exchange 2007 servers in the site where the user's mailbox is located. For Exchange 2013 RTM and CU1, the behavior is a redirect resulting in an FBA logon page being presented to the user from the Exchange 2007 server. This isn't an optimal user experience, but it's expected behavior. This was changed for the better when Exchange 2013 CU2 was introduced. From CU2 onward, Exchange 2013 sends a single sign-on (SSO) redirect, so that user does not get prompted for credentials twice when logging onto OWA.

When you have multiple site deployment with a non-Internet facing site where Exchange 2007 servers and mailboxes are located, Exchange 2013 redirects OWA users to the legacy namespace that's associated with Exchange 2007 servers located in the Internet facing site. Exchange 2007 servers from the Internet facing site then proxy the connection to a non-Internet facing site and the user is presented with their mailbox in OWA.

The deployments with multiple Internet facing sites containing Exchange 2007 servers require multiple namespaces configured to allow users to connect to their appropriate location. This is determined by ExternalURLs configured on relevant Exchange 2007 CAS servers, as appropriate. In the Exchange 2013 coexistence scenario, when a user logs on to OWA, Exchange 2013 determines the location and correct namespace assigned to Exchange 2007 servers in the site where the user's mailbox is located. An SSO redirect is then issued if Exchange 2013 servers are running CU2 or later. A redirect without SSO is issued if Exchange 2013 is running RTM or CU1 versions.

When dealing with ActiveSync clients, Exchange 2013 no longer issues a 451 redirect. This means that when an ActiveSync client connects to an Exchange 2013 server, Exchange 2013 proxies the connection, even if the mailbox is located in an Internet facing site with an external URL configured on Exchange 2007 server. If an ActiveSync device was already configured to connect to the Internet facing site using its external URL, unlike Outlook clients, ActiveSync doesn't periodically check for changes. It continues connecting to the namespace it was configured for when set up. If you retire the namespace that was in use when the device was set up, it results in an interruption of service to the client, and then the client must reestablish ActiveSync partnership with the server.

EXAM TIP

ActiveSync devices continue using the namespace even after the user is moved to a different site. The device will change the namespace it connects to only when it receives a 451 redirect. Since Exchange 2013 servers do not issue a 451 redirect, ensure that the Exchange 2007 CAS servers and associated namespace are preserved until migration of all users is complete and no ActiveSync devices are connecting to the Exchange 2007 servers.

For an Exchange Web Services (EWS) connection to be successful, the clients must connect to the appropriate version of CAS servers. This is usually addressed by an Autodiscover response, which includes the appropriate CAS server for the given user mailbox. However, for clients that are not configured to use Autodiscover, you must ensure that the clients are connecting to the correct CAS server. If a user whose mailbox is located on Exchange 2007 connects to Exchange 2013 CAS, the EWS connection fails because Exchange 2013 won't proxy the connection.

If both IMAP and POP service are in use, coexistence is quite simple. If an Exchange 2013 CAS server receives a POP/IMAP request for a user hosted on Exchange 2007 server, Exchange 2013 CAS determines the FQDN of the Exchange 2007 CAS server and proxies the request. Because IMAP and POP services don't have health checking, you must ensure that POP/IMAP services are running on Exchange 2007 servers.

Coexistence with Exchange 2010

One of the important differences between coexisting with Exchange 2007 and Exchange 2010 is that Exchange 2013 servers don't require legacy namespace when coexisting with Exchange 2010 servers. As long as no Exchange 2007 servers are in the mix, you can move the primary namespace to Exchange 2013 CAS servers. Then all client connectivity for users whose mailboxes are located on Exchange 2010 are handled by Exchange 2013 CAS servers.

For Outlook Anywhere and ActiveSync clients, the logic of their connection doesn't change at all when compared to the logic used with Exchange 2007 servers. Clients can connect to the primary namespace associated with Exchange 2013. Exchange 2013 CAS servers then proxy the connection to Exchange 2010 CAS servers. The same configuration requirements apply as described earlier. Outlook Anywhere must be enabled on Exchange 2010 CAS servers, and the IIS authentication method must include NTLM.

The logic for OWA connections is a bit different when a user's mailbox is located on Exchange 2010. Because there's no legacy host name requirement for coexistence with Exchange 2010, the Exchange 2013 CAS server receiving a OWA request from a user simply proxies the request to an Exchange 2010 server if it's located in the same site. If Exchange 2010 is located in a non-Internet facing site, the proxy behavior is the same. The behavior is different when a user mailbox is located on the Exchange 2010 server in an Internet facing site that has its own namespace. This is different from the primary namespace associated with Exchange 2013. In this case, Exchange 2013 CAS servers receiving the user's OWA request issues a redirect to the namespace associated with the site where the user's mailbox is located. Whether the redirect is SSO or requires the user to logon again, is dependent on whether the Exchange 2013 servers are running the RTM/CU1 or CU2 version.

ActiveSync behavior, when coexisting with Exchange 2010, isn't different from what was covered earlier in the coexistence scenarios for Exchange 2007. Regardless of the namespace configuration of Exchange 2010 servers, if a partnership existed before introducing the Exchange 2013 servers, then ActiveSync clients connect to the namespace they were configured for and they'll continue to connect to their mailboxes accordingly. If a new partnership is being established, ActiveSync connects to the namespace returned by Autodiscover, which is normally associated with the primary namespace, which, in turn, is associated with Exchange 2013 servers. In this case, Exchange 2013 CAS servers proxy the ActiveSync request, regardless of the location of the Exchange 2010 servers and their configured external URLs. This change was designed to eliminate issues with different ActiveSync implementations that didn't always honor 451 redirect and resulted in connectivity errors.

When an EWS client connects to the Exchange 2013 CAS servers and the target mailbox is located on Exchange 2010, Exchange 2013 CAS servers send a proxy request to Exchange 2010 CAS servers. This behavior is different from Exchange 2007 coexistence scenarios. If Exchange 2010 servers are located in another Internet facing site, while Exchange 2013 CAS servers won't send a redirect, the Autodiscover process would provide an appropriate external URL to the client and the client would connect to the servers associated with the given namespace.

When compared to Exchange 2007 coexistence, POP and IMAP connectivity to Exchange 2010 differs slightly. If the target server is Exchange 2010 CAS, Exchange 2013 CAS server enumerates POP/IMAP property InternalConnectionSettings. The value of this property should be set to a server FQDN and not a load-balanced FQDN. Once the value is determined, Exchange 2013 CAS proxies the connection to the selected Exchange 2010 server.

Configuring Office Web Apps server

Office Web Apps server delivers browser-based file viewing and editing services for Office applications, such as Word, PowerPoint, and Excel. Through the Web Application Open Platform Interface (WOPI) protocol, Office Web Apps server works with products such as Exchange 2013, Lync 2013, and SharePoint 2013. It allows these applications to offload online Office documents rendering and editing functionality to the dedicated Office Web Apps server farm.

You can configure Exchange 2013 to use the Office Web Apps server farm for previewing Office file attachments that aren't protected using Information Rights Management (IRM). When configured, OWA users can preview Office file attachments in the browser without downloading files before viewing them. This is also helpful for traveling or kiosk users who might not have access to locally installed Office applications.

To configure Exchange 2013 integration with the Office Web Apps server, you must first ensure that Office Web Apps server is installed and configured appropriately. The Office Web Apps server can be configured to accept unencrypted HTTP connections, encrypted HTTPS connections, or even offloaded SSL connections where a load balancer or a proxy device accepts encrypted Secure Sockets Layer (SSL) connections from clients and sends unencrypted data to the Office Web Apps servers. As an Exchange administrator, you need to gather this information, along with the internal URL as configured on the Office Web Apps server farm.

Configure the Exchange 2013 organization before you can use Office Web App servers to render Office attachments. Exchange 2013 servers use the Office Web Apps discovery URL to determine the required configuration details of the Office Web Apps server or server farm. To configure the Exchange organization for the Office Web Apps discovery endpoint, run the Set-OrganizationConfig cmdlet with the WACDiscoveryEndPoint parameter. The value of the parameter is the Office Web Apps server discovery URL, which looks similar to *http(s)://(server* or farm *FQDN)/hosting/discovery*. Ensure that the URL is reflecting the expected protocol, and HTTP if encryption isn't configured on the Office Web Apps server farm, and HTTPS if encryption is required or offloaded to the load balancer/proxy device. After setting the URL on the Exchange 2013 organization configuration, recycle MSExchangeOWAAppPool on Exchange 2013 CAS servers. After doing so, Exchange 2013 CAS servers perform Office Web Apps discovery using the URL configured and, after successful discovery, OWA can use the Office Web Apps servers to render attachments. You can confirm setup and success of discovery using two events in the Application event log on Exchange 2013 Mailbox servers. Event ID 140 from source MSExchange OWA indicates that the Office Web Apps discovery URL was successfully read from the organization configuration. The second event from the same source can be either Event ID 141, indicating failure to complete discovery, or Event ID 142, indicating successful discovery. A failure event usually means the misconfiguration of a discovery URL, an incorrect load balancer or Office Web Apps farm configuration, or that a firewall is blocking required ports to the Office Web Apps servers.

If the discovery is successful, users are displayed an option to open the attachment in the browser. No further configuration is needed. Users should be able to click the link and open the document in the browser. Figure 2-2 shows an example email with an attachment.

FIGURE 2-2 Example of an email attachment in OWA

When a user opts to open the attachment in the browser, a new window opens and Office Web Apps server is invoked to render the document in the browser. When the Client Access server sends the request to render the attachment, and the Office Web Apps server is configured to require encryption using SSL, the request to render only succeeds if the certificate assigned to IIS on the Client Access server is trusted by the Office Web Apps server. By default, Exchange 2013 CAS servers use a self-signed certificate created during installation. You should assign a certificate obtained from a certification authority (CA) that is trusted by the Office Web Apps server.

Figure 2-3 shows a failure when the certificate presented by the CAS server is not trusted by the Office Web Apps server.

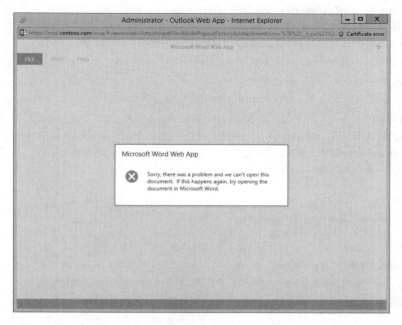

FIGURE 2-3 Failure to render an email attachment in OWA

Figure 2-4 shows a successful rendering of an attachment in the browser window when the CAS server is configured with a certificate issued by the CA trusted by the Office Web Apps server.

FIGURE 2-4 Email attachment successfully rendered in OWA

After enabling the organization configuration, you don't need to configure any additional properties before the user can view the attachment in the browser. This is because the default OWA virtual directory configuration allows OWA users on public and private computers to render the attachments using the Office Web Apps server. The settings also allow users to download the attachment before viewing the attachment in the browser.

The properties WacViewingOnPrivateComputersEnabled, WacViewingOnPublicComputers Enabled, ForceWacViewingFirstOnPrivateComputers and ForceWacViewingFirstOnPublicComputers on the OWA virtual directory allows the administrator to control the behavior of how attachments must be rendered or downloaded.

By default, WacViewing* parameters are set to $true. When set to $false, this can prohibit user from rendering the attachment in a browser on a public or a private computer, or both.

The parameters ForceWacViewing* are set to $false by default, allowing users to select whether to render the document in a browser or download the attachment in any order they choose. When set to $true, these parameters force the user to view the attachment in the browser before they can download the attachment.

Thought experiment

Coexistence

In this thought experiment, apply what you learned about this objective. You can find answers to these questions in the "Answers" section at the end of this chapter.

You are an Exchange administrator for Contoso, Ltd. Contoso plans to deploy Exchange 2013, which will coexist with the multisite deployment of Exchange 2007. Contoso has deployed Outlook clients using a manual configuration of user profiles via GPO. Many users have mobile devices with an established ActiveSync connection to their existing mailboxes. Most of the Exchange 2007 sites are connected to the Internet and are configured with a unique external URL for access to Exchange services.

When developing a deployment plan, you're required to ensure that Outlook clients aren't impacted when a primary namespace associated with Contoso HQ is moved to Exchange 2013 CAS servers. You are also required to ensure that existing ActiveSync clients aren't impacted when their associated mailboxes are moved from remote offices to centralized Exchange 2013 servers located in HQ.

1. What would you recommend to meet the requirements for Outlook clients?

2. What would you recommend to meet ActiveSync requirements?

3. If you're required to reduce the number of namespaces in use, can you avoid impacting Outlook and ActiveSync clients? How?

Objective summary

- When coexisting with Exchange 2007 and Exchange 2010, Exchange 2013 behavior is different for each version. The behavior is also different for each workload. It's important to understand how each workload, Outlook Anywhere, ActiveSync, and EWS are impacted during coexistence.

- Legacy namespace is required when coexisting with Exchange 2007. This impacts certificate requirements, as well as the process of moving a primary namespace to Exchange 2013 CAS servers. When moving a primary namespace to Exchange 2013 CAS servers, you must ensure enough capacity is available on Exchange 2013 CAS servers to service all users who are connecting to the existing primary namespace.

- When changing a primary namespace, you must account for impact of DNS infrastructure and caching. Propagation delays and caching can impact clients, and clients can continue connecting to previously associated Exchange 2007 servers until all the DNS servers are updated.

- The Office Web Apps server enables document rendering in a browser for OWA users. The integration must be enabled at the organization level and defaults must be accounted for to ensure it meets your requirements of desired user experience and behavior.

- When encryption is required, the Office Web Apps servers require SSL certificate presented by CAS servers to be from a trusted authority. There are default self-signed certificates assigned to IIS on CAS servers fail to meet this requirement, impacting the ability to render documents in the browser.

Objective review

Answer the following questions to test your knowledge of the information in this objective. You can find the answers to these questions and explanations of why each answer choice is correct or incorrect in the "Answers" section at the end of this chapter.

1. You are planning to migrate all users from an existing Exchange 2007 deployment to a planned Exchange 2013 deployment. All users connect internally and over VPN using Outlook clients. Users aren't allowed to connect from the Internet when they aren't using VPN. What must you do to deploy Exchange 2013? Select all that apply.

   A. Create legacy namespace and associate it with Exchange 2007 servers.

   B. Enable Outlook Anywhere on Exchange 2007 servers.

   C. Associate primary namespace with Exchange 2013 CAS servers.

   D. Configure ExternalURL property on Exchange 2007 servers.

   E. Configure ExternalURL property on Exchange 2013 servers.

2. You have deployed Exchange 2013 CU1 with the primary namespace mail.contoso.com, assigned to the New York location. The branch site is associated with the namespace London.contoso.com. When a user, whose mailbox is located on Exchange 2013 server in London, logs on to OWA by connecting to *mail.contoso.com/owa,* how will the Exchange 2013 server handle the request?

   A. A redirect is issued for the London.contoso.com namespace. The user is presented with a FBA logon page.

   B. Proxies the user request to Exchange 2013 CAS server at the London site.

   C. Proxies the user request to Exchange 2013 Mailbox server at the London site.

   D. SSO redirect is issued for London.contoso.com namespace. The user won't need to logon again.

3. You have deployed Exchange 2013 server and configured the organization properties to include the discovery endpoint of the Office Web Apps server farm. Exchange servers were installed using a GUI setup and no other properties were changed yet. You want users to be able to download attachments only after they have opened the attachment in the browser. What must you do? Select two.

   A. Set ForceWacViewingFirstOnPrivateComputers property to $true.

   B. Set WacViewingOnPrivateComputersEnabled property to $true.

   C. Set WacViewingOnPublicComputersEnabled to $true.

   D. Obtain a SSL certificate from a trusted authority and assign it to the Exchange 2013 CAS server.

Objective 2.2: Plan and configure namespaces and client services

A successful Exchange deployment is highly dependent upon careful planning and the deployment of namespaces for a given environment. User experience is also dependent on proper configuration of certificates in use. Without it, connectivity issues and certificate trust warnings become more than an annoyance for users.

Exchange 2013 has greatly simplified namespace configuration requirements. This helps reduce the number of namespaces needed for an environment, as well as simplifying SSL certificate requirements.

Designing namespaces for client connectivity

For each workload that Exchange 2013 supports, Exchange server provides you with the ability to configure a URL that can be used for both internal and external clients. The URL needs to be configured for each workload, such as OWA, EWS, and so on. Ideally, if split-brain DNS is deployed for a given environment, you can possibly associate a single FQDN to both internal and external URL parameters of the given workload.

To design a namespace configuration that best suits the environment, you must understand how client connectivity works in different environments. Most of this was covered earlier in Objective 2.1. Let's look at some Exchange 2013 specifics in a bit more depth.

Exchange 2013 workloads include HTTP-based protocols, which include OWA, ECP, EWS, EAS, OAB, RPC, MAPI, and AutoDiscover, as well as non HTTP protocols, which include SMTP, POP, and IMAP. In a simple, single site deployment, you have a minimum of two namespaces: one for AutoDiscover and the other for all other workloads. The AutoDiscover namespace is used for clients capable of using the AutoDiscover service to find appropriate connection endpoints and URLs for different workloads. Once the discovery process is complete, the client uses discovered namespaces to connect to the relevant workload, such as Outlook Anywhere, Exchange Web Services, or ActiveSync.

Unlike OWA, ECP, and other workloads, you can't just configure internal and external URLs for AutoDiscover virtual directories. Even if you did, would it really help clients find the Autodiscover service? Thinking logically, the purpose of the Autodiscover process is to find the configuration for user profile and connection end points for each client type. Because the process is about finding the URLs that aren't known to the client, you can't just configure internal and external URLs on the AutoDiscover virtual service and expect clients to know where to connect for Autodiscover. Some static information must exist that every client can use to get to the AutoDiscover service. Autodiscover logic for Exchange 2013 clients is a well-defined process that every client should follow. This ensures that just by providing the user's primary email address and authentication information, the client can connect to the AutoDiscover service and, in turn, can download the user profile and connection endpoint information from the Exchange 2013 servers.

For internal Outlook clients that are installed on domain joined computers, the process starts with looking up the Service Connection Point (SCP) in Active Directory. The Outlook client is hard coded to look for well-known globally unique identifiers (GUIDs) of SCP URLs stored in the configuration container of Active Directory. The search results of SCP lookup include Active Directory site information and the URL for the AutoDiscover service. On an out-of-box configuration of an Exchange server, this URL is configured to the user server FQDN and looks similar to the following: *Server1.Contoso.com/Autodiscover/Autodiscover.xml*.

When multiple Exchange servers are installed in the environment, the client receives multiple URLs it can connect to. It then prioritizes the URLs. The first preference is given to the SCP record that belongs to the same Active Directory site as the client computer. If no such SCP record is found, SCP records that contain an Active Directory site keyword are given preference. If both conditions fail to find an appropriate SCP record, the SCP records that don't contain an Active Directory site keyword are used.

Once an SCP record is selected, the AutoDiscover URL from the SCP record is used to connect to the AutoDiscover service on the given Exchange 2013 server. Upon a successful connection, the client obtains profile information needed to connect to the user's mailbox and other available Exchange features.

When starting the Outlook client for the first time, it provides you with an option to connect to an email account. If you opt for it, the Outlook client automatically retrieves the user's name and email address from Active Directory. This only works if the user's account is enabled and associated with an Exchange mailbox. When you proceed to the next step, the Outlook client establishes a connection with an AutoDiscover URI it retrieved from SCP, as discussed earlier. This is where you can notice the first sign of trouble!

As mentioned earlier, a default configuration contains the server FQDN of Exchange 2013 CAS server in the AutoDiscover URI. The server also has a self-signed certificate associated with IIS by default. This results in an Outlook client not trusting the certificate and prompting the user with a security alert. Figure 2-5 is an example of such an error.

FIGURE 2-5 Security alert in Outlook client

The resolution to this problem brings us to our first namespace: the AutoDiscover namespace. Even for internal clients, this namespace should be something other than a server FQDN. The most commonly used namespace for this purpose is autodiscover.contoso.com, where contoso.com is the SMTP domain name of the user's primary email suffix.

To change the URL associated with the SCP record, use the Set-ClientAccessServer cmdlet and change the AutoDiscoverServiceInternalUri parameter. When changing the value of this parameter, it's important to include a complete Autodiscover URI, such as *autodiscover.contoso.com/Autodiscover/Autodiscover.xml*. You must run this cmdlet for each Exchange 2013 CAS. Figure 2-6 shows the SCP record as seen using LDP.exe before and after changing the URI.

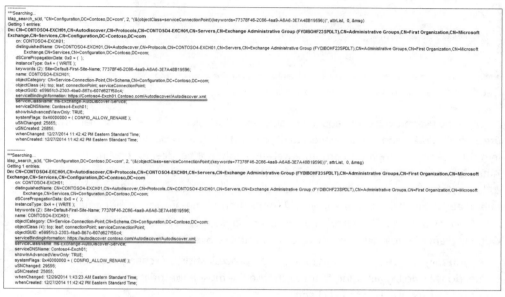

FIGURE 2-6 SCP record for AutoDiscover, before and after updating the SCP

Resolving the security alert is a two-part process. The first step is to change the AutoDiscover URI to an appropriate namespace similar to what we did earlier. The second step is to obtain an SSL certificate that contains the AutoDiscover namespace from a trusted CA. You learn more about certificates in "Planning for certificates" later in this chapter. It might not be as obvious, but the namespace assigned to the AutoDiscover URI must also exist in DNS and it must be associated with an appropriate IP address, ideally resolving to a load balanced IP.

The process for an external client or a client not connected to the domain is different. Because the computer is external or not domain joined, it doesn't have the ability to look up SCP records. It must resort to hard coded logic to search for the AutoDiscover endpoint. This process starts with the Outlook client requesting the user's name, the email address, and the password. Figure 2-7 displays an external Outlook client requesting user details before the AutoDiscover process can commence.

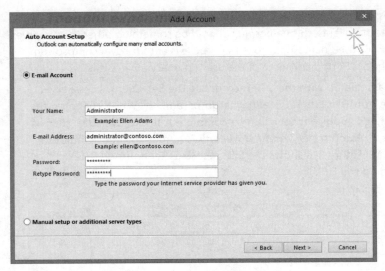

FIGURE 2-7 External Outlook client requesting user details

Once the user provides the required information, Outlook uses the SMTP domain from the user's email address and tries to connect to *https://<SMTP domain>/autodiscover/autodiscover.xml*. In most cases, the company's corporate website might not be ideal for hosting the AutoDiscover service and this step could fail. If it does fail, the Outlook client tries to connect to *https://autodiscover.<SMTP domain>/autodiscover/autodiscover.xml*. If the Outlook client fails again, it then tries the unencrypted connection to the Autodiscover namespace, *http://autodiscover.<SMTP domain>/autodiscover/autodiscover.xml*. If all of these steps fail, then the Outlook client tries to locate the SRV record for AutoDiscover *autodiscover._tcp.<SMTP domain>*.

As you might have noticed, this hard-coded process affords Exchange administrators tremendous flexibility, allowing them to choose the most appropriate way to provide the AutoDiscover service to external clients.

The second namespace usually addresses all other web-based workloads, as discussed earlier. These workloads include OWA, ECP, EWS, EAS, OAB, RPC, and MAPI. Depending on how the load balancing is configured, and if the deployment spans more than one datacenter, you might be able to use a single namespace for all HTTP protocols, as well as non-HTTP protocols, such as SMTP, POP, and IMAP.

Going from a simple, single-location deployment to multiple locations, whether designed as a primary and standby datacenter configuration or as multiple active sites, the namespace planning becomes more involved. You need to account for all of the different ingress points and decide whether you can use a single namespace for a multiple datacenter or should you deploy a regional namespace model.

When you deploy a single namespace for a pair of datacenters serving a single set of users and acting as an active/passive pair, this is known as an *unbound model*. User mailboxes are protected by DAG, and the DAG spans two datacenters to provide site resilience. DNS resolves the name (for example, mail.contoso.com) to load the balanced IP address of CAS servers in each site. CAS servers located in any site can serve client requests. If a client request lands on a CAS server located in a different site than where the user's mailbox is active, CAS simply proxies the request across the site. The benefit of this model is a simplified namespace and certificate planning.

EXAM TIP

When using a single namespace for both internal and external clients, there is a common scenario when split-brain DNS infrastructure is in use. The authentication value for both internal and external Outlook Anywhere settings must be the same. This is because Outlook gives priority to the internal settings when a single namespace is used for both internal and external clients. The Outlook client utilizes internal Outlook Anywhere authentication settings even when the Outlook client is connected externally.

In a similar deployment that contains two datacenters, but contains active users in both sites that are usually protected by two different DAGs, a bound model is usually preferred. In a *bound model,* each datacenter is assigned a unique namespace. This design aims at keeping user connections to their local datacenter, reducing cross datacenter traffic over WAN connections between datacenters. For example, mail.contoso.com might be assigned to one datacenter, while mail2.contoso.com could be assigned to another. Users receive their relevant namespace in the AutoDiscover response and can connect accordingly. If a failure causes the user's mailbox to fail over to a second site, the user continues to connect to the CAS servers in their site and CAS servers proxy the client connections to the appropriate Mailbox server, which isn't active in a different site. If a disaster affects the entire site, the DNS change is necessary to send traffic associated with the affected namespace to CAS servers located in a second site.

Configuring URLs

The Exchange 2013 CAS server installation configures internal URLs to use server FQDN by default. External URLs are always left null. One of the first steps is to configure CAS servers to use the correct internal and external namespaces, as discussed previously.

Configuring internal namespaces requires you to use EAC or Shell to configure each workload's virtual directory. The change needs to be made on every Client Access server associated with the given namespace. If configuring external URLs, Exchange provides a wizard to configure the external URL. The wizard configures external URLs on all virtual directories on a given server and also enables you to select multiple CAS servers. You can select all CAS servers that are associated with a given namespace to configure the external URL. To launch the wizard, from EAC, select Servers, and then select Virtual Directories tab. Then, click the Configure External Access Domain link, which is represented by an icon that looks like a wrench. Figure 2-8 shows the resulting dialog box that allows you to configure the external domain name.

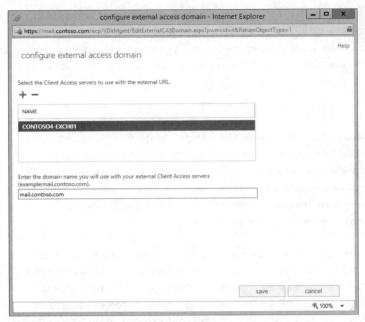

FIGURE 2-8 Wizard to configure external URLs on a CAS server

Notice that the wizard only asks for the domain name associated with external URLs. Once the external domain name is provided, the wizard automatically configures an appropriate external URL for each virtual directory. Looking at cmdlet logging, it looks similar to the following:

Cmdlets issued by the Configure External Access Domain Wizard

```
Set-PowerShellVirtualDirectory -ExternalUrl 'https://mail.contoso.com/powershell'
Set-EcpVirtualDirectory -ExternalUrl 'https://mail.contoso.com/ecp'
Set-OABVirtualDirectory -ExternalUrl 'https://mail.contoso.com/OAB'
Set-OWAVirtualDirectory -ExternalUrl 'https://mail.contoso.com/owa'
Set-WebServicesVirtualDirectory -ExternalUrl 'https://mail.contoso.com/ews/exchange.asmx'
-Force:$true
Set-ActiveSyncVirtualDirectory -ExternalUrl 'https://mail.contoso.com/Microsoft-Server-
ActiveSync'
```

While the identity parameter isn't visible in the log, you won't be able to simply copy-and-paste these cmdlets and run them without an error. This is because an identity parameter is required and must be supplied. Also note the absence of the MAPI virtual directory. Future updates should address the lack of the MAPI virtual directory configuration. Until then, you must set an external URL on it manually.

You can also use the cmdlets listed earlier and switch the ExternalUrl parameter with the InternalUrl parameter to configure an internal URL on each virtual directory. The following example shows how to set the internal URLs on each virtual directory, including the MAPI virtual directory:

```
Set-PowerShellVirtualDirectory -InternalUrl 'https://mail.contoso.com/powershell'
Set-EcpVirtualDirectory -InternalUrl 'https://mail.contoso.com/ecp'
Set-OABVirtualDirectory -InternalUrl 'https://mail.contoso.com/OAB'
Set-OWAVirtualDirectory -InternalUrl 'https://mail.contoso.com/owa'
Set-WebServicesVirtualDirectory -InternalUrl 'https://mail.contoso.com/ews/exchange.
asmx' -Force:$true
Set-ActiveSyncVirtualDirectory -InternalUrl 'https://mail.contoso.com/Microsoft-Server-
ActiveSync'
Set-MAPIVirtualDirectory -InternalUrl 'https://mail.contoso.com/mapi'
```

You might have noticed that in the previous examples, the same DNS name, mail.contoso.com, was used for both internal and external URLs. This simplifies the namespace planning, but requires split-brain DNS infrastructure, as discussed earlier.

When you change an internal or external URL on either a OWA (or ECP) virtual directory using Shell, you also get a warning, informing you that you changed URL on the OWA virtual directory and you must also change it on the ECP virtual directory.

As we configure all required URLs, there's one more URL to configure. And this is also one of the very important URLs. It's the Outlook Anywhere URL, used by Outlook clients to connect. This URL can be changed from the EAC from Client Access server properties. Figure 2-9 shows the default configuration of Outlook Anywhere in which the external URL is empty and the internal URL is set to FQDN of the Client Access server.

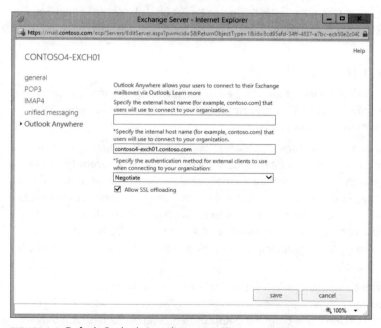

FIGURE 2-9 Default Outlook Anywhere on a Client Access server

You can simply change URLs for Outlook Anywhere clients from here or use the Shell. If using Shell, the cmdlet you issue would look similar to the following:

```
Set-OutlookAnywhere `
-ExternalHostname 'mail.contoso.com' `
-InternalHostname 'mail.contoso.com' `
-ExternalClientsRequireSsl:$strue `
-InternalClientsRequireSsl:$true `
-ExternalClientAuthenticationMethod 'Negotiate' `
-Identity 'Server01\Rpc (Default Web Site)'
```

You need to configure this for each Exchange 2013 Client Access server in the environment. Also, when deploying in a coexistence environment where an older version of Exchange servers exist, it's important to note that negotiated authentication isn't supported by earlier versions. If the user mailbox is located on Exchange 2013 server and the user tries to connect to public folders or a shared mailbox located on the Exchange servers running Exchange 2010 or Exchange 2007, the users can encounter issues. These issues include a repeated authentication prompt and the inability to access the resource if the authentication is set to negotiate. In the coexistence environment, set the authentication method to other valid choices, such as NTLM.

URL management couldn't be simpler in Exchange 2013, despite the existence of the Exchange Back End website, as visible in IIS. While this website is essential and is used to proxy traffic from the CAS server to the Mailbox server, with the Mailbox server being the back end, you only need to configure URLs on the Default Web Site. Protection against error is provided by surfacing only the relevant virtual directories when using EAC or the Get-*VirtualDirectory cmdlets. The virtual directories that exist in the Exchange Back End website are not visible when running Get-*VirtualDirectory cmdlets.

Planning for certificates

Certificate planning for any deployment is directly tied to the planning of namespaces. When it comes to selecting the right type of SSL certificate, knowing the required namespaces and the type of certificate makes the process efficient.

Besides the namespaces discussed earlier, you also need to consider whether split-brain DNS is in use. If the environment uses an internal domain name that is different from the external domain name, and the internal domain name isn't a publicly registered domain name, such as contoso.local, you also need to account for the new certificate requirements set forth by the CA/Browser forum. These new requirements state that certification authorities (CAs) cannot issue new certificates that contain an internal server FQDN that can't be externally verified as owned by the organization requesting the certificate, if the certificate expires after November 1, 2015.

This requirement creates a unique problem for environments with internal private namespaces. Because you can only assign one certificate to a given service, such as IIS, you can't have two different certificates, one containing appropriate internal names issued by an internal CA and another containing appropriate external names issued by an external CA.

One solution is to rename the internal domain. This is a daunting task at best, considering all the dependencies a domain name might have not only limited to an Exchange organization, but also with other systems and business applications in use.

Another, and a more elegant solution, is to create appropriate certificates containing internal names, issued by the internal CA. Assign these certificates to Client Access servers. Obtain certificates containing public names from a trusted third-party CA. These certificates are assigned to all external access points, which can be a reverse proxy solution, such as a TMG server or even a load balancer that's designated to handle external client traffic. Using this approach, external clients negotiate with an endpoint that's presenting certificate issued by a trusted CA and containing only externally verifiable domain names. The connection from a reverse proxy device or a load balance to the Client Access server is encrypted using the certificate containing the internal private domain name issued by the internal CA and assigned to the appropriate services on Exchange server, including IIS.

Another consideration when planning for certificates is a wildcard certificate. While a wildcard certificate is supported by Exchange 2013, you must ensure all of the applications integrating with Exchange and whether they support wildcard certificates. For example, when you enable the Unified Messaging integration with Lync server, the Subject Name (also known as Certificate Principal Name) as presented by the certificate must be a non-wildcard name. You can, however, have a wildcard in the Subject Alternate Name (SAN).

When using the wildcard certificate with Outlook Anywhere, you must set the Outlook provider settings to indicate that the certificate principal name is a wildcard. You must set the same for both EXCH and EXPR providers. EXCH setting is used for the Exchange RPC protocol used internally and includes internal URLs. EXPR refers to HTTP protocol used by Outlook Anywhere clients and includes external URLs. The cmdlets to configure EXCH and EXPR for use with a wildcard certificate are as follows:

```
Set-OutlookProvider EXCH -CertPrincipalName msstd:*.contoso.com
Set-OutlookProvider EXPR -CertPrincipalName msstd:*.contoso.com
```

When considering a simple configuration that is using only two namespaces, autodiscover.contoso.com and mail.contoso.com, and isn't planning to use wildcard certificates, you need to use a SAN certificate that contains both names and is issued by a trusted CA.

The same also applies when you have multiple regional namespaces. The difference, however, is that you have more than two names. You have one for Autodiscover, and one or more names for each regional datacenter. The number of names per location depends on which of the namespace design models, as discussed earlier, is in use.

You also need certificates for TLS used for transport, whether opportunistic or mutual. You can use a self-signed certificate if mutual TLS negotiation isn't required. Mutual TLS negotiation only passes when the certificate assigned to SMTP service is issued by a trusted CA.

Lastly, you need to consider Unified Messaging (UM) certificate requirements if you plan to deploy UM with Lync servers. UM has two components: Exchange UM service is located on Mailbox servers, whereas UM call router service is located on CAS servers. For each service, you must include server FQDN in the certificate. If the server FQDN contains an internal private domain name, a trusted third party CA might not issue the certificate due to the restrictions discussed earlier. You might need to issue a separate certificate for UM using internal CA that's mutually trusted by Exchange and Lync servers.

To avoid confusion and misconfiguration, Exchange 2013 provides a wizard to create and assign certificates. The wizard also makes the process of creating and assigning certificates much easier when compared with cmdlets that you must manually issue if you were to use Exchange Management Shell. You can access the certificate wizard user interface (UI) from EAC using the Servers menu item and by selecting the Certificates tab. Click New (+) to start the New Certificate Wizard. The first dialog box presents you with a choice to create a self-signed certificate or to create a request that can be submitted to a CA. After selecting to create a request, you're presented with a field for a friendly name. The name you use here is visible in the Name column of the Certificates tab. The next option is to request a wildcard certificate, if desired. When you proceed without selecting the check box, you're presented with selecting the Exchange server where you want to store the certificate. Select one of your Client Access servers and proceed further. Next, you're presented with a dialog box that provides a list of client types and associated FQDN. If you populated all of the URLs discussed earlier, this dialog box reflects both the internal and external namespaces you configured. The dialog box also includes both POP and IMAP namespaces, which defaults to the server name, which isn't a server FQDN. If you haven't deployed POP and IMAP, these namespaces can be removed in the next step. You also need to remove all internal namespaces if your internal namespace is a private domain name that can't be resolved externally and you plan to obtain a certificate from the external certificate authority due to restrictions discussed earlier. The Domain Name Selection dialog box looks similar to Figure 2-10.

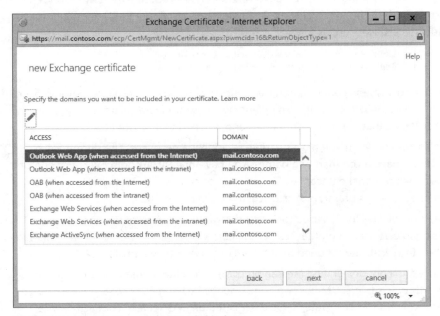

FIGURE 2-10 Domain Name Selection dialog box

While this dialog box lists the same domain name mail.contoso.com multiple times, when you proceed to the next step, the duplicates are removed to create a list of unique namespaces derived from this dialog box. This would normally contain an Autodiscover namespace, a primary namespace such as mail.contoso.com, and a server name for POP/IMAP. You can safely remove the server name if POP/IMAP isn't in use. You might have more namespaces displayed if you used different domain names for each workload when configuring URLs, as discussed earlier.

You can also select which one of the listed namespaces should be the common name, also known as the subject name or the certificate principal name. Usually, this is your primary namespace, such as mail.contoso.com.

In the next dialog box, you're required to provide organization information, such as Organization Name, Department Name, and Address details. Third-party certificate-issuing authorities require this information to be accurate for verification.

The next step requires you to select a shared location where the request is to be stored. Ideally, this location is an Exchange server because it has required file level permissions. If you chose a server that isn't an Exchange server, ensure that the Exchange Trusted Subsystem has permissions to write to the share specified.

The entire wizard can be summed up into the following cmdlet:

```
New-ExchangeCertificate `
-PrivateKeyExportable:$true `
-FriendlyName 'Trusted Certificate' `
-SubjectName 'C=US,S="WA",L="Redmond",O="Contoso",OU="IT",CN=mail.contoso.com' `
-DomainName @('mail.contoso.com','AutoDiscover.Contoso.com') `
-RequestFile '\\contoso4-exch01\c$\certreq.txt' `
-GenerateRequest:$true `
-Server 'Contoso4-Exch01' `
-KeySize '2048'
```

At this point, you now have a certificate request file that can be submitted to the certificate issuing authority. The server you selected in the process also contains a private key that corresponds to the certificate request. The Certificates tab of EAC will display a certification with a pending request.

When the CA issues the certificate, you can click complete on the pending request or issue the following cmdlet:

```
Import-ExchangeCertificate -PrivateKeyExportable:$true -FileName '\\contoso4-exch01\c$\
certnew.cer' -Server 'Contoso4-Exch01'
```

When complete, the certificate request process is finished. You can now assign the certificate to the appropriate services using the Enable-ExchangeCertificate cmdlet. You can also now export the certificate and import it on other Exchange servers, either using the cmdlets or the Certificate Export/Import Wizards from EAC.

As discussed earlier, both the Client Access servers and the Mailbox servers have self-signed certificates created and assigned during the installation. However, you don't need to manage certificates installed on the Mailbox servers. All clients connect through Client Access servers and are presented with a certificate installed on the Client Access server. The Client Access server connects to the Mailbox server and it automatically trusts the self-signed certificate on the Mailbox servers. So the clients won't receive a certificate trust warning due to a self-signed certificate on the Mailbox servers as long as trusted certificates are correctly installed on the Client Access servers.

Configuring authentication methods

When configuring the Exchange 2103 environment, one of the key considerations is what authentication method to use to authenticate the clients. Most commonly, the default configuration of each virtual directory is sufficient and shouldn't need to be changed. However, there are scenarios that occur when you might want specific authentication configuration for a given workload.

The authentication methods available in general are Negotiate, NTLM, and Basic. The *Negotiate process* allows clients to select between Kerberos and NTLM authentication. *NTLM* is selected for authentication when the Outlook client provides insufficient information to use the Kerberos authentication. When an Outlook client connects from an internal domain-joined machine, it can connect to the Exchange server and provide Kerberos with the authentication information required to connect.

When an external client connects to the Exchange server, because it doesn't have connectivity to the domain controller, even if it's a domain-joined laptop user working from home, it falls back to NTLM authentication. This is because the required Kerberos information isn't present.

By default, however, Outlook Anywhere is configured to use Negotiate as an external client authentication method and NTLM as an internal client authentication method. If you're using a single namespace for internal and external clients, as discussed earlier, Outlook uses the authentication method configured for internal clients.

EXAM TIP

Pay close attention to the namespace configuration and client configuration, such as domain joined laptop vs. user's personal computer at home running Outlook client. These factors affect your selection of authentication mechanisms and which ones can be effective for a given scenario.

The configuration of firewalls, load balancer devices, or reverse proxy solutions, such as Microsoft TMG, also affect Kerberos and NTLM functionality. For example, if a firewall examines HTTP traffic and modifies it in any way, the trust of authentication is broken due to "man in the middle" configuration. In such configurations, Kerberos and NTLM don't work due to protocol security requirements. Without an additional server configuration to account for such networks, only Basic authentication can work. For NTLM to work for external clients in such a scenario, additional configuration, such as Kerberos Constrained Delegation, is required to trust the intermediary device that sends authentication to servers on the client's behalf.

Another consideration for selecting the appropriate authentication is user experience in environments where reverse proxies such as Microsoft TMG are deployed and configured to use pre-authentication. In such scenarios, the client authenticates to the reverse proxy device and the reverse proxy, in turn, sends authentication to the servers. If the user is logging into OWA, for example, then the user is presented with the FBA form that is generated by the reverse proxy server. When the user provides the authentication information, the reverse proxy sends the information to the Exchange server. The default configuration for OWA, however, is to use FBA. If the configuration isn't changed from the default, the user will see the FBA logon screen generated by the Exchange server. This makes up for unpleasant and undesired user experience. To remove the extra authentication prompt, you must configure Exchange servers to use basic authentication, so that reverse proxy devices can send the authentication to the servers and authenticate users without an additional authentication prompt. When using basic authentication, you must also ensure the connection between the reverse proxy device and the Exchange server is also encrypted with SSL for security.

Also consider user experience when connecting internally. Internal clients usually don't connect to reverse proxy devices described earlier when connecting to Exchange servers internally. Because they could connect directly to Exchange servers bypassing reverse proxy, and FBA logon experience presented by reverse proxy, they might now get the basic authentication prompt when connecting to OWA if you configured Exchange to use basic authentication for the OWA virtual directory.

While it's beyond the scope of the exam and thus, this book, configuring Exchange 2013 Service Pack 1 is also possible, and later, using Active Directory Federated Services (AD FS) to provide authentication for Exchange 2013 clients. When configuring Exchange for AD FS authentication, you can benefit from advanced claims functionality offered by AD FS, which allows you to set restrictions on client location and other behavior. You can also use smart card authentication or Azure two-factor authentication to further secure access to Exchange environment.

Also worth noting is that while you can change authentication methods on IIS directly, the configuration is managed by Exchange server and is periodically overwritten with parameters configured on Exchange servers. The preferred mechanism to manage Exchange client authentication parameters is to configure them using Exchange Shell or EAC.

Thought experiment
Namespace planning

In this Thought experiment, apply what you learned about this objective. You can find answers to these questions in the "Answers" section at the end of this chapter.

You are an Exchange administrator for Contoso, Ltd. Contoso plans to migrate Exchange 2010 environment to Exchange 2013. The current deployment consists of three datacenters. Each datacenter is configured to use the regional namespace: na.contoso.com, eu.contoso.com and asia.contoso.com.

Contoso wants to reduce namespaces used after the migration is complete. Network connectivity between the datacenters is adequate to accommodate additional client traffic.

1. Is it possible to use a unified namespace in such deployment?

2. What is the minimum number of namespaces required?

Objective summary

- Namespace planning, certificate planning, and load-balancing configuration are interdependent for any Exchange 2013 deployment.
- Configuring appropriate authentication methods must account for the configuration of intermediary devices, such as firewalls, reverse proxy servers, and load balancers.
- Exchange 2013 CAS server proxy logic is applied differently to different versions of legacy Exchange servers. This directly impacts namespace planning and configurations in coexistence environments.
- The wizard-driven configuration of an external namespace simplifies administration. Internal namespaces must be configured manually, however, either using Shell or EAC.
- Certificate configuration is simplified in Exchange 2013 by certificate management user interface (UI). Creating an appropriate certificate request is easier if internal and external namespaces are configured before using the Certificate Wizard.

Objective review

Answer the following questions to test your knowledge of the information in this objective. You can find the answers to these questions and explanations of why each answer choice is correct or incorrect in the "Answers" section at the end of this chapter.

1. You are an Exchange administrator for Contoso, Ltd. You just deployed an Exchange 2013 server running CAS and Mailbox role. You haven't changed load balancer and reverse proxy servers to include the new CAS server. Internal users are reporting that they're receiving popups regarding an untrusted certificate. Select two actions you must perform to resolve the issue.

   A. Run the Set-ClientAccessServer cmdlet.

   B. Run the Set-AutodiscoverVirtualDirectory cmdlet.

   C. Request a certificate from a trusted CA and assign it to IIS.

   D. Configure internal namespace to resolve to load balanced IP.

2. Contoso has deployed Exchange 2013 in multiple locations. You need to change the external URL for all locations to use the unified namespace. What must you do to complete the task? Select all that apply.

   A. Configure the External Access Domain Using Wizard from EAC; select all CAS servers from multiple locations.

   B. Configure the External Access Domain Using Wizard from EAC; select CAS servers from each location. Run the wizard once per location.

   C. Run the Set-OutlookAnywhere cmdlet.

   D. Run the Set-MapiVirtualDirectory cmdlet.

3. Contoso has deployed Exchange 2013 and Lync 2013. Multiple locations are assigned regional namespaces. Lync will be integrated with UM for voicemail. You need to determine the appropriate certificate type. Which certificate should you choose?

   A. A self-signed certificate.

   B. A Unified Communications (UC) SAN certificate from internal CA.

   C. A UC SAN certificate from external CA.

   D. A wildcard certificate.

Objective 2.3: Deploy and manage mobility solutions

Mobile access to email has become increasingly important to organizations of all sizes. Exchange was an early leader, first by delivering the first full-featured web client (Outlook Web Access made its debut in Exchange 5.5), and then by delivering the first truly integrated email sync system, delivered in Exchange 2003 Service Pack 1 (SP1). That system, known as Exchange ActiveSync (EAS), is still a key part of Exchange 2013 and Exchange Online, although the EAS code and the sync protocol itself have evolved quite a bit since their introduction.

One thing you should know about EAS is that it combines two different aspects of mobile device access: synchronization and device management. EAS is normally used to synchronize data between the server and the devices, but it also includes management policies that you can use to control which users are allowed to sync, what types of devices can connect to your Exchange servers, and what policies (such as password strength) those devices must apply. Most of the questions you are likely to see on the 70-341 exam relate to device and policy management. This is because the basic sync operations don't require any setup or adjustment once you enable a user for EAS and they've paired their device with Exchange.

Another thing to remember is that a multistep process is required before a device is allowed to synchronize. First, the device must be able to connect to an Exchange CAS. Second, once it connects, the device must be able to supply a valid set of credentials for a user who has an Exchange mailbox. And, third, that user must have permission to use EAS. If all three of these requirements are true, then the device can attempt to synchronize. It might be unable to, though, depending on what limits you set on which device types are allowed.

EAS itself isn't the only mobility solution that Exchange supports, of course. First, Outlook Web App still runs well on a wide variety of tablets and mobile devices. For example, you can comfortably use OWA 2013 on an Apple iPad running iOS, a Windows desktop running Google Chrome, or a Google Android tablet. Second, in 2013, Microsoft introduced its own line of email clients for Apple iOS and Google Android devices. These clients are collectively known as "OWA for Devices," but internally (and on the 70-341 exam), Microsoft refers to this family as ""Mobile OWA" or just "MOWA." In 2015, Microsoft released a new Outlook app (based on their acquisition of Acompli) for iOS and Android devices, followed by a touch-friendly "universal" version of Outlook for Windows 10. Finally, there are a number of device management tools (including the Microsoft InTune and products from Good Technologies and others) that either supplement or replace the device management and policy features of EAS. These products won't be discussed any further.

> **This objective covers how to:**
> - Deploy Mobile OWA (MOWA)
> - Configure OWA policies
> - Configure Microsoft ActiveSync policies
> - Configure allow/block/quarantine
> - Deploy and manage Office Apps

Deploying Mobile OWA

OWA for Devices is designed as a replacement for the built-in mail and calendar clients on iOS and Android. By releasing OWA for Devices, Microsoft is trying to simultaneously address two weak areas of Exchange support for these devices. First, a number of features are included in OWA and/or EAS that aren't included in the built-in apps. Apple and Google have little incentive to support new features in Exchange as Microsoft deploys them, so features such as support for Office 365's Clutter feature have not been available on mobile clients. Second, the way that remote device wipes are implemented in EAS means that the device manufacturers have chosen to erase the entire device when a valid remote wipe command arrives. This is very user-unfriendly because it erases all of the data on the device, not just data that was being synchronized with Exchange—so family photos, personal email, photos, and applications that belong to the device user vanish along with data belonging to the user's workplace. Because OWA for Devices includes its own separate storage mechanism, a wipe command or removing the app from the device removes all of the data synchronized with Exchange.

Microsoft has made OWA for Devices available in the Apple App Store and the Google Play Store. As an administrator, you can push these applications to managed mobile devices if you are using a device management solution that supports application push, or users can install the application themselves. Setup is simple. The user needs only to enter an email address and password, and the app then uses Exchange Autodiscover to locate the appropriate CAS server and connect. Interestingly, OWA for Devices looks to Exchange as a sort of an OWA client, rather than a pure EAS client. This is because OWA for Devices consumes the same rendering code that OWA uses. As new features are added to OWA, they immediately become visible in OWA for Devices. For example, as soon as Microsoft added the People view to Office 365 Exchange Online, the People view appeared in OWA for Devices for users who connected to an Exchange Online mailbox.

By default, every user in your Exchange organization can connect to their mailbox with OWA for Devices. If you want to change this, use the Set-CASMailbox cmdlet with the OWAforDevicesEnabled parameter. For example, to disable OWA for Devices for all members of the Research distribution group, you could use something like the following:

```
Get-DistributionGroupMember "Research" | `
Set-CASMailbox -OWAforDevicesEnabled $false
```

Disabling a user who already has OWA for Devices installed doesn't remove the app (or your synchronized data) from their devices. If you want to ensure that the data was removed, you must issue a wipe command to the device using the Clear-MobileDevice cmdlet or the Mobile Devices tab in EAC.

Configuring OWA policies

Exchange 2013 enables you to define Outlook Web App policies to control the OWA features that users have access to. Just like the other policy types that Exchange supports, Outlook Web App policies let you create a group of settings; and then apply those settings to mailboxes without having to modify the settings on the individual mailboxes. All of the features Outlook Web App policies can control can also be controlled by changing settings on an individual Mailbox server. Many of them can be modified by changing settings on user mailboxes.

Speaking of settings: Table 2-1 shows the policy settings available in OWA mailbox policies. Remember that the features you enable or disable in a policy only control whether the user can access those features in OWA. They don't grant or deny those features to the user. For example, if you have an OWA mailbox policy that enables unified messaging and you assign it to some users, those users won't see any UM UI unless their mailbox is enabled for UM.

TABLE 2-1 Outlook Web App features controllable through Outlook Web App policies

Feature	Meaning	Feature available in
Instant messaging	If enabled, and if you configured Lync properly, users who have Lync access can use IM functionality from within OWA. If disabled, these features are unavailable.	Outlook Web App
Text messaging	If enabled, users can create and send text (SMS) messages from Outlook Web App. If disabled, this feature is removed. This feature requires a separate SMS gateway or service on your Exchange server.	Outlook Web App
Unified messaging	If this feature is enabled and the mailbox is enabled for UM, users can access and manage their UM settings through Exchange Control Panel (ECP). If disabled, the option is removed.	ECP
Exchange ActiveSync	If enabled, users can access details of the mobile devices they have synchronized, including the ability to wipe devices if they are lost and retrieve logs containing details of synchronization operations. If disabled, the option is removed from ECP.	ECP
Contacts	If enabled, users can access their Contacts folder in Outlook Web App. If disabled, the icon is removed from Outlook Web App.	Outlook Web App
LinkedIn contact sync	Controls whether Office 365 users are allowed to synchronize their LinkedIn contacts with their Exchange contacts folder.	Outlook Web App
Facebook contact sync	Controls whether Office 365 users are allowed to synchronize their Facebook contacts with their Exchange contacts folder.	Outlook Web App
Mobile device contact sync	Controls whether users running Outlook Web App for Devices are allowed to sync their Exchange contacts to the device using the app.	Outlook Web App for Devices
All Address Lists	If enabled, users can see all defined address lists in the directory. If disabled, they can see the Global Address List (GAL) only.	Outlook Web App
Public Folders	If enabled, users can access and work with public folders. If disabled, the icon is removed from Outlook Web App.	Outlook Web App
Journaling	If enabled, users can see the Journal folder in their folder list. If disabled, Outlook Web App hides the folder.	Outlook Web App
Notes	If enabled, users can see and modify note items in Outlook Web App. If disabled, Outlook Web App hides the Notes icon.	Outlook Web App
Search Folders	If enabled, users can access search folders created by Outlook. If disabled, these folders are suppressed.	Outlook Web App

Inbox rules	If enabled, users can create and modify rules through ECP. If disabled, the option is suppressed. However, Exchange continues to respect any rules created with Outlook.	ECP
Recover Deleted Items	If enabled, users can recover deleted items. If disabled, users can't recover deleted items with Outlook Web App, but Exchange continues to preserve these items in the Recoverable Items folder.	Outlook Web App
Change password	If this feature is enabled, users can change their account password from Outlook Web App. If disabled, Outlook Web App will not prompt users when their password is approaching its expiry date (prompts start 14 days in advance), and they cannot see the option to change their password in ECP.	Outlook Web App /ECP
Junk email filtering	If enabled, users can access the options to control junk mail processing, such as blocked and safe user lists. If disabled, the option is removed from ECP.	ECP
Themes	If enabled, users can select a theme other than the default and apply it to Outlook Web App and ECP. If disabled, the option is suppressed.	Outlook Web App /ECP
Premium client	If enabled, users can use the premium client with a browser that supports this client. If disabled, users are forced to use the standard client no matter what browser they use.	Outlook Web App
Email signature	If enabled, users can access the option to create or modify email signatures and apply them to outgoing messages. If disabled, the option is removed from ECP.	ECP
Calendar	If enabled, users can access the Calendar application. If disabled, the icon is removed from Outlook Web App.	Outlook Web App
Tasks	If enabled, users can create and manage tasks in Outlook Web App. If disabled, the option is suppressed.	Outlook Web App
Reminders and notifications	If enabled, Outlook Web App provides users with notifications of new messages, meeting reminders, and so on. If disabled, these notifications are suppressed.	Outlook Web App

Exchange includes a default Outlook Web App policy, but that default isn't applied to any mailboxes. You have to manually apply the policy if you want to use it. You can create as many Outlook Web App mailbox policies as you like, and then apply a maximum of one Outlook Web App policy to each mailbox. If you don't apply any policies to a mailbox, a user's access to Outlook Web App features is controlled by the segmentation properties defined for the Outlook Web App virtual directory on each CAS server by Set-OWAVirtualDirectory.

Figure 2-11 shows the EAC view for Outlook Web App mailbox policies, which you use to create and modify policies. To get there, open EAC, switch to the Permissions slab, and then select the Outlook Web App Policies tab.

FIGURE 2-11   OWA policies section of EAC shows you which policies are defined and what settings are part of the currently selected policy

Creating and managing policies in EAC

The easiest way to control what users can do in OWA, assuming you want all users to have the same settings, is to modify the policy named Default, and then apply its settings to users. If you prefer, you can create a new policy with the + icon. In that case, you get the OWA mailbox policy dialog box shown in Figure 2-12. This dialog box contains nearly all of the OWA mailbox policy settings listed in the previous Table 2-1. The settings that aren't shown become visible when you click the More Options link.

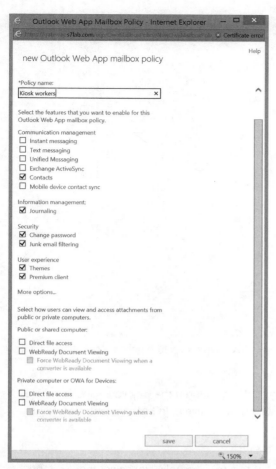

FIGURE 2-12 Use the New OWA mailbox policy to create a policy with the settings you want applied to recipients of the policy.

For any OWA policy you create, you can edit it by selecting it in EAC and clicking the pencil icon in the toolbar, or just by double-clicking it. This brings up a different dialog box, as shown in Figure 2-13. This dialog box contains the same policies as the version in Figure 2-12, but they are arranged into a slightly less-confusing tabbed interface.

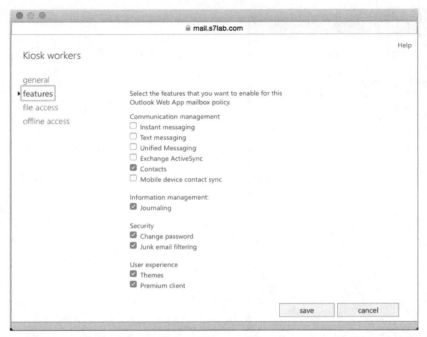

FIGURE 2-13 The New OWA mailbox policy section of EAC shows you which policies are defined and what settings are part of the currently selected policy

In either case, once you have the policy settings configured the way you want them, the next step is to apply the policy to the users who should have it. In EAC, the only way to do this is to do the following:

1. Open EAC and switch to the Recipients slab.

2. Double-click the user to whom you want to apply the policy (or select the user, and then click the pencil icon). The user's mailbox properties dialog box opens.

3. Switch to the Mailbox Features tab.

4. Scroll down until you see the Email Connectivity section, and then click View Details.

5. A dialog box opens (Figure 2-13) so that you can select the policy you want to apply to this mailbox. Select it, and then click Save to close this dialog box.

6. Click Save in the mailbox properties dialog box to save your policy selection.

Obviously, this process would be quite tiresome if you had to do it for large numbers of users. In such a case, you'd probably be better off using EMS, as described in the next section.

Creating and managing OWA policies in EMS

A new policy can also be created with EMS. For some odd reason, this is a two-step process. First, you create the new policy with the New-OWAMailboxPolicy cmdlet, and then you use the Set-OWAMailboxPolicy cmdlet to define which features are enabled or disabled by the policy. For example, here's a policy that allows users to use the premium client, while removing some of the more esoteric or less-used features:

```
New-OWAMailboxPolicy -Name 'Limited OWA features'
Set-OWAMailboxPolicy -Identity 'Limited OWA features' `
-ActiveSyncIntegrationEnabled $True `
-AllAddressListsEnabled $True `
-CalendarEnabled $True `
-ContactsEnabled $True `
-JournalEnabled $True `
-JunkEmailEnabled $True `
-RemindersAndNotificationsEnabled $True `
-NotesEnabled $false `
-PremiumClientEnabled $True `
-SearchFoldersEnabled $False `
-SignaturesEnabled $false `
-ThemeSelectionEnabled $False `
-UMIntegrationEnabled $False `
-ChangePasswordEnabled $True `
-RulesEnabled $True `
-PublicFoldersEnabled $False `
-SMimeEnabled $false `
-RecoverDeletedItemsEnabled $True
```

A number of Outlook Web App mailbox policy settings are also only available through EMS, including settings for controlling whether users are allowed to use delegate access permissions if they have them (DelegateAccessEnabled and ExplicitLogonEnabled), plus various other settings that are described in the Set-OWAMailboxPolicy documentation on TechNet (see *https://technet.microsoft.com/library/dd297989.aspx*).

To apply an OWA mailbox policy to a user or a set of users, you use the Set-CASMailbox cmdlet. The beauty of this approach is that you can quickly apply OWA mailbox policies to large collections of mailboxes based on OU or a distribution list membership, or any other criterion that you can think of. For example, to grab all the mailboxes that belong to the Huntsville organizational unit and apply the Factory OWA mailbox policy, you only need one line of code:

```
Get-Mailbox -OrganizationalUnit 'Huntsville'| `
Set-CASMailbox -OwaMailboxPolicy 'Factory'
```

Configuring Exchange ActiveSync Policies

You don't have to do anything to enable your users to synchronize their mobile devices by using EAS. Exchange already enables the protocol for all users by default. However, you have some fairly flexible options for controlling which devices are allowed to sync and what they can do once they do (as described in the section "Configure allow/block/quarantine policies" later in this chapter).

Turning EAS on or off

No global Off switch exists for EAS. If you want to disable EAS for all users, you have two options:

- You can use Get-CASMailbox | Set-CASMailbox -ActiveSyncEnabled:false to turn off EAS for all existing mailboxes. However, as soon as you create a new mailbox, it's enabled for EAS by default, unless you use a cmdlet extension agent to run a script to disable it (or you do so manually). See *http://eightwone.com/2012/06/19/postconfiguring-mailboxes-cmdlet-extension-agents-part-2/* for a primer on how to work with cmdlet extension agents.

- You can use a firewall product such as Kemp Technology ESP or various products from F5 (or even the venerable ISA/TMG product line) to block or allow access to the EAS virtual directory based on user ID or group membership. This approach enables you to let users on the corporate network sync, while preventing sync from the Internet except for permitted users.

Three other ways of disabling EAS will work and you might see them mentioned in exam questions. They aren't good choices for use with Exchange 2013. This is because Managed Availability interprets them as an application failure and then tries to "fix" your changes, possibly by rebooting your servers we advise you *not* to use them, but they're included here for completeness:

- You can remove the EAS virtual directory on all your Internet-facing CAS servers with the Remove-ActiveSyncVirtualDirectory cmdlet. This is easy to do, but it requires you to re-create the virtual directory later if you ever want to use EAS again. You can do this with the New-ActiveSyncVirtualDirectory cmdlet.

- You can disable all authentication methods on the EAS virtual directory of all Internet-facing CAS servers. This effectively prevents any client from connecting through EAS, and it's easy to change back if you want to enable it in the future.

- You can use the Internet Information Services (IIS) management tools to stop the MS-ExchangeSyncAppPool application pool. This prevents the EAS server component from running. You must do this on all servers, and it might restart when the server restarts.

Mobile device mailbox policies

Exchange starts with a single default mobile device mailbox policy. You can create new policies and assign them to users but, by default, every user gets the default policy. For many organizations, that's enough because they want to apply the same policies to all users. However, if you want different settings for different users, you can do that by creating multiple policies and apply them. You can change the policy that is applied to a mailbox at any time. For example:

```
Set-CASMailbox -Identity 'Shukla, Bhargav' -ActiveSyncMailboxPolicy "Research"
```

Most of the settings included in mobile device mailbox policies are self-explanatory. Figure 2-14 shows the window that appears when you create a new policy. The same settings are available when editing a policy through EAC, but they're separated into two tabs (General and Security). Selecting the This Is The Default Policy check box tells Exchange to apply this policy to all mailboxes that are EAS-enabled going forward, and it applies that policy to any device that doesn't currently have an explicitly assigned policy on its owning mailbox. However, checking that box doesn't change any existing mobile device mailbox policy assignments.

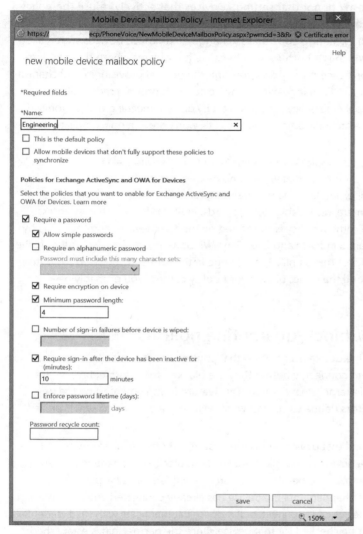

FIGURE 2-14 Creating a new mobile device mailbox policy, so you can choose the password policy that will apply to the device

The Allow Mobile Devices That Don't Fully Support These Policies To Synchronize check box (and the corresponding AllowNonProvisionableDevices parameter to the Set-MobileDeviceMailboxPolicy cmdlet) is important. A device that recognizes and applies

100 percent of the settings in a policy is said to be fully compliant. Devices that can't apply some policy settings are partially compliant. They accept the policy, but at least one policy setting can't be applied, either because it doesn't apply (for instance, a policy that turns off the camera applied to a device with no camera) or because the device doesn't honor that particular policy setting (for instance, a policy that turns off Wi-Fi on Apple iOS devices, whose EAS client doesn't honor that setting). Devices that actively refuse the policy (usually because the user cancels policy application) or that can't apply the policy are said to be noncompliant. In Exchange 2007 and Exchange 2010, these devices were called *nonprovisionable devices,* which is a better name because it indicates where the problem lies—the device can't or won't accept the policy through the normal provisioning mechanism. When this check box is selected, Exchange allows any device with proper credentials to synchronize, even if it can't apply the policy. This box is set by default, meaning that customizing the default policy to apply the security settings you want still won't prevent noncompliant devices from syncing.

Many more policy settings are available when you use the Get/Set-MobileDeviceMailboxPolicy cmdlets, however, it's important to note that virtually no modern devices actually support the majority of these settings. For example, some policy settings enable you to restrict the use of Bluetooth, the on-device camera, removable storage cards, POP/IMAP, and Internet-access tethering. Of these, only the camera policy is supported on modern devices, and then only by iOS 5+ and Android Ice Cream Sandwich and later. Even Windows Phone 8 doesn't support the majority of existing EAS policies. This is unlikely to change in the future. If you need to control mobile device behavior beyond the basics of password policy control, you probably need a third-party solution.

Configuring allow/block/quarantine policies

Exchange 2013 lets you define device access rules that control whether specific devices or device families are allowed to connect, whether they are blocked from connecting, or are quarantined until an administrator releases them. This feature is implemented by the device access rules that administrators define to control what devices are allowed to synchronize with the Exchange server.

It's important to understand that device access rules control whether a given device is allowed to talk to the server at all. If a device access rule exists to allow, block, or quarantine a given device explicitly, that rule controls whether the client can establish an EAS sync partnership. However, this decision doesn't happen until the device has already connected and authenticated to the Exchange CAS. If the device can't connect, or if it doesn't authenticate with valid credentials, the device access rules won't be checked for that device. Once the partnership is established, mobile device mailbox policies (described in the previous section) are applied to control the settings and the behavior required or banned on the device, but first it must go through the allow/block/quarantine (ABQ) process.

ABQ depends on the fact that each device that connects has a unique ID, known as a *DeviceID.* Some devices might also provide other unique identifiers, such as a phone number or International Mobile Equipment Identifier (IMEI). You can see these other identifiers in the sync logs, but the DeviceID is the primary key that makes decisions about which devices can connect. Apart from device-unique identifiers, there are other ways to identify devices, such as the device operating system, friendly name, or model. This sample of output from the Get-MobileDevice cmdlet shows these identifiers as provided by the device:

```
FriendlyName            : Yellow Lumia 920
DeviceId                : 3A50E6862817DB02477264117CD3F0F6
DeviceImei              : 353680056015391
DeviceMobileOperator    : AT&T
DeviceOS                : Windows Phone 8.10.14219
DeviceOSLanguage        : en
DeviceTelephoneNumber   : XXX-XXX-XXXX
DeviceType              : WP8
DeviceUserAgent         : MSFT-WP/8.10.14219
DeviceModel             : RM-820_nam_att_100
FirstSyncTime           : 7/26/2014 5:18:07 PM
UserDisplayName         : betabasement.com/Users/Paul Robichaux
DeviceAccessState       : Allowed
DeviceAccessStateReason : GlobalPermissions
ClientVersion           : 14.1
ClientType              : EAS
```

When a device connects and authenticates, Exchange then uses the process shown in Figure 2-15 to decide whether it should be allowed to connect. Restrictions can be applied in three places:

- A device or device family can be allowed, blocked, or quarantined for an individual user. This is often used to allow certain individuals to use unsupported devices (perhaps for testing) in organizations that normally block nonstandard devices. User-level blocks or allows take precedence over device access rules and the generic rule. Unfortunately, there's no good way to allow a single user to sync with an entire device family. You have to specify the devices individually.

- A device class or device family can be allowed, blocked, or quarantined. For example, you might put a block rule in place to keep old versions of Apple iOS devices from connecting because those versions have bugs that can lead to corrupt or missing calendar appointments. You could also use this feature to block beta versions of a given operating system to keep your early adopters in check until the device operating system has been tested.

- Devices or families for which no specific rule exists can be allowed, blocked, or quarantined.

This last point is worthy of a bit more discussion because it's where most organizations define their device connection policy. The default is that any device not specifically blocked elsewhere is allowed to connect. This is perfect for organizations that want to allow unrestricted

Bring Your Own Device (BYOD). However, you can choose to configure that default rule to block all devices that aren't specifically approved elsewhere. This gives you a simple way to control which users and devices are permitted to use EAS. You can also have the default rule quarantine devices that don't have a specific match, which is useful if you want to be flexible about allowing devices, while retaining some control over new devices. By using this approach, you can allow any device to sync after you approve it.

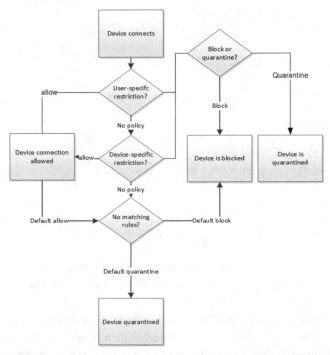

FIGURE 2-15 The device rule evaluation process starts by checking for user-specific restrictions, and then device access rules. If none of these are triggered, the default organizational rule is triggered

Managing device access rules

New mobile devices and operating system updates appear all the time, and users buy them. Once they get a shiny new device, it's natural that they'd want to connect it to their Exchange mailbox. Often, these connections occur without the knowledge or the intervention of an administrator—that's pretty much the nature of BYOD. This isn't a problem if everything works properly, but it can become a problem when the device misbehaves in some way. Perhaps, like the original Palm Pre, it doesn't enforce some part of your EAS policy. Perhaps, as with several versions of the Apple iOS, it contains a bug that hammers your server with excess traffic. At that point, you have a problem to solve.

The way many organizations choose to solve this problem is by using device access rules to control which devices are allowed to connect. This decision can be made based on a very specific combination of device type and operating system, just on the device type, or just on the operating system. For example, you could block all traffic coming from Android 3.x devices, but allow newer devices to connect. Or, you could create a rule that says that any device is quarantined and can't synchronize until an administrator approves it.

The simplest way to apply this restriction is to click the Edit button in the Mobile Device Access tab of the Mobile slab in EAC. This brings up the EAS global configuration dialog box shown in Figure 2-16. In this dialog box, you can choose the default behavior that should apply to any device that doesn't match a specific rule or exemption. In Figure 2-16, we chose the Quarantine option, meaning that any new device that connects is quarantined unless it matches a rule or exception that allows it.

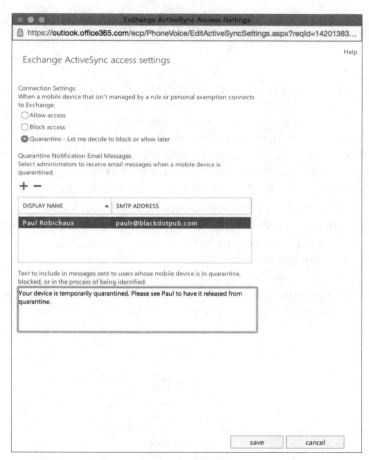

FIGURE 2-16 Modifying the global EAS configuration is the fastest way to block or quarantine all devices that aren't explicitly approved

After you configure the default behavior, if you chose to quarantine devices that aren't specifically allowed, you'll see a list of quarantined devices when you open the Mobile Device Access page in EAC (see Figure 2-17). The icons above the list of devices display device statistics (the pencil icon), allow the device to connect, block it permanently, or create a device access rule.

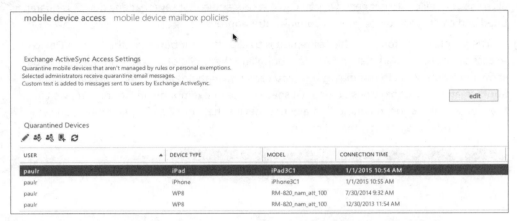

FIGURE 2-17 Quarantined devices show up in EAC and can be individually blocked or freed

You can create access rules based on the device type, model, user agent, or operating system. Examples of these values for a third-generation Apple iPad are shown in Figure 2-18. For this specific device, the device type is iPad, the device model is iPad3c1, the user agent is Apple-iPad3C1/1202.435, and the device operating system is iOS 8.1.1 12B435. A little thought shows that you can block all iPads (using the device type), all iPads of a similar vintage to mine (using the device model), or all revisions of a specific device operating system.

You can find these entries in the IIS logs on the CAS, but it's hard to pick out a specific device among all the noise in those logs. The easiest way to retrieve the most useful subset of this information is to use the Get-ActiveSyncDeviceClass cmdlet, which returns several interesting properties for each synchronized device (including the device model and device type) that your Exchange organization has seen so far. For example, running Get-ActiveSyncDeviceClass | ft DeviceType, DeviceModel in our test lab produces output like the following:

```
DeviceType                    DeviceModel
----------                    -----------
EASProbeDeviceType            EASProbeDeviceType
iPhone                        iPhone
iPhone                        iPhone3C1
WP8                           WP8
WP8                           RM-820_nam_att_100
iPad                          iPad
iPad                          iPad3C1
```

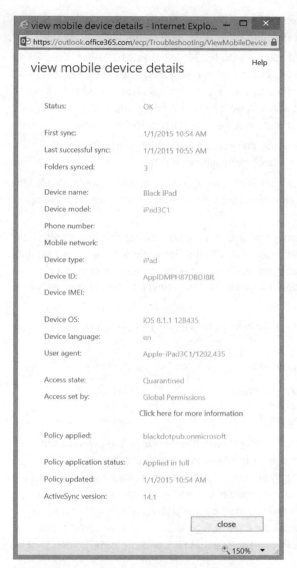

FIGURE 2-18 The device details for a specific device tell you what manufacturer-set user agent, device operating system, and device family the device reports

Microsoft has provided two ways to create device access rules. First, the easy way. When you click the + icon in the Device Access Rules section of the Mobile Device Access page, shown in Figure 2-16, the resulting New Device Access Rule dialog box includes buttons that enable you to browse through the list of device families and models that Exchange already knows about (based on devices that were synchronized successfully). If you want to quickly create a device access rule based on one of these characteristics, you can easily do so from EAC, as long as you don't want to use the operating system or user agent fields to make decisions.

The second way to create device access rules is with the New-ActiveSyncDeviceAccessRule cmdlet, which gives you a very flexible system for creating rules using any of the supported criteria. To create a rule, you need to specify a characteristic (that tells the rule what to base its decisions on), a query string (the value that will be matched by the rule), and an access level (that tells the rule what to do when it matches). Here are two quick examples:

- New-ActiveSyncDeviceAccessRule -characteristic DeviceModel -queryString "iPad" -AccessLevel block blocks all iPad devices from synchronizing.

- New-ActiveSyncDeviceAccessRule -characteristic UserAgent -queryString "Apple-iPad3C1/*" -AccessLevel block blocks all third-generation iPad devices from synchronizing, no matter what version of iOS they're running.

Sadly, device access rules don't have names that you can set, but you can see the names, characteristics, and so on for any rules in your environment with the Get-ActiveSyncDeviceAccessRule cmdlet. For example, this output shows that the organization has three device access rules in place. All iPhones and Windows Phone 8 devices are allowed to connect, but other devices are blocked by the default rule:

```
Get-ActiveSyncDeviceAccessRule | Format-Table Name, Characteristic, QueryString,
AccessLevel -AutoSize


Name                            Characteristic     QueryString       AccessLevel
--------                        --------------     -----------       -----------
iPhone (DeviceType)             DeviceType iPhone                    Allow
WP8 (DeviceType)                DeviceType WP8                       Allow
EASProbeDeviceType (DeviceType) DeviceType EASProbeDeviceType        Allow
```

When a user's device is blocked by a device access rule, the device isn't allowed to synchronize at all. If a device access rule or the default rule causes a device to be quarantined, the device is allowed to synchronize just long enough to receive a quarantine warning message, such as the one shown in Figure 2-19. This message shows all the device-specific data, along with an indication that the device is quarantined by the global default setting, not a specific device access rule. The policy specified earlier in Figure 2-16 included some custom text to be included in quarantine mails, and you can see that text present in the screen shot in Figure 2-19.

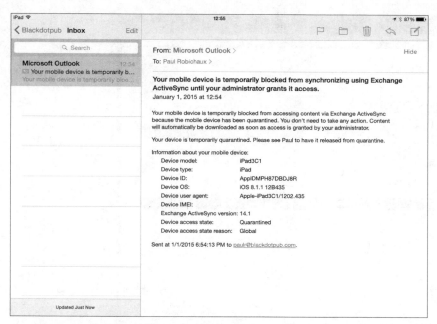

FIGURE 2-19 A quarantine message sent to a device after its initial connection

Controlling individual users' devices

In addition to creating device access rules to control the types of devices that can be connected to ActiveSync, you can allow or block individual devices for a user's mailbox. Microsoft refers to these mailbox-level allow/block settings as personal exemptions. They're checked first, so that if you block or allow a device for a given user, that choice takes precedence over the device access rules you have in place.

By selecting the target mailbox in EAC, and then clicking the View Details link under Mobile Devices in the right sidebar, you see the Mobile Device Details dialog box (Figure 2-20).

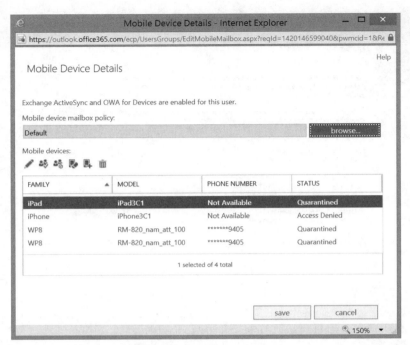

FIGURE 2-20 The Mobile Device Details dialog box through which to change the assigned mobile device mailbox policy and manage devices associated with the mailbox

The toolbar over the device list enables you to allow or block the selected device for this mailbox only, so you can remotely wipe the device, see the device details, or create a new device access rule based on the selected device. This last capability is the easiest way to create a new device access rule based on a particular device or device type. First, sync the new device to your own mailbox, then log in to EAC and then use that device to create a device access rule to allow or block the target device family.

If you prefer, you can use the Set-CASMailbox cmdlet to set the ActiveSyncAllowedDeviceIDs and ActiveSyncBlockedDeviceIDs parameters with a list of device identifiers that should be allowed or blocked for a mailbox. The default value for these parameters is $Null, meaning any device can synchronize with a mailbox. Using Set-CASMailbox requires you to know the device ID, however. You can get it by selecting a device in the Mobile Device Details box and clicking the pencil icon. In addition, some devices show the device ID (for example, Apple iOS 8.x devices label the field as Exchange Device ID in the account settings dialog box). You can also use the Get-ActiveSyncDeviceStatistics cmdlet to retrieve details about users' ActiveSync activity, including the identifiers for each mobile device they have connected to Exchange. For example:

```
Get-ActiveSyncDeviceStatistics -Mailbox 'Orton, Jon'
```

You can add multiple device identifiers to the list, separating the identifiers with semicolons. For example, this command allows just one specific device to synchronize with Jon Orton's mailbox.

```
Set-CASMailbox -Identity 'Orton, Jon' -ActiveSyncAllowedDeviceIDs
'4B9207650054671AD0AEE83A424BCD7F'
```

To clear the device identifier, so that any device can connect to the mailbox:

```
Set-CASMailbox -Identity 'Orton, Jon' -ActiveSyncAllowedDeviceIDs $Null
```

If you have a list of devices and want to remove only a single device from the list, export the list to a variable, update the list in the variable, and then write it back with Set-CASMailbox.

```
$Devices = Get-CASMailbox -Identity 'Orton, Jon'
$Devices.ActiveSyncAllowedDeviceIDs -= '4B9207650054671AD0AEE83A424BCD7F'
Set-CASMailbox -Identity 'Orton, Jon' -ActiveSyncAllowedDeviceIDs
$Devices.ActiveSyncAllowedDeviceIDs
```

The same techniques can be used to block devices. Simply update the ActiveSyncBlockedDeviceIDs parameter instead of ActiveSyncAllowedDeviceIDs. Grab the device ID, and then use Set-CASMailbox -ActiveSyncBlockedDeviceIDs on the target mailbox.

Another device blocking-related trick you might need is to adjust the number of devices an individual user is allowed to synchronize with their mailbox. By default, Exchange allows 10 device partnerships per mailbox. Depending on your user population, you might want to raise or lower this number. For example, the average user probably doesn't have more than three or four devices. To change this, you must update the EasMaxDevices setting on the policy by using Set-ThrottlingPolicy. If you have users who need more than 10 devices, you should create a separate throttling policy for them and apply it as needed, rather than modifying the default policy.

Managing organization-wide ABQ settings

You don't really set organization-wide settings for EAS, apart from controlling which types of devices are allowed to connect. Almost all of the parameters available to the Set-ActiveSyncOrganizationSettings cmdlet relate to how the device access rules you set up are interpreted. You can change the default behavior that is applied to new devices that aren't specifically managed by a device access rule or personal exemption. When a new device connects to Exchange, you can choose to allow it to connect, to block it, or to put it in quarantine. You can specify one or more email addresses that should receive quarantine notifications. The user who syncs the quarantined device always gets one. Finally, you can specify some text to be included in the quarantine message. To change settings at this level, you can use either the Set-ActiveSyncOrganizationSettings cmdlet or the Mobile Device Access page in EAC.

Deploying and manage Office Apps

Office Apps are a new feature in Exchange 2013, SharePoint 2013, and Office 2013. Rather than requiring you to download and install executable code on client computers, you install Office Apps, which are written using HTML5 and JavaScript on your servers. They can then be used by any client that supports them. As of this writing, that includes OWA for Devices, Office 2013, Outlook Web App, and Outlook for Mac (the 2014 version for Office 365, not Outlook 2011). When you install an Office App and make it available to a user or group, the app shows up in the user's clients. For example, if you deploy the Message Header Analyzer app, it appears in OWA, as shown in Figure 2-21. Microsoft has created an app store for Office Apps, and users can install their own apps through OWA or their local browsers if you give them permission to do so.

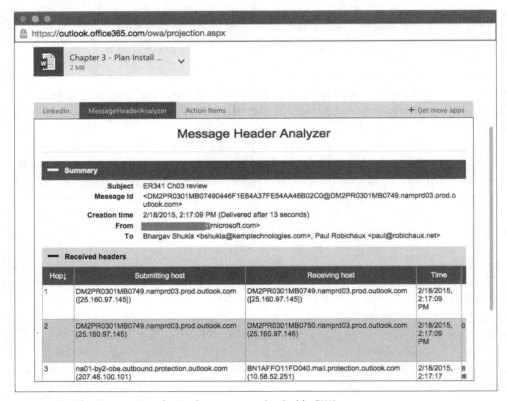

FIGURE 2-21 The Message Header Analyzer app running inside OWA

Installing and removing apps

You can get access to apps that run in Outlook and OWA in three ways:

- If you have permission, you can install them directly from within OWA or Outlook

- You can download and install apps from within EAC

- You can download apps and use EMS cmdlets to install and provision them

Exchange 2013 provides four RBAC roles that control app installation and usage. The Org Marketplace Apps role grants permission to install and configure apps that come from the Microsoft Office Store. The Org Custom Apps role grants the ability to install and manage apps that come from internal enterprise distribution points. Normally, administrators should have these roles, not users. The My Marketplace Apps user role and the My Custom Apps user role grant users the ability to install and manage their own apps and are, by default, available to all users in the organization.

MANAGING APPS IN EAC

As an administrator, you can control apps through the Apps tab of the Organization slab in EAC (see Figure 2-22). This tab shows the installed apps, whether each app is available to users, and which users have access to the apps. Selecting an individual app displays the app details (including which permissions the app requires) in the details pane on the right side of the EAC window.

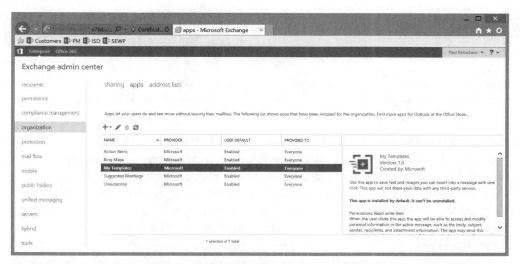

FIGURE 2-22 The Apps tab in EAC shows the apps available to all users in the organization

You can add or remove apps by using the icons in the toolbar. You can add apps from the Office Store or by providing a URL to the app. This URL can be used to install custom apps inside an enterprise from a SharePoint app catalog, or a local or shared directory. When you install an app, EAC prompts you to confirm that you want to install the app. The confirmation dialog box includes a summary of the permissions that the app has requested.

When you add an app, it's disabled, so users can't use it until you grant them permission. To change the app's availability, click the pencil icon to open the settings' dialog box, shown in Figure 2-23. The app can be made available to users by selecting the Make This App

Available To Users In Your Organization check box. Just making it available doesn't mean that users are necessarily able to use it, however. The group of three option buttons in this dialog box lists the states an individual app can take on: optional and enabled by default, optional and disabled by default, or mandatory. The "by default" in the first two options is there because users can enable or disable optional apps themselves, whereas apps marked as mandatory are always enabled. Exchange doesn't notify users when new apps are available, and clients only load the list of available apps when they start, so newly installed apps won't appear until the next time users launch their preferred client.

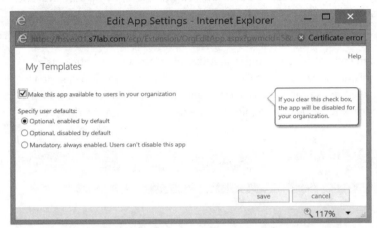

FIGURE 2-23 Editing an app's properties allows you to control whether it's available to users

INSTALLING AND MANAGING APPS WITH THE EXCHANGE MANAGEMENT SHELL

The Exchange Management Shell (EMS) offers six primary cmdlets for working with apps: New-App and Remove-App for installing and removing apps, Enable- and Disable-App for controlling app availability, and Get-App and Set-App for managing application settings. Each app has a display name and an AppId (basically a GUID), but the management cmdlets require use of the AppId for pretty much everything, although it isn't visible to users or used commonly in EAC.

To install a new app, you use the New-App cmdlet. When you install an application using this cmdlet, you need to provide the XML application manifest that Exchange uses to correctly install the application's components. You can provide a URL using the Url switch (although this is primarily useful when you're installing custom apps inside your organization), or you can read the manifest data from its file into a PowerShell variable, and then pass it to New-App, like this:

```
$myApp = Get-Content -Path "c:\dev\apps\ScreenShotCheckerApp.xml" `
-Encoding Byte `
-ReadCount 0
New-App -FileData $myApp
```

To get a list of the installed applications in your organization, you can use a command such as this:

```
Get-App -OrganizationApp | ft DisplayName, AppId

DisplayName                    AppId
-----------                    -----
LinkedIn                       333bf46d-7dad-4f2b-8cf4-c19ddc78b723
MessageHeaderAnalyzer          62916641-fc48-44ae-a2a3-163811f1c945
Bing Maps                      7a774f0c-7a6f-11e0-85ad-07fb4824019b
Suggested Meetings             bc13b9d0-5ba2-446a-956b-c583bdc94d5e
Unsubscribe                    d39dee0e-fdc3-4015-af8d-94d4d49294b3
Action Items                   f60b8ac7-c3e3-4e42-8dad-e4e1fea59ff7
```

Note, the Bing Maps, Suggested Meetings, Unsubscribe, and Action Items apps are installed as part of Exchange 2013 SP1. In this example, we added the free LinkedIn and MessageHeaderAnalyzer apps and made them available to the organization. Get-App won't show applications installed by individual users unless you use the Mailbox switch. For example, Get-App -Mailbox paulr returns the list of applications installed for the user with the specified mailbox.

You use Enable-App and Disable-App to change the application state both for individual users and the entire organization. If you use these cmdlets alone (for example, Enable-App -Identity 62916641-fc48-44ae-a2a3-163811f1c945) the app is enabled or disabled for the entire organization. Add the Mailbox switch if you want to enable or disable the app for a specific user. You have the same three choices for enabling apps when you use EMS as you do in EAC, although it's a little harder to distinguish among them because they're so similar.

- To enable an app by default, but to let users turn it off, use Set-App -Enabled $true -DefaultStateForUser Enabled.

- To disable an app by default, but to let users turn it on, use Set-App -Enabled $true -DefaultStateForUser Disabled.

- To enable an app by default, and not let users turn it off, use Set-App -Enabled $True -DefaultState AlwaysEnabled.

PROVIDING AN APP TO SPECIFIC USERS

Enabling an application means users can add it themselves (as described in the upcoming section, "Self-service app management for users"). You might need to assign an application to a group of users, instead of to everyone in the organization, without waiting for users to set up apps for themselves. If you want to do this, you can use the Set-App cmdlet with its ProvidedTo parameter. You can either enable an app for every user (Set-App -ProvidedTo Everyone) or for a specific set of users (Set-App -ProvidedTo SpecificUsers -UserList). In this latter case, you must also provide a list of users with the UserList parameter. Suppose you want to load a new app named ScreenShotChecker and assign it to all members of the Production group. You could do something like this:

```
$myApp = Get-Content -Path "c:\dev\apps\ScreenShotCheckerApp.xml" -Encoding Byte
-ReadCount 0
$installedApp = New-App -FileData $myApp
$theUsers = Get-DistributionGroupMember Production
Set-App -OrganizationApp -Identity $installedApp.appID -ProvidedTo SpecificUsers
-UserList $theUsers
```

When you use Set-App -ProvidedTo SpecificUsers, that prevents other users from seeing the installed app, although they can install it themselves if they have access to the app. However, users who are specified with this command can't install or remove the app.

SELF-SERVICE APP MANAGEMENT FOR USERS

Users can manage apps from Outlook Web App by clicking the Options icon (the gear in the upper-right corner of the window) and choosing Manage Apps. Or, they can manage apps from Outlook 2013 by opening the backstage view and choosing the Manage Apps link. In either case, the view similar to that shown in Figure 2-24 appears. One important difference between this view and the one shown earlier in Figure 2-22 is this view includes a user-installed app (as indicated by the value of *User* in the Installed By column).

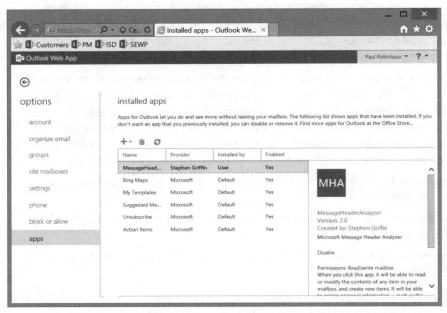

FIGURE 2-24 Users can see and change their app settings with the Apps tab in OWA Options

Blocking or allowing apps

By default, Office Apps are enabled for all clients that can display them. You can use Set-OrganizationConfig -AppsForOfficeEnabled to change this. When this parameter is set to $false, no new apps can be activated for or by any user in the organization. Changing this setting doesn't remove any existing apps or keep users from using them. If you want to disable user access to apps completely, you must remove any apps you added, and then disable the built-in apps (Action Items, Unsubscribe, Bing Maps, and Suggested Meetings).

Objective summary

- OWA for Devices is intended to be the Microsoft replacement for vendor-specific mail and calendar clients from Apple and Google. Users install it on their iOS or Android devices, and then they use it to sync mail, calendar, and contact data. To control its use, you can enable or disable it for the entire organization or for specific users.

- OWA mailbox policies control which specific features of OWA a given user can access. Each mailbox can have zero or one OWA mailbox policy assigned to it. Exchange creates a default policy for you, but it turns on all features and isn't assigned to any mailboxes.

- To customize OWA for your users, you can edit the default policy or create new ones. Either way, you need to apply the policies to the mailboxes before they take effect.

- While you can create and manage OWA mailbox policies from either EAC or EMS, it's much faster to do so with EMS.

- Exchange ActiveSync has a system of device access rules that you can use to control which types of devices specific users, or all users, can sync with Exchange.

- Device access rules can allow, block, or quarantine devices based on the device family, the device operating system, or the user agent string. You can allow exceptions for specific users that allow or block specific devices, families, or types just for those users.

- There's a single organization-wide access rule that will allows, blocks, or quarantines any device that isn't targeted by a more specific rule.

- Administrators or users can install Office Apps that run inside Outlook, OWA, and OWA for Devices. User-installed apps are stored in users' mailboxes and are only available to that user, while organizational apps are available to the users you select.

- You can control whether individual apps are available, blocked, or mandatory. Apps that you mark as available can be enabled or disabled by default, but users can change that state on their own. When you block an organizational app, users can still download and install it themselves, unless you turn off app access.

■ You can install apps from EAC or EMS. In the case of EMS, you can specify a URL or read the app contents from a file using the Read-Content cmdlet, and then pass that to New-App.

Objective review

Answer the following questions to test your knowledge of the information in this objective. You can find the answers to these questions and explanations of why each answer choice is correct or incorrect in the "Answers" section at the end of this chapter.

1. You need to install an app named ScreenShotChecker from a file at *appsrv03**ssc*\ *screenshotchecker.xml* and make it available to your users. Which of the following commands would you need to use? (Choose all that apply.)

   A. Set-App -OrganizationApp -Identity $sscApp.appId -ProvidedTo Allusers.

   B. $sscApp = New-App -FileData $myApp.

   C. New-App -OrganizationApp -Url \\appsrv03\ssc\screenshotchecker.xml.

   D. $myApp = Get-Content -Path \\appsrv03\ssc\screenshotchecker.xml -Encoding Byte -ReadCount 0.

2. You want to allow users of any Android or iOS device to connect and sync using Exchange ActiveSync, but you want to block all other devices. Choose the solution to accomplish this with the minimum administrative effort.

   A. Create device access rules for the device types you want to support, and then set the organizational default rule to block other devices.

   B. Set the organizational default rule to allow all devices, and then create device access rules to block the device types you don't want users to use.

   C. Set the organizational default rule to quarantine all devices, and then approve only those devices that meet your organizational guidelines.

   D. Use Get-ActiveSyncDeviceStatistics to get a list of device IDs, and then use Set-CASMailbox -AllowedActiveSyncDeviceID to assign them to user mailboxes.

3. You're asked to apply a new mobile device policy with a stronger password requirement for users who have a CustomAttribute1 value of "Manager". You create the new policy and start writing an EMS command to accomplish this task, beginning with "Get-Mailbox | where {$_.CustomAttribute1 -match "Manager"}". Which of the following cmdlets should come next in your command pipeline?

   A. Set-Mailbox.

   B. Set-ActiveSyncVirtualDirectory.

   C. Set-CASMailbox -OwaMailboxPolicy.

   D. Set-CASMailbox -ActiveSyncMailboxPolicy.

Objective 2.4: Implement load balancing

High availability is provided by many of Exchange's features. Features such as DAG use clustering features provided by the operating system, while connectivity to CAS must be managed through separate a load-balancing mechanism. This could be an external load balancer whether it's software, such as a virtual machine running on hypervisor, deployed on your server hardware, or a hardware-based offering. While Microsoft Windows NLB is also supported, it isn't a preferred choice due to limitations documented by Microsoft.

Deploying a load balancer allows you to handle more connections than a single server might be able to handle, thus distributing them to healthy servers, as appropriate. With health checks, a load balancer can detect a failed CAS server and remove it from the distribution of client connections automatically, providing clients with uninterrupted access to the Exchange environment.

With simplified load balancing in Exchange 2013, Layer 7 load balancing configuration is no longer a requirement. Because of changes in Client Access logic, a Layer 4 load balancer can serve the clients efficiently without requiring additional configuration and the management complexity of a Layer 7 load-balancing mechanism. Layer 4 load balancing also results in reduced resource usage requirements. This makes load balancer more efficient in handling large amount of requests compared to a Layer 7 load-balancing configuration.

Exchange 2010 introduced the concept of CAS arrays. The CAS array was created per each Active Directory site that the Exchange servers were in. Client Access servers from given Active Directory site automatically belonged to the CAS array for that site. In Exchange 2013, CAS arrays are no longer required. You don't need to create a CAS array object. Changing mailbox database properties to configure appropriate CAS array FQDN is no longer necessary. You simply need to configure internal and external URLs for different workloads appropriately, and then configure DNS to resolve the namespaces to the load balancer IP address.

> **This objective covers how to:**
> - Configure namespace load balancing
> - Configure Session Initiation Protocol (SIP) load balancing
> - Configure Windows Network Load Balancing (WNLB)

Configuring namespace load balancing

Earlier, in Objective 2.2, you learned how to configure different namespaces. Once you correctly configure all the namespaces, you can configure load balancer to accept traffic on a given IP address that the namespace resolves to. Then, you can add CAS servers to the pool that load balancer monitors for health and distributes client connections to. Before discussing the configuration requirements, let's discuss some load balancing basics.

In Exchange 2010, client connections and processing were handled by Client Access servers. Many protocols required affinity, which ensured a client to server pairing is maintained throughout the lifecycle of a given connection. Breaking the pairing meant that the client must authenticate again to a different server and the server must then perform necessary processing and rendering of client data. This results in an inefficient usage of resources on load balancer, as well as Client Access servers.

Affinity requirements also meant that load balancer needed to be a Layer 7 load balancer, which works at application layer, gaining understanding of protocols in use and visibility into application layer traffic. To achieve the Layer 7 functionality, load balancer needs to decrypt SSL connections from the client and re-encrypt it when sending data to Client Access servers. SSL decrypt and re-encrypt functionality requires significant processing power, especially as larger keys for SSL certificates are preferred over weaker 1,024 bit and smaller keys used in the past.

In contrast, Exchange 2013 CAS servers simply proxy client connections to an appropriate Mailbox server where the client mailbox is active. Load balancers no longer need to maintain client to server pairing and provide affinity. Because affinity is no longer required, SSL decryption and re-encryption requirement becomes optional. A load balancer can simply pass the traffic to a healthy Client Access server and the server can take appropriate actions, based on information received from the client. Because the load balancer processes traffic at the transport layer instead of at the application layer, it's considered a Layer 4 load balancer.

Depending on the namespace model selection and the number of planned namespaces, a load balancer deployment in any Exchange 2013 deployment usually starts with load balancing at least two namespaces. The first one is Autodiscover namespace. The client connections received for Autodiscover are sent to a healthy server for further processing. The rest of the connections are sent to the appropriate namespaces as discovered through the Autodiscover process. These namespaces resolve to the load-balanced IP address, which could be the same IP address as Autodiscover.

For all HTTP workloads, Exchange 2013 leverages managed availability to create a dynamic healthcheck.htm page. For example, if OWA component state is healthy, as determined by managed availability, an HTTP GET request sent to /OWA/healthcheck.htm results in a 200 OK response from the server. The same logic applies to AutoDiscover, ECP, EWS, MAPI, RPC, OAB, ActiveSync, and PowerShell virtual directories. Figure 2-25 shows a response from a healthy CAS server for an /OWA/healthcheck.htm request. When leveraging a simplified Layer 4 load-balancer configuration, you can only perform one health check per server. This means when the health check on given URL fails, the entire CAS server is deemed unhealthy and the load balancer stops sending client connections until it returns to a healthy state.

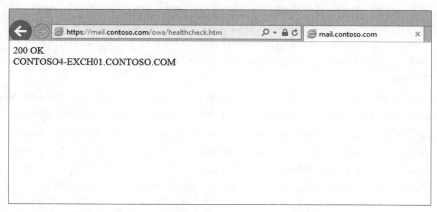

FIGURE 2-25 A healthy CAS server responding to an OWA health check request

Because the Layer 4 load balancer configuration means a single health check per server, it takes only a single workload failure to take the entire server out of the load-balanced pool. In the previous example where we're checking for OWA health, if the OWA process fails on the server or the administrator manually changes the OWA state to inactive using managed availability cmdlets, the load balancer sees that as an unhealthy server and stops sending clients connections to it. What if the other workloads are functional on that server? This is when a single namespace with the Layer 4 load balancer configuration results in inefficient server usage.

This scenario can be addressed in different ways. One of the ways is to create multiple namespaces, one per workload. Instead of mail.contoso.com for all workloads, for example, you can configure owa.contoso.com, ecp.contoso.com, and so on. Now you have a namespace for each workload. It can resolve to an individual load-balanced IP address per workload. Each IP configured to perform a health check for a given workload, such as */owa/healthcheck.htm*, */ecp/healthcheck.htm*, and so on. Now, if one workload is experiencing problems, it won't result in the entire server being removed from the load balanced pool. The downside is you have to allocate more IP addresses and maintain individual workload-based load-balancing configuration. If the load balancer is configured for external clients, this might mean multiple public IP addresses. Because publicly addressable IP addresses are limited in most deployments, this might be an undesirable configuration, despite its benefits.

Another option is to use the Layer 7 load balancer. In this configuration, you can utilize a single namespace, but unlike the Layer 4 configuration, you configure SSL termination on the load balancer. This allows the load balancer to become application-aware and differentiate between the traffic destined for different workloads. The load balancer can now perform a health check for any given workload, independently of each other, and maintain a separate pool of healthy CAS servers for a given workload. You can now gain the best of both worlds by allocating only a single IP for the namespace, while being able to perform health checks for individual workloads and distributing client connections accordingly. You can also achieve the best possible CAS server utilization, even when one of the components on the server is in an inactive or failed state. The tradeoff is a more involved configuration compared to Layer 4 configuration, and additional processing overhead of decrypting and re-encrypting the client to server connections.

As always, no solution is without tradeoffs. It comes down to unique design requirements of each deployment that should be used to determine the right approach for any given solution.

The Exchange 2013 CAS architecture changes enable you to configure load balancers with no affinity required. This translates to CAS servers built with required logic that identifies client requests and their authentication state to allow a client connection to be sent to any CAS server in the load-balanced pool, without the client repeatedly being requested for authentication. This is possible because when a client establishes a connection with any CAS server for the first time, the CAS server exchanges an authentication (auth) token, session keys, and other relevant information with the client. This information is encrypted by an SSL certificate installed on the CAS server. When the load balancer switches the client connection to different CAS servers for the subsequent requests, the same set of encrypted information is still embedded within the client request. As long as the CAS server receiving the client connection request is configured with the same SSL certificate, the CAS server can successfully decrypt the connection, read the relevant information, and process the connection. When the request lands on a CAS server configured with a default self-signed certificate or a different SSL certificate than the certificate used to encrypt the auth token and other information, the CAS server receiving the request fails to decrypt the required information and fails to identify the client request. This results in often-observed repeated logon prompts or the client's inability to successfully maintain the connection through the load balancer. Trying to remove the load balancer from the client connectivity for testing would be easy. When using a host's file for name resolution and sending all the client traffic to one CAS server, or using session affinity on a load balancer, resolves the issue, then it's incorrectly assumed the load balancer configuration is to blame for the problem. This is where the common logic of elimination doesn't always help pinpoint the actual problem. The correct understanding of requirements, however, always helps to quickly and accurately identify the issue.

As discussed in Objective 2.2 and in the previous paragraph, you're now armed with the understanding of why all the CAS servers in the same site or in the same load-balanced pool must be configured with the same SSL certificate.

Another important configuration aspect is how the load balancer presents the source IP address to the server. When a client connects to a load balancer, the source IP address is the IP address of the client and the destination IP address is that of the load-balanced namespace IP owned by the load balancer. The load balancer sends the packet from the client to the appropriate CAS server. If it's configured to network address translation (NAT) the client connections, the source IP of the request as seen by the CAS server is that of the load balancer. This setup simplifies the routing of packets. You don't need to use load balancer as the default gateway of the server, or configure the server for Direct Server Return, in which the server pretends to own the load-balanced IP address. Because the server only sees the load balancer

IP as source IP, it responds to the load balancer, which, in turn, responds to the client. The client receives the traffic from the load balancer as expected and communication carries on.

Load balancing also involves multiple different ways of configuring networking. For example, in a small environment where a single subnet is used for both servers and clients, the load balancer has a single interface connected to the network. This configuration is known as one-arm configuration. In *one-arm configuration*, configuring the load balancer to the NAT source IP address of the client becomes a necessity because the client and the servers are on the same subnet, and they can communicate directly without any additional routing. Configuring servers to use the load balancer as their default gateway doesn't help because servers never use the load balancer if the client IP is known to the server, as reflected in the source IP headers.

In larger networks where server subnets are dedicated and clients reside on separate subnets, the load balancer can be configured with two interfaces: one interface is connected to the client subnet and another is connected to the server subnet. In this configuration, servers can be configured to use the load balancer as the default gateway, and using NAT for client IP addresses becomes optional, although it's the preferred and recommended configuration.

Source NAT is the recommended configuration because in most routed networks it's desired to use the core router equipment for routing function. This is because the routers have a knowledge of the complex dynamic routes to different destinations within the enterprise network and are designed to handle all the routing traffic. When NAT isn't used, and servers are required to use the load balancer as a gateway, the routing configuration could become complex. Load-balancer sizing also needs to account for all the inter subnet traffic that must pass through the load balancer, regardless of the type of traffic and whether it's being load balanced.

When load-balancing CAS servers on the internal network, Kerberos doesn't work automatically. Additional configuration is required for Kerberos to work in a load-balanced CAS server environment. All load-balanced CAS servers must use the same account, known as the Alternate Service Account (ASA). The recommendation is that ASA is created in Active Directory as a computer account because a computer account doesn't allow interactive login. This results in better security. After an ASA account is created, you must associate it with all CAS servers, and then associate all the Service Principal Names (SPNs) with an ASA credential. To associate an ASA account with a CAS server, run Set-ClientAccessServer cmdlet with the AlternateServiceAccountCredential parameter. SPNs are a combination of service and workload FQDN. For example, there is *http/autodiscover.contoso.com*, where *http* is the service type and *autodisover.contoso.com* is the URL associated with the service. In a unified namespace configuration, you might have *http/mail.contoso.com SPN*, along with Autodiscover SPN, as described earlier. In a multisite environment with regional namespaces, you might need to associate additional SPNs with an ASA account. To associate ASA to a given SPN, run *"setspn -S http/mail.contoso.com Contoso\ExchangeASA$"*, where *http\mail.contoso.com* is SPN and the ASA computer account is ExchangeASA.

When considering load balancer vs. Windows Network Load Balancing (WNLB), it's important to note that while WNLB is supported, if you have multirole servers deployed with CAS and Mailbox roles installed on the same server and the server is a member of a DAG, you can't use WNLB. This is because installing clustering and WNLB on the same server isn't supported. In such a configuration, you must use the external load balancer.

Configuring Session Initiation Protocol (SIP) load balancing

Exchange 2013 deploys a different architecture for Unified Messaging (UM). The Client Access server runs the Microsoft Exchange Unified Messaging Call Router service. The UM call router service listens on TCP port 5060 and 5061. The TCP port 5060 is used in unencrypted communications with clients such as IP PBX, VOIP Gateway, or SBC. If secure configuration is in place, clients are expected to communicate over secure Session Initiation Protocol (SIP) port TCP 5061.

The Mailbox server runs Microsoft Exchange UM service, which listens on TCP ports 5062 and 5063. Similar to CAS servers, TCP port 5062 is used for unsecured SIP communications and 5063 is used for secured SIP communications. The Mailbox server also runs the UM worker process, which listens to TCP ports 5065 and 5067 when configured for unsecured SIP communications, and TCP ports 5066 and 5068 when configured for secured SIP communications.

The CAS servers are responsible for receiving all SIP client traffic and redirect the SIP client traffic to a Mailbox server where the user mailbox is active. The media channel, whether unsecured real-time transport protocol (RTP) or secure real-time transport protocol (SRTP), is established directly between the SIP client (VOIP Gateway, IP PBX, etc.) and the Mailbox server. For UM to function correctly, you must configure VOIP Gateway, IP PBX, and other SIP clients to use the CAS server as their entry point.

You only need to load balance TCP port 5060 and 5061 between SIP clients and CAS servers. Similar to other workloads, you don't need to configure any session affinity for SIP traffic because all of the incoming SIP INVITEs are redirected to the appropriate Mailbox servers, and the SIP client establishes RPT or SRTP channels directly with the appropriate Mailbox server.

Configuring Windows Network Load Balancing (WNLB)

Windows NLB is network load-balancing software included with Windows Server, and it's a common candidate for Exchange Server deployments. While WNLB is considered a free alternative to other load balancing solutions, it has several limitations.

One of the limitations briefly discussed earlier, is WNLB's incompatibility with Windows Failover Clustering. When DAG is deployed and Exchange servers are multirole servers running both CAS and Mailbox roles, Failover Clustering is in use, which rules out deployment of WNLB on the same servers. To deploy WNLB, you must have separate servers running only CAS role and this increases overall cost of Exchange deployment.

WNLB isn't service-aware. In case of service failures on a server that is part of the WNLB cluster, the client's connections could be distributed to a server with failed services, impacting client connectivity and user experience.

WNLB deployments often result in port flooding, which overwhelms network switches with broadcast traffic. This is both highly undesirable and problematic, considering its impact, which isn't limited to a server or a client, but to all traffic passing through the affected switch.

With all documented limitations in mind, it's supported to deploy WNLB to load balance Exchange 2013.

When considering deployment of WNLB, one of the recommended configuration items is the management adapter. While not required, it's highly recommended to configure a dedicated management adapter that isn't shared with any client networks or the cluster adapter.

To create an NLB cluster and join the first host to it, you must first install the NLB features on the server. You can use the Add Roles and Features Wizard from the server manager, or use Add-WindowsFeature to add the NLB and NLB tools. The installation using the Add-Windows feature can be accomplished using the following cmdlet:

```
Add-WindowsFeature -Name NLB -IncludeManagementTools
```

After the feature is installed on the server, create a new NLB cluster using the NLB manager. Figure 2-26 shows the new cluster dialog box. Connect to the first host that will join the newly created NLB cluster, and then select the interface to be used for management. In the following example, the server isn't configured with the dedicated management interface and uses a single available interface.

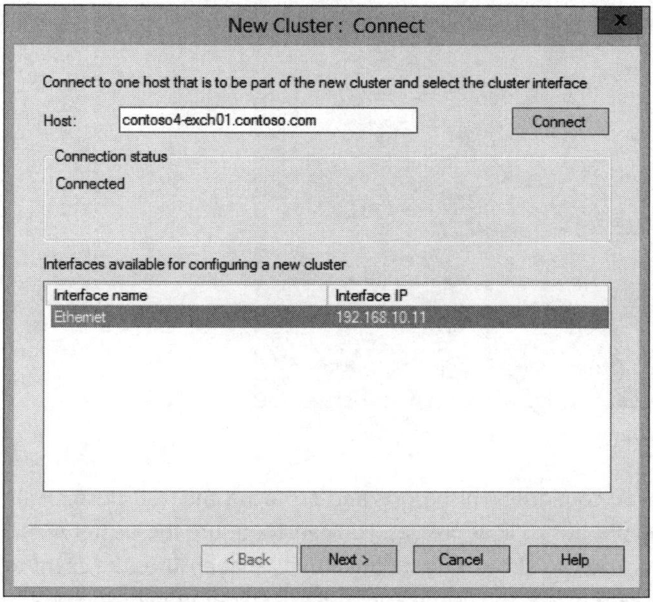

FIGURE 2-26 Creating a new NLB cluster and adding the first host

When you proceed to the next step, you're provided with a host parameter configuration screen. Here, you can configure the priority, which must be unique for each host participating in the cluster. The assigned value can be between 1 and 32. You can configure other parameters, such as a dedicated IP address, in the initial host state when the server is restarted. In the next step, you're required to provide a cluster shared IP address, which is the IP address clients connect to. You can assign multiple shared IP addresses, if needed. In this case, the first listed shared IP address is used for the cluster heartbeat.

In the cluster parameters screen, shown in Figure 2-27, you need to select each cluster shared IP created in the previous step and assign it the FQDN to be used by clients. You also need to configure the cluster operation mode. The default selection of the unicast mode is the recommended setting. Multicast changes the cluster mac address to the multicast address. Internet Group Management Protocol (IGMP) limits switch flooding by limiting the traffic to ports registered to NLB, instead of all switch ports, such as multicast. Careful planning is required if you plan to use multicast or IGMP multicast modes.

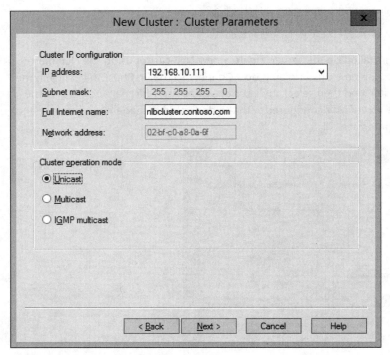

FIGURE 2-27 Configure NLB cluster parameters

In the next step, port rules let you configure which ports and protocols the NLB cluster will respond to. If you configured multiple cluster IP addresses, you can configure the cluster IP address the port range belongs to. You can also configure the affinity that ensures the client to server pairing will be maintained. Figure 2-28 shows the Port Rules Configuration dialog box.

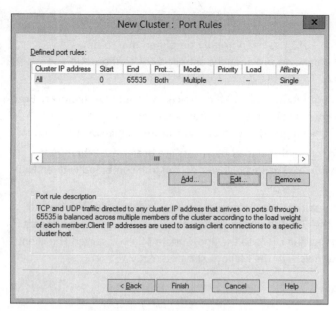

FIGURE 2-28 Configure NLB cluster port rules

Upon completing the new Cluster Wizard, NLB parameters are saved, NLB is restarted, and parameters are reloaded. During the first host configuration this isn't an issue, but be aware that this is a disruptive operation and it disconnects any connected clients. This is also why the recommendation is to complete the NLB configuration, add all the hosts, and after testing successful connectivity to the cluster IP, configure DNS to resolve the cluster name to the cluster IP and allow traffic to the hosts.

Also note that, while in this example, we only configured the server with a single adapter and a single IP address, in practice, this configuration could cause convergence issues. As the best practice, you should configure at least two adapters, with one adapter dedicated to management, as mentioned earlier.

Thought experiment
Load balancing

In this Thought experiment, apply what you learned about this objective. You can find answers to these questions in the "Answers" section at the end of this chapter.

You are planning an Exchange 2013 deployment for your client, Contoso, Ltd. Contoso wants to deploy supported cost-efficient fault tolerance in a unified namespace design. It plans to deploy multirole servers and DAG. The company wants to maximize server usage during failures that affect only certain workloads while the server is still operational and serving other workloads.

What would be your recommended load-balancer configuration?

Objective summary

- Load balancing in Exchange 2013 has been greatly simplified due to new CAS architecture. Layer 4 load balancing provides the simplicity of configuration and cost/performance benefits.

- Layer 7 load-balancing configuration is still a valid choice and might be deployed. Both Layer 4 and Layer 7 deployments have their own pros and cons, and depending on environmental factors and design goals, one might be a better choice over the other.

- Windows NLB is supported, but external load balancers are preferred. When multi-role servers are deployed with DAG, failover clustering can't be combined with an NLB cluster.

- Load-balancing UM sessions with UM architecture changes means you only need to load- balance SIP ports to the UM Call router service on CAS servers. CAS servers act as a SIP redirector and redirect the client to the appropriate Mailbox server. The client then establishes media channels with the Mailbox server directly.

Objective review

Answer the following questions to test your knowledge of the information in this objective. You can find the answers to these questions and explanations of why each answer choice is correct or incorrect in the "Answers" section at the end of this chapter.

1. You're deploying a load-balancing solution for a single namespace deployment. You need to determine the appropriate steps for Layer 4 configuration. All servers are located in a dedicated IP subnet or servers. The network policy states that core routing infrastructure must be used for routing any traffic that isn't load balanced. Select the actions you must perform. Choose all that apply.

   A. Configure the load balancer to pass the client traffic to CAS servers without decrypting and re-encrypting it on the load balancer.

   B. Setup the load balancer in a two-arm configuration.

   C. Install the same SSL certificate on all CAS servers.

   D. Configure NAT on the load balancer.

2. You're configuring load balancer for connections from IP PBX to Exchange 2013 UM. Which ports should you load balance? Select all that apply.

   A. TCP port 5060 and 5061.

   B. TCP port 5062 and 5063.

   C. TCP port 5065 and 5067.

   D. TCP port 5066 and 5068.

3. You're configuring Windows NLB to load balance client traffic to CAS servers. OWA, Outlook, and ActiveSync clients are deployed. UM isn't planned for the deployment. Which of the following actions must you take? Select all that apply.

    A. Configure the TCP port 443 in the NLB port range.

    B. Configure the TCP port 135 in the NLB port range.

    C. Configure the TCP port 5060 and 5061 in the NLB port range.

    D. Configure Network affinity in the NLB settings for the configured ports.

Objective 2.5: Troubleshoot client connectivity

Most of the time, when clients are unable to connect or users experience errors, basic troubleshooting methodology and available tools to test functionality become a great asset for the administrators.

> **This objective covers how to:**
> - Troubleshoot Outlook Anywhere connectivity
> - Troubleshoot POP/IMAP
> - Troubleshoot web services
> - Troubleshoot mobile devices

Troubleshooting Outlook Anywhere connectivity

When any of the Outlook clients connect to their mailboxes located on Exchange 2013 Mailbox servers, they use Outlook Anywhere as the only mechanism to connect because RPC no longer exists as a mechanism for client connectivity.

For the Exchange 2013 environment with no coexistence, the out-of-the box configuration uses the server FQDN as the internal hostname. As discussed in earlier sections, you need to assign the correct namespace to Outlook Anywhere, assign a trusted SSL certificate, and ensure the appropriate authentication method is configured.

After ensuring the internal clients are working as expected, the next step is to ensure that the external client access configuration is accurate. Microsoft provides a helpful test tool that helps not only with testing Outlook Anywhere, but also multiple other tests. The tool, Exchange Connectivity Analyzer (ExRCA), is a web-based tool that can be accessed at *https://testconnectivity.microsoft.com/.* Figure 2-29 shows the home screen of ExRCA. ExRCA provides the ability to test ActiveSync, EWS, and Outlook connectivity tests, including Autodiscover tests. It also provides the ability to test Inbound/Outbound SMTP email, POP, and IMAP email. ExRCA also provides other tests, such as Lync server and Office 365 connectivity tests. Note that this tool requires connectivity to configured external namespaces and must be able to resolve the domain name using public DNS servers. ExRCA doesn't provide offline testing capability, or testing of private or internal URLs that aren't resolvable on the Internet.

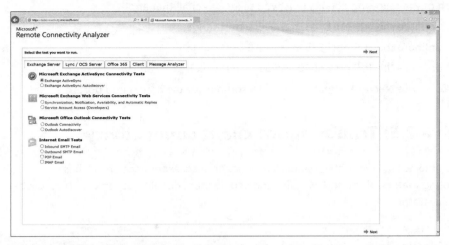

FIGURE 2-29 Microsoft Remote Connectivity Analyzer home page

Let's start with an example of the Autodiscover test. When you proceed to the next step after selecting the Outlook Autodiscover test, the screen you're presented with is common for almost all the tests. This page presents you with fields required to carry out the test, such as your email address, login information, password, and verification. Figure 2-30 shows the screen.

FIGURE 2-30 Microsoft Remote Connectivity Analyzer Outlook Autodiscover test page

After providing the required information, when you proceed to perform the test, ExRCA tests the required steps and reports the findings. In case of an Autodiscover test, the tool attempts to walk through the Autodiscover process, as discussed earlier in Objective 2.2.

Because the test is for an external client, you'll notice in Figure 2-31 that it doesn't try to find Autodiscover information using SCP. SCP discovery only applies to the internal domain-joined clients who are able to connect to the domain controllers containing SCP information. The external client tries to connect, using well-known URLs, as Figure 2-31 shows.

FIGURE 2-31 Microsoft Remote Connectivity Analyzer Outlook Autodiscover test page details

ExRCA flags all the errors and provides details that can help you determine the cause for the failure. For example, the first test that failed in the previous example, shows the failure to connect to *contoso.com:443/autodiscover/autodiscover.xml*. This is a common error in most deployments because the Autodiscover service isn't co-located with the website for the given domain.

Also, note all of the steps ExRCA executes to determine if the test is successful and the details it provides for each step. The test for Autodiscover in this example tried the known URL autodiscover.contoso.com after failing the first step. Upon a successful name resolution, it then tried to connect to SSL port, verified the certificate trust, and took additional steps to ensure the responding server is configured properly and the tool receives the successful Autodiscover response.

When you test Outlook Anywhere using ExRCA, it first tests Autodiscover. This is because Autodiscover is the only method for ExRCA to discover which namespace it must use to connect to Outlook Anywhere. Once the Autodiscover response is successful, it connects to the namespace received from the Autodiscover response for MAPI/HTTP and RPC/HTTP. After ensuring the port and certificate checks succeed, ExRCA then checks for connectivity to the mailbox over */mapi* and */rpc* URLs.

Each of these tests would reflect if the servers are configured with external URLs, if the authentication is configured as required, and if the virtual directories that allow Outlook clients to connect to the mailbox and address book services are accessible and responding as expected.

Exchange 2013 also includes the Test-OutlookConnectivity cmdlet, which tests end-to-end Outlook client connectivity for both RPC/HTTP and MAPI/HTTP connections. The following example tests connectivity to the Contoso administrator's mailbox:

```
Test-OutlookConnectivity -ProbeIdentity "OutlookRpcDeepTestProbe" -MailboxID
administrator@contoso.com
```

Note that no target server or credentials of a user are provided in this test. When credentials aren't provided, the test is carried out using the system's test credentials. If a user's credentials are provided using the Credential parameter, not only is the connectivity to the mailbox tested, but also the provided credentials and ability to access the mailbox using the provided credentials. Similarly, if a target server is provided, the test is carried out against the provided server to ensure the server can successfully provide connectivity to a given mailbox.

The test provides the ability to test using multiple probes to choose from. Self-test probes only test ability to connect to the RPC/HTTP or MAPI/HTTP endpoint on the server. Self-test probes don't log on to a given mailbox. Deep-test probe, like the one used in the previous example, tests connectivity to the endpoint and also tests logging on to the provided mailbox.

While the previous example provided a specific mailbox to test, this is optional. When you don't provide a mailbox ID, the test is carried out against the test account.

When you're in a coexistence environment with a previous version of Exchange servers, as discussed earlier in Objective 2.2, you must ensure Outlook Anywhere is enabled and the default authentication method on Exchange 2013 servers is changed from Negotiate to NTLM. This is because earlier versions of Exchange servers don't support negotiate authentication for Outlook Anywhere.

To change the authentication methods assigned to Outlook Anywhere, use the Set-OutlookAnywhere cmdlet. Using this cmdlet, you can configure the authentication methods for internal clients, external clients, and which authentication methods IIS will use. The parameters to configure the authentication methods are InternalClientAuthenticationMethod, ExternalClientAuthenticationMethod, and IISAuthenticationMethods. Valid values for these parameters are Negotiate, NTLM, and Basic.

EXAM TIP

Don't use the IIS management console to change IIS authentication methods for Exchange server. Exchange processes read the configuration set by Exchange cmdlets and periodically overwrite the IIS configuration. If changes are made to IIS directly and they conflict with the settings configured using Exchange cmdlets, they'll be overwritten.

When you use basic authentication for internal or external clients, logon information is sent by the client to the server in plaintext. Because of security implications, when you set client authentication to basic, you must also set SSL to required. The parameters you must use to set the SSL requirement are InternalClientsRequireSsl and ExternalClientsRequireSsl. Ensure that each is set to $True when basic authentication is configured.

Troubleshooting POP/IMAP

When it comes to POP3 and IMAP services, it's important to note that the services aren't enabled by default. This should always be the first step of troubleshooting when you work on POP3 and IMAP connectivity issues. The POP3 and IMAP services must be explicitly enabled on Exchange 2013 servers before users can connect to them.

To enable POP3 and IMAP services, you can use a services management console or Exchange cmdlets. The services you need to enable are msExchangePOP3, msExchangePOP3BE, msExchangeIMAP4, and msExchangeIMAP4BE. The services msExchangePOP3 and msExchangeIMAP4 are located on Client Access servers. The backend services msExchangePOP3BE and msExchangeIMAP4BE are located on Mailbox servers. On multirole servers, you'll find both front-end and back-end services installed on the same server. The following set of cmdlets demonstrates how you can enable POP and IMAP services:

Enabling POP and IMAP services

```
#Set service startup type to automatic
Set-Service msExchangePOP3 -startuptype automatic
Set-Service msExchangePOP3BE -startuptype automatic
Set-Service msExchangeIMAP4 -startuptype automatic
Set-Service msExchangeIMAP4BE -startuptype automatic

#Start services
Start-Service msExchangePOP3
Start-Service msExchangePOP3BE
Start-Service msExchangeIMAP4
Start-Service msExchangeIMAP4BE
```

By default, POP and IMAP access is enabled for all users. You can verify a user's POP and IMAP access status by running the Get-CASMailbox cmdlet and inspecting values of the PopEnabled and ImapEnabled parameters. Users who are allowed to use POP or IMAP features should have relevant values set to true. Or, you can also verify user properties from EAC, and enable or disable access to POP or IMAP features, as needed.

EXAM TIP

When you enable or disable a user for POP or IMAP, you must also restart POP or IMAP front-end and back-end services for the change to take effect.

POP3 and IMAP clients behave differently from the Outlook client that connects using RPC/HTTP or MAPI/HTTP. When POP clients connect to the server and receive messages, the messages are downloaded to the client and are deleted from the server. This might sometime catch users by surprise as they might be expecting to access their messages using OWA. POP/IMAP clients can be configured to change this behavior, so that client downloads the message, but also leaves a copy on the server.

When users need to configure their POP or IMAP clients to connect to an Exchange server, it's possible for the users to obtain the configuration values by logging into OWA and looking at the option, for POP and IMAP configuration information to be visible in the OWA options page, you must first configure it. For POP and IMAP, you must run the Set-PopSettings and Set-ImapSettings cmdlets. Both cmdlets offer the ExternalConnectionSettings parameter, which can be set with a value such as mail.contoso.com:995:SSL for a POP3 connection over SSL. Once configured, these settings are visible using account options in OWA, as Figure 2-32 shows.

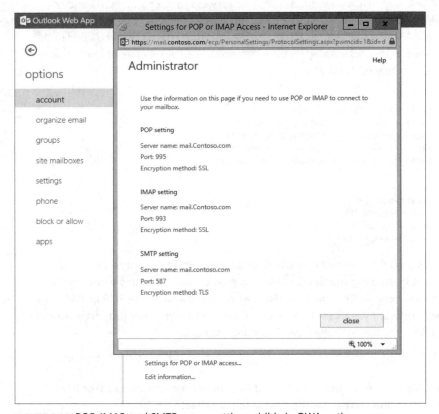

FIGURE 2-32 POP, IMAP, and SMTP access settings visible in OWA options

When using POP and IMAP clients, the user must also set outgoing SMTP server in their client to be able to send messages through the Exchange server. For the SMTP server, configuration to be visible in the settings dialog box, shown in Figure 2-32, you must set the server

FQDN that the user will use to connect and set the AdvertiseClientSettings to True on the client frontend receive connector on CAS servers. The following shows the relevant cmdlets.

Cmdlets to configure POP, IMAP, and SMTP settings so they're visible in OWA options

```
Set-PopSettings -ExternalConnectionSettings {mail.Contoso.com:995:SSL}

Set-ImapSettings -ExternalConnectionSettings {mail.Contoso.com:993:SSL}

Get-ReceiveConnector "*client frontend*" | Set-ReceiveConnector -Fqdn mail.contoso.com
-AdvertiseClientSettings $true
```

When enabling secure access to POP and IMAP, as shown in the previous examples, you must make sure that the trusted certificate is assigned to POP/IMAP services. A default self-signed certificate assigned to the services isn't trusted by clients and results in connectivity issues.

For external POP/IMAP client access, you must also ensure that you can connect through firewalls or reverse proxy servers that might be protecting the servers by inspecting external traffic. You can ensure external access by using the ExRCA tool discussed earlier or using the telnet client to test connectivity to the server. If you use the telnet client, you can connect to the server FQDN on a configured port and ensure that you're presented with an expected server banner. If you're unable to establish a connection to the server, investigate end-to-end connectivity including firewall rules, as needed.

Another troubleshooting tool that you can use when the client is able to connect, but is experiencing issues with POP/IMAP services, is protocol logging. By default, protocol logging is disabled. You can enable protocol logs by running the Set-PopSettings and Set-ImapSettings cmdlets, and setting the ProtocolLoggingEnabled parameter to True. When enabled, client connections are logged and contain detailed logging of client interactions with the server, which can be used for troubleshooting client connectivity issues.

Troubleshooting web services

Exchange Web Services (EWS) provide the ability to access information from Exchange mailboxes. The Outlook client and other applications can use EWS to access information such as Out of Office (OOF) settings, availability information of meeting invitees, mailtips, inbox rules, and message tracking. All such functionality that's dependent on EWS functionality must be able to access EWS services via the advertised EWS URL. By default, external URLs aren't set. You must set external URLs, as discussed in Objective 2.2.

When troubleshooting EWS, the concepts discussed earlier in the Outlook Anywhere and POP/IMAP section apply. Ensure that the URLs are configured and accessible, the assigned certificate is trusted by clients and contains FQDN configured for EWS services, and the firewall configuration allows access to the EWS services.

Configuring authentication on the EWS virtual directory is different compared to Outlook Anywhere settings. To configure authentication on the EWS virtual directory, you need to use the Set-WebServicesVirtualDirectory cmdlet. The parameters for each authentication mechanism are unique and must be specified individually. By default, NTLM and WindowsIntegratedAuthentication are enabled. You can enable Basic authentication by setting the BasicAuthentication parameter to True. You can also use EAC to configure a uthentication settings on the EWS virtual directory.

Troubleshooting mobile devices

Mobile devices connecting to Exchange 2013 servers can come from many vendors, running different mobile operating systems, and various implementations of Exchange ActiveSync protocol. Objective 2.3 discussed many details of deploying and managing mobile devices.

When troubleshooting mobile device connectivity, you want to start by ensuring the basics covered earlier, such as an external URL for ActiveSync virtual directory, certificate configuration, and so on. You can also use ExRCA for testing these configuration requirements.

When a device is unable to connect to the Exchange server, despite verification of all requirements, either manually or using ExRCA, you should look at the device capabilities and policies configured on the Exchange servers. Many times, policies dictate certain parameters, such as encryption to be required for a device to connect to the Exchange environment. When a device doesn't comply with such requirements, it can't be provisioned and fails to connect.

Exchange provides the ability for you to create mailbox policies that allow you to override provisioning issues when a device is deemed appropriate for the environment, despite if it's considered not compliant by another policy. You can create a separate mobile- device mailbox policy that has an AllowNonProvisionableDevices parameter set to True. When the policy is set to True, it allows mobile devices to connect to the Exchange servers, regardless of the device's ability to enforce the settings required by policy.

Another potential avenue to investigate when users are unable to connect using mobile devices, is a user's CAS mailbox settings. These can be set to disable ActiveSync devices for given users, or ABQ policies that could be putting the device in a blocked or quarantined state. Ensure that the user is enabled for ActiveSync by running the Set-CASMailbox cmdlet against the user mailbox and setting the ActiveSyncEnabled parameter to True. Also, verify quarantined devices and device access rules to ensure the device isn't getting blocked based on ABQ settings.

Thought experiment

Client connectivity

In this Thought experiment, apply what you learned about this objective. You can find answers to these questions in the "Answers" section at the end of this chapter.

You're assisting Contoso, Ltd in troubleshooting multiple client connectivity issues. The management states that the deployment project was left incomplete by the previous contractor and Exchange servers were installed, but not configured to meet connectivity requirements. The users state that they can connect to their mailboxes using Outlook clients internally. They receive certificate trust prompts, which they currently ignore and they connect anyway. Users are unable to configure Outlook client or mobile devices from external locations to connect to their mailboxes. They are able to use OWA externally and they successfully ignore certificate warnings to access OWA.

You need to address external connectivity issues. Which actions should be part of your action items?

Objective summary

- Troubleshooting client connectivity starts with a verification of the basics. Proper configuration of internal and external URLs, DNS servers, and certificates are paramount to a successful Exchange 2013 deployment.

- Firewalls, reverse proxies, and load balancers can cause unforeseen issues if they're configured to inspect Exchange traffic and filter hostnames and/or virtual directory paths.

- POP and IMAP services aren't enabled by default and must be configured manually, if required. While POP/IMAP services don't have specific URL configuration similar to HTTP workloads, you can configure POP and IMAP settings to include a URL to be used to make POP/IMAP access settings visible to the user using an OWA account options page.

- Because of a large variety of ActiveSync devices, each deployment must plan for an appropriate policy and allow/block/quarantine requirements. Implementing such policies and required exceptions must be carefully planned and addressed to avoid unexpected connectivity issues.

- Exchange Web Services provide critical feature access to Outlook and other clients. The inability to access EWS URLs successfully results in the loss of functionality, such as OOF, MailTips, message tracking, and a lack of visibility into the availability of meeting invitees.

Objective review

Answer the following questions to test your knowledge of the information in this objective. You can find the answers to these questions and explanations of why each answer choice is correct or incorrect in the "Answers" section at the end of this chapter.

1. You are required to configure POP and IMAP access for the Exchange 2013 environment. You must ensure that users connect to the services securely. Which ports must you configure? Select all that apply.

   A. TCP port 25.

   B. TCP port 995.

   C. TCP port 443.

   D. TCP port 993.

2. You are configuring Exchange 2013 servers in an existing Exchange 2010 environment. Exchange 2010 environment didn't provide external access. An Exchange 2013 environment is planned to provide external access to users. Which two actions must you take to ensure Exchange 2010 users can access their mailboxes using the Outlook client from external locations?

   A. Enable Outlook Anywhere on all Exchange 2010 servers.

   B. Enable NTLM authentication on Exchange 2013 servers.

   C. Enable Basic authentication on Exchange 2013 servers.

   D. Configure the DefaultAuthenticationMethod parameter on the Exchange 2013 server.

3. You're an Exchange administrator for Contoso, Ltd. Users reported they're unable to set OOF using their Outlook clients. The error message they receive states "Your automatic reply settings cannot be displayed because the server is currently unavailable. Try again later." What must you do to resolve the error? Select all that apply.

   A. Configure external and internal EWS URL.

   B. Configure DNS to resolve the EWS URL to the appropriate load-balanced IP.

   C. Obtain a trusted certificate that contains EWS FQDNs and assign it to IIS service on the Mailbox servers.

   D. Obtain a trusted certificate that contains EWS FQDNs and assign it to IIS service on the Client Access servers.

Answers

This section contains the solutions to the Thought experiments and answers to the objective review questions in this chapter.

Objective 2.1: Thought experiment

1. Outlook clients are configured to connect to the Exchange 2007 servers using manually created profiles. When changing a primary namespace to Exchange 2013 servers located in HQ, all the Outlook clients configured to use a primary namespace will connect to Exchange 2013 servers. Because Autodiscover isn't in use by Outlook clients, they won't connect to legacy namespace. This won't affect Outlook Anywhere connectivity because Exchange 2013 CAS servers proxy an Outlook Anywhere connection to the Exchange 2007 CAS servers. However, the OOF functionality that uses EWS is impacted because the EWS connectivity must exist from an Outlook client to the same version of the Exchange server where the mailbox resides. This won't be possible if Outlook clients aren't using Autodiscover. So, you must recommend changing Outlook clients to use Autodiscover before making the recommended changes to the primary namespace.

2. When ActiveSync clients are connected to Exchange 2007 CAS servers and the mailbox is moved to a different site, Exchange 2007 CAS servers issue 451 redirect. ActiveSync clients should connect to a new namespace provided by 451 redirect. The only requirement is the namespace can't be removed until after ActiveSync clients successfully connect to a new namespace.

3. To reduce the namespaces in use, you must account for the Outlook client connectivity logic, including the requirement for EWS and ActiveSync requirements, as previously mentioned. Ensure you have configured legacy namespace for Exchange 2007, configured Outlook clients for Autodiscover, and ensured all the ActiveSync clients have updated to new namespace before removing the old namespace to avoid impact.

Objective 2.1: Review

1. **Correct answers:** A, B, and C

   A. **Correct:** A legacy namespace is required for OWA, EWS, and ActiveSync during coexistence.

   B. **Correct:** Exchange 2013 CAS servers proxy Outlook Anywhere connections for mailboxes hosted on Exchange 2007 servers. You must enable Outlook Anywhere on Exchange 2007 servers for proxy functionality to work.

   C. **Correct:** You must associate the primary namespace with the Exchange 2013 servers, so users with mailboxes on Exchange 2013 can function correctly.

   D. **Incorrect:** ExternalURL isn't required for the given scenario where users don't connect from the Internet.

2. **Correct answer:** A

   A. **Correct:** Because the Exchange 2013 CAS server associated with the primary namespace is running Exchange 2013 CU1, it issues redirect without SSO. The SSO redirection login for OWA was introduced in CU2 of Exchange 2013.

   B. **Incorrect:** Because the site where the user's mailbox is located is associated with another namespace, Exchange 2013 CAS server won't proxy the request. The request is proxied only if the other site doesn't have a namespace or the URL is the same as the primary namespace.

   C. **Incorrect:** Because the site where the user's mailbox is located is associated with another namespace, Exchange 2013 CAS server won't proxy the request. The request is proxied only if the other site doesn't have a namespace or the URL is the same as the primary namespace.

   D. **Incorrect:** SSO redirection logic for OWA was introduced in Exchange 2013 CU2. Servers associated with the primary namespace are running CU1.

3. **Correct answers:** A and D

   A. **Correct:** The ForceWACViewingFirstOnPrivateComputers property is set to $false by default and must be set to $true to achieve the desired behavior.

   B. **Incorrect:** The default value of WacViewingOnPrivateComputersEnabled is $true and doesn't need to be changed.

   C. **Incorrect:** The default value of WacViewingOnPublicComputersEnabled is $true and doesn't need to be changed.

   D. **Correct:** Office Web Apps server must trust the SSL certificate presented by Exchange 2013 CAS servers to successfully render the requested document. Exchange 2013 CAS servers, by default, have a self-signed certificate assigned to IIS and must be changed.

Objective 2.2: Thought experiment

1. A unified namespace solution is possible for a given environment. When considering proxy scenarios for users connecting to a datacenter that is different from the datacenter where their mailbox is currently active. This requires bandwidth planning between datacenters to accommodate additional client traffic due to increased proxy traffic between Exchange servers. Because the bandwidth between datacenters isn't an issue, additional proxy traffic between datacenter isn't a problem. You don't need legacy namespace because the deployment doesn't consist of Exchange 2007 servers.

2. Considering the previously mentioned unified namespace, if SRV records are used for Autodiscover, a single namespace can suffice. This is based on the assumption that split-brain DNS is in use and the internal namespace is the same as the external. If the internal domain is a private domain, or different from the external namespace, then you need additional namespace for the internal clients.

Objective 2.2: Review

1. **Correct answers:** A and C

   A. **Correct:** A newly installed Exchange server creates SCP record in Active Directory using server's FQDN. Domain joined internal clients use SCP to find Autodiscover service URL and can possibly use newly created SCP. Using Set-ClientAccessServer allows you to change the Autodiscover internal URL to the desired Autodiscover namespace.

   B. **Incorrect:** Clients don't use URLs set by Set-AutodiscoverVirtualDirectory cmdlet for discovery.

   C. **Correct:** A default self-signed certificate assigned to IIS on a newly installed Exchange server isn't trusted by clients. A certificate issued by a trusted CA must be assigned to IIS and it must include FQDN provided by Autodiscover.

   D. **Incorrect:** Configuring an internal namespace to resolve to load-balanced IP address doesn't address certificate trust issue.

2. **Correct answers:** A, C, and D

   A. **Correct:** Because a unified namespace is used across all locations, selecting all CAS servers in the External Access Domain Wizard is the appropriate action.

   B. **Incorrect:** With a unified single namespace you don't need to run the External Access Domain Wizard for each location.

   C. **Correct:** The External Access Domain Wizard doesn't configure external URL for Outlook anywhere. It must be set separately.

   D. **Correct:** An External Access Domain Wizard doesn't configure the external URL for a MAPI virtual directory. It must be set separately.

3. **Correct answer:** C

   A. **Incorrect:** A self-signed certificate isn't trusted by clients and it causes connectivity issues.

   B. **Incorrect:** A UC SAN certificate from an internal CA can be trusted, but it isn't trusted by clients without an additional manual configuration.

   C. **Correct:** A UC SAN certificate from an external CA doesn't require an additional manual configuration on Outlook clients.

   D. **Incorrect:** While a wildcard certificate issued by a trusted CA can be a valid choice for Exchange 2013 environments, when integrating with Lync, you must have a certificate with a subject name that isn't a wildcard. A wildcard can be included in a subject alternative names (SAN) list on a UC SAN certificate.

Objective 2.3: Thought experiment

1. Contoso, Ltd. should consider whether it wants to allow any type of device, or whether it prefers to limit devices to a specific set of device families or types. In either case, the company should also decide what it wants to do with unsupported devices and devices that can't be provisioned by ActiveSync. Contoso should also consider whether it wants to allow, require, or block the use of OWA for Devices.

2. Contoso can control devices using device access rules to allow or block devices, the default organization rule to allow, block, or quarantine devices that don't match any rule, and EAS policies to control the length and strength of passwords required on devices. Depending on the device, the company might also be able to use other EAS policy settings, but this varies by device.

3. Users who are working remotely often have multiple devices. Many of them use OWA frequently alongside their mobile devices. Contoso might want to consider setting up OWA policies to control which users have which OWA features. Contoso should ensure that its administrators and users know how to remotely wipe lost or stolen devices.

Objective 2.3: Review

1. **Correct answers**: A, B, and D

   A. **Correct**: This command can make the app available to all users in the organization, but it can't be run until the app has been registered with New-App.

   B. **Correct**: This cmdlet registers the app, but it doesn't make it available to users. You can't specify a UNC path for an app file, which is why the Get-Content cmdlet is required.

   C. **Incorrect**: The Url flag to New-App requires an actual URL, not a UNC path.

   D. **Correct**: This cmdlet is required to read the contents of the app manifest file and put it in a format that the New-App cmdlet can handle.

2. **Correct answer:** C

   A. **Incorrect**: This solution can work, but it requires extra effort because you have to create a new device access rule to block each individual type of device you don't want. You won't know those devices have connected until you review the logs.

   B. **Incorrect**: This solution can work, but it requires extra effort. You (or another administrator) have to manually review each quarantined device and decide whether to release it.

   C. **Correct**: This is the simplest solution because you only need a single device-access rule for each device family. The default organizational rule blocks all other devices.

   D. **Incorrect**: This solution can work, but it requires you to get the sync statistics for each user, and then touch each user mailbox with Set-CASMailbox. It also doesn't prevent banned devices from syncing in the first place.

3. **Correct answer:** D

    A. **Incorrect**: The Set-Mailbox cmdlet can't be used to change ActiveSync settings for user mailboxes.

    B. **Incorrect**: This cmdlet can change a limited range of EAS settings for all users of EAS on a specific virtual directory and server, not only for the selected users.

    C. **Incorrect**: The Set-CASMailbox cmdlet is used to set EAS policy settings, but the specified parameter can only be used to change the OWA mailbox policy applied to a user.

    D. **Correct**: This cmdlet lets you specify which EAS device policy you want to apply to a specific mailbox.

Objective 2.4: Thought experiment

The requirements state that the servers are running both CAS and Mailbox roles. The DAG is also deployed. Because of this configuration, WNLB can't be used for load-balancing client access traffic. The requirements call for cost-efficient load-balancer deployment, which would require Layer 4 configuration. However, the conflicting requirement also states that server usage must be maximized during single workload failures. This requirement can be addressed with Layer 4 only if deploying multiple namespaces, but the requirements state a unified namespace design is selected, which rules out Layer 4 load balancing as an option. Layer 7 load balancing meets the requirements of achieving higher server efficiency during single workload failures when the server is operational.

Objective 2.4: Review

1. **Correct answers:** A, C, and D

    A. **Correct:** Configuring SSL decryption and re-encryption on load balancer is a Layer 7 configuration.

    B. **Incorrect:** Even though the servers are located on the dedicated subnet, two-arm configuration isn't a requirement. Clients can still connect through load balancer configured with one-arm setup. The answer is only incorrect because you have to select what you must do.

    C. **Correct:** You need to install the same certificate on all CAS servers, so the load balancer can distribute client connections without any affinity requirements.

    D. **Correct:** NAT is required to meet the routing requirements. Without configuring NAT, the server must use load balancer as a default gateway, which wouldn't meet stated requirements.

2. **Correct answer:** A

   A. **Correct:** UM call router service on CAS servers listen to TCP ports 5060 and 5061.

   B. **Incorrect:** Exchange UM service on the Mailbox server listens on TCP ports 5062 and 5063.

   C. **Incorrect:** The UM worker service on the Mailbox server listens on TCP ports 5065 and 5067 when configured for unsecured SIP communications.

   D. **Incorrect:** The UM worker service on the Mailbox server listens on TCP ports 5066 and 5068 when configured for secured SIP communications.

3. **Correct answer:** A

   A. **Correct:** All the stated workloads are HTTP workloads that use TCP port 443 to connect to Exchange CAS servers.

   B. **Incorrect:** TCP port 135 is an RPC endpoint mapper, which doesn't need to be load balanced for client connections.

   C. **Incorrect:** TCP ports 5060 and 5061 are UM ports. Requirements state UM isn't planned for the deployment.

   D. **Incorrect:** Affinity isn't required for client connections to Exchange 2013 CAS servers. Setting affinity on WNLB to "Network" sends all clients from a subnet to one CAS server, which won't achieve even client-connection distribution.

Objective 2.5: Thought experiment

Internally, if the client computers are domain joined, they can obtain Autodiscover information using SCP from domain controllers. Even if appropriate internal URLs aren't configured explicitly, default internal URLs that are configured to use server FQDN allow clients to connect. The SSL warnings are an indication of either incorrect URL configuration, the use of a self-signed certificate, or both. Also possible is that a trusted certificate is installed, but it doesn't contain appropriate FQDNs in the subject name or the subject alternate names, resulting in a certificate warning. Ensure internal URLs are configured to use the appropriate designed namespace. Also ensure that trusted certificate includes the appropriate namespaces and is assigned to IIS service on Exchange servers. This should resolve internal SSL certificate prompts.

External user connectivity issues indicate the possibility that no external URLs are configured. This is apparent in the problem statement because users are unable to configure their Outlook or Activesync clients. OWA works from outside, despite an SSL error that indicates that expected external URLs might be configured in DNS to resolve to Exchange servers. However, when Autodiscover fails to return the appropriate URLs, reported connectivity issues are expected. Configure appropriate external URLs for all workloads that need to be accessed externally. Also ensure that the appropriate certificate is obtained and assigned to IIS service on Exchange servers.

Objective 2.5: Review

1. **Correct answers:** B and D

   A. **Incorrect:** TCP port 25 is used by SMTP, which isn't required to secure the connection using SSL.

   B. **Correct:** TCP port 995 is assigned to POP3 services for secure access.

   C. **Incorrect:** TCP port 443 is used for secure web access.

   D. **Correct:** TCP port 993 is assigned to IMAP4 services for secure access.

2. **Correct answers:** A and B

   A. **Correct:** Outlook Anywhere must be enabled on all Exchange 2010 servers in a coexistence environment for Exchange 2013 servers to be able to proxy Outlook Anywhere connections successfully.

   B. **Correct:** Negotiate is the default authentication method used by Exchange 2013, which isn't supported by previous versions of Exchange servers. NTLM must be enabled for Outlook Anywhere to work with previous versions of Exchange servers.

   C. **Incorrect:** While Basic authentication can be assigned to Outlook Anywhere on Exchange 2013 servers, it isn't required for given requirements.

   D. **Incorrect:** Configuring the DefaultAuthenticationMethod parameter on Exchange 2013 server is ambiguous. Without the required authentication method it isn't addressing the requirements.

3. **Correct answers:** A, B, and D

   A. **Correct:** The error indicates the Outlook client is unable to connect to EWS URL. Configuring the appropriate URLs is one of the valid steps to address the issue.

   B. **Correct:** Configuring DNS to resolve EWS URLs to the appropriate IP address is a valid step to resolve the issue.

   C. **Incorrect:** In Exchange 2013, Client Access servers front-end all client traffic and present the SSL certificate that must be trusted by the client. The certificate assigned to the Mailbox servers is used and trusted by Client Access servers, even if it's self-signed.

   D. **Correct:** In Exchange 2013, Client Access servers front-end all client traffic and present a SSL certificate that must be trusted by the client.

CHAPTER 3

Plan, install, configure, and manage transport

Exchange 2013 has two primary roles: the Mailbox role is responsible for storing and retrieving messages, and the Client Access role provides interfaces for various clients and protocols to move mail around. The transport subsystem has parts that run on both roles. Together the combination of Exchange subsystems that touch messages in transit is known as the transport pipeline, as shown in Figure 3-1. Understanding how to design, manage, configure, monitor, and troubleshoot the transport pipeline is a key requirement for managing Exchange systems, and for passing the 70-341 exam.

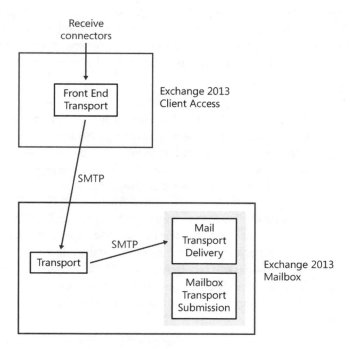

FIGURE 3-1 Transport pipeline for both inbound and outbound messages has services on both Exchange Server roles

Although there may not be questions about them on the exam, you'll need to understand the roles of the various services that make up the transport pipeline. That means you need to understand how messages are passed around. In Exchange 2013, we only have three server roles: Edge, Client Access, and Mailbox. Microsoft strongly recommends putting the Client Access and Mailbox roles on the same server, but whether or not they're physically separate, they're logically separate.

Inbound messages follow a four-step flow:

1. No matter whether they come from the Internet or another Exchange server, messages most often arrive on a receive connector on a client access server. They might also arrive in the server's drop directory or via an Exchange Web Services connection.

2. The Front End Transport (FET) service (MSExchangeFrontendTransport.exe) proxies the message from the CAS to the Transport service on a Mailbox server.

3. The Transport service (MSExchangeTransport.exe), which is the equivalent of the Hub Transport service in Exchange 2007/2010, accepts the proxied connection. The Transport service does much of the work of processing the message. This includes categorizing it, routing it, applying transport rules, and inspecting and modifying message headers and contents as needed.

4. The Transport service establishes a Single Mail Transfer Protocol (SMTP) connection to the Mailbox Transport Delivery service (MSExchangeDelivery.exe) on a Mailbox server. This service accepts incoming messages and delivers them to the information store, using a remote procedure call (RPC). The Transport and FET services don't communicate directly with the store service. All transport communications between servers use SMTP.

EXAM TIP

Some of the exam questions on the 70-341 and 70-342 exams may refer to Hub Transport servers. This can be a little confusing, because there's no Exchange 2013 Hub Transport role. If you see a reference to Hub Transport in a question or case study, read carefully to see whether the question is talking about an Exchange 2010 Hub Transport server or whether it's a leftover reference to the old name for the Transport service.

Outbound messages follow a similar flow. When a user sends a new message, the client first stores the message in a folder (Sent Items for users running Microsoft Outlook in cached mode, Outbox for users running Outlook in online mode, or the Drafts folder for Outlook Web App). The Mailbox Transport Submission service makes an RPC connection to the store and fetches the message from that folder. Then, it uses SMTP to send the message to the Transport service, either on the same server or on another, at which point it is treated like any other incoming message.

Another important thing to understand is the difference between the Set-Transport-Config and the Set-TransportService cmdlets. You use Set-TransportConfig when you want to make changes to the transport configuration *for the whole Exchange organization*. For example, if you want to block all your servers from accepting SMTP messages larger than 50MB, you could do that with the Set-TransportConfig -MaxReceiveSize 50MB cmdlet. The Set-TransportService cmdlet, along with its counterparts Set-FrontEndTransportService and Set-MailboxTransportService, only changes the setting on an individual server.

EXAM TIP

When you encounter a question where any of these cmdlets are among the proposed answers, stop and think whether the correct solution is to change a setting on one server or for the entire organization.

Objectives in this chapter:

- Objective 3.1: Plan a high availability solution for common scenarios
- Objective 3.2: Design a transport solution
- Objective 3.3: Configure and manage transport
- Objective 3.4. Troubleshoot and monitor transport
- Objective 3.5: Configure and manage hygiene

Objective 3.1: Plan a high availability solution for common scenarios

Reliable message transport is an extremely important part of the services Exchange provides. Exchange uses the SMTP for all its mail transport. SMTP doesn't provide any built-in features for high availability. Instead, the designers of SMTP required servers to be able to store mail and forward it later, so if a temporary connection failure prevented message delivery, the server could try again later. This type of retry behavior (known as store-and-forward) is better than nothing, but not really well- suited for modern enterprise messaging systems.

For the 70-341 exam, Microsoft expects you to understand how to manage high availability for message transport. This availability is provided by several methods, some of which are Internet standards (such as using redundant MX records) and some of which are specific to Exchange 2013.

> **This objective covers how to:**
> - Set up redundancy for intra-site scenarios
> - Plan for Safety Net
> - Plan for shadow redundancy
> - Plan for redundant MX records

Understanding transport high availability and message routing

Although there's no corresponding object in Exchange, the concept of a *transport high availability boundary* is central to understanding how Exchange 2013 transport high availability (HA) works. Within the transport HA boundary, Exchange tries to keep two redundant copies of each message as it moves through the transport system. Once a message leaves the boundary, Exchange no longer maintains redundant copies of the message. Figure 3-2 shows each of the types of transport HA boundaries and how they relate to each other:

- All the mailbox servers within a database availability group (DAG) are within the same boundary, so the four servers in the DAG-FABDAG01 box are all part of the same boundary. If the DAG spans multiple Active Directory sites, Exchange uses Active Directory site membership as a criterion when choosing a server for shadow redundancy. It always prefers a server in a remote site over a local one if one is available.

- All the mailbox servers in the same Active Directory site that are not members of a DAG are considered to be within a boundary, but not the same one as any DAG members in the same site. In Figure 3-2, AUSEX01 and HSVEX01 are within their own transport HA boundary.

- Messages sent to, or received from, servers outside the Exchange organization are considered to be in their own boundary, which Exchange ignores. In Figure 3-2, the Office 365 environment and any cloud-connected server are logically considered to be a part of their own boundary.

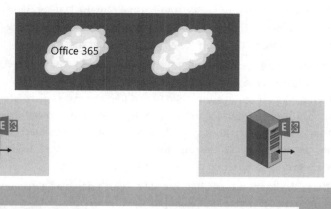

Active Directory site aus.fabrikam.com   Active Directory site hsv.fabrikam.com

FIGURE 3-2 Transport high availability boundaries in an Exchange organization

You can't configure or manage these high availability boundaries because there aren't any Exchange objects that represent them. Like membership in an Active Directory site, membership within a transport HA boundary is automatically computed based on the server's role and Active Directory site membership.

In Exchange 2010, the Active Directory site was the primary boundary for message routing. That is, Exchange 2010 servers within a single site assume they can communicate without restriction. Exchange 2013 builds on this approach by adding the DAG as a routing boundary, too. Standalone Mailbox servers use their Active Directory site membership as a routing boundary, while DAG members use DAG membership instead. The Exchange team assumed that servers within a DAG have good connectivity to each other, even if the DAG spans multiple Active Directory sites.

On standalone servers, an incoming message for a mailbox must be delivered only to the database that hosts that mailbox. However, in DAGs, incoming messages for a mailbox should only be delivered to the active copy of the database that contains that mailbox. Only the Mailbox Transport Delivery service can deliver messages to a mailbox database. This means the routing architecture needs to provide a way for a sending server to tell which server should be the target. That server's Mailbox Transport Delivery service should eventually get the message. The Active Manager subsystem of Exchange already tracks which copy of each database in a DAG is active, so it takes on that responsibility.

Using DAGs for message routing has another benefit: the DAG provides resilience for the Transport service. When you extend a DAG across multiple physical locations, any DAG member server can handle message transport for all servers in that site.

The Transport service is responsible for message routing. The *categorizer* determines the next hop for a message, and then delivers it to the appropriate queue for the selected destination. This queue might result in SMTP sending the message to another server or to the Mailbox Transport Delivery service for delivery to a local mailbox database. Exchange 2013 supports three types of destinations: mailbox databases, mail connectors, and distribution group expansion servers. Every message that leaves the Transport service on an Exchange 2013 Mailbox server is sent to one of those three objects.

Each of these destination types has a set of servers known as a *delivery group* that can accept mail for that destination. For example, the delivery group for a mailbox database contains all the servers of the same Exchange version as the server that holds the target mailbox database in the same Active Directory site. The delivery group for a connector contains all the Exchange 2013 Mailbox servers and Exchange 2010 or Exchange 2007 hub transport servers that could deliver messages to that destination.

For a deeper explanation of message routing, see the "Mail routing" topic in the Exchange 2013 online help (*http://technet.microsoft.com/en-us/library/aa998825(v=exchg.150).aspx*) or Chapter 2 of Exchange Server 2013 *Inside Out: Connectivity, Clients, and Unified Messaging* (Microsoft Press; 2013).

Planning for shadow redundancy

Shadow redundancy addresses a key area of potential message loss. When one SMTP server contacts another to send a message, the sending server has no way to see what happens to the message once the receiving server has accepted it for delivery. Without that knowledge, the sending server normally assumes that the message has been delivered and deletes its local copy. But if the message wasn't delivered properly, neither the sending nor the receiving server has a copy of the message to use when reattempting delivery. To solve this problem, shadow redundancy keeps a copy of a submitted message until the server at the next hop confirms receipt. Once Exchange has determined that the message has been delivered to its final destination, the last server to touch the message creates a discard notification. This signals any transport server with a copy of the message that it's safe to discard it. Discard notifications are small status indications that signal a particular server has received a message with a given Message-ID value.

Shadow redundancy only works when you have multiple Exchange Server computers in the organization. And it only protects against the case where one transport server at a time has failed.

How shadow redundancy works

Here's how the process works when Alice, who's using Outlook.com, sends a message to Bob, whose mailbox is on HSVMBX41 (see Figure 3-3).

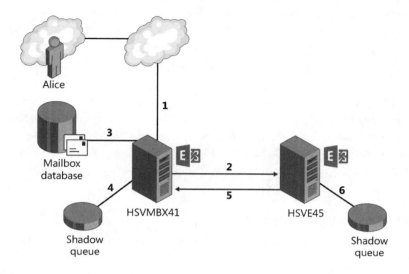

FIGURE 3-3 Shadow redundancy message flow

As shown in Figure 3-3:

1. Alice composes and sends her message. Outlook.com uses SMTP to transfer the message to HSVMBX41.

2. When HSVMBX41 receives the message, but before it sends its final 250 OK notification back to the Outlook.com server, it opens a connection to HSVEX45 and uses SMTP to submit a shadow copy of the message. HSVEX45 stores this message in its shadow redundancy queue.

3. HSVMBX41 transfers the message to the Mailbox Transport Service, which delivers it to the mailbox database containing Bob's mailbox.

4. Because it has accepted delivery, HSVMBX41 generates a discard notification for its copy of the message and stores it in the shadow redundancy queue. (It also moves the message to the primary Safety Net queue. More on that in the next section, "Configuring shadow redundancy options.")

5. HSVEX45 opens a connection to HSVMBX41 to check for a discard notification for the new message. By default, it does this every two minutes. But if HSVMBX41 opens an ordinary SMTP connection, it can use the XQDISCARD SMTP verb to query without making a separate connection.

6. Once HSVEX45 sees the discard notification, it moves the shadow copy of the message to its shadow Safety Net queue.

If HSVMBX41 fails before the message is delivered to Bob's mailbox, then the servers that hold shadow copies of its messages can resubmit them for delivery. Exchange contains code that can detect and suppress multiple copies of the same message, although multiple copies may still be sent (and may not be detected) to foreign systems. Discard notifications are passed during normal SMTP connections by use of the Exchange-specific XQDISCARD SMTP verb. So any two Exchange 2013 servers in the same organization that communicate can tell each other which messages have been confirmed as delivered, and which messages may be safely discarded.

For outbound messages, the flow is different. The last Exchange server in the organization to touch the message only holds the message until the receiving server acknowledges receipt, and then it moves the message to Safety Net. Shadow redundancy isn't involved with the outbound transport leg, although if one Exchange 2013 organization is sending to another across the Internet, the receiving organization will use shadow redundancy as described in the earlier steps.

Configuring shadow redundancy options

By default, shadow redundancy is on throughout the Exchange organization. You can use the Set-TransportConfig -ShadowRedundancyEnabled cmdlet to turn it on or off. This change applies to all the servers in the organization because it wouldn't make sense to enable or disable shadow redundancy only on some transport servers. For the feature to be useful, it needs to be enabled everywhere.

You can choose how you want to handle the case where a message cannot be persisted in the shadow redundancy system. For example, in a two-node DAG, when one node fails, the remaining node can't store messages in its local shadow redundancy queue, so if no other servers are reachable, the message won't be persisted in a shadow queue at all. You can force Exchange to reject any messages that cannot be stored in a shadow redundancy queue by using the RejectMessageOnShadowFailure parameter to the Set-TransportConfig cmdlet, like this:

```
Set-TransportConfig -RejectMessageOnShadowFailure $true
```

Once you turn shadow redundancy on, you can control a few other miscellaneous settings, as shown in Table 3-1.

TABLE 3-1 Shadow redundancy settings usable with Set-TransportConfig

Parameter	What it does
ShadowMessageAutoDiscardInterval	Specifies length of time the primary server keeps discard notifications for shadow messages. If the shadow server doesn't retrieve the notifications during this interval, the primary server throws them away. The default value is 2.00:00:00 (two days). You enter the time as dd:hh:mm:ss.
ShadowMessagePreferenceSetting	Controls where you want shadow copies of messages to be submitted. The default, PreferRemote, attempts to deliver shadow copies to a remote site if one is reachable, but will fail over to local if a remote site isn't reachable. Other permissible values are LocalOnly and RemoteOnly. Note that RemoteOnly will simply fail if no remote site is available.
ShadowResubmitTimeSpan	Indicates how long a server will wait before deciding that the primary server has failed and takes over processing queued shadow copies for the dead server. The default value is three hours (03:00:00).

Planning for Safety Net

Safety Net is designed to protect messages against failures that happen after a message has been delivered to the active copy of a mailbox database, but has not been replicated to the passive copies. You can think of it as what happens after shadow redundancy has processed the message—once the shadow redundancy system has detected that the message has been correctly delivered, Safety Net becomes responsible for ensuring the message is delivered to all copies of the mailbox database. Safety Net is implemented as a queue in the transport database, mail.que, so if anything happens to that database, you should assume the messages preserved by Safety Net in that database will no longer be available.

Consider the case when Alice sends a message to Bob, whose mailbox is stored on a database in a two-node DAG, consisting of servers HSVEX01 and HSVEX02. Alice's message arrives at the active mailbox database copy and is stored in Bob's mailbox. The instant the message is committed to the active database, that server fails catastrophically. Where did the message go? As far as the sending server knows it was successfully delivered. The message tracking logs will indicate that the message was delivered, too, because it made it to the then-active copy of Bob's mailbox. However, when Bob logs in to his mailbox, the active copy of which is now on HSVEX02, he won't see the message because it was never replicated. Safety Net solves this problem by preserving a copy of each message sent through a mailbox server until it has been delivered to the active mailbox database and replicated to all passive copies of that database.

Figure 3-4 shows what this process looks like.

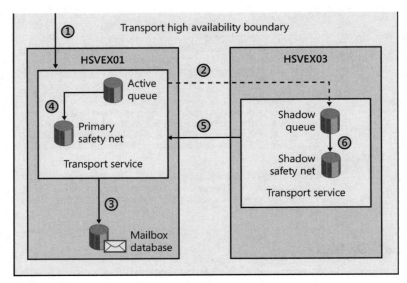

FIGURE 3-4 Message flow through Safety Net

Two separate Safety Net instances exist for any given message. The primary Safety Net copy of the message is held on the mailbox server that held the message before it was processed by the Transport service. The shadow Safety Net copy is held on the same server that got the shadow redundancy copy of the message. Once the transport pipeline determines the message has been delivered, and the shadow redundancy copy of the message is no longer needed, that message is moved to the shadow Safety Net queue on the same server.

By design, Safety Net has very few settings you can adjust. It's intended to be an automatic, self-configuring subsystem. You can control a few things:

- Whether Safety Net is redundant or not. If you turn off shadow redundancy with Set-TransportConfig -ShadowRedundancyEnabled $false, Safety Net still functions, but a shadow Safety Net copy won't be preserved because that depends on the existence of a shadow redundancy queue.

- How long messages will be kept in Safety Net. By default, messages are held for two days, which you can verify by looking at the SafetyNetHoldTime parameter returned by Get-TransportConfig. You can change this time with Set-TransportConfig -SafetyNetHoldTime. Shadow Safety Net messages may stick around longer if they haven't been acknowledged. They will remain in the queue for the sum of the SafetyNetHoldTime and the MessageExpirationTimeout value set on each server's transport service.

Planning for redundant MX records

SMTP servers use the Mail Exchanger (MX) record type in the Domain Name System (DNS). Every domain name that can receive email will have at least one MX record. When someone addresses a message to a recipient in that domain, the sending server looks up the target domain in DNS. It retrieves the MX record for that domain, and then performs a second DNS query using the name in the MX record to retrieve the associated DNS address (A) record and, thus, the IP address of the target.

MX records follow a standardized format. Each record contains the target domain, the host name to which mail for that domain should be sent, and a preference. A domain can have multiple MX records associated with it. If multiple MX records exist, the sending server is supposed to pick the record with the lowest preference and try it first. If there are multiple records with the same preference, the sending server is required to randomly pick one of the records and try it first.

Here's what the MX records for the outlook.com domain look like:

```
outlook.com      MX preference = 10, mail exchanger = mx3.hotmail.com
outlook.com      MX preference = 10, mail exchanger = mx4.hotmail.com
outlook.com      MX preference = 10, mail exchanger = mx1.hotmail.com
outlook.com      MX preference = 10, mail exchanger = mx2.hotmail.com
```

Note, in this case, all four of the returned records point to different hosts, but they have equal preference values. A server that's sending four messages in sequence to Outlook.com users would be expected to randomly pick one of the four hosts for each message.

If you configure multiple MX records with the same preference, you should expect incoming mail to be evenly distributed across all IP addresses associated with those records. For example, if you follow the previous Outlook.com example and create four MX records with preference 10, ¼ of your mail should go to each of the identified hosts. This gives you a primitive form of load balancing. But, remember, other servers on the Internet have no idea what the state of your internal network is. If one of the hosts pointed to by your MX records goes down, other SMTP servers continue to use it in rotation, although a well-written server retries after a waiting period. When the server does retry, it gets a different MX record that should allow it to deliver the mail normally.

> **REAL WORLD USING BACKUP MXING TO ENSURE MAIL FLOW**
>
> Many organizations use a technique known as *backup MXing*, where the primary MX records (those with the lowest preference) point to the organization's server and a set of secondary records, all with a higher preference, point to a service that can accept, hold, and relay mail if the primary servers are unavailable. I once had a customer who wanted to use this technique, but who accidentally reversed the preference numbers, so mail first went to their backup MX service, and only after that to their on-premises servers. The messaging team didn't have the ability to modify their DNS records, so this took some time to correct.; in the meantime, incoming email was delayed by a few minutes because the backup MXing service didn't instantly deliver messages it received.

Thought experiment

Planning for high transport availability

In this Thought experiment, apply what you have learned about this objective. You can find answers to these questions in the "Answers" section at the end of this chapter.

You are an Exchange administrator for Fabrikam, Inc. Fabrikam's automated order processing system routes mail through Exchange to send customer notifications, record support requests, and perform other similar tasks. You want to minimize the chances that an inbound customer mail will ever be lost or inadvertently rejected.

1. What are some of the issues you should consider when planning Fabrikam's inbound email infrastructure?

2. What are some steps you might include in the test plans for your deployment to verify that email delivery works properly?

Objective summary

- Shadow redundancy is designed to protect messages from losses that occur after a message has been delivered to the next hop. If the next-hop server fails, its replacement can request a new copy of the message from a shadow redundancy queue. There are primary and secondary shadow redundancy queues.

- Safety Net is designed to protect messages after they've been delivered to the active database copy containing the recipient's mailbox, but before that database has been replicated to all passive copies. Any passive copy of a database can request message replay from the primary or secondary Safety Net servers.

- Redundant MX records provide a simple but limited way to distribute inbound SMTP traffic across multiple servers. If the server pointed to by a particular MX record fails, servers that receive that MX record have to retry sending mail.

Objective review

Answer the following questions to test your knowledge of the information in this objective. You can find the answers to these questions and explanations of why each answer choice is correct or incorrect in the "Answers" section at the end of this chapter.

1. In an Exchange environment that contains a single two-node DAG, if one node fails, which of the following statements is true? (Choose all that apply.)

   A. Shadow redundancy will not preserve a copy of any messages sent.

   B. Shadow redundancy will preserve a copy of all messages sent.

    C. Shadow redundancy will preserve copies of any messages received from the Internet, but not messages from internal users.

    D. Shadow redundancy will only preserve copies of messages from internal users, but not messages from the Internet.

2. Your Exchange environment has two Internet-facing Exchange member servers, EX01 and EX02. You create two MX records for your domain and point one of them at the public IP of each server. However, you notice that no mail is flowing from the Internet to EX02. Which of the following is a possible cause?

    A. There are no user mailboxes on EX02.

    B. EX02 isn't configured for shadow redundancy.

    C. The preference in the MX record for EX02 is incorrect.

    D. EX02 cannot accept mail because it isn't part of a DAG.

Objective 3.2: Design a transport solution

Designing a transport solution is mostly about determining how you want messages to flow to and from the organization's servers, and then building a design that makes that flow possible. Exchange has sophisticated tools for routing messages efficiently in networks of all sizes.

> **This objective covers how to:**
> - Design inter-site mail flow
> - Design inter-org mail flow
> - Plan for Domain Secure/TLS
> - Design Edge transport
> - Design message hygiene solutions
> - Design shared namespace scenarios

Design inter-site mail flow

Because the Active Directory site is one of the primary items Exchange uses when deciding how messages will be routed, a thorough understanding of mail flow between sites depends on knowing how Exchange uses Active Directory sites to make routing decisions.

    The biggest thing to know about message routing in Exchange 2013 is this: an Exchange 2013 server always tries to connect to the target delivery group directly unless you have created a hub site. When you create a hub site, all mail will flow through servers in the Active Directory site if it's on the least cost path. If the source server can't, or isn't allowed to, establish a direct connection to the target delivery group, it will attempt to route the message using least-cost routing. Finding the least-cost route seems like a simple enough task, but a number of nuances in the process make it more complex, especially if the Active Directory administrators haven't paid much attention to site link costs. The process Exchange uses works like this.

1. Find the lowest-cost route to the destination by adding up the IP site link costs along each possible path. If the ExchangeCost value is set for an IP site link object, that cost is used. Otherwise, the normal IP site link cost value is used.

2. Sort the possible paths by cost, lowest cost first. The lowest overall path cost is the preferred route.

3. If there are multiple paths with the same cost, choose the one with the fewest number of hops.

4. If there are multiple paths with the same cost and the same number of hops, choose the path whose site name comes first in alphabetical order.

5. Determine whether a hub site exists. If so, mark it as the next hop for the message. If not, set the next hop to be the target delivery group.

6. If the message is addressed to multiple recipients, repeat steps 1 and 2 for each additional recipient. Then, compare the resulting paths to see whether there is a site in common with previous recipients. If so, mark that site as the next hop.

7. Try to deliver the message directly to the next hop.

If a direct connection to the next hop fails, and the message is not being delivered to a DAG, Exchange performs an operation known as *queuing to the point of failure*. Messages queue at the closest reachable site to the destination. Exchange determines this by reversing the least-cost routing path to find the delivery group closest to the destination. If no servers outside the home site can be contacted (normally due to a network outage), the message is queued on the server that currently has it. The message is then retried every minute until it is delivered or it expires from the queue after two days. (This one-minute interval is configurable with the TransientFailureRetryInterval parameter to Set-TransportService).

EXAM TIP

The clunky design of the Microsoft exam application means that, for case study questions, you'll often have to flip between tabs to refer to the textual description of the network while answering questions. Use the provided scratch board to draw a quick diagram that shows the Active Directory site and Exchange server topology and use it for reference instead. That way, you can annotate the diagram to make things easier.

When delivering to a mailbox that's stored in a DAG, Exchange tries to deliver the message to any DAG member on any Active Directory site that isn't the least-cost site. If those attempts all fail, it performs queuing to the point of failure.

It's important to know that least-cost routing happens repeatedly, not just once when the message is originally sent. Every time a message passes through a Mailbox server, its onward routing will be recalculated, so it may change.

Managing Active Directory site link costs

Because Active Directory site membership is such an important part of routing, you might find that you want to adjust the Active Directory topology in your organization to control how messages flow. Each Exchange server is assigned automatically to an Active Directory site based on the server's assigned IP address. If you want to change the topology, you would normally do it by splitting or consolidating Active Directory sites. But making site changes may also require you to add or move domain controllers and global catalog servers, which is often impossible. If you can't change the site topology, you still have two options. The first option is to adjust the Active Directory site link costs directly. However, doing this also affects Active Directory replication because that process relies heavily on site link costs. A better option is to set an Exchange-specific site link cost that Exchange uses for making routing decisions, but that Active Directory ignores. To do this, use the Set-ADSiteLink cmdlet with the ExchangeCost parameter. For example, to assign an Exchange cost of 10 to the Huntsville-Alexandria site link, you would use a command like this:

```
Set-ADSiteLink -Identity 'Huntsville-Alexandria' -ExchangeCost 10
```

When you set an Exchange-specific link cost, the Transport service immediately begins to use the new cost in its least-cost routing calculations. Adding or changing an Exchange-specific cost for a site link has no effect on Active Directory replication in any way.

Hub sites

Many messaging deployments were designed around hub-and-spoke networks in the days when wide area networking was expensive and unreliable. This is a less-popular design option today now that bandwidth is much more plentiful and much less expensive. Many companies are exploiting cheap bandwidth to centralize the delivery of IT services and applications in very large data centers. This centralization often reintroduces elements of hub and spoke routing. The data center is the hub and hosts the vast majority of computing resources; the spokes are branch offices or other facilities supporting users who cannot connect to the center to use IT services for whatever reason. Other instances occur when a firewall separates two parts of a company, each of which has its own Active Directory site, and all communications have to be channeled through a hub site between them.

The Set-ADSite cmdlet is used to mark an Active Directory site as a hub site. For example, this command marks the Huntsville Active Directory site as a hub site:

```
Set-ADSite -Identity 'Huntsville' -HubSiteEnabled $True
```

Design inter-org mail flow

The first two things you should be thinking of when you design inter-organization mail flow are simple: what domains will Exchange accept mail for, and what domains will Exchange send mail to? The third thing is slightly more complicated: do you need any rules to control message processing and, if so, what are they?

Accepted domains

Accepted domains specify the set of domains for which Exchange accepts mail. Your Exchange organization has a single accepted domain when you set it up: the FQDN of the forest root domain. You can add more domains at any time. Remember, accepted domains are global to the Exchange organization. So, when you change the set of accepted domains, that change propagates to all your servers, including subscribed Edge Transport servers.

There are three types of accepted domains: authoritative, internal relay, and external relay. The last two types get their names because they depend on SMTP relay behavior, where Exchange accepts mail for a domain that isn't necessarily part of the organization, and then sends it to the correct server. This is the same mechanism used for open relaying, but configuring internal or external relay domains doesn't provide open relaying, so it avoids the security and message hygiene hassles that come from operating an open relay.

AUTHORITATIVE DOMAINS

Authoritative domains are domains for which Exchange hosts mailboxes. In other words, if an Exchange server is directly delivering mail for contoso.com to local mailboxes, then contoso.com would be considered an authoritative domain for that organization. You need to create one authoritative accepted domain for each SMTP domain name you want to use to receive mail. For example, if Woodgrove Bank wanted to receive mail at woodgrovebank.com, woodgrovebankforyou.com, and woodgrovebankisawesome.com, Woodgrove's Exchange administrators would need to create MX records for each of those domains. Then, they would add them as authoritative accepted domains in Exchange, and then add email address policies to assign addresses for the accepted domains as appropriate.

INTERNAL RELAY DOMAINS

Internal relay domains are domains for which Exchange accepts mail for delivery within the same organization even if some, or all, of the recipients in that domain don't have mailboxes in the Exchange organization. For example, consider the very common case of a university where all incoming mail flows to the Exchange organization, but where individual departments may have their own separate Linux-based email systems. Figure 3-5 shows an example for Bellows College. Each of the accepted domains in the *bellowscollege.com* namespace is routed to either the Exchange organization or a separate server, but all of that mail initially passes through Exchange as an internal relay domain.

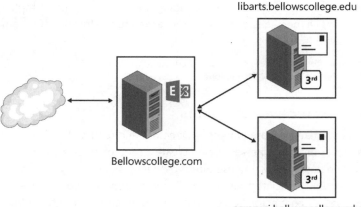

FIGURE 3-5 Internal relay domains pass through Exchange on their way to their destination domains

EXTERNAL RELAY DOMAINS

An external relay domain is what most administrators think of when they hear the words "SMTP relay": an external domain for which your Exchange organization accepts and forwards mail, without storing any of it in local Exchange mailboxes. For example, consider the organization shown in Figure 3-6 for Litware, a multinational firm formed by the merger of two smaller companies, one of which still maintains an IBM Lotus Domino environment. In this configuration, the proseware.com domain is an external relay domain for the litware.com Exchange organization.

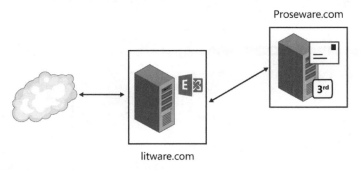

FIGURE 3-6 External relay domains

Remote domains

Remote domains are the set of domains that Exchange can send mail to. Think of them as the counterpart to accepted domains. By default, only one remote domain— "*"— matches any domain. You can define remote domains to control message format and message transport behavior to specific domains. For example, you might want to require that all messages sent to a particular domain be sent in plain text. Or, you might want to block out-of-office messages or non-delivery reports (NDRs) when sent to a particular domain. Exchange 2013 includes the *-RemoteDomain family of cmdlets for managing these settings. For example, if you want to prevent out-of-office messages from being forwarded to the fourthcoffee.com domain, you'd do it like this:

```
New-RemoteDomain -DomainName fourthcoffee.com -Name FourthCoffee
Set-RemoteDomain FourthCoffee -AllowedOOFType None
```

Understanding send and receive connectors

Connectors are logical objects that are stored in Active Directory and read by the Transport services. Think of *connectors* as pipes for messages: you create a send or receive connector to make messages take a certain path, just as you use pipes to direct water where you want it to go. Connectors aren't necessarily associated with a specific server, although you can restrict which servers can use a particular connector. You can manage connectors through the Mail Flow slab in the Exchange Admin Center (EAC) (see Figure 3-7) or with EMS. Note, many connector options can only be set in EMS, so you should be comfortable choosing the appropriate parameters and cmdlets to configure a connector in a certain way.

FIGURE 3-7 Managing send and receive connectors in the Mail Flow section of EAC

Exchange 2013 has two primary types of connectors: *send connectors* and *receive connectors*. Their names tell you exactly what they do, but there are some critical nuances you need to understand.

SEND CONNECTORS

Send connectors transmit outbound mail. When you create a send connector, its definition is stored in Active Directory, so send connectors may be used by any Mailbox server in the organization. The most obvious use for a send connector is to send mail out to the Internet. This requires you to create a new connector specifically for Internet delivery. However, you can create send connectors that route to any specific SMTP domain (or set of domains). The set of domains that a send connector can talk to is known as its *address space*. The address space for a connector can consist of the wildcard "*", which indicates it can send to anywhere, to a single SMTP domain, or to a domains whose names are made of a pattern combining the wildcard with a domain name. Exchange uses the most specific address space it can find when deciding what connector to use. Figure 3-8 shows an example with three send connectors, each with its own address space. Given this topology, the path a message takes depends on its recipient address:

- A message to dana@fourthcoffee.com uses the FourthCoffee connector because the SMTP address exactly matches the address space of the connector.

- A message sent to david@fineartschool.net uses the Education connector because its address space of *.edu is a closer match than the default.

- A message sent to accounting@fabrikam.com uses the Default Internet connector. No exact or partial match exists for "fabrikam.com", so the wildcard address space on that connector is "*", the only available match.

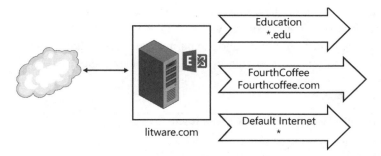

FIGURE 3-8 A single Exchange organization can have multiple send connectors with different address spaces

Exchange 2013 doesn't create any send connectors by default, so you need to create one before a newly created Exchange 2013 organization is able to send messages outside the organization. When you create a new send connector, you specify both the address space and a cost. If there is more than one connector whose address space matches the recipient address, Exchange chooses the one with the lowest cost. This can occasionally lead to unexpected behavior if you forget the cost factor because a distant connector with a lower cost is preferred over a closer one with a higher cost.

Send connectors also have a *type* that indicates the connector's intended purpose. You specify whether you want the connector to be used for sending messages within the Exchange organization, to the Internet, to specified partner domains, or for custom uses. Each of these types has a flag that goes with the Usage parameter to New-SendConnector.

Send connectors can deliver messages using two different schemes to find the target server: the connector can either look up the MX record for the target domain and send directly to it, or it can pass all messages for the connector to a single specified *smart host*. Not all connector usages support both of these methods. Generally, you would use smart hosting if you wanted to centralize all message flow to a particular server, and you would use MX delivery to improve the efficiency of delivery by allowing direct delivery to the target.

RECEIVE CONNECTORS

Each receive connector listens on the specific IP address and port you assign it, decides whether an incoming connection is from the range of IP addresses it's allowed to communicate with, and handles SMTP traffic when the connection is established. When you install Exchange 2013 on a server, you get up to five receive connectors installed by default, depending on whether you install both the Mailbox and CAS roles on the same server. The Default Frontend *ServerName* connector listens on the server's IP addresses on TCP port 25, so this is the connector that handles most normal traffic. There are also connectors for client connections (both proxy and direct) and a server-to-server connector that listens on TCP port 2525.

Receive connectors have permission groups associated with them. The *transport engine* checks the sender's permission to verify whether the sender is allowed to use the connector. Although they are implemented differently, Exchange permission groups (see Table 3-2 for an example) work similarly to Active Directory security groups: the group members are granted specific permissions by virtue of being included in the group. For a complete list of all the permission groups, and the permissions each includes, see TechNet at *http://technet.microsoft.com/en-us/library/jj673053(v=exchg.150).aspx*.

TABLE 3-2 Permission groups used for connectors

Permission Group	Security Principal	Included Permissions
AnonymousUsers	Anonymous User Account	Ms-Exch-SMTP-Submit Ms-Exch-SMTP-Accept-Any-Sender MS-Exch-SMTP-Accept-Authoritative-Domain-Sender Ms-Exch-Accept-Headers-Routing
ExchangeUsers	Authenticated User Accounts	Ms-Exch-SMTP-Submit Ms-Exch-SMTP-Accept-Any-Recipient Ms-Exch-Bypass-Anti-Spam Ms-Exch-Accept-Headers-Routing

Understanding transport rules

Transport rules are a flexible and useful tool for managing message flow in and out of Exchange. These rules enable you to specify conditions that, when met, allow a rule to take some action on a message. Rules can change the destination or addressing of messages, modify their contents, or take a number of other predefined actions. You can also specify exception conditions that, if met, exempt a given message from a rule.

The Exchange transport rule engine is often used to make sure messages comply with company policies or legal regulations. When you create or change a transport rule, its definition is stored in Active Directory and is used by every Mailbox server in the organization. So, you can create a rule once and know it will immediately take effect throughout the organization.

All *transport rules* share a basic structure and are composed of three parts: *conditions*, *actions*, and *exceptions*. When you create a new rule with EAC, its Rule Creation Wizard leads you through specifying each of these three items:

- The *conditions* of a rule tell the Transport service what criteria to use when deciding whether a message matches the rule. For example, Apply This Rule To All Outgoing Messages or Apply This Rule To Members Of A Specific Distribution Group. Each condition contains one or more *predicates, which are* similar to search terms. Table 3-3 contains a partial list of predicates available in Exchange 2013 SP1. (For the complete list of predicates, see *http://technet.microsoft.com/en-US/library/dd638183(v=exchg.150).aspx*.)

- The *actions* of the rule specify what the rule does when it's triggered by a message that matches its conditions. Actions can modify the message or its properties, or they can take some action, such as forwarding the message for moderation or dropping it and returning an NDR to the sender. (For the current list of actions available in Exchange 2013 transport rules, see *http://technet.microsoft.com/en-US/library/aa998315(v=exchg.150).aspx*.)

- *Exceptions* override conditions. For example, don't apply the rule if the sender is in a specified distribution group.

TABLE 3-3 Some of the Exchange 2013 transport rule predicates you can use

Predicate type	Predicates
Identify the sender	From a specific person From a member of a distribution list From users inside or outside the organization From a sender with a specific value in an Active Directory property From a sender in a specified range of IP addresses
Identify the recipient	When a recipient is a specific person (To, Cc, or Bcc) When any of the recipients is a member of a distribution list (To, Cc, or Bcc) When the recipient is inside or outside the organization or in a partner domain When a message is sent from one distribution list to another When a recipient has a specific value in an Active Directory property
Message characteristic	When the message has an attachment with a size greater than or equal to a limit When the message is marked with a specific importance When the message is a specific type When the message has a spam confidence level (SCL) that is greater than or equal to a limit When the message is marked with a specific classification When the message subject contains specific words When a message's attachment contains specific words When a message has an attachment that contains executable content

Apart from naming the rule and perhaps providing some comments so other administrators know why the rule was created and what it's supposed to do, all you need to do is answer three simple questions to create a rule. When should the rule be triggered (conditions)? When should it *not* be triggered (exceptions)? What should it do when triggered (actions)?

When you deploy the first Exchange 2013 server in an existing Exchange organization, any transport rules you've developed for Exchange 2007 and Exchange 2010 continues to work with Exchange 2013 because Exchange 2013 clones them, and then uses the clones. This cloning means you have two sets of transport rules stored in two different Active Directory objects. Changes you make to the original rules won't be honored by Exchange 2013. However, these older transport rules are very much a subset of the enhanced rules you can deploy with Exchange 2013. Upgrades such as the capability to make decisions about email processing based on Active Directory attributes for both senders and recipients make transport rules more powerful and flexible.

You can create your own rules in EAC or EMS. EMS gives you a great deal of control, but it's a little harder to figure out (and then type in) the exact syntax required for complex rules. EAC includes 10 predefined rule templates that you can use to set up common rules quickly, such as a rule to filter messages based on size or to apply disclaimers. You access the EAC rule creation interface through the Mail Flow section of EAC. If these predefined rule templates don't do what you want, you can use the Create A New Rule option to create a new blank rule that you can customize, or you can use the New-TransportRule and Set-TransportRule cmdlets in EMS to build the rules.

Transport rules are applied to messages by the transport rules agent after the full recipient list for the message is determined. The transport rules agent applies rules to every message from an anonymous sender, meaning that rules always apply to email received from the Internet. Rules also apply to messages originated by authenticated senders, of course, but depending on the type of message, the actual behavior of the agent might vary. For example, rules that require inspecting the content of a message or attachment can't be applied to messages encrypted with S/MIME, although messages protected with Active Directory Rights Management Services (AD RMS) may still be processed normally by the same rules.

Here's how Exchange processes rules when applying them to a message:

1. The message is passed to the transport rule agent. The agent checks the message type to see whether transport rules can be applied to the message. If not, the message is ignored.

2. The rule with the lowest priority is retrieved and evaluated. If the rule is active (meaning if activation and deactivation dates are set on the rule that the current date falls between them), evaluation continues.

3. If the rule has no conditions or exceptions, it's immediately applied. Otherwise:

   A. If the rule has one or more conditions, the conditions are evaluated to see whether the message matches. If there are multiple conditions, the message must match all of them. If a condition contains multiple values, any match of the condition applies. For example, a rule with a condition of The Recipient Is and values of Paul Robichaux or Bhargav Shukla will match any message when the recipient is either of those values.

B. If the rule has a matching condition, and one or more exceptions are defined, the exceptions are evaluated. If *any* part of *any* exception matches, the rule won't be applied to the message.

4. If the result of step 2 indicates the message should be processed by the rule, all the rule's actions are applied in the order in which they appear in the rule. Note, some actions might cause rule processing to stop. For example, if you delete the message, no further rules can process it.

5. The priority is incremented, and the process returns to step 2. When there are no more rules, processing stops and the message moves on.

Understanding data loss prevention rules

Exchange 2013 introduced an engine for applying data loss prevention (DLP) rules. *DLP rules* are intended to reduce the risk that a user or process will send out messages that contain sensitive information. You can configure DLP to block, report, or quarantine messages whose content matches a different set of sensitivity rules. Normally, you'd choose to deploy DLP rules when you want to prevent certain types of information, such as US Social Security numbers (SSNs) or credit card numbers from being sent in email.

This engine is based on the transport rule engine. In fact, when you create a new DLP policy, you can see new transport rules appear. Although you can modify these rules, remember by doing so, you might accidentally disable some aspect of scanning required for compliance with a particular DLP policy, so be careful.

To deploy DLP rules, you'll apply *DLP policies*, which act in two ways. A *DLP policy* can use rules that block certain patterns of data (such as credit card numbers or social insurance numbers, such as US Social Security numbers (SSNs) or UK National Insurance numbers). Or, it can trigger Policy Tips that appear in Outlook 2013 or Outlook Web App when users compose messages or add attachments that might violate whatever DLP policies are in effect. Both of these mechanisms piggyback on existing parts of the Exchange infrastructure.

> **MORE INFO   DLP RULES AND TRANSPORT RULES**
>
> DLP policy rules are based on the transport rule system, and Policy Tips are similar in behavior and implementation to the MailTips feature described in Chapter 5, "Mailbox management," of *Microsoft Exchange Server 2013 Inside Out: Mailbox and High Availability*.

A DLP policy is an XML file containing a package of settings that specifies what types and items of data the policy is supposed to look for. When you activate a DLP policy, that policy creates new transport rules (and related settings) that look for the kinds of content the policy is supposed to monitor. Matching is handled by a portion of the Transport service that performs what Microsoft calls *deep content analysis*, which applies several analytical methods, including keyword matches, matching of terms against dictionaries, pattern matches, and specific tests for individual data item types. Microsoft gives the example of calculating a checksum on certain number patterns to see whether they match the checksum rules for credit card numbers. This analysis is performed on message bodies and attachments. If a match is found, the action associated with that particular rule is triggered.

Plan for Domain Secure and TLS

The basic SMTP specification doesn't provide for encryption of email. This capability was added later through the addition of a new SMTP verb known as STARTTLS, which gets its name in part from the Transport Layer Security (TLS) cryptographic protocol. TLS is a derivative of the familiar Secure Sockets Layer (SSL) protocol. Exchange supports TLS for protecting client connections, but it also supports it for server-to-server communications.

Exchange can be configured to use TLS in three basic ways. The first two modes provide only confidentiality (through encryption), not authentication:

- With *opportunistic TLS*, Exchange accepts a STARTTLS request if it receives one from another server, and it attempts to establish a TLS connection by sending STARTTLS. However, Exchange in opportunistic mode still talks to servers that don't support or cannot accept a TLS request. This mode is the default.

- With *forced TLS* mode, Exchange only communicates with SMTP servers that can initiate or accept a TLS connection. To configure this mode, you need to create appropriate connectors (inbound and/or outbound) and configure certificates for them to use.

In both of these modes, the two SMTP servers use TLS to encrypt their communications but, generally, neither side authenticates the other. Some TLS implementations verify the certificate chain of a server that establishes a TLS connection, but many (including Exchange) do not. Exchange doesn't perform this verification step because doing so would make it more difficult to use self-signed certificates for encryption. By default, every Exchange server creates its own set of self-signed SSL certificates at installation time and uses them automatically to encrypt SMTP communications to other Exchange servers.

In *mutual TLS* (MTLS) systems, when two hosts communicate, each host verifies the certificate chain for the other host's certificate. This allows a server to ensure the other server's identity by verifying that its certificate is valid and unrevoked. Microsoft uses the name *Domain Secure* to refer to mutual TLS in Exchange (although Lync Server supports MTLS also). After you have Domain Secure enabled and configured properly, when a user receives a message from a sender over a trusted connection that's protected by Domain Secure, they see a special green check-mark icon in Outlook 2010 and Outlook 2013, which indicates the message was received over a Domain Secure-protected connection.

EXAM TIP

The exam objectives for 70-341 refer to "Domain Secure." Some of the Exchange 2013 documentation (both from Microsoft and third parties) calls this feature "Domain Secure." But, in other places, the same thing is called "Domain Security." No matter which name you see, both refer to the same feature set.

To make Domain Secure work, you need to do the following:

1. Decide which SMTP domains you want to securely exchange mail with. You have to set up Domain Secure for individual domains. You can't use the "*" wildcard to enable it for multiple domains. You can send and accept Domain Secure mail to different domains, that is, you can accept Domain Secure mail from contoso.com while you send it to fabrikam.com.

2. Each Exchange mailbox server using Domain Secure needs a valid SSL certificate. In this case, "valid" means the certificate must be issued by a certification authority (CA), must not be expired, and must be within its validity date range. You can use the same certificate on multiple Exchange servers.

3. You must assign the certificate for use with SMTP using the Enable-ExchangeCertificate cmdlet on all the servers that will exchange mail with your target domains.

4. You must use the Set-TransportConfig cmdlet to specify the list of sending and receiving Domain Secure domains. To specify sending domains, use Set-TransportConfig -TLSSendDomainSecureList. To specify the receiving domains, use Set-TransportConfig -TLSReceiveDomainSecureList.

5. You must configure the send and/or receive connectors you want to use Domain Secure on to enable the use of TLS, as described in the section "Configuring send and receive connectors" later in the chapter.

6. No other devices can be in between the sending and receiving servers. For example, if your inbound mail arrives at a message hygiene appliance such as a Barracuda, or if your outbound mail goes from the Mailbox server to a Client Access Server for outbound processing, Domain Secure can't be applied to mail going over that connection.

> **REAL WORLD** **DOMAIN SECURE IS RARE**
>
> Domain Secure is a nifty feature, and its complexity means it's great fodder for test questions, but relatively few organizations use it. I've never had a customer deploy it. However, both opportunistic and forced SSL are increasingly common and you are very likely to encounter them in the wild.

Remember, for Domain Secure to work, each side must be able to trust the other side's certificate. Many larger organizations have their own internal CA, which they use to issue certificates for internal use. Unless a trust relationship exists between the sending and receiving organizations, Domain Secure won't work. For that reason, most organizations that deploy Domain Secure use certificates issued by public CAs, such as Symantec/Verisign or DigiCert.

Design message hygiene solutions

Message hygiene is critical for Exchange. Spammers and criminals flood the worldwide Internet with malware and junk, and you want to filter as much of it as possible before it reaches your users' mailboxes. Many Exchange administrators use the Microsoft Exchange Online Protection

(EOP) service because it's included as part of the Exchange enterprise client access license (CAL). Others prefer to use perimeter message hygiene servers from third parties, such as Barracuda Networks. Whether or not you use an external message hygiene filter, you need to know how the native message hygiene features of Exchange 2013 work and how to configure them.

What gets filtered where

In Exchange 2013, message hygiene filtering is handled by code agents known as transport agents. These agents are called as part of the transport pipeline. They can inspect messages and their contents, make decisions about whether the message should be accepted or rejected, and modify message contents and headers as necessary. A number of transport agents implement various Exchange features. Message hygiene is only one of the activities these agents carry out.

The transport agents involved with filtering may be present on a Mailbox or Edge Transport server. They are all installed and enabled by default on the Edge Transport role. On Mailbox servers, some are installed by default, some are available but not installed, and some are not available. Table 3-4 shows the transport filtering agents that Exchange uses, where they're installed, and what they do.

TABLE 3-4 Transport filtering agents

Available on	agent name	What it does
Edge only	Connection Filter	Accepts or rejects connections based on the originating server's IP address and whether it appears on any explicit safe or block lists, or on a real-time block list (RBL) if Exchange is configured to use one.
Edge Mailbox	Sender Filter	Accepts or rejects messages based on the sender name, without checking to see if it's valid.
Edge	Recipient Filter	Accepts or rejects messages based on the recipient. This filter can optionally be used to reject messages sent to nonexistent recipients in the domain, with or without generating an NDR.
Edge Mailbox	Sender ID	Filters messages using the Sender ID standard to try to determine whether or not the mail is really from the domain it claims to be from.
Edge Mailbox	Content Filter	Filters messages based on the content in them. You can block or accept messages by specifying words or phrases that should trigger the filter.
Edge Mailbox	Protocol Analysis	Filters by looking at a reputation score calculated by Microsoft according to the behavior associated with the sender's IP address range. For example, an IP address that's previously sent out large volumes of spam has a negative reputation score.
Edge Mailbox	Malware Filter	Filters messages by scanning for signatures of known malware.
Edge only	Attachment Filter	Filters messages based on the file name, extension, or MIME type of the message attachments. The filter can be configured to block messages and attachments, allow messages but strip attachments, or to silently delete the message without delivering it.

All of these agents have settings you can configure, either through EMS or EAC. Some of the filters can be disabled, while others (notably the Malware Filter) cannot. Worth noting is that the Sender ID agent relies on a type of DNS record, known as a *sender policy framework* (SPF) record, to cross-check the actual and purported domains for a message. By default, the Sender ID agent will "soft fail" messages that don't match. *Soft fail* means it flags them as more likely to be spam, but doesn't reject them outright. Be careful when you change the settings for this filter, as many legitimate senders don't have SPF records. Changing the Sender ID agent to "hard fail" (or reject) messages may cause you to reject legitimate mail. For more details on how Sender ID filtering works and how to configure it, see *http://technet.microsoft.com/en-us/ library/aa996295(v=exchg.150).aspx*.

Installing the filter agents on a mailbox server

To install the available filter agents on a Mailbox server, you need to run the Install-AntispamAgents.ps1 script in the Exchange Management Shell. This script installs and enables the Content Filter agent, Sender ID agent, Sender Filter agent, and Protocol Analysis agent on the target Mailbox server role. Microsoft recommends that you only install these agents if you're not using any type of upstream filtering, because the specific tests performed by these filters are more useful if they're performed at the network edge than when the message is being delivered.

To install the additional filter agents on the Mailbox server, first you run the Install-AntispamAgents.ps1 script from the Scripts directory on the target Mailbox server. You need to do this using an account that has administrative privileges. After the script completes, restart the Microsoft Exchange Transport service on the target server. Until you restart the service, the newly installed filters won't run.

Because the Sender ID agent won't be able to retrieve the appropriate SPF records coming from your internal SMTP servers, it will incorrectly flag messages coming for those servers. To avoid this problem, you must use the Set-TransportConfig -InternalSMTPServers cmdlet to tell Exchange what internal servers it can safely ignore. You should specify the IP addresses of any servers on your internal network that might send mail to Exchange, including copiers/scanners, application servers, and any other server that might send mail. The syntax for the InternalSMTPServers parameter might seem a little odd because it involves multivalued properties. You need to use it like this:

```
Set-TransportConfig -InternalSMTPServers @{Add="10.7.29.71", "10.0.2.14"}
```

Design Edge Transport

Microsoft shipped the Edge Server role for Exchange 2013 as part of Exchange 2013 Service Pack 1, but you might still run across questions or exam prep materials that refer to the Exchange 2010 Edge Server role. That's OK because little functional difference exists between the Exchange 2010 and Exchange 2013 versions. Both versions do the same thing, and you connect to and manage them the same way.

Microsoft recommends that the Edge Server role be installed on a stand-alone member server. So the Edge Server can perform the full range of message, content, and recipient filtering that it's capable of, it has to have some information about the groups and users who might send or receive mail through the Edge Server. This is accomplished by creating Edge subscriptions that push information from the internal Exchange servers to the Edge servers. However, the Edge server should be placed in your perimeter network, so it can filter mail before it reaches the internal network. In general, it's a bad idea to put domain member servers in the perimeter when you don't have to.

The Edge role uses a pared-down version of Active Directory, known as Active Directory Lightweight Directory Services (AD LDS). There's a collection of processes, which Microsoft refers to all together as "EdgeSync," which pull data from your Active Directory forest to a single Edge server. Although you can use multiple Edge servers in your network, they stand alone and don't share configuration settings or directory data. There is no automatic load balancing or distribution for the Edge role, although you can easily use round-robin DNS, redundant MX records, or hardware or software load-balancing devices to load balance inbound Edge traffic.

Edge connectivity

The Edge Transport role is meant to be installed in your perimeter network, so you need to configure your firewall to allow both Internet servers and your internal servers to communicate with it. This is simplified by the fact that your Edge servers will (or should) have two network adapters: one for the internal network and one for the external network. You should plan to allow SMTP traffic in and out, using TCP port 25, on both network adapters. You must also allow TCP port 50636 from the Edge Transport server to the internal network. This port is used to allow synchronization between your internal Mailbox servers and the Edge Transport server. You may also want to allow TCP port 3389 from your internal network to the Edge Transport server, so you can use the Remote Desktop Protocol to manage the Windows installation on the Edge server. All the Exchange-related settings you might need to manipulate on the Edge server can be changed with the Exchange Management Shell, so you might want to consider allowing remote PowerShell traffic on TCP port 443 from your internal network to the Edge server.

The Edge role also requires DNS connectivity: each Edge server needs to be able to resolve host names from the public Internet on the Internet-facing adapter. The network adapter connected to the internal network either needs to have access to your internal DNS servers or have a hosts file configured, so the Edge server can resolve the names of your Mailbox servers. In addition, your Mailbox servers need to be able to resolve the names of your Edge servers. This can be accomplished either by adding A records for the Edge servers to your internal DNS or updating the hosts file on each Mailbox server with entries for your Edge Transport machines.

Understanding Edge subscriptions

Each Edge server must have a subscription to pull data from your internal network. An Edge server is affiliated with a particular Active Directory site via this subscription. Mailbox servers within the site use the subscribed Edge Transport servers to send messages outwards, and an

Edge Transport server sends inbound messages to a mailbox server in its subscribed site. Each Edge Transport server can be associated with only one Active Directory site.

The Edge Transport server is said to subscribe to the internal servers, but the process for creating these subscriptions might seem to go in the opposite direction. To create a new Edge subscription, here's what you have to do:

1. Identify which Active Directory site the Edge server will be associated with.

2. Configure the Mailbox servers in that Active Directory site with the transport settings and connectors you want them to have.

3. On the Edge Transport server, create an Edge subscription file and export it using the New-EdgeSubscription command. This leaves you with a subscription file that you must transfer to a Mailbox server in the target site. The Edge Transport server creates a new Active Directory LDS account called the *EdgeSync bootstrap replication account* (ESBRA) with a 24-hour expiration time, and then writes the ESBRA credentials, along with the public key of the Edge Transport server's self-signed certificate, to the subscription file.

> **NOTE   DON'T DAWDLE WHEN CREATING THE SUBSCRIPTION**
>
> Because the ESBRA account has a lifetime of 24 hours, you must complete the Edge subscription process within 24 hours of performing this step or the synchronization will fail and you'll need to repeat it.

If the Edge Transport server had been subscribed before, its configuration objects will be deleted, and all of the New- and Set- cmdlets related to send connectors and remote and accepted domains are disabled on the Edge server. That's because you have to manage those objects from the Mailbox servers on the internal network.

After you create the subscription file and move it to a location accessible from a Mailbox server in the target site, you can use the New-EdgeSubscription cmdlet and provide the path to the subscription file you created.

When the Mailbox server imports the subscription file, a complex chain of events starts.

1. The Mailbox server where you run the New-EdgeSubscription cmdlet creates the edge subscription object in Active Directory. All Mailbox servers in an organization subscribe to the same Edge container in Active Directory, so they receive notification any time an Edge subscription is added or removed in their home site.

2. The Mailbox server pulls the ESBRA credentials from the subscription file, encrypts them using the Edge Transport server's public key, and stores them in Active Directory. This encryption ensures only that specific Edge Transport server can decrypt the credentials, because only that server's private key can decrypt data encrypted with the public key.

3. Each Mailbox server in the target site encrypts the ESBRA with its own public key and stores a copy in its own configuration object.

4. Each Mailbox server creates a new *EdgeSync replication account* (ESRA). There is one ESRA for each Mailbox-Edge Transport pair. The ESRA is encrypted and stored in Active Directory within the Mailbox server's configuration object and in the Edge Transport configuration object. (For details on exactly how this encryption works, see the TechNet topic "Edge Subscription Credentials" at *http://technet.microsoft.com/en-us/library/bb266959(v=exchg.150).aspx)*.

5. The Mailbox server creates new send connectors: one for the Edge Transport server to relay messages outbound, and one for the Edge Transport server to send messages inbound to the Mailbox server. (There's no need to create separate receive connectors because those are automatically generated by default when the Mailbox and Edge Transport servers are installed.)

6. The Mailbox server uses the ESBRA credentials to make an encrypted LDAP connection to the Edge Transport server and pushes topology, configuration, and recipient data into the Edge Active Directory LDS. This push includes the ESRA credentials for that specific mailbox server.

7. The Edge Transport server's Exchange Credential Service installs the ESRA credentials into the local machine credential store.

8. The EdgeSync service on the Edge Transport server sets up the synchronization schedule. By default, synchronization occurs at various intervals for different types of data, but you can use the Set-EdgeSyncServiceConfig cmdlet to change those intervals.

As soon as this setup process is complete, the Edge Transport server can start accepting messages for inbound and outbound processing.

Inbound traffic processing

The point of the Edge Transport role is to filter your inbound mail. Normally, you configure the MX records for your SMTP domains to point at the public IP address of your Edge Server, using redundant MX records and multiple Edge servers where appropriate for redundancy and load balancing. The Edge server receives inbound mail, filters it (as described earlier in the "What gets filtered where" section), and send it onwards. What "onwards" means in this context depends on the next hop you have configured for the Edge server. If you're sending mail from the Edge role to a server that has both the CAS and Mailbox roles installed, the Edge server will connect to the Front End Transport server on the target machine. If you're routing mail from the Edge role to a Mailbox server, then it goes directly to the Transport service on the target server.

The Edge role can also perform *address rewriting*, meaning that it can modify inbound addresses to match a particular format you specify. For more on address rewriting, see the section "Configuring address rewriting" later in the chapter.

Outbound traffic processing

By default, all the Exchange servers in your organization route outbound mail through your Edge Server computer. When you create a new send connector, that connector information is included in the data that's synchronized with the Edge server. The internal servers all send mail to the Edge with the expectation that the Edge server will send it on to its eventual destination. In some cases, you might need to manually create connectors on the Edge server as described later in the section "Configure Send/Receive connectors."

Message hygiene processing

The Edge server's primary job is filtering inbound and outbound messages. To do so, it applies the filters listed in Table 3-2. For filter agents that run both on the Edge role and your internal servers, the settings are shared through the Edge subscription mechanism. For example, when your users mark individual senders as safe or blocked senders, those markings are aggregated into a combined safelist, and that safelist is replicated through the subscription mechanism. So, once a user marks a particular sender as "safe," all subscribed Edge servers honor that marking.

Design shared namespace scenarios

One common requirement for large email systems is to support multiple address spaces. You've already seen how Exchange supports multiple accepted domains, so a single Exchange organziation can handle incoming mail, not only for the organization's primary SMTP domain, but also for additional subdomains or stand-alone domains. However, consider a typical large company, which probably has multiple business units, possibly in separate locations. Some of these business units may have been acquired or merged over time. For business or organizational reasons, some of these business units might have their own email systems that they want to keep. This type of environment requires the use of shared namespaces, where one or more SMTP domains are shared between multiple email systems.

> **REAL WORLD**   **A SIMPLE COMPLEX EXAMPLE**
>
> Some years ago, I worked as part of the team that migrated a multi-billion dollar financial services company to Exchange 2010. In Japan alone, they had seven business units with different SMTP domain names, three of which had their own completely separate Exchange or Lotus Notes environments. Their US and EMEA environments were just as complex. We ended up with several dozen accepted domains, split pretty evenly between authoritative, internal relay, and external relay domains, and a heavy set of address rewriting rules to make sure that firstname.lastname@company.com would work for every user, no matter what country/region, business unit, or email system hosted their mailbox.

The process for designing a shared namespace is fairly simple.

1. Identify the SMTP domains you want to share. If you run the Get-AcceptedDomain cmdlet, you may see these domains listed as authoritative domains. If you don't see the domains listed at all and you need to add them, see the section "Configure accepted domains" later in the chapter. Don't forget to add or update MX records to your Internet-facing DNS server for any new domains you're going to accept mail for.

2. Decide how you want to assign addresses to users. For example, you might want to give every user a secondary proxy address, using a standardized name format and a single domain, no matter what their current address looks like. Then, v-probic@dogfood.contoso.com, danabirkby@us.contoso.com, and luis.bonifaz@contoso-latam.cl will all end up with the same firstname.lastname@contoso.com address format in addition to their existing address. If you prefer, you can make the newly assigned address the primary address instead.

3. Change the domain type of the target domains to either internal relay or external relay, depending on where the target mail will end up. Remember, internal relay domains are intended to route email received from Exchange to other systems inside the company, while external relay domains are for routing email from Exchange to external systems. You can make this change with the Set-AcceptedDomain -DomainType cmdlet.

4. Create one send connector for each of the target domains. For example, if you're setting up contosocanada.com, contosousa.com, and contoso-australia.com as accepted domains for the existing contoso.com domain, you'll want three new send connectors, one for each of the new domains.

5. Create email address policies to assign the correct domains to the correct users. For example, the users who work for Contoso Australia (and currently have addresses of @contoso-australia.com) need a new address policy that assigns them contoso.com addresses. Remember, the left-hand side of these addresses has to be unique. If you have a user named joe@contoso-australia.com and an existing joe@contoso.com address is assigned to another user, you have to manually tweak one of the user objects to eliminate the conflict.

6. Review the set of send and receive connectors you currently have, adding new connectors or changing existing ones as necessary.

If you're using recipient filtering, you have an additional step. You need to create contacts for any user in your SMTP namespace whose mailbox is on a non-Exchange system. Normally, any address in your accepted domains will be accepted, even if no mailbox exists for that address. Exchange will accept the message, relay it to the server for the target domain, and let that server return an NDR if the address is invalid. However, if recipient filtering is enabled, Exchange examines the target address, sees there is no Exchange mailbox with a matching proxy address, and rejects the message. To avoid this, each user in the remote system needs a contact where the contact address is the address you want Exchange to accept and the forwarding address is their real address on the remote system. For example, if you're using Exchange to share the adatum.com domain between Exchange and a Linux-based system that handles mail for *research.adatum.com*, a researcher named Steve needs a contact object where the primary address is steve@adatum.com and the forwarding address is *steve@research.adatum.com.*

Thought experiment
Planning for a migration from Linux

In this Thought experiment, apply what you have learned about this objective. You can find answers to these questions in the "Answers" section at the end of this chapter.

The Phone Company is moving from its existing Linux-based mail system to Exchange 2013 as part of a merger with Trey Research. The combined organization will use the treyresearch.com SMTP namespace. However, all users from The Phone Company need to continue receiving email at their existing @thephonecompany.com SMTP namespace during and after the migration to Exchange.

1. Describe the namespace design you'd recommend to meet these requirements.

2. How would you address the requirement to provide coexistence with the legacy Linux system during the migration?

Objective summary

- Exchange calculates routes according to their cost, and it always seeks the lowest-cost route for messages. Know the routing process to understand how a given message will flow.

- A DAG is treated as a delivery boundary. Exchange delivers a message for a mailbox hosted in a DAG to any server in the DAG, not only the server where the primary mailbox database copy is active.

- Exchange uses Active Directory site link costs to make routing decisions. You can use Set-ADSiteLink -ExchangeCost to apply Exchange-specific costs to use instead of the default costs.

- Accepted domains come in three types. Authoritative domains are domains that Exchange will accept mail for. Internal relay domains are those where Exchange shares the domain with an external system. And external relay domains are those where Exchange sends mail to an external system.

- All mail flows into and out of Exchange over connectors. Send connectors handle outbound traffic, and receive connectors handle inbound traffic. They don't have to be linked.

- Send connectors have address spaces that control which messages can travel over them. The connector with the most specific address space is used to send messages to a target domain.

- Transport rules can modify or inspect messages and attachments based on conditions you set. You can specify exceptions to those conditions.
- Exchange will try to use opportunistic TLS to encrypt SMTP connections. You can force the use of TLS on connectors.
- You can set up Domain Security so all messages to and from specific domains are encrypted and the connection itself is authenticated. This requires you to set the list of send and receive Domain Security domains using Set-TransportConfig, configure the connectors to take part in Domain Security, and ensure you have valid certificates correctly installed.
- Message hygiene filtering is performed by transport agents that run on the Mailbox and Edge Transport roles. The Connection Filter, Recipient Filter, and Attachment Filter agents only run on the Edge role.
- Edge Transport servers require subscriptions that synchronize their settings (including connectors and recipient data) with Mailbox servers in a specific Active Directory site.
- You can set up shared namespaces that split a set of SMTP domains between Exchange and foreign systems.

Objective review

Answer the following questions to test your knowledge of the information in this objective. You can find the answers to these questions and explanations of why each answer choice is correct or incorrect in the "Answers" section at the end of this chapter.

1. You have an Exchange infrastructure with three sites: SiteA, SiteB, and SiteC. You want to ensure that all mail is routed through the servers in SiteB. To accomplish this, you should:

    A. Set SiteB as a hub site using Active Directory Domains and Trusts.

    B. Set SiteB as a hub site using Set-ADSite SiteB -HubSiteEnabled $true.

    C. Add an Exchange hybrid server in SiteB.

    D. Set SiteA and SiteC as leaf sites using Set-ADSite sitename -LeafSiteEnabled $true.

2. You want to install the message hygiene filtering agents on a mailbox server named CD3-EX14. You would do this by:

    A. Copying the transport agent files from the Exchange install media to the $ExScripts directory on CD3-EX14.

    B. Running the Exchange setup tool with the /installhygieneagents switch.

    C. Running the command Set-TransportConfig -Server CD3-EX14 -HygieneFilters $true.

    D. Running the install-antispamagents.ps1 script on CD3-EX14.

3. To reduce the number of servers required on your network, an outside consultant has proposed removing the existing Edge Transport servers and configuring filtering on the Mailbox servers instead. Which types of filtering capabilities will you lose by doing this? (Choose all that apply.)

   A. Connection filtering.

   B. Attachment filtering.

   C. Content filtering.

   D. Sender ID filtering.

   E. Sender reputation filtering.

4. You run the Exchange organization for Litware, Inc. You want to configure Domain Security for mail exchanged with your business partner, Proseware. Which of the following steps are required? (Choose all that apply.)

   A. Set-TransportConfig -TLSSendDomainSecureList litware.com.

   B. Set-TransportConfig -TLSReceiveDomainSecureList proseware.com.

   C. Create a send connector for the proseware.com address space and enable TLS and Domain Security on it.

   D. Create a receive connector for litware.com and enable TLS and Domain Security on it.

   E. Request a new certificate for each user who will use the Domain Secure connection.

Objective 3.3: Configure and manage transport

The Exchange transport system has many different settings you can adjust, but Microsoft has designed its default behavior to handle the most common cases of mail transport. You want inbound and outbound mail to travel as efficiently as possible, with good security and effective logging, so you can quickly identify and fix problems.

After this lesson, you should be able to manage the major aspects of configuring and managing the Exchange transport system in your organization, including the following topics.

This objective covers how to:

- Configure Edge servers
- Configure Send/Receive connectors
- Configure transport rules
- Configure accepted domains
- Configure email policies
- Configure address rewriting

Configuring Edge servers

Much of the configuration that Edge servers need comes through the subscription mechanism. However, there are a number of specific tasksyou need to know how to perform on the Edge servers themselves, including creating and removing subscriptions, cloning configurations between Edge servers, and changing the settings for subscription updates.

Adding and removing Edge Transport servers

When you add a new Edge Transport server to your organization, the process you follow depends on how you want the new server to be configured. You might find yourself in three basic situations: you're installing the first Edge server in an organization, you're installing an additional Edge server and you want it to have the same settings as another existing server, or you're installing another Edge server and you want it to have unique settings.

INSTALLING YOUR FIRST EDGE SERVER

In the first case, you install the Edge Transport server role using the Exchange setup utility, and then do the following:

1. Run the New-EdgeSubscription cmdlet on the Edge server, specifying the path where you want the file to be stored, like this:

   ```
   New-EdgeSubscription -FileName "j:\HSVEDGE04-subscription.xml"
   ```

2. Move or copy the subscription file to someplace accessible to a Mailbox server in the target Active Directory site. (Remember, when you create a subscription, it applies to all the Mailbox servers in an Active Directory site.)

3. On the Mailbox server, run the New-EdgeSubscription cmdlet. You have to read the file data into a byte stream, and then pass that stream to the cmdlet, along with the name of the Active Directory site you're creating the subscription for. Here's an example:

   ```
   [byte[]]$subFile= Get-Content -Path "p:\HSVEDGE04-subscription.xml" -Encoding Byte
   -ReadCount 0
   New-EdgeSubscription -FileData $subFile -Site "Huntsville-West"
   ```

   After you create the subscription on the Edge server, the first synchronization pass copies recipient, connector, and configuration data from the Mailbox server to the Edge Transport server. Remember, a separate synchronization relationship exists between each Mailbox server in the subscribed site and the Edge server. The Edge Transport machine doesn't care which mailbox server in the site it talks to at any given synchronization.

ADDING MORE EDGE SERVERS

If you want to add more Edge Transport servers, you have a couple of choices: you can create each server and configure it individually, or you can clone the configuration of an existing Edge Transport server and apply it to the newly installed server. Cloning the server is much simpler and less error-prone than manually configuring additional servers. The cloning process requires five basic steps (not including copying the import and export scripts from a Mailbox server to the Edge Transport server).

1. Run the ExportEdgeConfig.ps1 script on the existing Edge server you want to clone. You specify a single argument, the path to an XML output file known as the *intermediate XML* file. This file contains information from the source server, including the number, type, and configuration of connectors, the paths used for log files, and the list of accepted and remote domains.

   ```
   .\ExportEdgeConfig.ps1 -CloneConfigData:"j:\HSVEDGE01.xml"
   ```

2. Copy the intermediate XML file to the target server, which should already have the Edge Transport role installed. Then run the ImportEdgeConfig.ps1 script, specifying the name and path of the intermediate XML file along with the **-IsImport:$false** switch. That switch tells the script you want to validate the intermediate XML and use it to produce an answer file that the script can use to complete the import. The validation process replaces some information specific to the original server with blanks in the answer file, so you can customize the answers. For example, the IP addresses on which receive connectors listen will be replaced with a blank line that you need to edit.

   ```
   ./ImportEdgeConfig.ps1 -CloneConfigData:"j:\hsvedge01.xml" -IsImport $false
   -CloneConfigAnswer:"c:\temp\hsvedge02-answer.xml"
   ```

3. Edit the answer file, completing any items that were removed during the previous step. You might not have any blank or invalid entries but, if you do, you need to fix them.

4. Run the ImportEdgeConfig.ps1 script again, this time specifying -**IsImport $true** and providing the path to the answer file. The script reads data from the answer file and uses it to configure the cloned copy of the server. If you left any incomplete items in the answer file, this step will fail and you'll need to repeat step 3 to get a clean configuration

   ```
   ./ImportEdgeConfig.ps1 -CloneConfigData:"j:\hsvedge01.xml" -IsImport $true
   -CloneConfigAnswer:"c:\temp\hsvedge02-answer.xml"
   ```

5. Create a new EdgeSync subscription from the newly cloned server. Existing subscriptions aren't copied as part of the cloning process because the certificates and credentials required for the EdgeSync ESBRA and ESRA accounts can't be cloned. When you create the new subscription, any items that are part of the subscription overwrite items configured by the cloning process.

Managing EdgeSync

The EdgeSync process is intended to be completely automatic. Configuration data is synchronized every three minutes, while recipient and topology data are synchronized every five minutes. These are the maximum intervals that can pass between synchronizations, so sync operations may happen at a shorter interval. You can force a new sync at any time using the Start-EdgeSynchronization cmdlet. This triggers an immediate update of the recipient, configuration, and topology data for all Edge servers in the organization. If you want to resynchronize only a single server, specify it with the TargetServer parameter. When you run Start-EdgeSynchronization, the targeted server (or servers) only synchronize changes that have occurred since the last synchronization. If you want to force a complete resyc, you can do so by adding the -ForceFullSync switch. Here's an example:

```
Start-EdgeSynchronization -ForceFullSync -TargetServer HSVEDGE03
```

Sometimes you may want to change the frequency or timing of synchronization without necessarily starting a new sync immediately. You can do that with the Set-EdgeSyncServiceConfig cmdlet and its ConfigurationSyncInterval and RecipientSyncInterval cmdlets. For example, to set both of these intervals to sync every eight hours, you'd use the following:

```
Set-EdgeSyncServiceConfig -ConfigurationSyncInterval 00.8:00:00 -RecipientSyncInterval
00.8:00:00
```

The intervals you specify apply to all Edge Transport servers. Currently, there's no way to set a different synchronization interval for an individual server.

Configuring Send and Receive connectors

Exchange 2013 lets you create and manage Send and Receive connectors in two ways: through the Exchange Admin Center or through the Exchange Management Shell. In general, it's a good idea to know how to do common tasks using either method, although many options can only be controlled or viewed through EMS. EAC doesn't implement the full set of connector options yet.

Creating and configuring Send connectors

The basic process of creating a new send connector requires four steps.

1. Give the connector a name and choose a type (Figure 3-9). You can choose to create a connector to be used for custom applications, to send mail to servers within your organization, to send mail to the Internet, or to send mail to trusted external domains such as business partners.

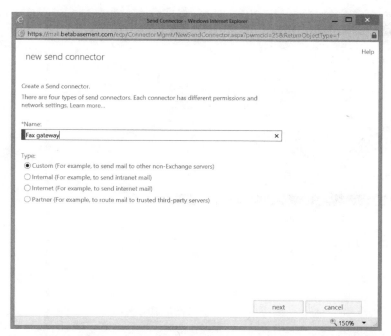

FIGURE 3-9 Creating a new send connector gives you four choices for the connector's intended use

2. Specify whether you want it to pass mail through a single smart host or to deliver mail by performing Domain Name System (DNS) MX record \lookups. Depending on the connector type you chose in the first step, you might not be able to enable smart host delivery. If you enable smart host delivery, you are asked to specify what kind of authentication mechanism to use when Exchange connects to the smart host. You might have an SMTP server set up as an open relay for general use within the company, in which case, you won't have to use authentication. Or, you might have to provide a username and password for basic authentication. The smart host can be another Exchange server. If this is the case, you'd use Exchange Server Authentication. Or, it might support IPsec for encrypted communication between the two servers.

Along with the choice of whether to use smart host or direct MX delivery is a new option, Use The External DNS Lookup Settings On Servers With Transport Roles, which appears on the second page of the New Send Connector process (see Figure 3-10). This check box controls whether Exchange uses the specific DNS settings associated with its source servers (as described later in this section) or the Windows-provided DNS servers configured on the server's network interface cards (NICs).

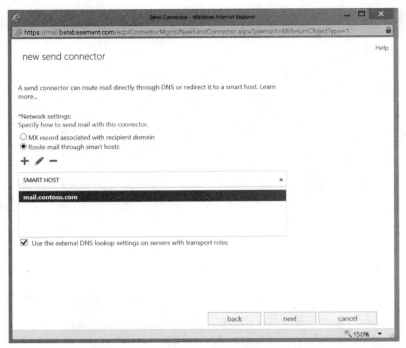

FIGURE 3-10 Creating a new send connector that specifies routing all mail through the mail. contoso.com smart host

3. Specify the address spaces you want this connector to handle. The simplest address space is "*", indicating that the connector can match any SMTP domain. Whichever address spaces you specify for the connector is used to define which messages the connector may accept. The Scoped Send Connector check box that appears on the address space page controls whether the connector is available for routing by any hub transport or Mailbox server in the organization. The default is to leave the check box cleared. If you select the check box, though, Exchange constrains the connector, so only Mailbox servers on the same site as the source server can use it for routing. Servers outside the site won't evaluate the connector as a possible target. You can always change the scoping setting or the list of source servers with Set-SendConnector or EAC later.

4. Specify which servers can send messages over this connector. The servers you define are considered source servers for the connector, so other servers can pass messages to them for onward routing.

When you complete these steps, the connector is added to Active Directory and becomes immediately available (pending Active Directory replication delays) for use by all the servers allowed to use it.

Most of the properties on send connectors (which you can retrieve with a simple Get-SendConnector command) have adequately descriptive names. For example, it's easy to imagine what MaxMessageSize and ConnectionInactivityTimeOut control are. If you need to change any settings, you can do it with the Set-SendConnector command. Assume you want to change the maximum message size that flows across the connector to 25 MB and change the time period after which a connection is dropped for inactivity to five minutes. The command is:

```
Set-SendConnector -Identity 'Default Internet' -MaxMessageSize 25MB
-ConnectionInactivityTimeOut 00:05
```

Normally, send connectors can direct mail straight to the target server, either because they're configured to send to a smart host or because they're able to perform an MX record lookup to find the target server, and then connect directly to it. However, this means messages may appear to originate from any mailbox server. Consider a network that has Exchange 2013 Mailbox servers on five physical sites, with multiple send connectors defined on each site for efficiency and redundancy. By default, that means messages leaving the network can appear to originate from the IP addresses of any of the Mailbox servers associated with the connectors. In such a situation, you could choose to force the Mailbox servers to pass their messages through a proxy beforehand. You can tell Exchange to do this by selecting the Proxy Through Client Access Server check box on the connector properties page or by using the Set-SendConnector -FrontEndProxyEnabled cmdlet. When this option is set, servers using the connector proxy their messages through the Front End Transport service on a CAS on the same Active Directory site. That mail appears to the outside as though it originated with the CAS.

Creating and configuring receive connectors

Exchange creates all the receive connectors you need for a basic setup when you install it, although you will often want to create additional connectors or customize the behavior of some of the default set. Which connectors you get depends on the server role you install because separate connectors are used by the CAS and Mailbox versions of the transport pipeline.

When you install the CAS role, you get three connectors. The first, named Default Frontend serverName, uses the Internet-standard TCP port 25 for SMTP traffic. In a welcome change from Exchange 2007 and Exchange 2010, the standard SMTP connector accepts anonymous inbound mail by default. This means you don't have to do anything to enable your CAS servers to receive email from the Internet. The Client Frontend serverName connector is intended for use by clients. It listens on TCP port 587 and only accepts Transport Layer Security (TLS)–protected or Secure Sockets Layer (SSL)–protected traffic. A third connector, named Outbound Proxy Frontend serverName, is intended to receive messages from send connectors on Mailbox servers.

Exchange 2013 automatically creates receive connectors for you as part of setup. Which connectors you get depends on which server roles you install. On a Mailbox server, two connectors are created.

- The Default *serverName* connector accepts SMTP traffic from servers inside the organization. On a multirole server, it listens on TCP port 2525. On a Mailbox-only server, it listens on TCP port 25.

- The Client Proxy *serverName* connector accepts connections on TCP port 465 from messages received by the Client serverName Receive Connector on CAS servers only.

Both of these connector types use nonstandard ports, and both have authentication settings that allow them to accept only messages from Exchange servers and authenticated users in the local Active Directory forest. However, they have no IP address restrictions. Clients shouldn't connect to them directly. Instead, clients should be configured to connect to the client connector that listens on TCP 587, and that connector will proxy connections as necessary to the Client Proxy connector.

If you run Get-ReceiveConnector on an unmodified server, the result shows all five default receive connectors, like this:

```
Get-ReceiveConnector -server hsv-exmbx02
```

Identity	Bindings	Enabled
HSV-EXMBX02\Default HSV-EXMBX02	{0.0.0.0:2525, [::]:2525}	True
HSV-EXMBX02\Client Proxy HSV-EXMBX02	{[::]:465, 0.0.0.0:465}	True
HSV-EXMBX02\Default Frontend HSV-EXMBX02	{[::]:25, 0.0.0.0:25}	True
HSV-EXMBX02\Outbound Proxy Frontend HSV..	{[::]:717, 0.0.0.0:717}	True
HSV-EXMBX02\Client Frontend HSV-EXMBX02	{[::]:587, 0.0.0.0:587}	True

Each receive connector also has an attribute known as TransportRole. This attribute can take on one of two values—HubTransport or FrontEndTransport—that indicate how the connector is to be used. You can't change this value for the default connectors, although you have to specify it if you create your own (and after specifying it, you can't change it there either).

Speaking of which, Microsoft mentions several times in its documentation that a "typical installation" won't need any additional receive connectors. As you can see from the listings, the Default Frontend HSV-EXMBX02 connector is ready to receive TCP port 25 traffic from all IPv4 and IPv6 addresses. However, you might want to create new connectors to enforce specific permissions or handle traffic from certain servers or ports in a particular way. Before you consider creating a new receive connector, ask yourself the following questions:

1. What server will host the new connector?

2. What transport role will the target server fulfill? If you have a multirole server, a transport listener already is on TCP port 2525. But if you create a new receive connector for transport bound to port 25, both FET and Transport will listen on port 25 at the same time. This can't happen, so whichever service finishes starting first grabs TCP port 25 and the other service can't, leading to unpredictable results. To avoid this problem, avoid creating receive connectors using the default ports on a multirole server. Instead, choose other port numbers

3. What function does the new connector serve? Will it connect two internal Exchange organizations, handle other internal SMTP traffic, connect Exchange 2013 to Exchange 2003, or have another use? Your answer here determines which of the connector purposes you specify.

4. Do you want to change any of the default settings, such as the maximum size of inbound messages allowed?

5. What permissions are necessary for clients who will use the receive connector?

After you answer these questions, you can create a new receive connector with EAC or EMS. The process for doing so in EAC is straightforward, as long as you understand what it's asking you. When you open the new Receive Connector page in EAC (Figure 3-11), you have to specify the connector name, whether it's a hub or FET connector, and its type. The type you pick determines the permissions Exchange initially applies to the connector, as well as its default settings. The New Receive Connector process offers the following types:

- **Custom** Allows the greatest flexibility over the use of the connector. A connector of this type can be used for many purposes, including cross-forest connections and connections to other SMTP-based mail systems that operate within the firewall.

- **Internal** Used for connections among this Exchange organization and other Exchange organizations that operate within the firewall. When you create an internal connector using EAC, you can't define the port on which it listens.

- **Internet** Used to allow connections from external SMTP servers.

- **Partner** Used for TLS-secured connections with specified partner domains using Domain Security.

- **Client** Used to support POP3 and IMAP4 client connections or, perhaps, devices such as scanners or copiers that can send mail by using SMTP. These clients usually connect on TCP port 587 because many Internet providers, hotels, and so on block TCP port 25 traffic to help reduce spam.

FIGURE 3-11 Creating a new receive connector for partner traffic from Woodgrove Bank

The New-ReceiveConnector cmdlet lets you specify the settings required to create a new connector, including the usage (which can be set with the Usage flag and a keyword, such as Usage Internal, or with the shortcut parameters Client, Internal, Internet, and Custom), the IP addresses and ports that the connector should listen on, and the range of IP addresses the connector accepts connections from.

The type you set on the connector is reflected in the settings visible on the Security page of the connector properties in EAC or in the output of Get-ReceiveConnector; each type of connector has its own characteristic combination of assigned permission groups and authentication methods. Receive connectors support seven authentication mechanisms, as shown in Table 3-5. The Default *serverName*, Client Proxy *serverName*, Default Frontend *serverName*, and Outbound Proxy Frontend *serverName* connectors all support the TLS, Integrated, BasicAuth, and BasicAuthRequireTLS methods. All except the Client Frontend connector also support ExchangeServer authentication.

TABLE 3-5 Authentication mechanisms for receive connectors

Authentication Mechanism	Description
None	No authentication.
TLS	The connector advertises that it supports TLS and will accept TLS requests. This mode requires you to configure the connector with a specific certificate, which will be offered to the remote end.
Integrated	NTLM and Kerberos (Integrated Windows) authentication. Only useful with other servers in the same forest.
Integrated	Basic authentication. Requires an authenticated logon, which is evaluated like any other domain logon.
BasicAuthRequireTLS	Basic authentication over a connection that has been secured with TLS. Requires a server certificate.
ExchangeServer	Exchange Server authentication (Generic Security Services application programming interface [GSSAPI] and Mutual GSSAPI).
ExternalAuthoritative	Causes Exchange to treat messages arriving on this connector as though they originated from an internal server. Normally, this connector type is used in conjunction with IPsec or other types of network transport encryption.

Suppose you need to create a receive connector to accept mail from a remote system running Linux qmail. You could easily create it with EMS, using a command similar to this:

```
New-ReceiveConnector -Name "Receive From Tailspin Toys" -Usage Custom -Bindings
'0.0.0.0:9925' -RemoteIPRanges '192.168.70.71' -Server HSV-EXMBX02
```

After the connector is created, you can see its properties with the Get-ReceiveConnector cmdlet. In particular, you might want to review a few specific settings:

- It can be useful to restrict a connector to listening only to a specific, known IP address that belongs to a partner. The RemoteIPRanges parameter lets you specify the remote IP addresses from which you accept messages.

- AuthMechanism controls what types of authentication the connector supports. You need to be sure this list includes TLS and BasicAuthRequireTLS if you want to use the connector to participate in Domain Security connections. If you only want opportunistic TLS, then you only need to specify TLS.

- The RequireTLS parameter is what you use to force the use of TLS on the connector. If you set RequireTLS $true, the connector drops connections from any server that can't negotiate TLS with it.

- DomainSecureEnabled indicates whether you want the connector to work with Domain Security (but see the section "Configuring connectors for TLS and Domain Security" later in the chapter to find out what other connector settings you need to apply for this to work).

- The MaxMessageSize and MaxRecipientsPerMessage parameters let you apply limits to messages passing through this connector. Remember, these limits apply along with, not instead of, any limits you've set with Set-TransportConfig (as described in the "Configuring Email Policies" section later in the chapter).

Notice there aren't any parameters for changing the connector usage. You can only do that when you create a new connector.

Configuring connectors for TLS and Domain Security

Your Exchange 2010 and Exchange 2013 servers already use TLS for passing mail internally. This is possible because each newly installed Exchange server generates and assigns its own set of self-signed SSL certificates to secure this traffic. However, these certificates aren't useful if you want your external connections protected with TLS. You need to answer a few questions before you can deploy TLS or Domain Security in your organization.

1. What connections or domains do you want to protect with TLS, which ones should use Domain Security, and which ones should remain unencrypted?

2. Of the list of connections or domains you identified in step 1, which ones are inbound, which are outbound, and which are both? For example, you might want to apply Domain Security to a connector that routes mail to and from your company's law firm, while also accepting encrypted mail from, but not sending it to, a business partner who sends your company orders.

3. For each of these three categories, which connectors provide send and receive connectivity?

Once you have the answer to these questions, you can set up your environment for the combination of sending and receiving using TLS and Domain Security that meets your requirements. You need to make changes both to the overall transport configuration and to individual connectors and servers. Here's what you need to do.

1. Use the Set-TransportConfig cmdlet to specify the list of domains you want to use with Domain Security using TlsReceiveDomainSecureList and TlsSendDomainSecureList. Remember, you have to specify both the domains you want to receive from and those

you want to send to. For example, if you're the admin for fabrikam.com and you want to set up Domain Security for connections to contoso.com, you'd do the following:

```
Set-TransportConfig -TlsReceiveDomainSecureList contoso.com
Set-TransportConfig -TlsSendDomainSecureList fabrikam.com
```

The administrator for contoso.com would use the same commands, but in reverse. You specify the send and receive domains separately because within your Exchange organization you might have multiple accepted domains, and Exchange needs to know which ones you want to use for Domain Security.

2. If you want to send mail to a specific domain using TLS or Domain Security, create a new Send connector with a usage type of Partner. Partner connectors are automatically configured to require TLS when sending to the connector's assigned address space. (You can check this with Get-SendConnector | ft name, DomainSecureEnabled). Specify the address space you want to use for the connector.

3. If you want to receive mail using TLS from a specific domain, create a new Receive connector and specify a usage type of Partner. Optionally, you can edit the address ranges assigned to the connector, so only your partner's SMTP servers are able to connect to it.

4. For any connector that you want to participate in Domain Security, make sure you've set its DomainSecureEnabled attribute to TRUE.

THE ROLE OF CERTIFICATES

For both send and receive connectors, it's important to know a few things about the role of certificates for TLS and Domain Security. The first thing you should know is you manage certificates for all TLS traffic over connectors on the Edge Transport or CAS roles, not the Mailbox server role. This distinction is unimportant if you're using multirole servers, but if you have separate roles, remember that changing the certs installed or assigned on the Mailbox roles won't have any effect on the certificates used by the CAS servers for their send and receive connectors.

Next, remember that whatever certificates you want to use for TLS or Domain Security need to be installed on all the Edge Transport or CAS servers that will host connectors to the domains you're protecting. You can install separate certificates for each server, although this can quickly become expensive if you buy commercial certificate for each server. If you try to use internally issued or self-signed certificates, you'll find other hosts won't speak TLS to you because they don't trust your certificates, which don't come from a trusted CA. A better alternative is to use the same set of certificates for all servers that will send or receive TLS-protected mail, whether through Domain Security.

The certificate you want to use for TLS must be assigned to the SMTP role using EAC or the Enable-ExchangeCertificate cmdlet. You can use the same certificate for multiple usages. It's important for you to specify a certificate the remote server will accept.

CONFIGURING SEND CONNECTORS FOR TLS

A send connector can participate in Domain Secure conversations if all of the following are true:

- The value of the DomainSecureEnabled parameter on the connector must be $true.
- The connector must be set to use direct MX delivery, not a smart host (that is, the DNSRoutingEnabled parameter is set to $true).
- The value of the IgnoreStartTLS parameter must be $false.

The requirements for setting up a connector to use TLS (as opposed to Domain Security) are a little different. If you set the RequireTLS parameter to $true, the connector only sends messages to a destination host if the destination server can accept a TLS negotiation. However, as long as IgnoreStartTLS is $false, the send connector will participate in TLS conversations whenever it can negotiate them.

CONFIGURING RECEIVE CONNECTORS FOR TLS

For a receive connector to be usable for Domain Security, you need to follow three specific rules. First, the DomainSecureEnabled parameter on the connector must be set to $true. Second, the AuthMechanism setting for the connector must be set to some form of TLS (and it may not contain ExternalAuthoritative). And, third, at least one of the domains in the address space of the connector must also appear in the list of domains you specified with Set-TransportConfig, TlsReceiveDomainSecureList, and TlsSendDomainSecureList in at least one send connector's address space.

The rules for TLS support on receive connectors are much more relaxed: if you want to require the use of TLS on the connector, Set-RequireTls $True. If you're willing to accept messages with TLS on a purely opportunistic basis, you don't have to do anything.

Configuring transport rules

You can configure transport rules using either EMS or EAC. For most uses, you'll probably find that EAC is a simpler, easier way to configure rules because you don't have to remember all the transport rule syntax. However, you need to know how to do both for the exam. The New-TransportRule and Set-TransportRule cmdlets are the primary tools you use for this task. However, you don't have to memorize the syntax for all the predicates and actions. Microsoft helpfully provides cmdlets that will list them: the Get-TransportRuleAction and Get-TransportRulePredicate cmdlets emit lists of their respective objects, so you can quickly find the predicate or action you're looking for.

SETTING RULE PRIORITIES

Each transport rule has a priority associated with it. The rule with the lowest priority is applied first to see whether its conditions and exceptions match. Once it's been processed, the next applicable rule is applied, and so on, until all rules have been evaluated or until a rule fires with the "stop further processing" action. It's *very* important for you to test new rules before you start to rely on them to make sure the priority order does what you expect. In particular, rule priority can act in ways that might surprise you because DLP rules are added at the bottom of the priority list. If you create a rule that applies a disclaimer and stops further rule processing, no lower-priority rules are run when that rule runs—including the DLP rules you wanted to apply.

You can see the rule priorities in your organization with the Get-TransportRule cmdlet, like this:

```
Get-TransportRule | ft Name, Priority
```

You can change the priority of any rule by specifying its name and the priority you want it to have. All the other rules with higher priority are then adjusted to match the new priority. For example, let's say you do this:

```
Set-TransportRule "Mail From Managing Consultants" -Priority 2
```

Whatever rule had priority 2 moves to priority 3, the rule formerly at priority 3 gets priority 4, and so on throughout all the rules you have defined.

CONFIGURING MODERATION

One common use for transport rules is to work together with Exchange's moderation functions. You can set the properties of any distribution group, so messages sent to it must be approved by a *moderator* before they're sent to distribution group members. However, this requires the moderator to review every message, which adds the potential for delay in getting messages out to people. Another alternative is to create a transport rule, which requires approval for messages that match certain criteria. For example, you might want to moderate all messages sent to a distribution group for a project unless they're sent by the project manager or her deputy. This is easy to set up by doing something like the following, which requires that Jane Doe moderate any message sent to the ProjectX distribution group, except for messages she sends herself:

```
New-TransportRule "Restrict sending to ProjectX DG" -AnyOfToCCHeader "ProjectX"
-ExceptIfFrom JaneDoe@contoso.com -ModerateMessgeByUser JaneDoe@contoso.com
```

You can instead use the ModerateMessageByManager parameter to send the message to the original sender's manager for moderation approval.

CONFIGURING ETHICAL FIREWALLS

Another common use for transport rules is to create what's known as an *ethical firewall*, a set of rules that prevents two groups of people from emailing each other except under certain conditions. For example, in many countries/regions, financial regulators don't allow employees of a company's investment banking division to communicate electronically with employees of the same company's brokerage division. Also common practice is to isolate individual product teams that are working on secret projects from communicating with some other internal users.

The general pattern for rules to implement ethical firewalls is you need to define two distribution or security groups that contain the people who aren't supposed to talk to each other. The New-TransportRule cmdlet has specific parameters for this case: betweenMemberOf1 and betweenMemberOf2 let you specify the two groups. For example, if you don't want members of Fabrikam's legal department to be able to communicate directly with the research team unless they're talking about Project Starburst, you could create a transport rule to block any messages between the two groups that didn't contain the phrase "Starburst Privileged" in the subject line.

```
New-TransportRule "Starburst Filter" -betweenMemberOf1 Legal `
-betweenMemberOf2 Research `
-ExceptIfSubjectContainsWords "Starburst Privileged" `
-rejectMessageReasonText "This message has been blocked because it may contain
confidential information"
```

You could use other actions in an ethical firewall rule, too. For example, RedirectMessageTo could be used to send the offending message to someone else (perhaps the head of the legal team for Project Starburst?), or AddManagerAsRecipientType Redirect could be used to send the message to the original sender's manager for review.

Configuring accepted domains

When you want to support receiving mail for multiple domains, you need to set up multiple accepted domains. You have to do four separate things to add support for a new accepted domain:

1. Decide on the SMTP domain name you want to use and whether the domain will be an authoritative domain or part of a shared namespace (that is, an internal or external relay domain). If you need a refresher on the difference between these types, see the section on accepted domains earlier in the chapter.

2. Create the appropriate domain entries in Exchange using the New-AcceptedDomain cmdlet or EAC.

3. Create addressable objects for the new domain. You can do this in two ways: create contacts where needed for relay domains or use email addressing policies to apply additional email addresses to existing objects for the new accepted domains.

4. For internal or external relay domains, create or configure a send connector to route mail to the target servers.

Creating accepted domains

To complete step 2, you can create new accepted domains in two ways: from the Mail Flow slab in EAC (Figure 3-12) or by using the New-AcceptedDomain cmdlet. In either case, you need to know the FQDN of the domain you want to accept and the type of domain you want it to be. To add a new accepted domain, go to the Mail Flow slab in EAC, and then switch to the Accepted Domains tab and click the + icon. When the New Accepted Domain dialog box appears (Figure 3-12), specify the display name, the FQDN, and the domain type, and then click OK to save the domain.

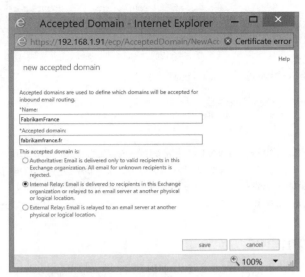

FIGURE 3-12 Creating a new accepted domain using EAC

If you want to create a new accepted domain with EMS, you use New-AcceptedDomain, which requires you to provide a name for the domain, the FQDN, and the type of domain (using DomainType): Authoritative, InternalRelay, or ExternalRelay. For example, this command creates a new authoritative domain for FabrikamFrance.com:

```
New-AcceptedDomain –DomainName FabrikamFrance.com –DomainType Authoritative –Name
FabrikamSA
```

Creating addressable objects

Whenever you create an accepted domain, you're telling Exchange it may accept mail for that domain—but that only covers the transport system. At some point, mail addressed to recipients in that accepted domain needs to be delivered to actual recipients. The way this happens depends on whether you're creating an authoritative domain, an internal relay domain, or an external relay domain:

- For an authoritative domain, you need to create a new email address policy (see the following paragraph) that assigns the new domain as an SMTP address. You can do this by assigning the new domain as the primary address (forcing the previous primary address into being a secondary address), or you can just add the new domain as a secondary address.

- For an internal or external relay domain, you generally don't need to change email addresses on the existing recipient objects in your Exchange organization because the purpose of the domain is for Exchange to accept mail and deliver it to someplace else. However, if you use recipient filtering, any mail for an unknown recipient will be rejected, so you need to create contact objects for recipients in the relay domain that you want to accept mail for.

If you need to create an additional email address policy, you can do so with the New-EmailAddressPolicy cmdlet or through EAC. In either case, you can pick one of the predefined address formats (such as *firstname.lastname*) or use the format specifiers defined in TechNet (see the topic "Create an Email Address Policy"). Remember, until you create or modify a policy so it adds the new accepted domain to the target recipient objects, they won't be able to receive mail at the new address.

Creating send connectors

When you create an internal or external relay domain, this tells Exchange it will be accepting mail and forwarding it on to another system. That means you need a route to get it there, and that means you need a send connector. You use the same process described earlier to create the send connector, although you need to remember a few specific things:

- You need the send connector you create to direct mail to the correct target server for the domains it handles. This means it should be configured to use a smart host instead of DNS delivery.
- The send connector needs to be created from a Mailbox server, not a client access server.
- If you're creating a send connector for an external domain, and you're using the Edge Transport role, you have to manually create a send connector on a Mailbox server, but specify the Edge Transport server as the source server. The Edge subscription process doesn't automatically create these connectors.

Configuring email policies

Setting limits and policies for email transport is an important part of running an Exchange organization. As Exchange has matured, Microsoft has added more configurable policy limits, and changed defaults as needed to reflect the realities of how people use Exchange. You often need to adjust these limits, though.

You can adjust limits and settings within the transport system in multiple ways. First, there are settings that apply to all transport items in the organization. Second, there are settings that apply only to individual servers, although you can use EMS to apply consistent settings to all your transport servers. Finally, there are settings that apply to connectors, no matter what servers the connector is actually hosted on.

Setting global policies with Set-TransportConfig

You view and set transport policies for the entire organization with the Get-TransportConfig and Set-TransportConfig cmdlets; the most interesting settings for Set-TransportConfig are shown in Table 3-6. You've already encountered some of these parameters elsewhere in the chapter, but some may be new to you. Many Exchange admins never have to adjust any of these settings. The most likely settings you'll need to change relate to three things.

- Message size limits. You can use the MaxSendSize and MaxReceiveSize parameters to control these. Remember, the limits you set with Set-TransportConfig apply to every transport server in the organization. For example, if you set a MaxReceiveSize of 15 MB (smaller than I'd recommend), even if you have a receive connector with a maximum receive size of 30 MB, a 17 MB message will be rejected because it's bigger than the global transport size limit. (When you set these limits, don't forget to account for the expansion of binary attachments when they're converted to MIME format for transmission.)

- Safety Net and shadow redundancy behavior, as described earlier in the chapter.

- The domains for which you want to enable Domain Security, configured with the TlsSendDomainSecureList and TlsReceiveDomainSecureList parameters.

TABLE 3-6 Key parameters you can set with Set-TransportConfig

Parameters	Meaning
ExternalDelayDSNEnabled	Specifies whether Exchange should create a DSN if messages from external recipients cannot be delivered immediately. The default is $True.
ExternalPostmasterAddress	This property specifies the email address that Exchange inserts into the From header field of a DSN sent to an external recipient. The default is $Null, meaning that Exchange uses the default postmaster address from the Mailbox or edge server that generates the DSN (postmaster@defaultaccepteddomain.com, where defaultaccepteddomain.com is the default accepted domain for the organization). If a value is entered in this property, Exchange uses it instead.
InternalDelayDSNEnabled	Determines whether Exchange creates DSNs for messages from internal senders that cannot be delivered immediately. The default is $True.
InternalSMTPServers	A list of IP addresses of SMTP servers that the anti-spam agents consider internal and, therefore, ignore as a potential source of spam.
JournalingReportNdrTo	Basic authentication over a connection that has been secured with TLS. Requires a server certificate.
JournalingReportNdrTo	The mailbox the journaling agent sends journal reports to if the journal mailbox is unavailable.
MaxReceiveSize	The maximum size of message the organization can receive.
MaxRetriesForLocalSiteShadow and MaxRetriesForRemoteSiteShadow	Controls the number of attempts an Exchange Mailbox server makes when submitting a shadow copy of a message in the same site (default is 2) or a remote site (default is 4).
MaxSendSize	Sets the maximum size of message that can be sent within the organization.
RejectMessageOnShadowFailure	Indicates whether failure to submit a shadow copy of a message should cause Exchange to reject the original message. Defaults to $True. When this parameter is set to $True, messages are rejected with the SMTP code 450 4.5.1. When this parameter is set to $False, the message is accepted without making a shadow copy.

Parameters	Meaning
SafetyNetHoldTime	Controls how long messages are stored in Safety Net after being successfully delivered. The actual time is the sum of the time you specify here and the time set with Set-TransportService -MessageExpirationTimeout.
ShadowMessageAutoDiscardInterval	Specifies how long a primary server maintains discard events for shadow messages. If the shadow server doesn't query the events within this interval, the primary server discards them. The default value is 2.00:00:00 (two days).
ShadowMessagePreferenceSetting	Controls where you want shadow copies of messages to be submitted. The default, PreferRemote, attempts to deliver shadow copies to a remote site if one is reachable, but will deliver shadow copies to a local site if no remote site is reachable. Other permissible values are LocalOnly and RemoteOnly. Note that when you use RemoteOnly, message delivery will fail if no remote site is reachable.
ShadowRedundancyEnabled	Specifies whether the shadow redundancy feature is enabled within the organization. The default is $True.
ShadowResubmitTimeSpan	Indicates how long a server waits before deciding that a primary server has failed and takes over processing shadow messages in the shadow queue for the unavailable server. The default value is 03:00:00 or three hours. This replaces the ShadowHeartbeatRetryCount parameter, which is still available for Exchange 2010 backward compatibility.
TLSReceiveDomainSecureList	Contains a list of domains that are configured for mutual TLS authentication through receive connectors.
TLSSendDomainSecureList	Contains a list of domains that are configured for mutual TLS authentication through send connectors.
TransportRuleAttachmentTextScanLimit	Sets the limit for the amount of text extracted and scanned for transport rule and DLP rule checks. The default is 150 KB. If the message contains attachments that have more than this amount of text, only the specified amount is checked.
VerifySecureSubmitEnabled	Set to $True to force MAPI clients to submit messages over a secure channel (encrypted RPCs). The default is $False. By default, Outlook 2007 and Outlook 2010 use a secure channel, but previous versions do not.

Setting server policies with Set-TransportService

The Set-TransportService cmdlet controls settings for the Transport service. While this might seem obvious, don't confuse it with the cmdlets that control settings for the Front End Transport (Set-FrontEndTransportService) or Mailbox Transport (Set-MailboxTransportService) services. Notable things you can change with Set-TransportService include:

- Various aspects of logging behavior, as described in the section "Interpreting message tracking and protocol logs."

- How long the server waits before it sends a delay notification. By default, Exchange keeps trying to deliver a message for four hours. If it can't deliver during that time, it sends a delay notification. Many organizations want earlier notification of delays, for example, to set the notification timeout to two hours, you could do this:

```
Get-TransportService | Set-TransportService -DelayNotificationTimeout 0.2:00:00
```

- How long the server waits before it sends a failure notification after a delivery delay. By default, Exchange keeps trying to resend a message for 72 hours, but once it reaches the end of that period, it sends a non-delivery report (NDR). You can use the MessageExpirationTimeout parameter to change this interval. This example sets it to two days:

```
Set-TransportService -MessageExpirationTimeout 2.0:00:00
```

- The IP address used in the Received header for the local server. Normally, the actual address of the network adapter is used, but Microsoft recommends using the IP address associated with your public MX record. For example, if your public MX record pointed to a load balancer at 203.0.113.55, you'd set the IP address with Set-TransportService -ExternalIPAddress 203.0.113.55.

Setting policies on connectors

The primary settings of interest on send and receive connectors are different, as you might expect, but they have some commonalities. Table 3-7 lists some common tasks you might want to perform with connectors and describes how to accomplish them for send or receive connectors (or both, where applicable).

TABLE 3-7 Common connector policies and how to apply them

Desired task	Receive connector	Send connector
Limit the max message size	Use the MaxMessageSize parameter with Set-ReceiveConnector or Set-SendConnector	
Allow the connector to be used for Domain Secure conversations	Use the DomainSecureEnabled $true parameter with Set-SendConnector or Set-ReceiveConnector	
Force the connector to use TLS at all times	Set-SendConnector or Set-ReceiveConnector -RequireTLS $true	
Limit the rate of messages that can pass through the connector	Set-ReceiveConnector -MessageRateLimit	
Change the address spaces that the connector can use		Set-SendConnector -AddressSpaces
Control which servers can use the connector		Set-SendConnector -SourceTransportServers, with the list of Mailbox servers you want to be enabled for this connector

Configuring address rewriting

Address rewriting is a great example of a very narrowly focused feature in Exchange: most organizations never need address rewriting, but for those who do need the feature, it's invaluable. You can use address rewriting on the Edge Transport role to modify inbound and/or outbound email addresses for a variety of purposes, including making multiple address spaces look like a single one or applying a consistent format for addresses on mail that might originate from multiple systems inside the organization.

Address rewriting depends on two additional transport agents that only exist on the Edge Transport role: the Address Rewriting Inbound Agent and the Address Rewriting Outbound Agent. To enable or disable it, then, you have to set the appropriate state of the agents using Enable-TransportAgent or Disable-TransportAgent. For example, to enable address rewriting on a single Edge server, you use these commands:

```
Enable-TransportAgent "Address Rewriting Inbound Agent"
Enable-TransportAgent "Address Rewriting Outbound Agent"
```

Although no rewriting takes place unless the agent is active, you should wait to enable it until after you create the address rewriting entries you want. Each entry requires three parameters: a name, the internal address you want to use, and the external address you want to use. A fourth, optional, parameter specifies whether the entry should be applied to rewrite both inbound and outbound mail, or only outbound messages. Depending on the direction of the message, the internal address is converted to the external address format, or vice versa.

Here's a simple example. Suppose you want any mail sent to ceo@fabrikam.com to arrive in the mailbox of Ann Beebe, the CEO, without giving out her email address. A single address rewriting rule does the trick:

```
New-AddressRewriteEntry -Name "Mail to CEO" -InternalAddress ann.beebe@fabrikam.com
-ExternalAddress ceo@fabrikam.com
```

Because this command didn't specify OutboundOnly $false, it is applied for mail that Ann sends and receives. If you only want inbound mail to ceo@fabrikam.com to be rewritten, adding OutboundOnly $false would achieve that result. Outbound mail from Ann's mailbox would keep her ann.beebe@fabrikam.com address.

The next case where address rewriting can be useful is in rewriting addresses for an entire domain or subdomain. Suppose that Fabrikam, under Ann Beebe's visionary leadership, becomes so profitable that it acquires Northwind Traders. After the merger is complete, the new company wants all the Northwind employees to receive email with an @fabrikam.com address, but without rendering the existing email addresses invalid. It's trivial to do this with a single address rewriting rule:

```
New-AddressRewriteEntry -Name "Northwind to Fabrikam" `
-InternalAddress northwindtraders.com
-ExternalAddress fabrikam.com
```

Once this rule is in place, any message arriving for a recipient in the northwindtraders.com domain is rewritten so the left-hand side of the address remains the same, but the right-hand side is replaced with *fabrikam.com*.

You can use the "*" wildcard, too, with three specific restrictions. First, you can only use the wildcard for a complete subdomain (so "*.fouthcoffee.com" is acceptable, but "*fourthcoffee. com", with no period to delimit the subdomain, is not OK). Second, you can only use the wildcard with the InternalAddress parameter. Finally, you must set -OutboundOnly $true. The net result is you can create a single rule to quickly rewrite multiple subdomains. For example, suppose that after years of having country/region-specific subdomains, Litware has decided to consolidate to a single SMTP address space. This can be easily accomplished by a command like the following:

```
New-AddressRewriteEntry -Name "Litware Consolidation" `
-InternalAddress *.litwareing.com
-ExternalAddress litwareinc.com
```

Thought experiment
Deploying Edge Transport

In this Thought experiment, apply what you learned about this objective. You can find answers to these questions in the "Answers" section at the end of this chapter.

Fourth Coffee is deploying Edge Transport servers as part of their migration from Exchange 2007 to Exchange 2013. They also want a complete review of their mail system to ensure they are meeting all their compliance and governance requirements.

1. Describe the process you'd use to ensure that mail flows smoothly during and after the Edge deployment.

2. What changes might you consider making to existing connectors as part of the deployment?

3. What are some suggestions you might make to Fourth Coffee about their compliance and governance infrastructure?

Objective summary

- The Edge Transport role lets you create subscriptions that synchronize data from your Exchange organization to the non-domain-joined Edge Transport servers.

- When you install an Edge Transport server, you must complete four steps: install Edge Transport on the server, run the New-EdgeSubscription cmdlet, copy the resulting subscription file to a Mailbox server in the target site, and run New-EdgeSubscription on the Mailbox server to import the subscription file.

- You can clone Edge Transport configurations, but the cloned servers need their own subscriptions.

- You can control the frequency at which the EdgeSync process updates its data with the Set-EdgeSyncServiceConfig cmdlet.

- When you create a new Send connector, you must specify a purpose (Internet, partner, internal, or custom) and indicate whether you want outbound mail to be funneled through a smart host or delivered through MX lookups. You also must specify the address spaces the connector can route messages for.

- When you create a Receive connector, you must specify a purpose (Custom, Internal, Internet, Partner, or Client), which determines the security settings and ports used on the connector. You might also need to apply permissions to the connector.

- Both send and receive connectors can be allowed to use TLS (the default state), forced to use TLS (-RequireTLS $true), or prevented from using TLS (-IgnoreStartTLS $true).

- Transport rules can be used to create ethical firewalls, add disclaimers, and trigger Exchange moderation.

- To add accepted domains in Exchange, you need to create the domain itself (along with specifying a type) and make sure addressable objects are in the domain. You can do this by creating new email address policies for the new domain or creating contact objects.

- Set-TransportConfig lets you configure options that apply to all transport servers in the entire organization, such as the delay periods before NDRs are sent and the maximum permitted size for sent and received messages.

- Set-TransportService lets you control settings on an individual server, including settings that control protocol logging.

- Address rewriting is only available on Edge Transport servers. You must first enable the inbound and outbound address rewriting agents to use it. You can create address rewriting entries that rewrite a single mailbox's addresses, all addresses for a single subdomain, or all addresses for a domain. You can also specify whether you want addresses rewritten for outbound messages, inbound messages, or both.

Objective review

Answer the following questions to test your knowledge of the information in this objective. You can find the answers to these questions and explanations of why each answer choice is correct or incorrect in the "Answers" section at the end of this chapter.

1. Your company is upgrading from Lotus Notes. Your current Exchange organization uses fourthcoffee.com as its only accepted domain. You want to continue accepting email for that domain while you transition to Exchange 2013. But you also want to ensure that incoming email is routed to Exchange 2013 and redirected to the legacy Notes system if the target recipient hasn't moved to Exchange yet. You update your firewall to send SMTP traffic to Exchange 2013. What should you do next?

A. Add a new external relay domain for fourthcoffee.com and create a new Receive connector.

B. Add a new internal relay domain for fourthcoffee.com and create a new Receive connector.

C. Modify the existing accepted domain for fourthcoffee.com and create a new Receive connector.

D. Add a new email address policy for fourthcoffee.com and create a new Send connector.

E. Modify the existing accepted domain for fourthcoffee.com and create a new Send connector.

2. Your company has factories in Huntsville, Orlando, and New Orleans. Each physical site contains two Exchange servers: one CAS and one mailbox server. Only the CAS servers have Internet access. You need to ensure all outbound mail from each site is routed through the CAS servers. Which of the following actions can best accomplish this?

A. Add the CAS role to each of the existing Mailbox servers.

B. Remove the mailbox servers from the list of internal SMTP servers with Set-TransportConfig.

C. Create new Send connectors from the Mailbox servers to the CAS servers.

D. Use Set-SendConnector on the existing Send connectors and specify the -FrontEndProxyEnabled $true parameter.

3. You want to ensure your Exchange 2013 users get quick notification when outbound messages are delayed for more than 30 minutes. Which cmdlet should you use to accomplish this?

A. Set-TransportConfig.

B. Set-TransportService.

C. Set-FrontEndTransportService

D. Set-Mailbox.

4. You receive a request from your company legal department to block incoming mail from the Internet to the Project Sunburst distribution list. In addition, the legal department wants to block any inbound mail messages that contain the words "syzygy" and "stellerator." Which cmdlets should you use to accomplish this? (Each correct answer presents part of the solution. Choose all that apply.)

A. Set-ReceiveConnector.

B. Set-TransportConfig.

C. Add-ContentFilterPhrase.

D. Set-RecipientFilterConfig.

E. New-MalwareFilterPolicy.

Objective 3.4: Troubleshoot and monitor transport

Once you understand how the transport system works, you'll be able to answer questions about where mail is going, and why it sometimes doesn't go where you want it to. Given the importance of transport in a properly running Exchange system, you should expect to get these questions a lot. To troubleshoot transport, you'll need to become familiar with reading message tracking and protocol logs and troubleshooting inbound and outbound SMTP mail flow.

This objective covers how to:

- Interpret message tracking logs and protocol logs
- Troubleshoot a shared namespace environment
- Troubleshoot SMTP mail flow
- Given a failure scenario, predict mail flow and identify how to recover
- Troubleshoot Domain Secure/TLS
- Troubleshoot the new transport architecture

Predicting mail flow

One of the most useful skills you can develop as an Exchange administrator is a sense of where messages should go under given circumstances. That is, if Alice sends Bob a message, you need to be able to understand and predict what route that message will take as it traverses your organization. To do this, you need to understand the concepts of message routing as described earlier in the chapter. You also need to understand your own messaging environment well enough to know which connectors are likely to come into play in different scenarios. Here are a few rules that can help you predict where messages should be flowing, so you can apply that knowledge to look for outages or stoppages along the way:

1. If the message was inbound from the Internet, then consider that

   - The message may have passed through a perimeter filtering service before it got to you, and this may have delayed or prevented delivery.

   - If you're using an Edge Transport server, the message tracking logs will reflect the message's arrival. If you don't see it arrive at the Edge server, it was blocked before reaching your organization.

2. If the message was outbound from your organization, you should be able to identify the originating server and use this information to trace its progress.

3. At each hop, Exchange chooses the lowest cost route to the destination. If you have multiple sites, remember, separate site link and Exchange-specific costs might be associated with each site link.

4. Any time a server can't connect to the next hop for a message, the message is queued. When you change the routing topology (perhaps by changing the set of

available connectors), Exchange recalculates routes for queued messages and retries them, if necessary. You can sometimes help this process along when you detect that messages are stuck somewhere by making a change in the environment. For example, in Figure 3-13, if the ATLEXMBX02 server in Atlanta is down, creating a new send connector in Boston or changing the existing connector to be hosted on ATLEXMBX01 allows messages to flow outwards.

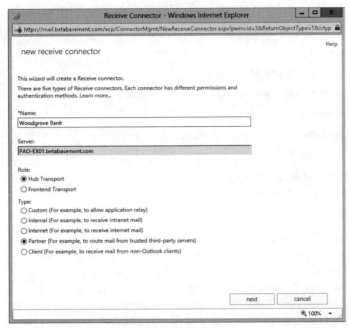

FIGURE 3-13 An example of the message tracking log display in EAC

Interpreting message tracking and protocol logs

Sometimes the best way to determine what's wrong with a mail conversation is to use logs to inspect what's actually happening, as opposed to what you think might be happening. The Exchange Transport services can each log information about a variety of activities, over and above the normal status, warning, and error messages they might register in the system's Windows application event log. Their contents can be invaluable when you're trying to understand why a message didn't arrive when and where it was supposed to. Although you probably won't use these logs on a daily basis, they are useful whenever you need to understand why messages aren't being transported as you expect.

All three of the Transport services can independently maintain four types of logs:

- Message tracking logs (Figure 3-14) show the flow of messages from sender to recipient. This flow is displayed at a fairly high level. Rather than showing the nuts and bolts of the SMTP protocol conversation, or the exact TCP/IP connection history, it focuses on which parts of the Exchange transport pipeline touched the message. Message tracking logs are on by default. Message tracking logs are kept on each server and shared in an automatically created folder, so the EAC and EMS tools for processing and searching these logs can automatically include all pertinent logs in the organization.

FIGURE 3-14 An example of the message tracking log display in EAC

- Connectivity logs capture the date, time, source, destination, and direction of all connections to a server. Connectivity logging is on by default. If you look at the server connectivity logs in their default path of C:\Program Files\Microsoft\Exchange Server\V15\TransportRoles\Logs\Hub\Connectivity, you see entries for shadow redundancy submissions, ordinary SMTP delivery, and every other significant server-to-server connectivity event. Other parts of Exchange might log different data in the connectivity logs, too, although connectivity logs don't show the details of protocol-level conversations.

- Receive protocol and send protocol logs that show the details of conversations: which party to the conversation said what and what the response was. These logs are off by default. You normally enable them only if you identify or suspect problems with a specific protocol's connectivity because the logs are quite verbose. However, it might be a good idea to enable the logs and keep the log lifetime short, so you have log files you can refer to in the event of a problem. Turning on the protocol logs after you have a problem might not give you the information you need to identify the fault.

Using message tracking

Message tracking is the most direct way to see how an individual message, or where messages to or from a specific user or group, has passed through your servers. The tracking logs use the Message-ID header, which is assigned by the sending server and is unique to each message, to correlate message flow. At each stage of the transport pipeline, and on each server that touches a message, the state of the message is recorded. This state indicates which transport event fired (receive, deliver, etc.) and what action, if any, was taken. For the simplest example of message transport—a mail sent by one user to another on the same server—the tracking logs show RECEIVE events followed by a single DELIVER event. More complex message flows result in more entries in the tracking logs. You also see other transport actions, such as distribution group expansion, in these logs.

You can search the tracking logs in three ways. First, you can use the "Delivery reports" tab in EAC (or the Search-MessageTrackingReport and Get-MessageTrackingReport cmdlets in EMS) to look for tracking information for one or more specific mailboxes. You can search for messages to or from these mailboxes, but not both, or you can filter the search by key words in the subject line. When you open one of the search results, you see a neatly formatted human-readable summary of the delivery events, as shown in Figure 3-15.

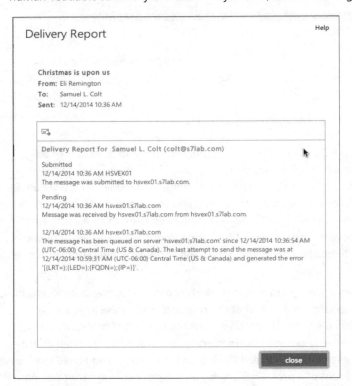

FIGURE 3-15 Delivery report showing major message delivery events for this specific message

Second, users can search for their own messages from within Outlook Web App (OWA) by using the Delivery Reports tab. This is the same functionality as administrators have except it's restricted to the specific user's mailbox. Users who know how to use the delivery report search function spend less time asking you for help in locating messages, so it's worth the time to explain how it works.

And, third, administrators can use the Get-MessageTrackingLog cmdlet from EMS. This is by far the most flexible way to search, because you can search for mail to or from specific mailboxes, restrict the search by time and date, filter on the subject line, or follow a specific message by searching for its Message-ID header. For example, this command displays all the messages, including sender, received date, and subject line, sent to colt@s7lab.com on the specified date (Figure 3-16):

```
Get-MessageTrackingLog -Server PAOEX01 -Start "12/14/2014 08:00:00" -End "12/14/2014
12:00:00" -recipient "colt@s7lab.com"
```

FIGURE 3-16 Message tracking results

When you use Get-MessageTrackingLog, the message tracking results by default include all the events for all the messages that match the search criteria, including the message subject and the list of recipients. This can be a bit confusing. For example, the sample in Figure 3-16 includes an event tagged HAREDIRECTFAIL, indicating that no shadow redundancy copy of that message was created. If you didn't know that this particular Exchange server is the only one in its organization (and, thus, thatshadow redundancy is ineffective because there's no second server), you might find that result worrisome.

Using protocol logging

Protocol logging tracks the steps that occur in SMTP conversations to transfer messages between Exchange and other servers. The logging is at a lower level than what you see in the message tracking logs because it captures details, such as the authentication between servers and the SMTP verbs used in the conversations. Protocol logging is disabled by default, so you have to enable logging on a per-connector basis before Exchange generates logs. All the logs for a given server go into the protocol logging directory whose location you specify with the

ReceiveProtocolLogPath and SendProtocolLogPath parameters to Set-TransportService, Set-MailboxTransportService, and Set-FrontEndTransportService.

Each transport service maintains its own set of protocol logs, and so does each server. In fact, eight total sets of protocol logs exist: SMTP send and receive on the Front End Transport service, SMTP send and receive on the Transport service, and separate SMTPReceive and SMTPSend logs for both the delivery and submission portions of the Mailbox Transport services. (Note, no logs are generated for the Mailbox Transport submission for SMTP receive because the submission service never receives SMTP email.) This might seem confusing, but having so many logs gives you a great deal of flexibility in troubleshooting because you can enable logging and review data from only the parts of the transport process that are giving you trouble.

Like the other log types, protocol log output is in comma-separated value (CSV) format. Figure 3-17 illustrates typical content from an SMTP receive log (some steps have been removed from this extract for the sake of clarity). The example shows how two Exchange transport servers set up an SMTP connection between each other to exchange messages. After the normal SMTP interchange of supported verbs, the connection is encrypted with TLS, and then the sending server begins to transmit the message header fields, beginning with the sender information (MAIL FROM). The receiving server validates thatthe recipient is OK by checking that the sender is not blocked. (The recipient might be a restricted address that only accepts messages from a defined set of senders.) You can also see the new XSHADOW ESMTP (extended SMTP) verb that sends information for the shadow redundancy feature of the transport dumpster. The message content was transmitted with a binary transfer (BDAT). The final step disconnects the link between the two servers.

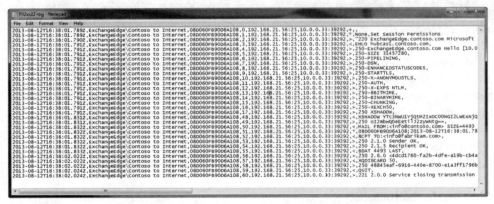

FIGURE 3-17 A protocol log showing an SMTP conversation between two Exchange servers

The content of the send and receive protocol logs are similar. For example, if you look at the transactions generated to send a message through an external SMTP relay, you see Exchange identifying itself with EHLO, sending the STARTTLS verb, and then creating a TLS-secured connection if this is supported by the relay server, sending the message, and closing the link.

When you're trying to troubleshoot a transport problem, one of the first steps is determining which log has the information you want. Here are a few tips.

■ The message tracking logs are generally the best place to start because they tell you where the message originated and which Exchange servers touched it en route. You can see whether a given message ever made it into or out of your organization.

■ The protocol logs are primarily useful when you're troubleshooting inter-organizational mail flow. Transport problems between Exchange servers in the same organization are quite rare.

■ You have to identify which connector carried the message you want. The message tracking logs can help you determine this, but understanding how message routing works (as described in the section "Predicting mail flow" earlier in the chapter) is also important. The two connectors in which you're most interested are the Default Frontend *Servername* and Client Frontend *Servername* connectors, which listen on TCP ports 25 and 587, respectively.

Because protocol logging is off by default, it may be off when you need it. When you suspect a transport problem, you need to turn on protocol logging on the suspect connectors. The following commands enable protocol logging on these two receive connectors on a server named AEX-EXCAS07:

```
Set-ReceiveConnector -Identity 'AEX-EXCAS07\Default Frontend AEX-EXCAS07'
-ProtocolLoggingLevel Verbose
Set-ReceiveConnector -Identity 'AEX-EXCAS07\Client Frontend AEX-EXCAS07'
-ProtocolLoggingLevel Verbose
```

For a send connector, of course, you'd use the Set-SendConnector cmdlet instead.

Just as with connectivity logs, Exchange uses a circular logging mechanism to keep the protocol logs under these thresholds. The following command shows how to configure the various settings:

```
Set-TransportService -Identity ExServer2 `
-ReceiveProtocolLogPath 'C:\Logs\SMTPReceive' `
-SendProtocolLogPath 'C:\Logs\SMTPSend' `
-ReceiveProtocolLogMaxFileSize 20MB `
-SendProtocolLogMaxFileSize 20MB `
-ReceiveProtocolLogMaxDirectorySize 500MB `
 -SendProtocolLogMaxDirectorySize 500MB `
-ReceiveProtocolLogMaxAge 15.00:00:00 `
-SendProtocolLogMaxAge 15.00:00:00
```

As with connectivity logging, using the same settings for all transport servers in the organization is the best practice. This is easily accomplished as described in the previous section to configure the connectivity log settings by using Get-TransportService to fetch a list of all hub transport servers and using that list as input to Set-TransportService to implement the settings.

Troubleshooting SMTP message flow

Troubleshooting SMTP message flow is a critical skill. It involves three steps: identifying that messages aren't going where they are supposed to; identifying the reason they aren't going where they are supposed to; and remedying the root cause, so that normal message flow is restored.

The first step can take place in multiple ways, but the two most common are that you notice an individual mail failure (perhaps because of an unexpected NDR, or because a user calls you and asks "Where's my mail?") or you notice a change in the normal flow of mail. Perhaps this is an unexpected increase in delays, or your monitoring software may alert you to steady growth in a message queue. In any case, once you become aware that a problem exists with message flow, you can proceed to identify the root cause, and then fix it.

Understanding queues

The basic behavior of queues is simple: messages enter a queue and remain there until they are retrieved and processed by one of the transport services. Any time more messages are arriving into a queue than are leaving that queue, you should expect mail delivery delays.

If you look at the set of queues for an Exchange 2013 server (which you can see with a quick run of the Get-Queue cmdlet), you see that the queues break down into a few well-defined groupings. Each mailbox database has its own destination queue, as does each DAG and Active Directory site. Somewhat surprisingly, Active Directory forests have their own queues, as do external SMTP domains. These two groups could be combined because delivery to a remote forest uses SMTP, but Microsoft evidently sees some advantage in keeping them separate.

When the Transport service processes messages in a queue, it attempts to deliver the first message in the queue. If the message delivery succeeds, it updates Safety Net and the shadow redundancy system, described earlier in this chapter, to indicate that delivery was successful. If not, the message remains queued and is retried at a later time. After a preset number of retry attempts, or after the retry interval expires, the message is considered undeliverable and returned to the sender with an NDR.

You need to be familiar with several different types of queues:

- The *submission queue* holds and organizes messages awaiting processing by the transport categorizer. All arriving messages on a server are delivered to this queue, and the categorizer processes each of them, redirecting them to other queues as appropriate.

- *Delivery queues* are the most familiar type. They contain messages being sent using SMTP. The destination can be remote or local. Each destination has one delivery queue. For example, if you have messages concurrently flowing to 17 remote SMTP domains through the Internet, you have at least 17 delivery queues.

- Messages that can't be delivered might end up in two additional, delivery-related queues. The *unreachable queue* contains messages for destinations that can't be routed to. For example, if Nicole addresses a message to an SMTP domain with no MX record, that message eventually ends up in the Unreachable queue. Messages with invalid recipients can end up here, too. Exchange periodically retries messages from this queue, so each message eventually is either returned with an NDR or delivered. Interestingly, this queue is hidden in both EMS and EAC unless messages are in it. Likewise, the *poison message* queue is normally invisible and empty. It receives and holds any message that made a Transport service crash. The idea is that such messages can be stuffed into this queue and kept out of the way before they cause further harm. Poison messages aren't automatically resubmitted, and the poison queue is never automatically cleared.

Viewing queues

You can view queues in Exchange 2013 in three primary ways. First, you can use the Get-Queue cmdlet, which gives you information about the queues on a specific server. Second, you can use Get-QueueDigest, which gives you a summary of queues across multiple servers. Or, third, you can use the Exchange Queue Viewer tool, a holdover from Exchange 2010.

USING GET-QUEUE

The following sample shows the output from the Get-Queue cmdlet on an Exchange 2013 server with the Mailbox and Client Access roles installed.

```
Get-Queue -Server PAO-EX01 -SortOrder: -MessageCount
```

Identity NextHopDomain	DeliveryType	Status	MessageCount	Velocity	RiskLevel	OutboundIPPool
PAO-EX01 \Submission Submission	Undefined	Ready 5		0	Normal	0
PAO-EX01\15	SmtpDeliv...	Retry 1		0	Normal	0	pao-ex02
PAO-EX01\16 robichaux.net	DnsConnec...	Active 1		0	Normal	0
PAO-EX01\17 microsoft.com	DnsConnec...	Active 1		0	Normal	0
PAO-EX01\18 summit7systems.com	DnsConnec...	Con... 1		0	Normal	0
PAO-EX01\3	SmtpDeliv...	Ready 0		0	Normal	0	pao-ex01
PAO-EX01\19 gmail.com	DnsConnec...	Ready 0		0	Normal	0

In this instance, the queues are sorted by the number of messages on the queue—that's what the SortOrder parameter in the sample command is for. The minus sign in front of the MessageCount parameter means you want to sort in descending order. Put a plus sign (+) in front of the parameter to sort in ascending order.

The Filter parameter is also available to select queues from the full set. For example, here's how to select the queues that hold more than 20 messages:

```
Get-Queue -Server ExServer1 -Filter {MessageCount -gt 20} -SortOrder:-MessageCount
```

You can only see queues while they're active. The Transport service creates queues as needed, and then deletes them when no messages are queued for that destination. If you look at a server during a period of heavy demand, you might see queues for every database in the local site, plus queues for servers in all the other Active Directory sites within the organization. If you look at the queues on the same server at a time of low demand, all the queues might have disappeared, except for the submission queue that submits messages to the categorizer.

USING GET-QUEUEDIGEST

The Get-QueueDigest cmdlet gives you a summary view of all active queues on multiple servers. You can use it to get an overview of queue activity for all servers in the forest, all members of a DAG or Active Directory site, or all servers on a specified list. Get-QueueDigest supports the Filter flag, so you can perform server-side filtering. It's very simple to use:

- The Forest flag shows queues for all servers in the current forest.
- The Dag option accepts a comma-separated list of one or more DAG names. For example, Get-Queue -DAG "Alexandria,Huntsville,Pensacola" shows all active queues on all servers that are members of any of those DAGs.
- Use Server to specify a comma-separated list of server names and show their queues.
- The Site option takes a comma-separated list of Active Directory site names.

These options are mutually exclusive, so you can only specify one at a time.

USING THE EXCHANGE QUEUE VIEWER

EAC doesn't include any way to see the contents of queues, so you have to use the EMS cmdlets previously described or use the Exchange Queue Viewer to examine the contents of the transport queues. The Queue Viewer is a Microsoft Management Console (MMC) that was part of the Exchange 2010 EMC toolbox collection and is now a standalone tool. The major advantage of the Queue Viewer is it provides an easy-to-use method to see what's happening on queues and to examine the properties of messages that are currently in a queue. The Transport service is capable of quickly processing even large messages, so the Queue Viewer refreshes its display every five seconds or so to provide an up-to-date picture of what's happening on a mailbox server.

Fixing queueing-related problems

Once you determine that message queue lengths are growing, the next step is to learn why. Remember, Exchange always tries to use the lowest-cost path to send messages. If you see messages backing up in a queue that can mean one of several things.

- The destination can't be reached at all. For example, if you only have one send connector, and it routes to a smarthost, and the smarthost is down, no outbound mail will flow.
- There is no available next hop. For example, if you have a topology with offices in Austin, Boston, and Chicago, where Austin and Chicago both route messages to Boston for connectivity to the Internet, and the Austin-Boston link fails, messages will queue in Austin, even though the Boston and Chicago sites are unaffected.

- The rate of delivery is slower than the rate of arrival. This might indicate a problem sending messages, such as a DNS problem on a server that makes DNS queries take exceptionally long to complete. This might also indicate a sudden spike in the number of messages arriving at that server, perhaps because another "upstream" server has just had a blockage resolved. (Think of what happens on a river when a dam breaks!)

The key thing to know when solving these problems is this: changing the set of possible routes that Exchange has access to, allows it to recalculate routes and frees the queued messages. For example, during a site outage that involves a server hosting a send connector that points to a smart host, you could allow messages to start flowing by taking any of several actions.

- Creating a new send connector with the same address spaces as the old connector, optionally removing the old connector.
- Changing the existing send connector to use MX record delivery instead of tying it to a specific smart host.
- Changing the smart host that the connector points to (assuming that connectivity to the smart host is the problem in the first place).
- Modifying costs on send connectors (and possibly Active Directory site links) to create a new, lower-cost alternate route.

Another common case is where Exchange can't find a workable route to the outside world because of connector settings. If you, for example, configure a Send connector to require TLS, it won't send mail to any domain that can't negotiate TLS. There's a tricky setting on the General slab of the Send connector property dialog box in EAC labeled Proxy Through Client Access Server. If you enable that setting, the Send connector routes all its outbound mail through a CAS server, causing it to exit your network with the IP of the CAS. Because most CAS servers are connected to the Internet, this may be useful to make sure your outbound mail has the correct IP address on it when you're not using a smart host or Edge Transport servers. The problem arises if there is no available CAS server: mail that would usually go over that Send connector instead queues because there's no way to satisfy the requirement that outbound traffic go through a CAS. To solve this problem, turn off the option and restart the Transport service. Then, mail over that Send connector should start flowing again.

Fixing other SMTP flow problems

When you're trying to troubleshoot SMTP mail flow, one of the first questions to ask is which mail flow is affected: mail into your servers from the Internet, outbound mail to the Internet, or both? If the answer is both, the first suggestion is to look at your Internet connection, because most of the parts of the Exchange transport system distinguish between inbound and outbound traffic.

For problems with inbound messages, you can use the message tracking system, plus protocol logs, to verify whether or not the messages made it to your servers in the first place. If they didn't make it, you should focus your efforts on verifying that your external mail infrastructure is set up properly. Look at your MX records, load balancer configuration, and external hygiene filtering (if any) to verify that a sender's server can reach your server without interruption.

For problems with outbound messages, remember Exchange queues messages at the point of failure. When you look at the queues on your server (probably using Get-QueueDigest), you can see where messages are building up. You can use the methods described in the previous section to create an alternate path to get the messages out.

Troubleshooting Domain Secure and TLS

For a server to participate correctly in Domain Security, you need to verify the following points.

1. The RequireTLS flag must be sent on the send and receive connectors for the participating domain. In other words, if you want to exchange TLS mail with contoso.com, whatever send and receive connectors you have configured for that domain must have RequireTLS $true set.

2. The IgnoreStartTLS flag must *not* be set on the connectors you want to participate.

3. The DomainSecureEnabled flag must be set on the send and receive connectors that carry traffic to your partner domains. If you don't set this, but you do set -RequireTLS $true on those connectors, they might still send or receive TLS-encrypted mail, but you won't see the Domain Secure icon in Outlook.

4. The target Send connector must be set to use MX record for delivery (Set-SendConnector -DNSRoutingEnabled $true). Using smart hosts for Domain Security isn't supported because the smart host is effectively a "man in the middle."

5. The domains you want to use for Domain Security must appear in the TLSReceiveDomainSecureList and TlsSendDomainSecureList parameters when you do a Get-TransportConfig. If they don't appear, you need to add them.

6. You must have valid certificates available to all the participating connectors.

This certificate requirement sometimes trips people up. The moment you no longer have a valid certificate for any connector involved in Domain Security or TLS, that connector no longer takes part in TLS conversations, either because the sending or the remote end recognizes it's invalid. If you configured your connectors to require TLS, mail queues until you replace the invalid certificate with a new one using EAC or the Enable-ExchangeCertificate cmdlet. You also need to restart the Transport service on the server hosting the connector where the mail is blocked.

Troubleshooting shared namespaces

Troubleshooting shared namespaces is a special case of SMTP troubleshooting because shared namespaces add two more layers of complexity. You have to make sure the messages are reaching your Exchange servers. The first extra layer is you have to verify the accepted domains you're using are properly configured. The second layer involves address rewriting. If you're using it, you must ensure the inbound or outbound addresses are being handled in the way you expect. Let's deal with each of these issues in turn.

You can see whether messages for any accepted domain are reaching your servers. A simple Get-AcceptedDomain cmdlet gives you the list of all the domains Exchange is willing to accept mail for. If you don't see the correct domains listed there, then you need to add them using the procedures described earlier in the chapter. Once you're confident the correct domains are being accepted (and that each domain has the correct type: authoritative, internal relay, or external relay), you can begin tracing the flow of messages using the protocol logs and message tracking logs. For inbound messages, you should see the message arrive from the Internet, and then flow over the appropriate connector if the domain is a relay domain. Sending a test message to a known good address in one of the accepted domains might also be helpful for two reasons. First, if an NDR is returned, it often gives you enough detail to pinpoint the nature of the failure. Second, using a single address (and a unique subject line) makes it easier to follow messages through the tracking logs by giving you an easy phrase to search for.

If you're using address rewriting, the primary thing you'll need to look for when troubleshooting is to verify that the rewriting entries exist and are correct. Use Get-AddressRewritingEntry to check these: if you don't see addresses being rewritten as you expect, it may be because there's no rewriting entry that matches the address you're using, or it may be that the rewriting entry exists but isn't generating the results you expect.

Thought experiment
Figuring out where mail went

In this Thought experiment, apply what you learned about this objective. You can find answers to these questions in the "Answers" section at the end of this chapter.

You're the email administrator for Contoso. One day you notice mail seems to have stopped flowing out from one of your Mailbox servers. Inbound mail appears unaffected.

1. What are some troubleshooting steps you might take to identify the source of the problem?

2. During your troubleshooting, can you do anything to get mail flowing again sooner?

Objective summary

- Users and administrators both have access to track messages in Exchange. Users can only track their own messages through OWA. Administrators can use ECP or the Get-MessageTrackingLog cmdlet.

- Message tracking logs show which parts of the Exchange transport pipeline, on which servers, took what actions on a message, and what the results were. Searching the tracking logs causes Exchange to correlate logs across servers.

- Several of the transport services also have the capability to log protocol-level transactions in protocol logs. This feature is off by default. When enabled, the protocol logs shows you the exact SMTP conversations that took place between the sending and receiving server, including the SMTP verbs used and the IP addresses of both ends.

- Every Exchange message passes through a sequence of queues from which the various transport services fetch them for processing. When messages build up in a queue faster than they can be sent, or if some kind of problem prevents them from being sent, delivery problems result.

- Because Exchange queues messages at the point of failure, when messages are queued, you can change the cost or availability of connectors to trigger rerouting.

Objective review

Answer the following questions to test your knowledge of the information in this objective. You can find the answers to these questions and explanations of why each answer choice is correct or incorrect in the "Answers" section at the end of this chapter.

1. You have three Active Directory sites: Site1, Site2, and Site3. Each site contains an Exchange 2013 CAS/Mailbox server. Site2 is set as a hub site. You notice that mail from Site1 users to Site3 users is queueing for delivery on the server in Site1. You investigate and find the server in Site2 has failed. You want to resume normal mail flow as quickly as possible. What should you do first?

   A. Create a new Send connector from Site1 to Site3.

   B. Remove the hub site.

   C. Restart the Microsoft Exchange Transport service on all servers in Site1.

   D. Modify the Active Directory site link costs between Site1 and Site2.

2. Your boss comes to your office and says she is trying to determine what happened to a message she was expecting, but hasn't received. What should you do first?

   A. Check the protocol logs on your Edge Transport servers.

   B. Tell your boss to have the sender resend the original message.

   C. Check the message tracking logs for the time period during which the message was expected.

   D. Restart the Transport service in case messages are stuck in a queue.

3. You receive a report that mail from a business partner is being rejected. When you investigate, you find the partner's domain is configured to use Domain Security but the certificate assigned to the SMTP service on the Mailbox server handling that traffic has expired. What should you do? (Choose all that apply.)

A. Set-SendConnector -IgnoreStartTLS on the Send connector that handles the partner's traffic.

B. Request and install a new certificate on the server.

C. Send the certificate to the administrator of the partner domain.

D. Use Enable-ExchangeCertificate to assign the new certificate to the SMTP service.

E. Create a new Receive connector and assign the partner's domain to it as an accepted domain

Objective 3.5: Configure and manage hygiene

Maintaining good message hygiene is a critical part of running Exchange. Email has become such a common method of attack that allowing unfiltered mail from the Internet to reach your end users is both dangerous and foolish. The message hygiene system built into on-premises Exchange 2013 servers includes filter agents that can check incoming messages for malware and spam. It has a fairly flexible set of controls that let you manage many aspects of the filtering process.

If you run the Get-TransportAgent cmdlet on a Mailbox server that has the full set of filtering agents installed, you see results similar to the following:

```
[PS] C:\Windows\system32>Get-TransportAgent


Identity                            Enabled         Priority
--------                            -------         --------
Transport Rule Agent                True            1
Malware Agent                       True            2
Text Messaging Routing Agent        True            3
Text Messaging Delivery Agent       True            4
Content Filter Agent                True            5
Sender Id Agent                     True            6
Sender Filter Agent                 True            7
Recipient Filter Agent              True            8
Protocol Analysis Agent             True            9
```

The agents are in this order for a reason: the Transport Rule agent has to run first to ensure messages are journaled (or otherwise processed by transport rules as appropriate), and then the Malware Filter agent runs. Then, the Content Filter, Sender ID, Sender Filter, and Recipient Filter agents run, followed by the Protocol Analysis agent. This ordering reflects the relative importance of each filter agent. For example, the Malware Filter agent needs to run before the others, so any infected messages can be filtered out of the pipeline as early in the process as possible.

Managing connection filtering

Connection filtering depends on the allow and block lists that you specified. The IP address the connection comes from is used as the basis for making the filtering decision. All the Connection Filter agent does is compare the IP address against the block and allow lists you configured, and then decide whether or not to allow the connection. Connection filtering happens before any of the other filtering stages because you can control how connection filtering is applied in one of four ways:

■ You can manage individual entries on the lists with the *-IPAllowListEntry and *-IP-BlockListEntry set of cmdlets. For example, running Add-IPAllowListEntry -IPRange 216.82.250.0/24 cmdlet results in the following output:

```
Identity       IPRange            ExpirationTime         HasExpired
--------       -------            --------------         ----------
   2           216.82.250.0/24    12/31/9999 3:59:59 PM  False
```

To create an entry, you can specify a single IP address or a range (either by using CIDR notation, as in this example, or by specifying start and end addresses). When you create the entry, you can also provide a comment and an expiration time after which the entry is automatically removed. You can't modify allow or block list entries individually after you add them. If you get something wrong, you have to delete the individual entry, and then re-add it.

■ You can specify list providers that Exchange will query. Examples of well-known list provider services include Spamhaus (*http://www.spamhaus.org/sbl*) and DNSBL (*http://www.dnsbl.info*). To use a provider, you have to create a provider by using the Add-IPAllowListProvider or Add-IPBlockListProvider cmdlet. This requires you to specify the name of the list provider, the DNS server the provider requires you to use, and whether the provider returns explicit status codes or a bitmask indicating why the target server is on the list. Normally, you use the AnyMatch:$true parameter for block list providers to indicate you want to treat any answer from the server as an indication you shouldn't be accepting mail from that particular IP address. You can also use Add-IPBlockListProvider -RejectionResponse to specify a custom string to be delivered as part of the "now go away" message that Exchange returns as part of the SMTP conversation when a sender's IP appears on the block list. Many sites set the custom message to a short phrase including the URL of the RBL provider, so senders whose messages are inadvertently blocked know what to do about it. Corresponding Get-, Set-, Remove-, and Test- cmdlets exist for both allow and block lists, too.

- You can change the configuration that applies to the allow or block lists themselves with the Set-IPAllowListConfig and Set-IPBlockListConfig cmdlets. You can enable or disable the use of the server-specific block list by using the Enable switch. When filtering is enabled, you can further control whether the allow or block list is used for external or internal email with the ExternalMailEnabled and InternalMailEnabled switches.

  The Set-IPBlockListConfig cmdlet adds two parameters specific to block lists. You can configure separate text responses that are returned when the message is rejected. The MachineEntryRejectionResponse text is included in the NDR generated when a block list entry based on SRL scoring rejects a message, whereas the text specified in StaticEntryRejectionResponse is sent back as an SMTP response when the connection is blocked because of an entry on the block list.

- You can change the settings that configure how Exchange uses allow or block list providers by using the Set-IPBlockListProvidersConfig and Set-IPAllowListProvidersConfig cmdlets. With either type of list, you can turn the use of providers on or off with the Enabled switch. You can also set whether the block or allow list providers you specified should be used for internal mail, external mail, both, or neither. To accomplish this, use the ExternalMailEnabled ($true by default) and InternalMailEnabled ($false by default) switches. The Set-IPBlockListProvidersConfig also has an additional switch. -BypassedRecipients accepts a multivalued list containing the SMTP addresses of senders whose mail should never be filtered, even if the originating address fails a provider list check.

Managing content filtering

Content filtering blocks or allows messages based on the contents of the message. Depending on the settings you apply to the Content Filter agent, messages can be rejected, held for further processing, or allowed to pass on to the recipient. You can specify phrases to block messages or exempt them from further filtering. These phrases are shared, so all servers in the organization use consistent settings. In addition, the Content Filter agent automatically downloads updates to its existing SmartScreen database of phrases.

> **NOTE LARGE MESSAGES DON'T GET FILTERED**
> Exchange 2013 only filters messages smaller than 11MB in size. Larger messages are ignored by the Content Filter agent.

You can also specify specific recipients or domains that should be exempt from filtering. For example, you might choose to specify a business partner's SMTP domain as an exempt domain. Then, no matter what they send you, their messages pass through the Content Filter agent with a flag value indicating they originated from an exempt sender and shouldn't be filtered.

The Content Filter agent also uses the aggregated Safe Senders, Blocked Senders, and Blocked Domains lists that Outlook and Outlook Web App users can create. Mailbox servers aggregate entries from different users into a single consolidated list, and that list is synchronized with Edge Transport servers as part of the EdgeSync process.

Specifying a quarantine mailbox

Message hygiene systems usually include some way to quarantine messages, so a user or administrator can examine them to see whether or not they should have been filtered. Some third-party systems provide a per-user quarantine function. However, instead of providing quarantine folders for each individual user, Exchange 2013 lets you specify a single quarantine mailbox for the entire organization. Messages quarantined by the spam or malware filters are placed in this mailbox, so an administrator can either review and release them from quarantine, or delete them in place. To set the quarantine mailbox, use the Set-ContentFilterConfig cmdlet with the QuarantineMailbox parameter, like this:

```
Set-ContentFilterConfig m -QuarantineMailbox joe@contoso.com
```

The quarantine mailbox you specify doesn't have to be an Exchange mailbox, it only has to be a valid SMTP address.

EXAM TIP

The Exchange 2013 quarantine functionality is pretty weak. All you can do is designate a single quarantine mailbox and a single SCL threshold for putting messages in it. The quarantine features of Exchange Online Protection (EOP), as well as most third-party message hygiene systems, are much more advanced. Don't let your knowledge of those systems mislead you into wrongly answering questions about the Exchange 2013 feature set.

Managing Spam Confidence Level (SCL) thresholds

The original spam filtering systems were primitive by today's standards. Their filtering was crude, and they could only label a message in one of two ways: spam or not. It didn't take long to recognize that a more granular scale for evaluating spam might be useful. Exchange implements this notion with a 10-point scale called the *spam confidence level* (SCL). Many of the Exchange anti-spam agents do their work by setting the SCL for a message. As an administrator, you can choose what happens to messages based on their assigned SCL.

An SCL of 10 indicates a message that is positively known to be spam. A value of 1 indicates a message that's very unlikely to be spam. All the numbers in between indicate how spam-like the Exchange filtering system thinks a message is. An SCL value of -1 indicates the message is known to be good because it matched a specific rule or exception, such as coming from a trusted sender. You can set thresholds that remove messages, quarantine them, or deliver them directly to users' individual junk mail folders based on the message SCL.

The Content Filter agent can act on a message based on its SCL. You can set levels at which three actions take place with the Set-ContentFilterConfig cmdlet:

- -SCLRejectThreshold specifies the SCL at which the message is rejected with an NDR (optionally including a message if you specify one with the RejectionResponse parameter).

- -SCLQuarantineThreshold specifies the SCL at which the message is quarantined for inspection and possible release. Messages are only quarantined if you also specify the SCLQuarantineEnabled $true parameter. Simply setting the threshold by itself won't filter anything.

- -SCLDeleteThreshold sets the SCL at which the message is silently deleted. Use this parameter to instruct Exchange to throw away messages. If you want the sender to get a notification, use SCLRejectThreshold instead.

Setting these thresholds doesn't do anything unless you enable the corresponding behavior with the SCLRejectEnabled, SCLDeleteEnabled, or SCLQuarantineEnabled parameters. For example, you can specify that messages with an SCL of six should be quarantined, messages with an SCL of seven should be rejected, and messages with an eight or above should be deleted with this command:

```
Set-ContentFilterConfig -SCLQuarantineEnabled $true `
-SCLQuarantineThreshold 6 `
  -SCLRejectEnabled $true `
-SCLRejectThreshold 7 `
-SCLDeleteThreshold 8 `
  -SCLDeleteEnabled $true `
-QuarantineMailbox junk@contoso.com `
  -RejectionResponse "Contoso does not accept spam messages"
```

Note this command enables the SCL quarantine and rejection behaviors, sets thresholds for them both, and adds an optional message included in the NDR returned to the sender. Because you enabled quarantine, you must also include the SMTP address of the quarantine mailbox you want to use.

Exempting specific senders, recipients, and domains

You can force the Content Filter agent to allow specific senders, recipients, or domains. Microsoft refers to these as "bypassed" items, so you use the BypassedSenders, BypassedSenderDomains, and BypassedRecipients parameters to Set-ContentFilterConfig. When you set a sender, recipient, or domain as bypassed, then those messages are exempt from any other content filtering. Remember, other agents in the filter pipeline still run against messages that are exempt from content filtering.

Blocking or allowing specific words or phrases

Content filtering based on the message text can be useful if you can identify specific phrases or words you want to block or exempt consistently. These phrases might vary between different organizations. For example, Woodgrove Bank might not want to filter messages that mention the phrase "mortgage loans," while Tailspin Toys might filter messages with that phrase because of its frequent use by spammers.

The Add- and Remove-ContentFilterPhrase cmdlets let you specify how individual phrases should be treated. When you add a content filter phrase, you must specify the phrase and whether you want to treat it as a good or bad influence on the filter. A "good" phrase receives an SCL of zero, while a "bad" phrase gets an SCL of nine. For example, the following cmdlets block any messages containing the phrase "Cheap Pharma" while exempting the phrase "Project Starburst" from filtering:

```
Add-ContentFilterPhrase -Phrase "Cheap Pharma" -Influence BadWord
Add-ContentFilterPhrase -Phrase "Project Starburst" -Influence GoodWord
```

Controlling which types of mail are filtered

By default, content filtering is active on every Mailbox and Edge Transport server, and it filters only mail originating outside the organization. That means you have a few options for controlling what the filter actually does:

- To disable content filtering altogether, use Set-ContentFilterConfig -Enabled. This doesn't disable the Content Filter agent, it just tells it to run without filtering anything.

- To have content filtering applied to mail originating inside the organization, use Set-ContentFilterConfig -InternalMailEnabled $true. By default, this switch is off.

- To filter content originating from external servers (the defaut), use Set-ContentFilterConfig -ExternalMailEnabled $true.

Remember, these settings only apply to the Mailbox server where you run them. If you want the same settings applied on all Mailbox servers, you need to apply those settings on all servers.

Managing recipient filtering

In a normal SMTP conversation, the next command sent by the sender after MAIL FROM is one or more RCPT TO commands listing the intended message recipients. The Exchange Recipient Filter agent can filter messages by checking the list of recipients against a block list of recipients who should never receive mail from unauthenticated senders, or by verifying that the target recipient exists in the Exchange organization. Messages sent to blocked or unknown recipients are rejected. Messages sent to legitimate recipients are accepted and sent to the next stage in the transport pipeline.

Exchange can perform two types of recipient filtering. First, it can use an administrator-defined, organization-specific list of recipients that should never receive external email. This is often used for internal addresses (such as service desks) that should never receive mail from the outside world. Second, recipient filtering can look up recipients in Active Directory to see whether they exist, rejecting or ignoring any message sent to a nonexistent recipient. Using this second method is especially valuable on Edge Transport servers because it lets the Edge role screen out bogus recipients before they make it inside.

You use the Get- and Set-RecipientFilterConfig cmdlets to manage recipient filter behavior. Recipient filtering is enabled by default, but you can disable it using the Enabled:$false switch, although this leaves the Recipient Filter agent in the transport pipeline.

After recipient filtering is enabled, you can choose whether it applies to internal or external email by using the InternalMailEnabled and ExternalMailEnabled switches, the same as connection filtering. You can also specify blocked recipients by specifying a comma-separated list to the -BlockedRecipient switch (for instance, Set-RecipientFilterConfig -BlockedRecipient helpdesk@contoso.com,CEO@contoso.com) and setting the -BlockListEnabled flag to $True. By default, recipient blocking is turned off, which is fine because it's not a terribly useful feature for most organizations.

The most useful setting for Set-RecipientFilterConfig is probably RecipientValidationEnabled. When it's set to $True, the Recipient Filter agent performs directory lookups for each recipient specified in an RCPT TO command, rejecting or blocking messages to nonexistent senders.

Managing Sender ID

Sender ID was designed to be flexible because Microsoft realized that the usefulness of having a protocol to help verify senders' information had to be weighed against the fact that many senders wouldn't or couldn't adopt it so that automatically blocking mail from sending systems that don't use Sender ID would result in high numbers of false positives. The key aspect of this flexibility is thatthe Sender ID agent persists information about the nature of the failure when a message fails a Sender ID check, so later stages in the pipeline can use that information to help decide what to do.

You configure the Sender ID agent's behavior with the Set-SenderIdConfig cmdlet. The Sender ID agent understands three actions: it can stamp the Sender ID status of the message on the message (the default behavior), it can reject the message with a 5xx SMTP error, or it can silently delete the message. You can specify separate actions for outright failures (corresponding to a Sender ID status of Fail) and temporary failures (corresponding to a Sender ID status of TempError) with the SpoofedDomainAction and TempErrorAction parameters to Set-SenderIdConfig.

As with most of the other filtering agents, you can specify senders or recipients whose mail should be exempted from Sender ID filtering, in this case by using the BypassedRecipients and BypassedSenderDomains parameters to Set-SenderIdConfig. These work identically to the bypass switches for Set-ContentFilterConfig: the recipients or sender domains you pass to Set-SenderIdConfig are exempt from that specific filter only.

Managing anti-malware

The Set-MalwareFilteringServer cmdlet lets you control the behavior of the malware filtering agent on an individual server. Although you can't directly change the way filtering works, you can use the parameters for Set-MalwareFilteringServer to control the following.

- Whether malware filtering actually acts on incoming messages. If you use -Bypass-Filtering $true, the filter still scans incoming messages, but it won't take any action on suspicious messages. Use -BypassFiltering $false to re-enable message actions. You might need to do this to temporarily reduce the load on your servers, or to allow troubleshooting to verify that malware filtering isn't accidentally filtering legitimate messages.

- How often malware signatures are updated. By default, each server downloads signature updates every 60 minutes. Depending on what other filtering solutions you're using, you may want to change this interval, which you can do with the UpdateFrequency parameter. You need to specify the number of minutes you want the updates to be pulled, for example, Set-MalwareFilteringServer -UpdateFrequency 1440 specifies daily updates (because 24 x 60 = 1440).

- How many times to retry a message that can't be scanned for some reason. The DeferAttempts parameter controls this. Acceptable values are from one to five, with a default of three. After the set number of deferrals has been reached, the action varies according to why the message was deferred. If the scan engine failed or timed out, the message is returned with a non-delivery receipt (NDR). For all other errors, the message is retried for up to 48 hours. The first deferral retry is after one hour; the next, two hours after that; and then three hours after that, and so on.

- How long to wait between scan attempts for a deferred item. Set the DeferWaitTime parameter to a number of minutes between 0 (meaning that items are immediately re-submitted) and 15. On the first deferral, the filter waits for the specified interval before retrying. On the second deferral, it waits for double the specified interval, and so on. When the item has run out of deferral attempts (as set by the DeferAttempts parameter), the timing described in the preceding bullet kicks in.

- How long to wait before deciding that a scan attempt has failed. Set the ScanTimeout parameter to the number of seconds (between 10 and 900; the default is 300) that must elapse before the engine decides the scan attempt has failed.

- What to do if a message fails all its deferred scan attempts. The default is to block the message. You can use the ScanErrorAction switch to allow those messages through instead, although that probably isn't a great idea from a security perspective.

- Whether you want to rescan messages that have already been scanned by Exchange Online Protection (EOP). If ForceRescan is set to $True, every incoming message is scanned, even if it's stamped with the X-MS-Exchange-Organization-AVStamp-Enterprise or X-MS-Exchange-Organization-AVStamp-Service scan headers that EOP stamps on messages when it scans them.

- How often to fetch signature updates. The default is to do so once per hour. By changing the value of the UpdateFrequency parameter to the number of minutes you want to pass between updates, you can vary the interval up to 27 days or down to one minute. An hour is a reasonable default.

- Where to get signature updates. The PrimaryUpdatePath and SecondaryUpdatePath parameters control this behavior. You would typically use them when Exchange servers don't have direct access to the Internet to fetch signature updates from an internal staging server. To load the updates on the server in the first place, you can use the URLs contained in the Update-MalwareFilteringServer.ps1 script (included in the Exchange scripts directory) to download updates onto a staging server, and then move them over to the server that needs them. The UpdateTimeout parameter specifies the interval—in seconds—that you want the server to wait before switching from the primary to the secondary update path.

You might find it useful to manually update malware signature updates on a specific server. While there's no direct cmdlet to do so, Microsoft provides a script as part of each Exchange installation (in the $exscripts directory) named Update-MalwareFilteringServer. ps1. Run this script and specify the FQDN of the target server. It downloads the current set of definitions and applies them to the server you specify.

Managing attachment filtering

Attachment filtering, which is only available on Edge Transport servers, lets you filter messages based on their attachments. According to the list of file names, file extensions, or MIME file types you specify, you can delete messages that contain a blocked attachment, reject them with an NDR, or allow the message through while stripping the offending attachments. The basic tasks involved with attachment filtering break down into three categories: enabling or disabling filtering, changing the types or names of attachments that should be filtered, and choosing a filter action (which must be the same for all filtered attachments).

To enable or disable filtering, use the Enable-TransportAgent or Disable-TransportAgent cmdlets, specifying "Attachment Filtering Agent" as the target, like this:

```
Enable-TransportAgent "Attachment Filtering Agent"
```

Remember, like any other time when you enable or disable transport agents, you have to restart the Microsoft Exchange Transport service on the Edge Transport server before this change takes place. While the service is being restarted, that server won't process any inbound mail.

If you want to see the list of attachment types the filter is currently set to block, you can use the Get-AttachmentFilterEntry cmdlet. Just running the cmdlet by itself dumps the list of filtering entries on the current server. You can use the ContentType or FileName parameters to specify that you only want to see filter entries that match the wildcard you specify. However, these parameters have an unusual syntax: you don't specify them with the "-" that normally precedes Exchange Management Shell parameters. To specify that you want to see the entries for all image file filters, do this:

```
Get-AttachmentFilterEntry ContentType:image/*
```

To add a new filtering entry, you use Add-AttachmentFilterEntry. You can specify the new entry is based on a MIME content type or a file name pattern with the Type ContentType and Type FileName parameters, respectively. Whichever you specify, you must also include the Name parameter to indicate what pattern the filter entry should match. Here are two different ways to attempt to block RAR archives:

```
Add-AttachmentFilterEntry -Type ContentType -Name application/x-rar-compressed
Add-AttachmentFilterEntry -Type FileName -Name *.rar
```

You can also remove filtering list entries with the Remove-AttachmentFilterEntry cmdlet (for example, Remove-AttachmentFilterEntry -Identity FileName:*.rar).

To control what happens when a message contains an attachment that matches a filter list entry, use the Set-AttachmentFilterListConfig cmdlet. You can't set an action for individual file types. The action you pick applies to any attachment that matches. You can strip messages with the Action Strip parameter, reject messages with Action Reject (in which case you can specify an NDR message the sender receives using the RejectResponse parameter), or silently delete the message with Action SilentDelete.

> ### Thought experiment
> #### Deploying message hygiene
>
> In this Thought experiment, apply what you learned about this objective. You can find answers to these questions in the "Answers" section at the end of this chapter.
>
> You're the email administrator for Litware, Inc. As part of your upgrade to Exchange 2013, you've been asked to recommend message hygiene settings for Exchange.
>
> **1.** What would you recommend, and why?

Objective summary

- Message hygiene services are provided by a set of several transport agents. Some of these agents can run on the Mailbox or Edge Transport roles, while the Connection, Attachment, and Recipient Filter agents only run on the Edge Transport role.
- The filtering agents work together to assign a spam confidence level (SCL) to each incoming message.
- You can set thresholds for the SCL that, when exceeded, cause the message to be quarantined, rejected with an NDR, or silently dropped.
- Content filtering works by assigning specific phrases as "good" or "bad." Good phrases are exempted from filtering, while bad phrases automatically receive an SCL of nine, the highest level.
- Recipient filtering lets you reject messages to nonexistent recipients. However, you have to be careful when using it together with relay domains to avoid inadvertently bouncing mail for relay domains.

- Connection filtering can allow or block messages based on the originating IP address, either directly or because the IP address appears on a block list you specify.
- Exchange includes malware filtering, which you can temporarily bypass for trouble-shooting purposes, but which should normally be allowed to run even if you're using an external scanner.

Objective review

Answer the following questions to test your knowledge of the information in this objective. You can find the answers to these questions and explanations of why each answer choice is correct or incorrect in the "Answers" section at the end of this chapter.

1. While troubleshooting a message delivery problem, you want to temporarily disable malware scanning on a server. The best way to accomplish this is to:

   A. Use Set-TransportConfig to disable filtering.

   B. Run the Disable-MessageFiltering.ps1 script on the target server.

   C. Use Set-MalwareFilteringServer to disable filtering.

   D. Use New-MalwareFilterPolicy to create an empty policy and apply it to the target server.

2. You are asked to ensure that incoming messages containing the phrase "Project Oxcart" are never treated as spam. To do this, which of the following actions should you take?

   A. Set-ContentFilterConfig -SCLQuarantineLevel 7.

   B. Add-ContentFilterPhrase -Phrase "Project Oxcart" -Influence GoodWord.

   C. Set-ContentFilterConfig -EnableFiltering $true.

   D. Run the Install-AntispamAgents.ps1 script on the Edge Transport server.

3. You want to specify the quarantine mailbox. Which of the following commands should you use?

   A. Set-ContentFilterConfig -QuarantineMailbox.

   B. Set-MalwareFilteringServer.

   C. Set-Mailbox -Quarantine.

   D. New-Mailbox -Identity Quarantine.

Answers

This section contains the solutions to the Thought experiments and answers to the objective review questions in this chapter.

Objective 3.1: Thought experiment

1. Because Fabrikam depends on inbound mail flow for order processing and handling, high availability of inbound messages is critically important. Your design should take this into account by using redundant DNS records or, preferably, a load balancer to handle inbound traffic. Ensure you have enough servers properly situated to take advantage of Safety Net and shadow redundancy, and provide adequate logging and traceability for verifying message flow.

2. Your test plan should include tests for internal mail flow between users in the same mailbox database, on different mailbox databases within the same DAG, between users in different DAGs, and between Active Directory sites. You should also plan to thoroughly test mail flow to and from the Internet.

Objective 3.1: Review

1. **Correct answer:** A

   A. **Correct:** Shadow redundancy requires at least two servers to function: messages arrive at one server, which contacts its shadow redundancy partner to persist the message.

   B. **Incorrect:** With only a single server, shadow redundancy won't be able to preserve any messages.

   C. **Incorrect:** Internet and internal messages are treated the same way by the shadow redundancy subsystem, so if shadow redundancy is disabled or inoperative, no messages is persisted.

   D. **Incorrect:** Internet and internal messages are treated the same way by the shadow redundancy subsystem, so if shadow redundancy is disabled or inoperative, no messages is persisted.

2. **Correct answer:** C

    A. **Incorrect:** A Mailbox server can accept mail for a non-local mailbox, and its local Transport service routes the message to another server for delivery.

    B. **Incorrect:** Shadow redundancy isn't required to be enabled to receive mail from the Internet.

    C. **Correct:** When you configure redundant DNS MX records, each record must have an equal preference value. Any record with a higher preference value assigned gets proportionally less traffic than the group of records that all have the same preference.

    D. **Incorrect:** Standalone Exchange servers can accept and send mail without being part of a DAG.

Objective 3.2: Thought experiment

1. The requirement to keep thephonecompany.com indicates you should add it as an accepted domain to the Exchange server. Configure it as an internal relay domain and add a Send connector to the existing Linux system.

2. The Send connector provides mail flow from Exchange to the Linux system. You need to ensure the correct email addressing policies are in place, so users have the right email addresses.

Objective 3.2: Review

1. **Correct answer:** B

    A. **Incorrect:** You manage the designation of an Active Directory site as an Exchange hub site with Set-ADSite, not any of the Active Directory management tools.

    B. **Correct:** Set-ADSite lets you designate a hub site.

    C. **Incorrect:** The number or type of servers in a given site doesn't influence whether the site is marked as a hub site.

    D. **Incorrect:** This answer is a distractor. There is no LeafSiteEnabled parameter to Set-ADSite.

2. **Correct answer:** D

    A. **Incorrect:** The transport agents aren't packaged as individual files and can't be copied between servers.

    B. **Incorrect:** This answer is a distractor. There is no such parameter to the Exchange setup utility.

    C. **Incorrect:** This answer is a distractor.

    D. **Correct:** The Install-AntispamAgents.ps1 script is the only way to enable the additional message hygiene agents on a Mailbox server.

3. **Correct answers:** A and B

    A. **Correct:** Connection filtering is only available on the Edge Transport role.

    B. **Correct:** Attachment filtering is only available on the Edge Transport role.

    C. **Incorrect:** Content filtering is available on the Mailbox and Edge Transport roles.

    D. **Incorrect:** Sender ID filtering is available on the Mailbox and Edge Transport roles.

    E. **Incorrect:** Sender Reputation filtering is available on the Mailbox and Edge Transport roles.

4. **Correct answers:** A, B, and C

    A. **Correct:** To participate in Domain Security, you have to define your own domain as a TLS sending domain with Set-TransportConfig.

    B. **Correct:** To participate in Domain Security, you have to define the partner domain as a TLS receiving domain with Set-TransportConfig.

    C. **Correct:** You need a Send connector with type Partner, the correct address space, and a valid certificate to send mail to the partner domain.

    D. **Incorrect:** The existing receive connectors can receive TLS mail unless you specifically disabled that feature.

    E. **Incorrect:** Domain Security doesn't require certificates for individual users, just for the servers that host participating connectors.

Objective 3.3: Thought experiment

1. The key to a smooth Edge deployment is verifying that inbound mail flow works before pointing the full inbound mail stream to the Edge servers. Don't change the MX record until your testing is complete. You want to verify that inbound messages are filtered as appropriate (in other words, that you tested all the filtering settings you put into place), that failure of your Edge servers doesn't interrupt mail flow (unless they all fail, which you should also plan for), and that any address rewriting rules you plan to use are working properly.

2. You might want to review your connectors to consolidate existing connectors into a smaller number or change the endpoints. In addition, while you're at it, a good idea is to review whether any of the domains you communicate with is a candidate for forced TLS or Domain Security.

3. Exchange includes a wide variety of compliance and hygiene features. You might mention to Fourth Coffee that they review all their existing transport rules, modifying them as necessary to provide disclaimers, ethical firewalls, auditing, or moderation as needed.

Objective 3.3: Review

1. **Correct answer:** E
   A. **Incorrect:** The legacy system is part of a shared namespace, not an external entity, so it wouldn't use an external relay domain.
   B. **Incorrect:** The legacy system is part of a shared namespace, not an external entity, so it wouldn't use an internal relay domain.
   C. **Incorrect:** It isn't necessary to create an additional Receive connector.
   D. **Incorrect:** There's no need to create an additional address policy because you want all incoming mail to be routed without changing addresses.
   E. **Correct:** Creating a new Send connector for unresolved recipients allows incoming mail for legacy users to be properly routed.

2. **Correct answer:** D
   A. **Incorrect:** This solution would work, but it isn't the best solution because it's significantly more complex than the correct answer.
   B. **Incorrect:** This answer is a distractor. The only entries that should appear in the internal server list are those that relay mail through Exchange.
   C. **Incorrect:** You can't create Send connectors to an Exchange CAS unless you designate the CAS as a smart host, which wouldn't achieve the desired result.
   D. **Correct:** the FrontEndProxyEnabled setting, when set, forces outbound mail to pass through a CAS server, so it achieves the desired result.

3. **Correct answer:** B
   A. **Incorrect:** You have to set delay notification timeouts on individual servers, not on the organizational transport system.
   B. **Correct:** Set-TransportService -DelayNotificationTimeout will allow you to change the delay notification value as requested.
   C. **Incorrect:** This answer is a distractor. There is no such cmdlet.
   D. **Incorrect:** This answer is a distractor. You can't set timeout values for individual mailboxes.

4. **Correct answers:** C and D
   A. **Incorrect:** You can't set filtering options directly on the receive connector.
   B. **Incorrect:** This answer is a distractor. There are no relevant filtering options that you can set with Set-TransportConfig.
   C. **Correct:** You need to use Add-ContentFilterPhrase to block the target words using Influence BadWord.
   D. **Correct:** Set-RecipientFilterConfig lets you block mail from the Internet to the target distribution list by specifying its SMTP address.
   E. **Incorrect:** Malware filtering policies can't be used to control filtering messages based on their contents or recipients.

Objective 3.4: Thought experiment

1. The first step in troubleshooting a problem like this is normally to localize the problem to a particular server or site. In this case, if you know a single server is affected, you should review the queues on that server and see if the blockage affects all of them or a subset. Once you have an idea of the extent of the blockage, you can make configuration changes as needed.

2. You could change the costs on your existing connectors (and possibly on site links), or create or remove the connectors accessible to the problem server. The fastest route to get mail flowing is probably to raise the cost on the misbehaving connector and create a new connector to a different endpoint with a different cost.

Objective 3.4: Review

1. **Correct answer:** B

   A. **Incorrect:** Creating a send connector doesn't remove the restriction that all mail flows through the hub site, so the blockage will remain.

   B. **Correct:** Removing the hub site eliminates the restriction that all mail must pass through the hub site, so Site1 can send directly to Site3 once this restriction is gone.

   C. **Incorrect:** Restarting the Transport service won't do anything except interrupt normal mail flow.

   D. **Incorrect:** The site link costs aren't used to calculate routing in this case because Site2 is specified as a hub site, so changing the link costs won't resolve the problem.

2. **Correct answer:** C

   A. **Incorrect:** The protocol logs might tell you whether or not the message arrived at your perimeter, but they don't provide as much useful detail as the message tracking logs. You probably wouldn't rely on them first.

   B. **Incorrect:** This would be a terrible first troubleshooting step to take!

   C. **Correct:** The message tracking logs are on by default, and they contain information (including the subject line) that should let you quickly determine whether or not the message arrived at your network and, if so, what happened to it after that.

   D. **Incorrect:** Restarting the Transport service interrupts normal mail flow. With no evidence that an actual transport problem exists, this would be a poor troubleshooting choice.

3. **Correct answers:** B and D

   A. **Incorrect:** Changing this setting on the send connector won't have any effect on inbound mail flow.

   B. **Correct:** You need to get and install a valid certificate before the remote system will accept a mutual TLS session with your servers.

   C. **Incorrect:** The remote administrator doesn't need your certificate. Your Exchange servers present it as part of TLS negotiation.

   D. **Correct:** After you obtain the new certificate, you have to register it with Exchange by assigning it to the SMTP service.

Objective 3.5: Thought experiment

1. The filtering capabilities in Exchange 2013 are designed to do a good job screening mail without requiring any adjustments. Because you're just deploying Exchange 2013, and probably aren't familiar with how the filtering works, your best course of action is to leave the default filtering settings in place and see how well Exchange does at filtering the specific mix of mail you get. Once you have some practical experience with what is, and is not, being filtered in your environment, you can start changing SCL thresholds, adding content filtering phrases, and configuring the other filtering agents as appropriate.

Objective 3.5: Review

1. **Correct answer:** C

   A. **Incorrect:** This answer is a distractor. This cmdlet won't change the state of malware filtering.

   B. **Incorrect:** This answer is a distractor. There is no provided script by that name.

   C. **Correct:** Set-MalwareFilteringServer can be used to temporarily disable, and then re-enable, malware filtering on the suspect server.

   D. **Incorrect:** Malware filtering policies can't pause or disable malware scanning for a server.

2. **Correct answer:** B

   A. **Incorrect:** This command sets the SCL threshold for quarantining a message, but won't exempt messages with the key phrase from filtering.

   B. **Correct:** Tagging a phrase with Influence GoodWord forces the content filtering agent to set its SCL to -1, indicating that the message is known good and should not be filtered further

   C. **Incorrect:** This answer is a distractor. This cmdlet doesn't have an EnableFiltering parameter.

   D. **Incorrect:** The antispam agents are already installed on the Edge Transport role, so this command won't accomplish anything.

3. **Correct answer:** A

   A. **Correct:** This command sets the quarantine mailbox to the specified SMTP address.

   B. **Incorrect:** This answer is a distractor. There is no such cmdlet.

   C. **Incorrect:** This answer is a distractor. This cmdlet doesn't has no parameters that can be used to change quarantine-related settings.

   D. **Incorrect:** This answer is a distractor. This command creates a new mailbox named Quarantine, but it won't be used as a quarantine mailbox until it's set with Set-ContentFilterConfig -QuarantineMailbox.

Design and manage an Exchange infrastructure

S ome Exchange administrators inherit complete Exchange environments that already have everything set up and running, while others have to upgrade or migrate from another system, or an old version of Exchange, to Exchange 2013. Whenever you deploy Exchange 2013, there are several areas you need to be mindful of:

- Making sure that your Active Directory Domain Services (AD DS) and Domain Name System (DNS) environments are configured, and sized, appropriately for your Exchange deployment;

- Knowing how to monitor Exchange performance and how to respond if users complain of unusually slow client performance;

- Taking full advantage of role-based access control, the security system that Exchange uses to control which Exchange features users and administrators can access; and

- Designing your Exchange environment to meet a specific service level agreement (SLA)

Objectives in this chapter:

- Objective 4.1: Plan for impact of Exchange on Active Directory services
- Objective 4.2: Administer Exchange workload management
- Objective 4.3: Plan and manage role based access control (RBAC)
- Objective 4.4: Design an appropriate Exchange solution for a given Service Level Agreement

Objective 4.1: Plan for impact of Exchange on Active Directory services

Exchange depends completely on Active Directory. One lesson that many Exchange administrators have had to learn the hard way is that any interruption in, or problem with, the Active Directory service inevitably leads to problems with Exchange. Most of the time when you deploy Exchange, it's in an environment that already has a stable, properly functioning Active Directory environment, but that environment might not be designed or sized correctly for the specific requirements of Exchange 2013. In this lesson, you will learn how to size and configure Active Directory and Domain Name System (DNS) to support Exchange 2013 installations. You also learn how to prepare an existing Active Directory environment for Exchange 2013 by extending its schema and setting permissions.

> **This objective covers how to:**
> - Plan the number of domain controllers
> - Plan the placement of global catalog (GC) servers
> - Determine DNS changes required for Exchange
> - Prepare domains for Exchange
> - exEvaluate the impact of the schema changes required for Exchange
> - Plan around Active Directory site topology

Planning Active Directory deployment

The US Navy SEALs have a saying: "Two is one, and one is none." This just means that for critical equipment, you'd better have adequate redundancy because if you have only one of anything, it represents a single point of failure. Exchange administrators haven't exactly adopted this saying, but it is certainly true for Active Directory. Knowing how many domain controllers and global catalog (GC) servers you need, and where to put them, is critical in getting good results from your Exchange deployment.

Planning placement of GC servers

The basic planning guidance from Microsoft on where to put Active Directory servers has long been based on three guidelines:

- Put at least one GC in every Active Directory site that contains an Exchange server. Because having a single domain controller or GC represents a single point of failure, this guideline calls for putting at least two GCs in each site.

- Put at least one GC in every Active Directory site that contains computers that run Outlook.

- Don't install Exchange on GCs servers or domain controllers. Doing so makes disaster recovery much more complicated.

Interestingly, for older versions of Exchange, Microsoft used to provide separate prescriptive guidance around the number of domain controllers and GCs required. Microsoft no longer does that. The documentation (and the code) assume that every domain controller that Exchange might talk to is also a GC. This is not an unreasonable assumption.

EXAM TIP

If you see a question or case study that includes Exchange running on a GC, or an answer that suggests that you do so, be wary. Although this configuration is supported, it's a bad idea. Look for the answer that involves keeping Exchange on its own separate servers.

When an Exchange 2013 server starts, it randomly chooses a GC in the same Active Directory site and attaches to it. You can override this behavior with the Set-ExchangeServer cmdlet, which allows you to define a set of GCs that a particular server should use. However, if you find yourself having to use this cmdlet, stop and consider why you want Exchange to use GCs that aren't in its local site. If the reason is that there aren't enough in-site GCs, you should add some, rather than forcing cross-site access in most cases.

EXAM TIP

The introduction of read-only domain controllers (RODCs) doesn't change these guidelines. This is because Exchange won't use RODCs even when they're in the same Active Directory site. Because Exchange won't use RODCs, one favorite tactic of exam writers is to give you a question or case study where some sites have RODCs, and then ask you to figure out how Exchange will use a particular Active Directory resources. Remember, when it comes to RODCs, Exchange just ignores them.

Planning the number of domain controllers

For most deployments, the number of domain controllers doesn't matter as long as you have enough capacity to authenticate users and apply group policies at a reasonable speed. Domain controller performance is often less important to users and admins than domain controller reliability and availability (in the previous section). However, Microsoft does have sizing guidelines for Active Directory when it's used to supporting Exchange, and you'll be expected to know these guidelines for the 70-341 exam. These guidelines are also useful when you're planning large Exchange deployments.

The basic rule is simple: for every eight cores dedicated to Mailbox server operations, you need at least one 64-bit core dedicated to GC processing. However, you still have to observe the guidelines in the previous section. If you have a single 8-core Mailbox server, that doesn't mean it's safe to have a single 2-core GC server. If that GC fails, your Exchange server will stop working. Even for small deployments, the guidance of Microsoft is to have at least two Mailbox servers and two GCs.

Planning around Active Directory site topology

In Chapter 1, you learned how Exchange 2013 uses site topology when making decisions about how to route messages. Unless you change its behavior by setting Exchange-specific site link costs, or modifying the underlying Active Directory topology, Exchange routes messages between Active Directory sites as it did with older versions, treating each Active Directory site as a separate physical site. You can create connectors to shape mail flow to and from specific domains, but you need to understand your internal Active Directory site topology and modify it, if necessary, to affect internal message routing.

Determining DNS changes required for Exchange

There's good news and bad news when it comes to DNS and Exchange. The good news is that DNS is a stable, robust part of virtually every network, and Exchange's impact on DNS is fairly low. The bad news is that proper DNS configuration and setup is critical for Exchange. If DNS doesn't work, you might not be able to send inbound or outbound mail. There are two aspects to configuring DNS to support Exchange: first, adding the necessary records to allow inbound mail flow, and, second, ensuring that your DNS infrastructure is available to Exchange when it needs to resolve the names of servers to which outbound mail is being sent.

DNS configuration for inbound mail

The mail exchanger (MX) record discussed in the section "Planning for redundant MX records" in Chapter 1 is a critical requirement for inbound mail with Exchange. Unless you have at least one MX record that is configured to route traffic to your Exchange system, you won't receive any inbound mail. More accurately, you need to have at least one MX record that points to a service or server that can deliver mail to your Exchange environment. For example, if you're using Microsoft Exchange Online Protection (EOP), which is included with the Exchange enterprise client access license (CAL), your MX records point at whatever servers Microsoft tells you to direct mail to, and those servers are then separately configured with connectors that point to your on-premises Exchange servers.

   As described earlier, you need at least one public MX record. That is, there must be an MX record that other servers on the Internet can resolve to an IP address. The MX record contains the name of the server to which you want mail for your domain sent. You also need an associated CNAME and A record pair that maps the name specified in the MX record to the IP address of your server. Exchange doesn't care what type of DNS server hosts this record. You can use a public DNS registrar such as Joker.com or GoDaddy, the Windows DNS server included in all Windows Server editions, or a Linux- or UNIX-based DNS server. No special or additional configuration is required for Exchange 2013 inbound mail flow compared to previous versions. If you have an existing MX record setup that works to deliver mail to whatever mail system you currently have, as long as you get the IP address on the MX records correct, mail will continue to flow to your Exchange 2013 environment.

DNS configuration for outbound mail

While the DNS configuration required for inbound mail is simple, the configuration required for outbound mail is a little more complex. That's because you need to be aware of three separate DNS-related configuration items for outbound mail.

DEFAULT WINDOWS DNS SETTINGS

The first set of important settings for Exchange are the DNS resolution settings in place on your server (Figure 4-1). Remember that if you don't make any configuration changes in Exchange, any server can send mail to the Internet by looking up the MX record for the destination domain, and then connecting to the target server. Your servers do this by using the DNS server settings on the server's network adapters. Normally, you set these as appropriate for your server's network connections, and then leave them alone. This is because Windows itself and other applications on the servers need the ability to resolve names in DNS.

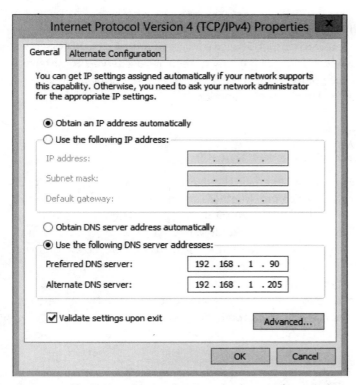

FIGURE 4-1 The DNS settings on the network adapters of your Exchange servers are used by default

FORCING EXCHANGE TO USE SPECIFIED DNS SERVERS

Exchange itself can also use its own DNS settings. One common configuration involves the use of split-brain DNS, where you have a server pointing to separate internal and external DNS servers. *Split-brain DNS* usually happens when your servers are multihomed to both an internal network and the Internet, as transport servers often are. Older versions of Exchange always use the system DNS settings, but Exchange 2013 allows you to customize DNS lookup settings—for Exchange only—on individual servers. To see these settings, open EAC, navigate to the Servers tab, and double-click a server to open its Properties dialog box. On the DNS

Lookups tab (Figure 4-2), you see two sets of controls. One is for external DNS lookups, which are performed for MX record resolution, and the other is for internal DNS lookups for queries, such as finding other Exchange servers. You can specify if you want Exchange to use the network adapter's settings for resolution. Or, you can provide the IP addresses (not an FQDN, although you might use either an IPv4 or IPv6 address) of DNS servers you want Exchange to use. When these settings are in place, Exchange performs DNS queries only against the servers you set, ignoring the normal settings on NICs. This feature is a mixed blessing. It is convenient to be able to tell Exchange exactly which DNS servers to use, but if you make a mistake here, or if another administrator makes a change without your knowledge, it can be tricky to troubleshoot.

You can see and change these settings for multiple servers by using the Exchange Management Shell using the Set/Get-TransportService cmdlets with the ExternalDNSServers and InternalDNSServers parameters. This makes it easy to keep all your servers consistent. For example, this cmdlet sets each of the Exchange 2013 servers in your organization to use the popular OpenDNS service for external DNS resolution.

```
Get-TransportService | `
Set-TransportService -ExternalDNSAdapterEnabled $false
-ExternalDNSProtocolOption Any `
-ExternalDNSServers 208.67.222.222,208.67.220.220
```

The ExternalDNSAdapterEnabled and InternalDNSAdapterEnabled parameters don't do what their names might indicate. They control whether Exchange uses the system-provided DNS settings on the adapter for queries. You must set the corresponding value to $false if you want to specify your own settings. If you provide values for ExternalDNSServers or InternalDNSServers, they'll be ignored unless you set the matching AdapterEnabled parameter. In addition to changing these settings on the Transport service, you can make the same changes to the Front End Transport service by substituting Set-FrontEndTransport in the preceding command. Both services also accept parameters for choosing which NIC the settings apply to and whether you want to use UDP, TCP, or both for DNS queries.

EXAM TIP

Be sure you know the difference between Set-TransportService and Set-FrontEndTransport, and when you would use each one. In particular, remember that you use Set-TransportService to control DNS resolution (and other settings) on an Edge Transport server.

FIGURE 4-2 Optionally configure individual Exchange servers to use specific DNS servers for internal and external message traffic

CONFIGURING DNS ON SEND CONNECTORS

As you learned in Chapter 1, individual transport connectors can have wildly different options. Send connectors, whether homed on a Mailbox or an Edge server, have a single DNS-related setting. Set-SendConnector -DNSRoutingEnabled controls whether the connector routes mail to target domains by doing MX record lookups (-DNSRoutingEnabled:$true) or by sending all messages to a smarthost (-DNSRoutingEnabled:$false). If it's the latter, then none of the settings you put into place with Set-TransportService matter, and Exchange only performs a DNS lookup to find the smarthost if you supply an FQDN instead of an IP address (the usual practice).

Configuring SPF records

In Chapter 1, you saw that Exchange can use sender policy framework (SPF) records to filter incoming mail. That might lead you to wonder where SPF records come from, how they're used, and why you might need them. If other organizations are using SPF for filtering, you need to ensure that you have the correct records to keep your messages from being blocked by other organizations.

SPF records are how the vendor-neutral Sender ID standard is implemented. Sender ID was designed to address a major problem with Simple Mail Transfer Protocol (SMTP): How do you know that a message came from a particular sender? Consider the case of a postal letter. If you receive a letter with a return address of One Microsoft Way, Redmond, Washington, DC, you might believe that it came from Microsoft. However, if the address is written in crayon, or if the postmark indicates that the letter was mailed from Mountain View instead of Redmond, you might (rightly) doubt the accuracy of the address. SMTP itself doesn't provide a way for a recipient to crosscheck any aspects of the sender's identity, so Sender ID was born in 2006.

Sender ID works by comparing the IP address that the message came from with the SPF records registered for the SMTP domain in the return address. The SPF record for an organization is supposed to contain the IP addresses of all the SMTP servers that are authorized to send mail on behalf of that organization. For example, say that all of Contoso's email originates from 172.16.250.32 and 172.16.250.34. To create an SPF record, Contoso's administrator uses the handy SPF Record Wizard on the Microsoft website *(http://www. microsoft.com/mscorp/safety/content/technologies/senderid/wizard/),* plugs in those IP addresses, and tells the wizard that no Contoso email will ever originate from any other server. She gets the following result.

```
v=spf1 ip4:172.16.250.32 ip4:172.16.250.34
```

This record says that the only IP addresses that will ever send out Contoso mail are the two listed in the record. By creating a text (TXT) resource record (RR) on Contoso's public DNS server, any server that uses Sender ID can check mail that arrives with contoso.com in a MAIL FROM header against the SPF record. The receiving server might query DNS for the SPF record, parse it to see the addresses from which Contoso says it will send mail, check those addresses against the sending server's actual address, and then decide what to do based on whether those addresses match. If the receiving system is Exchange, an administrator could configure it to accept the message, reject it with an NDR, delete it silently, or mark it as having failed the Sender ID filter, so that other filters (including the Outlook junk mail filter) can decide what to do.

Sender ID defines seven statuses, as shown in Table 4-1, that an SPF lookup can generate. These are mostly self-explanatory, although the "soft fail" result needs a little more explanation. If you add "~all" at the end of your SPF record, it specifies that any other IP address that your mail appears to come from should be treated as a possible match, but not a definite one. This essentially means that a spammer who fakes your domain will have its messages tagged as soft fail because its IP addresses don't match the contents of your SPF record. A better idea is to omit "~all" in your SPF records to force failure of any messages sent from IP addresses not included in your SPF record. If you change the IP addresses that can originate messages, however, you must first add them to the SPF record and wait for the record to propagate through DNS.

TABLE 4-1 SPF check statuses

Status	What it means
Pass	The IP address and sender address match the SPF record.
Neutral	The SPF record didn't explicitly specify that the sender IP is or is not acceptable.

Status	What it means
Soft fail	The sender's IP address isn't in the SPF record, but the SPF record contains "~all" so the IP address is still acceptable.
Fail	The sending domain has an SPF record, and the sender's IP isn't listed in it.
None	The sending domain doesn't have a matching SPF record.
TempError	The DNS SPF record couldn't be retrieved because of a temporary problem.
PermError	The DNS SPF record was found, but it's malformed and can't be used.

EXAM TIP

If you run into any exam questions involving Sender ID, make sure you check the TXT record for that "~all" at the end. It's a subtle detail and many exam takers don't read the TXT record all the way to the end. If "~all" is *not* there, the record is telling any server that reads it to fail any message from any IP address that isn't in the record. If it *is* there, then the receiving server is allowed to soft fail that message, so that it can be accepted and processed.

DNS configuration for client access

While we don't want to repeat the extensive guidance from the section "Design namespace for client connectivity" in Chapter 2, it is worth mentioning that whatever namespace you want to use for Exchange needs to have an appropriate set of DNS records for Autodiscover. This can include SRV records for clients inside your network or conventional CNAME Autodiscover records for internal or external clients.

EXAM TIP

Be sure you understand how to use the Remote Connectivity Analyzer *(http://testconnectivity. microsoft.com)* and the Test-OutlookWebServices EMS cmdlet to verify that your Autodiscover configuration is correct.

Preparing Active Directory for Exchange

Before you can install Exchange 2013, you must prepare Active Directory to support it. This is true no matter which version of Windows Server you're using or what domain and forest functional levels you're using. Exchange 2013 can use domain controllers and GC servers from Windows Server 2003 onward. Also, it supports domain and forest functional levels of Windows Server 2003 and higher (although you should check the requirements matrix at *https://technet.microsoft.com/en-us/library/ff728623(v=exchg.150).aspx* to make sure you have the correct service pack for older versions of Windows). Once you verify that your Active

Directory environment is healthy and that replication is working correctly, you're ready to start the preparation process. This process consists of three steps.

- **Preparing the Active Directory schema by adding new classes and attributes to support Exchange-specific objects**   As Microsoft adds new features to Exchange, these new features often require changes to the schema that represent new or changed object types. Because schema changes alter the physical layout used in the Windows directory information tree (.dit) file, changing the schema even by adding a single attribute causes Active Directory to re-replicate every attribute on every object in most versions of Windows Server. This can cause a significant amount of Active Directory traffic, which you need to plan for. (If you're curious about the specific changes that a given version of Exchange makes to the schema, Microsoft maintains a list *at https://technet.microsoft.com/en-us/library/bb738144(v=exchg.150).aspx).*

- **Preparing Active Directory forests, domains, and container objects**   For example, installing Exchange 2013 into an Exchange 2007 environment adds new containers for security groups that are used by the role-based access control (RBAC) mechanisms described later in this chapter. This step can involve creating objects such as security groups or organizational units (OUs), changing the names or locations of existing objects, and changing permissions on objects to match Exchange's requirements.

- **Preparing individual domains that will contain Exchange servers or mail-enabled users**   This step is required because it creates containers (and sets permissions on them) for the Exchange servers and related objects within the domain. Even though Exchange's global configuration data is stored in the configuration naming context, there are still objects that have to be stored in individual domains.

REAL WORLD   **SCHEMA EXTENSIONS ON DEMAND**

You have to update the schema before you update Exchange, but you don't have to do it *right* before you update Exchange. We worked with a large customer that wanted to minimize the impact of their Exchange deployment, and they had already planned an Active Directory and Windows Server upgrade for about four months before their Exchange upgrade was planned to start. We performed the schema update as part of the Active Directory update, so that all the replication traffic generated by the schema update was rolled in with the other network disruptions caused by the Active Directory upgrade. Because schema changes are additive, it was safe to update the schema even though the Exchange upgrade wasn't scheduled for some time. When the time came to install Exchange 2013, no changes were necessary to the Active Directory environment, and the planned upgrade went off without a hitch.

You can accomplish these preparation steps in two ways. The first, and most simple way is to run the Exchange setup utility and let it figure out what needs to be done. It checks for a variety of semaphore values on various Exchange configuration objects (as described in the section, "How do you know this worked?" of *https://technet.microsoft.com/en-us/library/bb125224(v=exchg.150).aspx*) and uses those values to decide which prep steps, if any, still need to be performed. The installer is smart enough to perform the steps in order, and then install Exchange, so you can run the installer once to go from an empty environment to one that is prepared and has an Exchange server installed in it. The second way, if you prefer, you can also perform each preparation step individually. It won't hurt anything if you accidentally perform any of the prep steps more than once. In fact, you might find that re-preparing Active Directory or individual domains could be necessary to fix permissions issues after installing Exchange if an administrator later changes permissions on something they should have left alone.

Preparing the schema

To prepare the schema, you need to run Exchange Setup with an account that is a member of the Schema Admins and Enterprise Admins security group. This is by design, so that the schema can be prepared by Active Directory administrators in organizations that use a split-permissions model. The computer from which you run Setup also needs to be in the same Active Directory domain and site as the schema master. To perform the schema update, you use the /PrepareSchema switch to Setup, like this:

```
Setup.exe /PrepareSchema /IAcceptExchangeServerLicenseTerms
```

Around 1,100 schema changes are required to install Exchange 2013 SP1, so applying the changes can take a few minutes. Before you proceed with the other preparation steps, you should ensure that all of the schema changes have replicated to all of your domain controllers. You can check this with the repadmin tool, or you can just wait for a sufficient period (the duration of which will vary depending on your replication topology and network connectivity).

Preparing Active Directory

Preparing Active Directory sounds like a vague description for what is one of the most important parts of the Exchange installation process. Many of the settings that Exchange relies on are stored in the *Exchange organization object,* and it is so called because it is named after the organization name you supply as part of the Exchange setup process. Figure 4-3 shows an example Exchange organization object in its proper location: within the forest configuration naming context inside the "Services" container.Several restrictions exist on the organization name. It can contain spaces, upper- or lowercase letters, numbers, and dashes, but not other special characters, such as commas, underscores, or quotation marks. The most important thing to remember about the organization name is that you can't change it once it's set. The second most important thing to remember is that users won't ever see it, so if you accidentally misspell it, or if a merger or acquisition changes the name of the organization that owns the Exchange server, it's no big deal.

If you install Exchange into an Active Directory forest that hasn't contained Exchange before, this preparation step creates the organization object and sets appropriate permissions on it. If you're upgrading from any previous version of Exchange, that object already exists, so Exchange 2013 Setup adds the necessary version-specific attributes to it and sets the permissions as required.

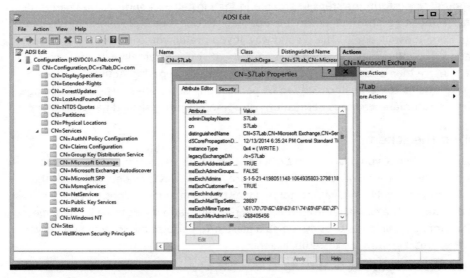

FIGURE 4-3 The Exchange organization object in ADSIEdit.

To perform this preparation step, you use the /PrepareAD switch to Setup, like this.

```
Setup.exe /PrepareAD /IAcceptExchangeServerLicenseTerms
```

As with the schema preparation step, you should wait for the Active Directory preparation to complete before proceeding with the domain preparation.

Preparing domains

The simplest way to prepare your domains for Exchange 2013 is to use the /PrepareAllDomains switch to Setup. This does what its name suggests: it creates the needed Exchange security groups and permissions in every domain in your forest. The account used to run this command must be a member of the Enterprise Admins group.

In complex Active Directory environments, you might not want to prepare certain domains (for example, a resource domain that contains only desktop workstation computer accounts wouldn't need to be prepared). Microsoft gives you this degree of control if you want it with the /PrepareDomain switch, which you use to specify the FQDN of the specific domain you want to prepare. (Note that the domain where you ran the /PrepareAD switch doesn't need to be separately prepared.) Unlike the schema and Active Directory preparation steps, preparing an individual domain doesn't require any forest-level permissions. The account from which you run /PrepareDomain just needs to be a member of Domain Admins in the target domain.

The documentation of Microsoft points out an interesting case that many admins won't encounter. Suppose you install Exchange 2013 in a forest, and then add new domains after you run PrepareAD. If you want to put Exchange servers into the new domains, you need to prepare the new domains before you can install Exchange into them by using the /PrepareAD switch. However, in this case, the account you use must be a member of the Exchange Organizational Management role group and a member of Domain Admins in the target domain.

Thought experiment
Active Directory and DNS planning

In this Thought experiment, apply what you have learned about this objective. You can find answers to these questions in the "Answers" section at the end of this chapter.

The Phone Company (TPC) is upgrading its existing Exchange 2007 system to Exchange 2013. They asked you for a comprehensive review of their DNS and Active Directory infrastructure before proceeding with the upgrade.

1. What items would you check for TPC's public-facing DNS?

2. Explain how you would evaluate TPC's Active Directory infrastructure to ensure that it's suitable.

Objective summary

- Exchange is completely dependent on a functioning Active Directory infrastructure.

- You need at least one Active Directory global catalog server in each Active Directory site that contains an Exchange server or computer running Outlook. Having two or more for redundancy and scalability is better.

- The standard ratio for processor cores is to have one 64-bit processor core dedicated to GC service for every eight processor cores running Exchange mailbox workloads.

- Although installing Exchange on a GC or domain controller is supported, try to avoid doing so.

- Your Exchange servers use the DNS settings on their network adapters by default. You can configure Exchange to use specific servers for internal or external traffic with Set-TransportService or EAC.

- Each Send connector can have its own DNS settings, which are used instead of the Windows or server-specific settings.

- You should plan to create SPF records for your domains, so that recipients can correctly filter mail sent from your servers.

- Even if you've ever had Exchange installed in your Active Directory forest, you'll still need to prepare the forest, schema, and domains before installing Exchange 2013.

- There are three separate preparation steps: updating the schema (schema prep), preparing Active Directory (AD prep), and preparing domains that contain Exchange servers or mailbox-enabled users.

- The Exchange Setup utility automatically tries to carry out any preparation steps that have not yet been done.

- Extensive changes to the Active Directory schema are required, but you can update the schema at any time before you start installing Exchange. Remember that these changes take time to replicate.

Objective review

Answer the following questions to test your knowledge of the information in this objective. You can find the answers to these questions and explanations of why each answer choice is correct or incorrect in the "Answers" section at the end of this chapter.

1. You are installing Exchange 2013 into a new Active Directory forest. You already updated the Active Directory schema. Which of the following steps should you take next?

    A. Wait 24 hours for all schema changes to replicate fully.

    B. Install the Exchange mailbox role.

    C. Prepare the domain you're installing Exchange into with the /PrepareDomain switch.

    D. Prepare Active Directory by running Exchange Setup with the /PrepareAD switch.

2. You manage an Exchange 2010 network with two physical sites: Huntsville and Flint. Currently, no GC servers are in the Flint site and one is in the Huntsville site. Each site has an additional domain controller. You want to increase reliability of the Exchange deployment at the lowest possible cost. As part of your Exchange 2013 upgrade, which of the following actions should you take? (Choose all that apply.)

    A. Convert the existing Flint domain controller to a GC.

    B. Convert the existing Huntsville domain controller to a GC.

    C. Add a GC server in the Flint site.

    D. Install a read-only domain controller in the Flint site.

3. You notice that outbound mail that should flow over a particular send connector is remaining queued. When you examine the connector queues, you see that the listed errors indicate that the computer cannot reach the remote server. You verify that DNS is working properly on the Exchange server hosting the send connector. Which of the following is likely to be the cause?

    A. An intermittent DNS failure is making outbound MX records lookupsfail.

    B. The network adapters on the server have incorrect DNS settings or one of the configured servers is not responding.

C.   The send connector is set to use specific DNS servers and either the configuration is wrong or the target servers are unreachable.

D.   The address space on the connector is wrong.

Objective 4.2: Administer Exchange workload management

Rather than write a unique explanation of what "workload" means in the context of Exchange, it's probably more useful to lift the Microsoft description from the Exchange 2013 SP1 documentation:

> An Exchange workload is an Exchange Server feature, protocol, or service that's been explicitly defined for the purposes of Exchange system resource management. Each Exchange workload consumes system resources such as CPU, mailbox database operations, or Active Directory requests to run user requests or background work. Examples of Exchange workloads include Outlook Web App, Exchange ActiveSync, mailbox migration, and mailbox assistants.

The workload management features in Exchange are mostly self-tuning. Microsoft sets default limits on how many resources individual users can consume, and how many server resources individual workloads can take up. This ensures that server performance stays predictable. When a given user or workload exceeds these limits, the system slows processing for that user or workload, a process known as *throttling*.

This objective covers how to:

- Monitor system workload events
- Monitor user workload events
- Manage workload throttling settings

Workload management explained

If you only had one Exchange server, and that server was accessed only by a single client, then you probably wouldn't have any use for workload management. At the other extreme, if you ran a global service with tens of millions of active users, as Microsoft does with Office 365, you would be intensely interested in tools to make sure that you could monitor and control resource usage and performance on all your servers. That's why Microsoft developed the workload management features in Exchange 2010 and improved them in Exchange 2013. Microsoft needed these features for Office 365, and the rest of us have benefited.

The goal of Exchange workload management is twofold: watch workloads to ensure that they're not using too much of any system resource and set limits to control resource usage by selected workloads. However, in Exchange 2013 SP1 RU6, Microsoft made a major change and removed the system workload management cmdlets: *-ResourcePolicy, *-WorkloadManagementPolicy, and *-WorkloadPolicy. TechNet now includes this ominous statement at the bottom of the page:

> The *-ResourcePolicy, *-WorkloadManagementPolicy and *-WorkloadPolicy system workload management cmdlets have been deprecated. System workload management settings should be customized only under the direction of Microsoft Customer Service and Support.

Even with this change, it's still useful to understand the basic concepts behind workload management. Let's start with *workload policies;* these objects identify how a specific workload should be treated by the system. The workload policy contains a classification, which specifies an increasing priority: Discretionary, InternalMaintenance, CustomerExpectation, or Urgent. Creating a workload policy allows you to set a priority for that workload, and to change it later. If you think about the performance and stability implications of changing the priority of internal maintenance workloads, you'll start to see why Microsoft deprecated this capability.

Next come *resource policies,* which set limits on how much of a particular resource (such as processor time) can be consumed by a given workload policy. For example, a resource policy might specify that a workload with a classification of Discretionary might be able to consume no more than 75 percent CPU without being throttled back. Resource policies specify a range of values that signal when the resource should be considered underloaded (so it can take on more work), overloaded (so that it has to defer any additional work until its resource usage drops), or critical.

Finally, you have the *workload management policies,* which are container objects that are used to connect workload policies with specific servers. When you use system-level workload management (which, of course, you only do if Microsoft CSS tells you to), you create a workload management policy, create or assign workload policies to it, and then use Set-ExchangeServer to apply the workload management policy to a set of servers.

Monitoring system and user workload events

You can monitor workload events, both for the system and for individual users, in three primary ways. The first way, of course, is to use the system event log. If you see these events, they tell you exactly what's wrong, provided you read the description carefully. Here's an example for a user who's gone over their preset budget for OWA access.

> Process w3wp.exe () (PID=9270). User 'paulr' has gone over budget '17' times for component 'OWA' within a one minute period. Info: 'Policy:DefaultThrottlingPolicy_d7d68d93-9490-4fa7-f00e-901072974e2f, Parts:AD:13;'. Threshold value: '10'.

The key item to note here is that the "threshold value" message is *not* the limit that's been exceeded, it's the number of times that the user must exceed the throttling limit before the system logs event 2915. In this case, the user has gone over budget 17 times, and the system starts logging event 2915 when the user has gone over budget 10 times or more.

The second way to monitor user workload events is to watch the Internet Information Services (IIS) logs. This is complicated because the format of the log entries varies according to which workload is generating the log entry. This is not a useful method for an ongoing monitoring plan, but it can be useful when you're trying to identify the cause of a specific problem. Searching the IIS logs for the term overbudget is a good way to quickly find specific instances where a workload has gone over budget.

One case where workload events are often generated is when you use a single service account for tasks, such as synchronizing mailboxes or providing mobile device access or management. The activity of that single account might lead Exchange to think that the account is over-consuming resources. For example, BlackBerry Enterprise Server (BES) often requires administrators to adjust their workload throttling policies to account for the resources it uses when synchronizing.

The third way to monitor user workload events is to use the native Windows performance monitoring tools to look at workload-related performance counters. You might find several counters useful:

- **MSExchange Throttling counter** Provides monitoring instances for EWS, EAS, PowerShell, OWA, replication, and RPC client access workloads on the entire server.

- **MSExchange User Throttling counter** Provides the same information as MSExchange Throttling, but for user workloads.

- **MSExchange WorkloadManagement Classification counter** Breaks down performance data for the Exchange service host process, the mailbox assistants, and mailbox replication into the workload classifications, described earlier in the chapter (internal maintenance, customer expectation, and so on). This can be a useful way to see whether discretionary or internal maintenance workloads are taking more of your server's time than you expect.

- **MSExchange Workload Management counter** Shows you how many total workloads are currently running in each of three categories: the service host process, the mailbox assistants, and mailbox replication. This gives you a quick look at how many of each of these workloads is running at a given time on your servers.

- **MSExchange WorkloadManagement Workloads counter** Provides information about all the system workloads (including services such as the Calendar Assistant and the offline address book generator). If you have reason to suspect that an individual system workload is being throttled, you can use the instances for this counter to pinpoint if that's the case.

One important part of troubleshooting Exchange is learning to determine whether a problem reported by a user is limited to that specific user, to all users on a mailbox database, to all users on a server, or to users across a set of servers. When a user reports performance problems, a good idea is to make a quick check of overall performance on that user's mailbox server to see if the problem is likely related to the individual user being throttled or to poor overall server performance. For example, if you're moving a large number of mailboxes, you might find that the MSExchange Throttling RPC client access counter shows over budget, but that the MSExchange User Throttling RPC client access counters are not.

One particular area exists where users (whether human or service accounts) tend to get throttled. The message rate sending limits, described in the next section, especially MessageRateLimit and RecipientRateLimit, can be exceeded by users who run mail merges, send out large numbers of notifications, or run other types of automated services that generate lots of mail.

Managing workload throttling settings

Individual clients can occasionally place an excessive load on an Exchange server. This can happen for a variety of reasons, including bugs in a particular client (such as the famous bug in Apple iOS 6.1 that caused excessive transaction log growth on Exchange servers) or unexpected spikes in load (perhaps a user sets up several new devices in quick succession and they all try to sync the user's mailbox at once). Older versions of Exchange gave us very limited tools for identifying and solving problems caused by excessive client resource consumption, but those tools don't scale well. To help protect against misbehaving clients in Office 365, Microsoft introduced a feature in Exchange 2010 known as *client throttling,* which enables administrators to set proactive limits on how much work a client can ask the server to do. Don't confuse client throttling with the system throttling policies described earlier in this chapter. Although they have the same basic concept, client throttling policies only affect resource consumptions by clients working against client-facing workloads.

Client throttling policies control what resources, and how many of them, clients can use for various workloads. When a client exceeds the limit for resource usage, it's not usually blocked altogether. Instead, its requests are delayed. The net effect is that clients who are using more than their fair share of any particular resource have their access to that resource reduced, with a gradual reduction in the amount of slowdown that allows the client to recharge.

Exchange 2013 client throttling policies can be applied to several workloads:

- Outlook connectivity
- Exchange Web Services (EWS) (this category includes Unified Messaging users and users running Entourage or Outlook for Mac OS X)
- Exchange ActiveSync (EAS)
- Push notifications
- Outlook Web App
- POP3 and IMAP4
- Discovery searches
- Cross-forest access (including hybrid access between on-premises and Office 365 tenants)
- Sending messages using SMTP

- Windows PowerShell and PowerShell Web Services

When you install Exchange 2013, you automatically get a default policy, named GlobalThrottlingPolicy_GUID, which is meant to be the baseline policy for any user who doesn't have a more specific policy applied. You can't remove or rename this policy. You can change the limits enforced by the default policy. However, Microsoft instead advises that you create additional policies that provide more granular control over resource usage, and then assign those policies to users. Any throttling setting not explicitly specified in a policy is inherited from the global policy, so you can quickly build policies that control exactly the resources you want, while allowing other resources' usage to be governed by the global policy.

The policy comes into effect when the percentage of CPU usage by Exchange exceeds the threshold defined in the CPUStartPercent property of the default policy. This setting is applied on a per-service basis. The default value for CPUStartPercent is 75. When one of the Exchange workloads monitored for client throttling reaches this threshold, Exchange begins to apply any throttling restrictions that are defined in the default policy or on a per-mailbox basis. This ensures that the server can continue to provide a reasonably smooth service to all clients.

Four different limits are associated with each workload's resource usage. It might help to think of these limits as though they are tied to a bank or credit card account. Here's what the limits are and what they mean:

- **CutoffBalance**   Controls the level at which Exchange starts denying access to a resource. Think of this as a hard maximum limit for using the resource. After the client hits this limit, it is blocked from that resource until it recharges. For bank accounts, this would be the credit limit on the account.

- **RechargeRate**   Is the rate at which the user's resource budget refills. For example, a client that sends a large number of messages and hits the recipient rate limit eventually falls below the limit, recharges at the specified rate, and regains full access as time passes. For a credit card or bank account, this rate reflects how fast the account refills with money.

- **MaxBurst**   Controls how far above the standard resource limit a client can go in short bursts. Think of this like a temporary bank loan.

- **MaxConcurrency**   Sets the limit for how many concurrent connections or actions a single client might take. Unfortunately, no good equivalent to this exists in the bank account metaphor, but it's important for Exchange because multiple concurrent connections to the same user's mailbox (or to the same workload on a single server) can be a major source of performance problems.

Individual workloads can also have additional settings. For example, the Discovery workload has limits you can set on the maximum number of keywords that a user can include in a single search and the maximum number of mailboxes that can be searched at once. See the TechNet documentation for the New-ThrottlingPolicy cmdlet for a complete list of all limit settings for all workloads.

If you want to reduce the load imposed on your server by a particular workload, the best way to do this (as previously mentioned) is to create new policies, set the limits you want them to have, and then apply them to users as needed. This is the same way that you manage other types of policies in Exchange, of course. The difference here is that, unlike mailbox, mobile device access, and OWA policies, you can only manage throttling policies through EMS.

You can view details of the default policy with this command:

```
Get-ThrottlingPolicy | Where {$_.IsDefault -eq $True} | Format-Table
```

This gives you a great deal of data, probably more than you can use. It might be more useful to look at the settings for individual workloads, which you can do with a command such as this.

```
Get-ThrottlingPolicy | Select Ews* | Format-List
```

```
EwsMaxConcurrency              : 27
EwsMaxBurst                    : 300000
EwsRechargeRate                : 900000
EwsCutoffBalance               : 3000000
EwsMaxSubscriptions            : 5000
```

This output tells you that the maximum concurrency for any user is set to 20 (the range is from 0 to 100), meaning that a user can have up to 20 active EWS sessions. A connection is maintained from the time a request is made to establish it until the connection is closed or otherwise disconnected by a user action (logging off). If a user attempts to establish more than the allowed maximum, that connection attempt fails. The EwsMaxBurst, EwsRechargeRate, and EwsCutoffBalance limits are set, too, indicating that limits for specific resource usage are in place. The max burst and recharge rate are both expressed in milliseconds. The user can have a burst of up to five minutes of heavy EWS activity before being blocked.

Similar groups of settings are available for the other client categories. For example, you can find those applying to Outlook Web App with:

```
Get-ThrottlingPolicy | Select OWA* | Format-List
```

In addition to the workload-specific settings, three throttling policy limits aren't associated with a specific workload because they have to do with what users are doing, not what protocol they're using to do it:

- **MessageRateLimit** Governs the number of messages per minute that a user can submit to the transport system for processing. Messages over the limit are placed in the user's Outbox until the server can accept them. The exception is for clients, such as POP3 and IMAP4, that submit directly to the transport system using SMTP. If these clients attempt to submit too many messages, their request is declined, and they are forced to reattempt later.

- **RecipientRateLimit**   Controls the number of recipients that can be addressed in a 24-hour period. For example, if this value is set to 1,000, the user can address messages to up to 1,000 recipients daily. Messages that exceed this limit are rejected.

- **ForwardeeLimit**   Sets a limit for the number of recipients that can be configured in Inbox Rules for the forward or redirect action.

You can create your own policies with the New-ThrottlingPolicy cmdlet. It's important to remember that you only need the policy you create to specify the settings that are different from those in the global policy. For example, suppose you wanted to set a policy to restrict the number of discovery search keywords and mailboxes that a user could submit at once. You'd probably do something like this:

```
New-ThrottlingPolicy -Name RestrictedDiscovery `
-DiscoveryMaxKeywords 10 `
-DiscoveryMaxMailboxes 100 `
-DiscoveryMaxSearchQueueDepth 10 `
-ThrottlingPolicyScope Regular
```

Notice that in this example the ThrottlingPolicyScope parameter is added. This optional parameter can take on two values. Regular specifies that the policy is applied to users you specify, and Organization specifies that you want the policy to apply to all users in the organization.

Speaking of applying policies to users, you can do so in one of two ways. The easiest way is to use the Set-ThrottlingPolicyAssociation cmdlet, which takes a target object and a throttling policy as parameters. The target object, specified with the Identity parameter, can be a mailbox-enabled user, a user, a contact, or a computer account. The policy name is self-explanatory. To apply the RestrictedDiscovery policy to your own account, you could do this:

```
Set-ThrottlingPolicyAssociation -Identity paulr -ThrottlingPolicy restrictedDiscovery
```

Or, you could do this instead:

```
Set-Mailbox -Identity paulr -ThrottlingPolicy RestrictedDiscovery
```

This latter approach has the advantage of being easier to use with commands that fetch large numbers of mailboxes, filter the resulting pipeline, and then apply settings.

Thought experiment
Pinpointing the cause of performance problems

In this Thought experiment, apply what you learned about this objective. You can find answers to these questions in the "Answers" section at the end of this chapter.

Users on a particular server are complaining about slow performance in Outlook. What are some things you might check to identify possible causes for the problem?

Objective summary

- Microsoft defines an Exchange workload as a specific feature, protocol, or service whose resource usage can be monitored and controlled. The Exchange developers have identified a few dozen workloads. You don't get to create your own.

- The purpose of workload management is to let Exchange slow down, or throttle, requests from users or processes that are consuming more than their budgeted allocation of some resource.

- A workload policy specifies how a particular workload should be treated by the system and what its priority (or classification) is.

- Resource policies limit how much processor time, RAM, or other resource can be used by workloads that are part of a specific workload policy.

- A workload management policy applies a workload policy with one or more specified servers.

- Microsoft deprecated the cmdlets for managing system workloads by yourself. Exchange administrators are only supposed to modify those workload settings under the direction of Microsoft product support.

- You can define client throttling policies that specify how much CPU time or system resources can be consumed by users for a specific workload, including Outlook connectivity, sending mail, or using Exchange ActiveSync.

- By default, Exchange creates a global client-throttling policy that's applied to all clients. You can create your own client throttling policies and apply them to users. The policies you create only need to contain the settings that are different from those in the default policy.

Objective review

Answer the following questions to test your knowledge of the information in this objective. You can find the answers to these questions and explanations of why each answer choice is correct or incorrect in the "Answers" section at the end of this chapter.

1. A user complains that sending mail from her workstation slows down dramatically around the same time each day. No other users have complained. You investigate and find that she is sending approximately 5,000 automated emails per day from her workstation. Which of the following is the most likely cause of the slowdown?

   A. The transaction logs on her mailbox server are stalling.

   B. A scheduled backup or other task is slowing the server.

   C. Her account is being throttled because it's exceeding the limits set for the number of messages that a user can send.

   D. Resource contention on the network is slowing her work.

2. You want to limit how many keywords your users can include in a discovery search. To do this, you should:

   A. Change RBAC settings on the Discovery Management group to control who can perform complex searches.

   B. Modify the global user-throttling policy.

   C. Create a new user throttling policy and apply it to the target users.

   D. Remove the global user-throttling policy and create a new one with the desired limits.

3. You want to reduce the amount of time that it takes for one group of users whose use of a specific workload has been throttled to become unthrottled. The best way to do this is to:

   A. Increase the RechargeRate setting for the policy that applies to that workload for the users.

   B. Raise the CutoffBalance setting for the policy that applies to that workload for the users.

   C. Increase the RechargeRate setting for that workload in the global policy.

   D. Create a new policy with no limits set for that workload, and then assign it to the target users.

Objective 4.3: Plan and manage role based access control

Ever since Exchange 2000 was released, Active Directory became a critical part of an Exchange deployment. Exchange objects are stored in Active Directory and permissions on Active Directory play an important role to define which operations an Exchange administrator can perform on an Active Directory object.

Exchange 2000, 2003, and Exchange 2007 provided a simplified way to assign appropriate permissions using the *Administration Delegation Wizard*. This wizard was designed to reduce the need to evaluate applicable ACEs/ACLs on Active Directory objects for given roles and permissions. The wizard provided pre-defined management roles to select from, however, it was limited in nature and if any customization was needed, the wizard and built-in management roles weren't very effective.

Exchange 2010 introduced *role based access control (RBAC)* to provide granular control over access and assigned administrative permissions. Exchange 2013 continues building on the functionality and introduces new cmdlets to accommodate new functionality. However, the fundamentals of RBAC remain unchanged.

The RBAC model of permissions consists of three important entities: Who, What, and Where.

Who, represents the administrative users responsible for maintaining Exchange server objects. This includes server configuration, recipient objects, or end users who might be required to maintain their own information, such as home address and mobile phone number, and so on. Members of a Role Group or, if permissions are directly assigned to a user instead of a group, the Role Assignees represent the *Who*.

What translates to the objects or configuration steps that administrative users, or end users, should be able to manage. For example, an administrator might be responsible for maintaining the mailbox configuration. The collection of cmdlets and parameters, known as *Management Role Entries*, form pre-defined or custom Management Roles. These Management Roles define what the assignee is allowed to do.

Where represents the scope of permissions that are assigned to an administrator or an end user. The scope of access where operations can be performed by administrators and end users is called the *Management Scope* or the *Management Role Scope*. An example of a scope is an OU or a set of users defined by a common attribute value, such as department equals Sales.

While Who, What, and Where define the assignees, the cmdlets and parameters, and the scope, this is not effective until they are all bound together by Management Role Assignments, making them effective. Until permissions and scopes are assigned to assignees (group or user), the permissions aren't effective.

This objective covers how to:

- Determine appropriate RBAC roles and cmdlets
- Limit administration using existing role groups
- Evaluate differences between RBAC and Active Directory split permissions
- Configure a custom-scoped role group

Determine appropriate RBAC roles and cmdlets

Exchange 2013 provides multiple built-in management roles. Each role represents a set of administrative functions. For example, the Mail Recipients role includes cmdlets and parameters that allow an administrator to create and manage recipient objects, such as a user mailbox. When a defined job function requires access to a set of cmdlets and an assigning built-in role might exceed the required authority over managed objects, the creation of customized roles might be required.

A pre-requisite to creating a custom role is to define a set of cmdlets and parameters required for the defined job function. The default Organization Management role group allows an administrator to manage everything within an Exchange organization, so membership to this role group should always be restricted. To provide restricted access to an administrator based on their job function, you need to determine which roles are appropriate. The other consideration is, for a selected role, are there any cmdlets and parameters that provide undesired access to the administrator and should be removed? For example, if an administrator is allowed to manage mail recipients, but shouldn't be able to disable any mail recipient objects, then you need to remove cmdlets that can disable mail recipient objects when creating a custom management role.

The first step in this process is to identify built-in roles. More than 80 built-in management roles are created based on different job function definitions, ranging from an organization administrator to a helpdesk admin and others. To list management roles, you can simply run the Get-ManagementRole cmdlet. Running this cmdlet returns all management roles, including built-in roles and any custom management roles if they exist. Each management role consists of a property named IsRootRole. All the built-in roles have the property value set to true. If you want to list only built-in roles, you can run the following in the Management Shell:

```
Get-ManagementRole | where IsRootRole -eq true
```

Each role consists of role entries. Each role entry represents a cmdlet and related parameters that are associated with the management role. This can provide a great starting point for an administrator to determine whether the built-in role provides required functionality for given requirements and if any of the cmdlets provide more functionality than desired. You can list associated role entries for a given management role. The following example shows all associated cmdlets for management role named Mail Recipients.

```
Get-ManagementRole "Mail Recipients" | Select -ExpandProperty RoleEntries | Format-Table Name
```

In the previous example, notice that the associated cmdlets allow the administrator, who is assigned this management role, to view the mailbox user or mail- enabled objects properties with cmdlets, such as get-mailbox, change the properties of the objects using cmdlets, such as set-mailbox, disable mailbox, and other recipient objects.

When trying to determine a role for a given task, you need to account for the type of access required. For example, if you need to provide access to an administrator to allow management of certain Exchange objects, you need to look for roles, such as Recipient Policies, Message Tracking, or Mail Recipient Creation. In contrast, if you need to assign permissions to a user so that the user can manage their own information or related Exchange features, you need to use roles that start with My, such as MyPersonalInformation, MyVoiceMail or MyDistributionGroups.

Exchange server also provides specialty roles that enable specialty tasks, such as application impersonation, server diagnostics, or the use of non-Exchange cmdlets or custom scripts. You can also create unscoped top-level roles. *Unscoped top-level roles* are special roles that must be created by an administrator and that contain no cmdlets on creation. An administrator must add cmdlets and scripts to the newly created unscoped top-level role manually.

Limit administration using existing role groups

Selecting from one of the many built-in roles can be challenging. However, assigning permissions does not have to be challenging. Exchange provides built-in groups that are created when deploying Exchange servers. These built-in groups associate appropriate roles and cmdlets with a Universal Security Group (USG) created in Active Directory, known as a *role group* or a *management role group*. You can always create additional role groups if needed.

The purpose of built-in role groups is to simplify the task of determining and associating appropriate roles and cmdlets for the most common job functions related to the management of an Exchange deployment. For example, *Organization Management* provides a member of the role group with access to almost all built-in management role groups and associated cmdlets. This allows the organization administrator to effectively carry out their duties as related to the management of an Exchange deployment. The *Help Desk role group,* in comparison, provides access to roles and cmdlets that allow a member of the group to change properties of a user, such as the display name. The two roles associated with the Help Desk role group are the User Options Role and the View-Only Recipients Role.

If built-in roles meet the requirements of the job function for a given administrative account, it simplifies the assignment of permissions by simply adding an administrative account to the appropriate built-in role group. This can be achieved by using the Add-RoleGroupMember or the Update-RoleGroupMember cmdlet from the Shell, or, you can use the role group membership using EAC. When using the cmdlets from the Shell, the difference between using the Add-RoleGroupMember cmdlet and the Update-RoleGroupMember cmdlet is this. The Member property for the Add-RoleGroupMember cmdlet expects the Security Principal ID as a value, whereas the Members parameter for the Update-RoleGroupMember cmdlet is a multi-valued property, allowing you to add or remove multiple users at once.

EXAM TIP

While using Update-RoleGroupMember is a convenient option when adding or removing multiple members of the group, note that the Members parameter overwrites the existing membership of a role group with the members specified by the parameter. If the role group contains members that must be retained while adding or removing other members, they must be included in the provided member list.

Let's look at two administrators, Jason Carlson and Jeff Hay, who are going to assist you with installation of new Exchange servers in your Exchange deployment. You determined that the existing role group, Delegated Setup, provides sufficient access to the required cmdlets and parameters. You can add Jeff and Jason to the existing role group, as shown in the following example.

```
#Add members using Add-RoleGroupMember cmdlet
Add-RoleGroupMember -Identity "Delegated Setup" -Member jeff@contoso.com
Add-RoleGroupMember -Identity "Delegated Setup" -Member jason@contoso.com

#Add members using Update-RoleGroupMember cmdlet
Update-RoleGroupMember -Identity "Delegated Setup" -Members jeff@contoso.com,
"jason@contoso.com"
```

If you want to retain existing membership of the role group while adding Jeff and Jason to the group, the previous example is not appropriate as it does not retain existing members and, instead, it will replace the role group membership with Jeff and Jason as the only members of the group. To retain the existing membership, you should use the following syntax instead.

```
#Add members using Update-RoleGroupMember cmdlet, while retaining existing members
Update-RoleGroupMember -Identity "Delegated Setup" -Members
@{add="jeff@contoso.com","jason@contoso.com"}
```

Notice the use of code block @{} and the operator *add*, which adds specified users to the group, while retaining the existing members of the group. Similarly, you can use the *remove* operator if you need to remove existing members from the group.

When you assign permissions to a user by leveraging built-in role groups, the scope of effective permissions is inherited based on the definition of the associated roles. Built-in roles always have the organization as the scope. This allows the administrator to perform actions determined by associated roles and cmdlets anywhere within the organization. Assigning custom scopes is discussed in the upcoming section, "Configure a custom-scoped role group."

When using EAC, this process becomes simpler. You only need to navigate to Permissions, Admin Roles where the existing role groups are listed. You can select the appropriate role group and manage members and other properties, as needed. Figure 4-4 displays the dialog box to add users to the existing role group.

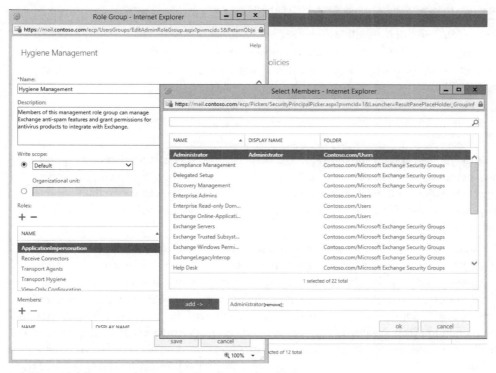

FIGURE 4-4 Adding members to a role group using EAC

The previously described steps are appropriate when you want to assign required permissions to an administrator using built-in role groups. However, the same process doesn't work if you need to assign permissions to individual users to manage their own mailbox-related tasks. To assign permissions to end users, you must use management-role assignment policies. Similar to management role groups, *management-role assignment policies* are a collection of end-user management roles. These *management role assignment policies* allow users to manage their own mailbox configuration and the distribution group membership for the distribution groups they own. By default, the built-in role assignment policy is associated with all mailbox objects. If the built-in policy does not meet the needs of permissions you need to assign to your users, you can create a new role assignment policy and associate with mailboxes that require them. For both built-in and custom-role assignment policies, the scope is always "self" because the mailbox user is only allowed to manage their own mailbox properties and features.

You can create a new role assignment policy by using the New-RoleAssignmentPolicy cmdlet, as shown in the following example. You can also define if the new policy will replace the current default policy going forward. If you specify the IsDefault parameter, the newly created policy is applied as a default policy to any mailboxes created after the creation of the new policy.

```
#Create new role assignment policy and set it as new default policy
New-RoleAssignmentPolicy "Limited Mailbox Configuration" -Roles MyBaseOptions,
MyAddressInformation, MyDisplayName -IsDefault
```

Creating a new default role-assignment policy does not change the currently assigned role assignment policy on the existing mailboxes. You must change it manually, if desired. To change a policy assigned to an existing mailbox, you can use the Set-Mailbox cmdlet, as the following shows.

```
#Set a role assignment policy on existing mailbox
Set-Mailbox -Identity jason@contoso.com -RoleAssignmentPolicy "Limited Mailbox
Configuration"
```

While you can add an administrator to multiple role groups, effectively assigning cumulative permissions, the same isn't true for a role assignment policy. You can only assign a single role assignment policy to a mailbox at any given time. You can create multiple-role assignment policies for different types of users and assign an appropriate policy to a relevant mailbox object, however.

You might have previously noticed in this section the mention of Organization Management role-group members having access to *almost* all built-in management role groups. Why *almost*, and why not all when Organization Management is the top-level group of administrators for any given Exchange deployment? It is because there are certain permissions that allow administrators far-reaching access into user mailboxes, which might not be desired due to privacy reasons, or access to the diagnostics cmdlets that must be used under the direct supervision of Microsoft support staff. Roles providing access to such cmdlets are built-in, but they are not assigned to organization administrators for their use. They do, however, have the ability to assign such permissions to any group or users as needed. This is because two types of role assignments exist. One is called Regular assignment and the other is known as DelegatingOrgWide permissions. The *Regular assignment* allows the role assignee to have access to the cmdlets and parameters that are part of the management role group being assigned. The *DelegatingOrgWide permissions* allow the assignee to delegate permissions defined by the management role, but it does not provide access to cmdlets and parameters defined by the management role being delegated.

Evaluate differences between RBAC and Active Directory split permissions

When you start a new deployment of an Exchange organization, after the preparation of the organization, you might have noticed that the only member of the Organization Management group is the Active Directory account that actually prepared schema for the Exchange organization. This provides the administrator full access to Exchange objects. If an Exchange administrator is a different person, the Active Directory administrator must add the user account of an Exchange administrator to the Organization Management USG in Active Directory. The Exchange administrator can then remove the Active Directory administrator from the Organization Management group, if needed.

For organizations that want stricter separation of duties between different roles, you need to implement split permissions. *Split permissions* enable organizations to assign only relevant permissions to specific groups within the organization. The separation helps enforce appropriate access for different administrative groups, and it can help maintain accountability and change control for the environment.

The split permission in the context of an Exchange deployment typically aims at providing a distinction between the creation of security principals—such as users and groups within Active Directory—and the creation and management of Exchange-related objects—such as mailbox, which depends on the Active Directory object. In the split-permission model, only Active Directory administrators should be able to create security principals, while other administrators, such as Exchange administrators, should only be able to manage specific attributes on existing Active Directory objects.

If split permissions aren't configured during setup, the RBAC model is deployed as a shared permission model. In this configuration, Exchange administrators are allowed to create security principals in Active Directory. For example, when an Exchange administrator creates a new mailbox using the New-Mailbox cmdlet, a new user is created in Active Directory based on information provided by the Exchange administrator. After the creation of a user in Active Directory, the mailbox is created for a given user. In contrast, using Enable-Mailbox cmdlet requires that the user exist in Active Directory before the mailbox can be created.

In a default Exchange deployment where split permissions aren't configured, when preparing the organization, setup creates a USG named Exchange Windows Permissions Group, and then another USG named Exchange Trusted Subsystem is added as a member. Appropriate permissions on Active Directory are assigned, so that the Exchange Windows Permissions

Group has the ability to create and modify objects as necessary for the Exchange environment. When a new Exchange 2013 server is installed in the organization, it's added to the Exchange Trusted Subsystem group.

When an Exchange administrator launches Exchange Management Shell or uses EAC, the RBAC permissions are evaluated based on the assigned management roles. Exchange server only surfaces the cmdlets and parameters that the administrator has access to. When using Shell, this is apparent when an administrator tries to run a cmdlet that they don't have access to. If using PowerShell's tab complete feature, you might notice that the administrator is unable to tab complete a known cmdlet when they do not have access to it. If an administrator types a complete cmdlet instead, upon trying to run the cmdlet, the error suggests that the cmdlet does not exist. This is a valid error because the cmdlet might exist in the organization configuration, but it does not exist for the session established by the administrator.

When a valid cmdlet is executed by an administrator, RBAC then modifies the Exchange and the Active Directory objects as needed using the Exchange server's Active Directory account. This account has permissions on Active Directory, as previously described.

While the Active Directory administrator might have Enterprise Admin or Domain Admin permissions, they cannot modify Exchange objects unless they use Exchange Management tools and are also provided with appropriate permissions using RBAC, either by assigning management roles directly to their Active Directory user account, or by adding them to the appropriate management role groups.

Understanding these RBAC basics helps determine what changes are necessary when you need to achieve separation of roles using split permissions.

To achieve split permissions, you can use one of the two models: RBAC split permissions or Active Directory split permissions.

The *RBAC split-permissions model* modifies the default management role assignments. This is so the administrators who can create security principals in the Active Directory domain partition are separated from those who administer the Exchange organization data in the Active Directory configuration partition. This is achieved by restricting assignment of the Mail Recipient Creation and Security Group Creation and the Membership management roles. These roles provide the ability to create security principals, such as users and security groups.

These permissions are separated from the permissions required to create security principals outside the Exchange management tools. Exchange administrators who aren't assigned the Mail Recipient Creation or Security Group Creation and Membership role will not be able to create a new user of a group object in Active Directory. However, they can still modify Exchange-related attributes on existing security principals. Active Directory administrators can also use the Exchange management tools to create Active Directory security principals.

Active Directory split-permissions model is much more restrictive. The RBAC split- permissions model might be desired if third-party programs that integrate with RBAC and depend on the ability to create security principals in Active Directory are deployed. The *RBAC split-permissions model* is used when Exchange administrators are required to maintain group membership of distribution groups and role groups. Management of group membership is not possible when Active Directory split permissions are deployed.

Switching from shared permissions to RBAC split permissions is a manual process. You must remove the permissions required to create security principals from the role groups that are granted them by default. The steps you must take are similar to the following list:

1. Create a role group, which contains the Active Directory administrators that will be able to create security principals.

2. Create regular and delegating role assignments between the Mail Recipient Creation role and the new role group.

3. Create regular and delegating role assignments between the Security Group Creation and Membership role, and the new role group.

4. Remove the regular and delegating management role assignments between the Mail Recipient Creation role, and the Organization Management and Recipient Management role groups.

5. Remove the regular and delegating role assignments between the Security Group Creation and Membership role, and the Organization Management role group.

The first three steps assign permissions to a new role group that grants the ability to create and manage security principals, such as users and security groups in Active Directory using the Exchange Management tools. Steps 4 and 5 modify the existing Organization Management role group's assignments, so that they no longer have access to cmdlets that allow the creation of security principals in Active Directory. While this is a manual process, the steps achieve a similar separation effect while providing Exchange System and third-party programs to be able to create security principals when proper RBAC roles are assigned. Because delegating role assignments are also removed in Step 5, the Organization Management role will not allow Exchange administrators to grant the permissions to anyone else. Only Active Directory administrators who are members of the new role group created in Step 1 are able to assign permissions and manage memberships to the appropriate role group that allows the creation of the security principals in Active Directory.

The split permissions model of Active Directory provides much more restrictive configuration. In this model, changes are made to permissions granted to the Exchange Trusted Subsystem and Exchange servers to limit their ability to create and modify objects in Active Directory. You can implement the Active Directory split permissions when installing an Exchange server by running setup and selecting Active Directory split permissions in the wizard, or by running setup.exe from the command line and using the ActiveDirectorySplitPermissions parameter. When set to true, this parameter instructs Exchange setup to implement Active Directory split permissions. When it's set to false, it removes Active Directory split permissions if it exists. You can also run setup.exe and specify the ActiveDirectorySplitPermissions parameter after an Exchange server has already been installed. When specifying the ActiveDirectorySplitPermissions parameter during an Exchange server setup, you must also specify the PrepareAD parameter.

When Active Directory split permissions are implemented, Microsoft Exchange Protected Groups OU is created in Active Directory. After this OU is created, Exchange Windows Permissions group is moved to this OU. Exchange Trusted Subsystem, which is normally a member of Exchange Windows Permissions group, is removed from the membership. Also, the Access Control Entries (ACEs) for the Exchange Windows Permissions group that grant it the ability to create objects in Active Directory are neither added nor removed if split permissions are being implemented after the installation of Exchange server. Regular management role assignments that allow Organization Management role group members the ability to create users and manage group memberships are not created for Mail Recipient Creation and Security Group Creation and Membership management roles.

EXAM TIP

If you have co-located an Exchange server with a domain controller, the split permissions can't be enabled due to interdependencies of this unique deployment.

When implemented, Active Directory split permissions requires that Active Directory user creation, group creation, and management of group membership including security and distribution groups must be performed using Active Directory tools by an Active Directory administrator who is assigned appropriate permissions. Exchange administrators are unable to use Exchange Management tools to perform any such tasks. The only permission they have on Active Directory is the ability to manage Exchange attributes on existing Active Directory objects. For example, an Exchange administrator can create and manage a transport role object, and can create a mailbox for an existing user, but they cannot create or delete a user, or change distribution group membership.

If you are implementing Active Directory split permissions in a forest that contains multiple domains, you must also prepare every domain that will host Exchange servers, mail-enabled objects, or GC servers that can be accessed by an Exchange server. You can either use the PrepareAllDomains parameter or run setup with the PrepareDomain parameter in each domain.

Some Exchange cmdlets, such as Add-ADPermission, allow you to modify both user- and Exchange-related objects. When split permissions are implemented, the cmdlet still exists, but it fails to take action on a user object. This is because changing permissions on an Active Directory object is not allowed when split permissions are implemented. However, an Exchange administrator can use the same cmdlet to manage an Exchange object, such as a receive connector. Similarly, when using EAC, certain GUI elements might be accessible, but they will result in an error if they are used to create or modify a user, another security object, or properties in Active Directory.

Configure a custom-scoped role group

While Exchange provides many management roles and few built-in role groups that can be used to provide permissions to administer Exchange-related objects, it might not meet needs of the defined administrative job functions as it relates to each organization. Because of each organization's unique requirements, you might need to determine appropriate management roles and create an appropriate role group, as needed.

Using EAC provides an easy way to create and manage role groups. For example, if you need to create a group for help desk administrators who are able to perform more functions than allowed by the built-in help desk role group, you can do so from EAC. From EAC, select Permissions, and then Admin Roles. In the Admin Roles panel, click the + sign to create a new role group. This opens the dialog box shown in Figure 4-5.

FIGURE 4-5 Using EAC to create a new role group

Here, you need to provide the new name for the role group, its description if desired, as well as its scope, roles, and members. You can select from existing roles, either built-in or custom if one is created, add members who are performing administrative functions assigned to this role group, and the scope where they can carry out their assigned functions.

The EAC dialog box allows you to select one of the two write scopes: A *default write scope,* which represents the scope associated with roles being added, and an OU scope. You also have an option to use the drop-down box for the default write scope where you can select from other custom scopes, if they exist. The default write scope for built-in roles is Organization and OrganizationConfig.

Two different scopes are mentioned—the default write scope and the OU scope— because you have the ability to manage two different types of objects in an Exchange organization. One type of object is the recipients that reside in the domain partition of Active Directory. The other is the configuration objects that reside in the configuration partition of Active Directory. This is why each role has four different scope associations: ImplicitRecipientReadScope, ImplicitRecipientWriteScope, ImplicitConfigReadScope, and ImplicitConfigWriteScope. The read scopes cannot be changed and are always effective organization-wide. This is primarily because of the complexities of applying custom read scopes and the impact on the performance of Active Directory when such queries are frequently run. This leaves you with two scopes you can customize. A write scope for recipient objects, and a write scope you can use for configuration objects. Note that if you want to apply different scopes to the recipient and configuration objects, you must use the Shell. This is because EAC allows you to select only one scope from the drop-down menu, which it assumes has the required scope configuration for both types of the objects.

For the explicit configuration of scopes, you can create one of the three types of scopes. One is the obvious *OU scope, which* allows the assignee to modify only recipient objects within the specified OU in Active Directory.

A *recipient filter scope* is a more complex scope that can be created to encompass recipient objects that might not be located in a single OU. For example, if you want to allow management of all recipients whose department attribute matches a certain value (for example, department matches sales) throughout the entire Active Directory forest, regardless of which OU the recipient is located in, the recipient filter scope must be created as the OU scope does not contain all recipient objects.

The third type of scope is applicable to the configuration objects. This type of scope allows you to target a list of Exchange servers, a list of databases, or a filterable attribute that can allow you to define a list of servers or databases that meet the defined filter criteria, such as all Exchange servers in a specific site.

To define a custom recipient scope, you need to create an OPATH filter that uses defined filterable properties for the recipientfilter parameter. To create a scope that would apply to all recipients whose department attribute is set to Sales, you can use the following example.

```
#Create custom recipient scope that applies to users with department attribute "Sales"
New-ManagementScope -Name "Sales Users" -RecipientRestrictionFilter {Department -eq
"Sales"}
```

Figure 4-6 shows the new role-group creation dialog box, which uses the newly created scope and defines the appropriate roles that will be associated with the new role group.

FIGURE 4-6 Using EAC to create a new role group with custom write scope

Notice the roles associated with the new role group. While roles such as Mail Recipients apply to recipient objects, Databases role is also selected. Because a recipient write scope is selected, it does not apply to the Databases role. When the new role group is created, it will inherit the implicit scope defined in the built-in Databases management role. Because it is a built-in role, the scope is OrganizationConfig, which allows the role group members to manage all the database objects across the Exchange organization, while restricting their recipient-related operations to only users that match the filter criteria.

To create a custom configuration scope that matches all the databases with a name that contains Sales, you can use the following syntax:

```
#Create custom configuration scope to databases with name that contains "Sales"
New-ManagementScope -Name "Sales Databases" -DatabaseRestrictionFilter {Name -Like
"*Sales*"}
```

Notice the use of the like operator in this example, compared to the use of the eq operator in the recipient configuration scope example. When you need to find an exact match, you can use the eq operator in the filter. The word "Like" is used when you need to use a wildcard search in the filter.

When you create a scope using the database restriction filter, you cannot combine it with other filters, such as the recipient restriction filter used earlier. If you want to have the same set of administrators able to manage both the users defined by the recipient restriction filter and the databases defined by the database restriction filter, then here's what you have to do. You need to create two scopes, assign them to two separate role groups, and assign the appropriate roles to each role group. You can then add administrators to both of the role groups and the administrators have cumulative permissions allowing them to perform actions on databases and recipients' objects that are within the defined scope.

As you might have gathered, the RBAC permissions are cumulative. You can assign more than one role and role groups, so that administrators can perform different functions as their jobs require. However, what if you have a set of sensitive objects that must be managed exclusively by only a certain group of administrators?

This is what the exclusive scopes are for. You can create exclusive scopes using a similar syntax as the scopes you created earlier. You must, however, ensure the use of the Exclusive parameter when creating the exclusive scope. For example, say that Jeff is a vice president (VP) of sales and you want to create an exclusive scope for all the VPs, including Jeff. You want only Jason to manage the mailboxes and related properties for the group of VPs. You first need to create an exclusive scope. Once an exclusive scope is created, you need to create a role group as we did previously, using an exclusive scope, and then add Jason as a member of that role group. This allows Jason to manage all the VPs defined by the scope, exclusively. Also note that earlier, when a scope that encompasses all the users from the sales department was created, this scope would also include Jeff. However, administrators assigned to the role group created earlier will not be able to manage Jeff's recipient object. This is because despite having access to the object by the definition of their applicable scope, they were not assigned to the exclusive scope into which Jeff falls. Only administrators who are explicitly added to the role groups associated with the exclusive scope can manage objects that match the exclusive scope definition. The following example shows how to create an exclusive scope.

```
#Create exclusive scope for recipients whose title contains VP
New-ManagementScope -Name "VP Exclusive Scope" -RecipientRestrictionFilter {Title -like
"*VP*"} -Exclusive
```

 EXAM TIP

When creating scopes, you must account for replication delays for underlying Active Directory infrastructure. You may not see expected behavior applied to objects managed by exclusive scopes, for example, immediately after creating the exclusive scope if Active Directory replication has not completed.

Note the use of the Exclusive parameter in the previous example. When you create an exclusive scope, the objects managed by the scope become inaccessible to all Exchange administrators, including the administrators who are members of the Organization Management role group. This is because the exclusive scope requires explicit assignments. After creating an exclusive scope, until you create an assignment using a role group and add members to it, no one is explicitly assigned to the exclusive scope and it can't manage objects that fall under the exclusive scope definition. Do not forget to create appropriate role assignments after creating exclusive scopes!

Thought experiment
Principle of least privilege

In this Thought experiment, apply what you learned about this objective. You can find answers to these questions in the "Answers" section at the end of this chapter.

You are an Exchange administrator for Contoso, Ltd. Contoso is upgrading from Exchange 2007 to Exchange 2013. As part of its upgrade, Contoso wants to reevaluate current permissions assigned to administrators. The company wants to apply the principal of least privilege and apply only required permissions to administrators based on their job requirements. How would you create a list of available tasks and permissions through RBAC, and determine if you need any customizations?

Objective summary

- RBAC provides granular control over Exchange 2013 management and permissions. You can customize permissions not only based on existing roles, but also down to the level of individual cmdlets and parameters.

- Custom roles can be created by using existing roles as parents. By definition of this hierarchy, you cannot add cmdlets to a custom role if they did not exist in the parent role.

- The unscoped top-level role is an exception to the hierarchical nature of custom roles. The unscoped top-level roles have neither parent nor cmdlets associated with them. An administrator can add cmdlets and scripts to the empty role, however, they cannot assign any scope to it.

- While Exchange 2013 provides many built-in role groups and management roles, you can always customize roles to create one that meets each environment's unique needs.

- All administrative sessions using Exchange management tools leverage RBAC. They can only access the cmdlets and parameters the RBAC role assignments allow access to.

- Objects that meet the exclusive scope criteria can only be managed by administrators who have been explicitly assigned to the exclusive scope.

- You can use OPATH filters to create recipient and configuration filters. Not all Active Directory attributes can be used to create such filters. You must choose from a valid list of attributes that can be used for Exchange recipient and configuration filters.

- When using a database or server list, the management scope creation cmdlet does not validate a specified server or database names for accuracy.

Objective review

Answer the following questions to test your knowledge of the information in this objective. You can find the answers to these questions and explanations of why each answer choice is correct or incorrect in the "Answers" section at the end of this chapter.

1. You are tasked with configuring a policy that allows users to change their phone numbers, but that would not allow them to upload their photo to the user profile using OWA options. What must you do to meet the requirements?

   A. Create a new role that includes the Set-User cmdlet and assign it to users.

   B. Create a new role that includes Set-Mailbox cmdlet and assign it to users.

   C. Remove the Set-UserPhoto cmdlet from the default role-assignment policy.

   D. Create a new role assignment policy that includes the appropriate cmdlets and assign it to the user mailbox.

2. You are an Exchange administrator. Your account is member of Organization Management role group. You need to export a mailbox for legal discovery. What must you do?

   A. Create a role group and associate the Mailbox Import Export role. Add your mailbox to the newly created role group. Export the mailbox using the appropriate cmdlet.

   B. Run the Export-Mailbox cmdlet to export the mailbox.

   C. Run the New-MailboxExportRequest cmdlet to export the mailbox.

   D. Add your administrator account to the Discovery Management role group. Export the mailbox.

3. You are planning for RBAC permissions. Which of the following can be achieved with RBAC? Choose all that apply.

   A. North America helpdesk should only be able to view users located in the OU named NA.

   B. North America helpdesk users should be able to reset password for users located in the OU named NA.

   C. North America helpdesk users should not be able to modify executive users located in the OU named NA.

   D. North America helpdesk users should be able to move a user mailbox to a database named NA Users only if the user is located in OU named NA.

Objective 4.4: Design an appropriate Exchange solution for a given SLA

Successful adoption and effectiveness of any Exchange deployment depends on an organization's ability to plan, deploy, and maintain the solution based on a standards-based approach. Any solution is dependent on technology, underlying infrastructure, and the human element.

Technology can provide innovative solutions to age-old problems. Exchange 2013 provides multiple new features that can help increase both uptime and user productivity, as well as help identify and stop costly data leaks by utilizing Data Loss Prevention (DLP) features. All the features, by themselves, cannot provide effective solution until it is paired with appropriate hardware. You must deploy an appropriate amount of servers to provide redundancy and, during failures, provide uninterrupted service to users without degrading the performance to the point where the service becomes unusable. And then there is the human element. An administrator can only be as effective as he is knowledgeable about the solution, and he must have appropriate access to the environment to be able to effectively manage it.

When a solution is deployed without agreement and understanding between IT and its users, this usually results in friction between the two groups. The IT department might deploy the Exchange environment based on their knowledge of best practices or available budget to purchase required components. Users might be expecting a different set of features or higher availability, all without a formal agreement and understanding of the business requirement. IT departments do not have an unlimited budget and uninterrupted availability comes at a cost. The same applies to user expectations about the size of their mailbox or the IT department's ability to restore data after the user discovers it was lost. The agreement among users, business leaders, and the IT department in the form of service level agreements (SLAs) provides formal agreements that outline features provided by the deployed solution, the expected availability requirements, the ability to recover data in a given timeframe, and from a certain time period. The SLAs might also have to be drafted based on regulatory and compliance requirements.

This objective focuses on Exchange 2013 features that can help provide uninterrupted services, while meeting SLA requirements governing the Exchange deployment. While the features and functionality of Exchange 2013 are already covered in other objectives in this book, this objective focuses on when to utilize a particular set of functionality offered by Exchange 2013 for given SLA requirements.

> **This objective covers how to:**
> - Plan for change management and updates
> - Design a solution that meets SLA requirements around scheduled downtime
> - Design a solution that meets SLA requirements around RPO/RTO
> - Design a solution that meets SLA requirements around message delivery

Plan for change management and updates

Change management most commonly requires an administrator to document the change before it is made. The documentation requires the details of the nature of the change, the steps being taken to implement the change, and the way to identify any risks to the solution if the change does not go as planned. The change management process also serves as a historical reference, if needed.

When you're thinking of an Exchange deployment, depending on what you are changing, the change might be reversible. For example, if you made a change to a transport configuration, so an attachment larger than 25 MB is not allowed to be sent, it can be changed to a different size limit in the future, if necessary. In contrast, what if you were to upgrade a database availability group (DAG) member to the latest Service Pack of an underlying OS and move a database to an upgraded DAG member? You can't move the database back to a DAG member who isn't running the same Service Pack or later for an underlying OS. This is because changes made to the database are irreversible when it is moved to a newer version of the OS.

When documenting procedures for change management, you should account for such items because it not only serves as a reference point in the future, but it also provides administrators a critical reference point during the change window. This helps to ensure the proper steps are followed to avoid potentially disastrous situations.

When updating Exchange 2013 servers, cumulative updates (CUs) differ from update rollups and Service Packs of previous versions of the Exchange server. This is because any CU for Exchange 2013 server is a full installation package. When installing a CU, the Exchange server is uninstalled from the server, and then the new CU installation is performed. This would be similar to new install process, including updates to schema if necessary. The difference, however, is that the server configuration exists in Active Directory, which the update uses during the install and it retains any previous configuration settings that are stored in Active Directory. If, however, you made any changes to the configuration files on the server itself, or changed the OWA theme files, it will be lost. You must have a process in place for any such changes that might need to be accounted for anytime an Exchange update is applied.

You must also account for the times when CU installation is interrupted or doesn't complete successfully. In such occurrences, the server is left without the Exchange server installation on it. You must run setup.exe with the recoverserver switch to install the Exchange server. You might also need to address any underlying issues that might have caused the CU installation to fail in the first place.

When you are applying updates to a server, it is not available to serve any users, however, it still exists in the Exchange organization configuration. To avoid issues, you must also take appropriate actions on the Exchange server before you apply updates, so that the server is properly put in maintenance mode. Managed availability cmdlets are handy because they can mark Exchange server workloads as inactive and ensure clients are not referred to a server that is marked as inactive.

You must also ensure that enough capacity is planned for servers that will host the databases and users during planned maintenance. When a DAG is designed, the maintenance of a node is equivalent to the failure of a node. The remaining servers of a DAG must be able to serve the users without degradation of service below acceptable levels, which might be defined by SLAs.

Design a solution that meets SLA requirements around scheduled downtime

Most SLAs account for scheduled downtime and expectations around the scheduled downtime. In today's environment, most deployments implement high availability and redundancy in their Exchange 2013 infrastructure. This allows for scheduled maintenance to take place without an interruption to users.

When accounting for different Exchange 2013 roles and functionality, you must account for each of the roles, and ensure the redundancy is planned and implemented appropriately. When starting the scheduled maintenance on a server, you should make sure that the server workloads are put in maintenance mode using managed availability cmdlets.

Before you start maintenance on a Client Access server (CAS), you can set the server to inactive, so that it stops servicing client connections. When a load balance is configured to the user healthcheck page created by managed availability, setting the server in maintenance is also reflected in the healthcheck page. A load balancer should then update the server pool accordingly, so that no new service requests are sent to the server placed in maintenance. It is also recommended to drain client connections on the load balancer before putting the server in maintenance, so that there is no abrupt disconnection experienced by clients. The connection draining process on the load balancer can take some time because it waits for the client to complete ongoing transactions and close the session. New sessions from the same clients are distributed to other servers, but not to the server being drained. To put a CAS in maintenance, you can issue the following syntax.

```
#Set Client Access Server in maintenance
Set-ServerComponentState -Component ServerWideOffline -State Inactive -Requester
Maintenance
```

For a Mailbox server or a multirole server, you need to account for more workloads than you did on CAS. A Mailbox server is almost always busy sending and receiving email messages. Before performing maintenance, you should ensure that the transport queue is emptied and the server isn't receiving additional messages while the queues are being drained. To do so, you can use the following syntax.

```
#Drain the transport queues on a Mailbox server
Set-ServerComponentState -Component HubTransport -State Draining -Requester Maintenance
```

While the previous cmdlet stops accepting new connections and starts draining queues, you must wait and monitor the queues to make sure they are empty before you can start maintenance on the server. To expedite the process, you can use the Redirect-Message cmdlet to redirect all the existing messages from the server queue to a different server. This simply moves all messages from the queue to a different server, instead of trying to deliver the messages to its destinations to empty the queue. This might or might not always be a best option. This is because the time it takes to transfer the messages to the target server depends on the network connectivity to the target server and how busy the target server is. The following example redirects the existing messages to the defined target server.

```
#Redirect messages to a mailbox server
Redirect-Message -Server <Source Server FQDN> -Target <Target Server FQDN>
```

If the server is a member of DAG, you need to ensure that the server is not used to host Primary Active Manager (PAM) and if it is currently hosted on the server, it is moved to a different server. This can be achieved by suspending the cluster node. Next, you should move any database copies hosted on the server to a different server in the DAG. Finally, configure the server to block any further database activations in case of simultaneous maintenance or failures of other members in the DAG. The following cmdlets are an example of how you can perform the previously mentioned steps.

```
#Suspend cluster node, move active databases to different DAG member and block
activation
Suspend-ClusterNode
Set-MailboxServer -DatabaseCopyActivationDisabledAndMoveNow $true
Set-MailboxServer -DatabaseCopyAutoActivationPolicy Blocked
```

Or, you can use the script provided with the Exchange server. The script StartDagServer-Maintenance.ps1 is available in the scripts directory on the Exchange server, which you can access by issuing cd $exscripts on the Exchange Management Shell. The benefit of using the script is this: if any failures are detected in the previous steps, then all the steps, except moving the databases, are rolled back.

If you configured Unified Messaging (UM) and it is actively in use, you should also put the UM component in maintenance by draining the UM calls.

```
#Drain UM calls
Set-ServerComponentState -Component UMCallRouter -State Draining -Requester Maintenance
```

After ensuring that the transport queues are empty and the databases are moved to a different server in the DAG, you can set the entire server in maintenance mode by using ServerWideOffline as shown in the following example.

```
Set-ServerComponentState -Component ServerWideOffline -State Inactive -Requester
Maintenance
```

When maintenance is complete, the server can be put back in service by reversing the changes made previously. When doing so, ensure that the requester is the same that was used to put the server in maintenance. You must use the same requester to set the server out from an inactive state to an active state. For DAG members, you can use the StopDagServerMaintenance.ps1 script. The following syntax can be used to bring the server out of maintenance.

```
#Activate a Client Access Server or a Mailbox server
Set-ServerComponentState -Component ServerWideOffline -State Active -Requester
Maintenance
#Resume cluster node, and allow database activation on the mailbox server
Resume-ClusterNode
Set-MailboxServer -DatabaseCopyActivationDisabledAndMoveNow $false
Set-MailboxServer -DatabaseCopyAutoActivationPolicy Unrestricted
#Activate transport on a Mailbox server
Set-ServerComponentState -Component HubTransport -State Active -Requester Maintenance
#Activate Unified Messaging on a mailbox server
```

```
Set-ServerComponentState -Component UMCallRouter -State Active -Requester Maintenance
```

Managing servers properly by using available cmdlets or scripts can improve availability during scheduled maintenance and avoid accidental activation attempts on servers being maintained. This results in better user experience and service availability.

Design a solution that meets SLA requirements around Recovery Point Objective/Recovery Time Objective

When a problem is identified with a database copy or a user reports corruption or an accidental loss of mailbox data, administrators must resort to some sort of restore mechanism. Depending on the deployed Exchange 2013 features, you can improve response times and reduce the time it takes to restore the requested data. SLAs determine the expected maximum time to restore the data, known as Recovery Time Objective (RTO), and from how far back in the past the data can be restored, known as Recovery Point Objective (RPO). When drafting the SLAs, Exchange engineers should communicate realistic expectations based on the available hardware configuration and software functionality. These expectations should include Exchange 2013 features, such as single item recovery, legal hold and lagged database copy features, as well as the cost of associated hardware due to storage, processing, and other requirements. Ultimately, a good SLA can help strike the balance among realistic user expectations, compliance to regulatory requirements, and the cost of implementing technology to meet outlined requirements. The selection of features and functionality from different vendors make a considerable difference in the cost of deploying the solution, as well as meeting RPO/RTO requirements.

Single item recovery can provide a speedy recovery of accidental data loss. An administrator can completely eliminate the need of restoring data from backup if the deletion is within the configured retention period. The time to restore the data can sometimes be reduced from days to minutes.

Combined with the legal hold feature, single item recovery can provide recovery of data reaching as far back in the past as the date when the mailbox was put on legal hold using Exchange-provided functionality. It certainly comes at a cost of retaining additional data for a given user mailbox beyond quotas that might have been defined for your mailboxes.

For database corruption and other data loss situations you can also use lagged database copies. While it can only go as far back as maximum of 14 days, if the scope of recovery falls within the maximum limit, recovering a database can still be must faster compared to restoring from tapes. Database copies located in different datacenter can serve as a point of recovery when there is a disaster affecting main site.

The procedures associated with single item recovery, lagged database copy activation, and database restore are covered earlier in Chapter 2, "Install, configure, and manage the mailbox role."

Design a solution that meets SLA requirements around message delivery

SLAs for any Exchange environment should also cover the availability of transport components. The usual SLA requirements address the functionality, such as the guaranteed delivery of messages, the continued service of transport features during a planned or unplanned outage, and messaging hygiene.

Exchange deployments should account for higher availability for external mailflow using multiple ingress endpoints. This usually translates to deploying multiple edge transport of CAS/Mailbox server roles. It also translates to ensuring multiple MX records are configured in external DNS, so the senders can use standard SMTP logic and functionality to work around failures and still be able to deliver messages successfully. A load balancer to provide high availability to SMTP mail flow is also an option that many organizations deploy.

Exchange 2013 also introduces changes in how new transport functionality addresses redundancy. Safety Net functionality in Exchange 2013 improves on and replaces transport dumpster functionality from Exchange 2010. DAG dependency is removed, providing benefits of transport dumpster functionality when DAG is not deployed. Safety Net also guarantees message redundancy, instead of providing best effort redundancy, which was the case in Exchange 2010.

EXAM TIP

Because of changes in Exchange 2013 transport functionality and guaranteed message redundancy by Safety Net, you cannot configure the maximum size for Safety Net. You can only configure how long the messages are kept in Safety Net before automatic deletion.

During recovery situations, Safety Net can be leveraged to request the replay of messages for a specific time period. This can be useful when activating a lagged copy or restoring a database from tape.

Load balancing of internal mail delivery is automatic, based on the target delivery group. If multiple servers are available in the target delivery group, messages are sent in round-robin fashion to available servers without dependency on the external load balancing mechanism.

To provide higher availability and redundancy to outbound mail delivery, multiple outbound connectors do not serve as redundant, highly available routes. However, you can configure connectors to use smart hosts, which can be configured as MX records in DNS. This configuration ensures that a failed smart host is not used for outbound mail delivery. This method does not require manual intervention when a smart host is unavailable for outbound mail delivery.

Transport moderation and transport rules allow you to meet compliance and DLP requirements. They are designed to protect sensitive information from unauthorized access, both from within the organization and from external communications.

Thought experiment

RPO and RTO considerations

In this Thought experiment, apply what you learned about this objective. You can find answers to these questions in the "Answers" section at the end of this chapter.

You are planning an Exchange 2013 deployment for your client, Contoso, Ltd. Contoso wants to deploy a backup solution that can meet a one-hour RPO and a two-hour RTO requirement. They also want to meet the same requirement in case of a disaster at a primary site.

What factors should you consider to help meet the requirements?

Objective summary

- A change management process provides a sounding board to proposed changes, discusses risks associated with the proposed changes, and provides remediation or back out plans in case of failure to implement proposed changes.

- Built-in Exchange server functionality, such as Managed Availability cmdlets, maintenance mode scripts, and database copies can help meet availability requirements defined by SLAs during scheduled maintenance or unexpected failures.

- Single item recovery, legal hold, and lagged database copies can help reduce the time to recover from accidental deletions and data corruption. In case of database corruption, the time to recover the database can be reduced if the recovery period can be met by a maximum configurable lag of 14 days.

- Safety Net is improved over the transport dumpster functionality of Exchange 2010. Safety Net aims to provide guaranteed message redundancy compared to the best effort redundancy offered by Exchange 2010.

Objective review

Answer the following questions to test your knowledge of the information in this objective. You can find the answers to these questions and explanations of why each answer choice is correct or incorrect in the "Answers" section at the end of this chapter.

1. SLA requires you to guarantee mailbox availability for all users during scheduled maintenance or unexpected failures. All Exchange servers are multirole servers. DAG is deployed. You are planning to perform maintenance on one of the mailbox servers. Which steps must you take? Select all that apply.

   A. On load balancer, drain connections to the server.

   B. Drain hub transport.

   C. Run Redirect-Message cmdlet.

    D. Run StartDagServerMaintenance.ps1.

    E. Set ServerWideOffline to inactive.

2. You need to plan for SLAs that require the ability to restore from database corruption if corruption is detected within 10 days. The solution must reduce the time required to restore from backup, while reducing the cost. Which solution must you implement?

    A. Lagged database copies.

    B. VSS Shadow copy backups.

    C. Tape-based backup and restore solution.

    D. Offsite synchronous database copies using a third-party solution.

3. You are installing the latest CU on an Exchange 2013 server. You deployed a custom logon page for OWA. You also configured OWA integration with Lync IM. What must you do to ensure the existing functionality isn't affected after CU is applied? (Choose all that apply.)

    A. Edit the web.config file.

    B. Edit the OWA logon page to include customization.

    C. Set the OWA Mailbox policy.

    D. Run the Enable-CsTopology cmdlet.

Answers

This section contains the solutions to the Thought experiments and answers to the Objective review questions in this chapter.

Objective 4.1: Thought experiment

1. TPC needs to have at least one MX record pointing to their Exchange environment. They probably already have this because they are currently using Exchange. They should also investigate adding SPF records to ensure the correct outbound mail flow. They should verify that they have, or can add, all the records required for client access, including Autodiscover, as well.

2. You should evaluate the number of GC servers that TPC has deployed, their locations, and their CPU sizing to ensure that their Active Directory deployment can support the planned Exchange design. In addition, you should plan to check their Active Directory site design to make sure that it is correct and that it reflects how you want mail to be routed.

Objective 4.1: Review

1. **Correct answer**: D

   A. **Incorrect**: Allowing Active Directory replication to finish after updating the schema is necessary, but there's no fixed waiting period.

   B. **Incorrect**: You cannot proceed with installing Exchange until you finish preparing the schema, Active Directory, and domains.

   C. **Incorrect**: You cannot prepare domains until after the Active Directory preparation step is completed.

   D. **Correct**: After you prepare the schema, you must next prepare Active Directory using the /PrepareAD switch.

2. **Correct answers**: A, B, and C

   A. **Correct**: Converting the existing domain controller into a GC helps protect you against network outages that might otherwise keep the servers in Flint from working.

   B. **Correct**: Huntsville currently has a single GC. Converting the other domain controller to a GC will provide redundancy.

   C. **Correct**: Adding a GC in the Flint site will provide redundancy.

   D. **Incorrect**: Exchange cannot use read-only domain controllers, so adding one in the Flint site doesn't help.

3. **Correct answer**: C

   A. **Incorrect**: It's unlikely that an intermittent failure would happen consistently at the right time, and enough times, to cause the reported symptoms.

   B. **Incorrect**: If the network adapters on the server had bad DNS settings, or those servers weren't responding, other programs such as Internet Explorer on the affected server wouldn't work properly either.

   C. **Correct**: A send connector always uses its own connector-specific DNS settings if they exist, so if those settings are wrong the connector will be unable to deliver messages.

   D. **Incorrect**: If the connector had the wrong address space on it, messages that didn't match the address space would be delivered over another connector.

Objective 4.2: Thought experiment

If multiple users on a single server are complaining about poor performance, you might immediately assume that it's a problem with the server. Do not forget, however, that the users might have other things in common (such as poor network connectivity from their work site to the server) besides just the server. You want to check the server itself to see whether it is basically healthy and that its usage of RAM, CPU, network, and disk I/O is not excessive. It might just be overloaded. Checking the workload monitoring counters and the IIS logs can help identify whether individual workloads are going over budget.

Objective 4.2: Review

1. **Correct answer**: C

   A. **Incorrect**: Transaction log stalls occur when writes to the transaction logs take excessive time. Stalls tend to be short-lived and sporadic, and they probably wouldn't occur consistently at the same time each day.

   B. **Incorrect:** While this might be a possible cause, it's not the most likely cause given that no other users have complained.

   C. **Correct**: Because the default global-throttling policy includes rate limits on sending email, this is probably the cause of the user's performance complaint.

   D. **Incorrect:** While this might be a possible cause, it's not the most likely cause given that no other users have complained.

2. **Correct answer**: C

   A. **Incorrect**: Changing RBAC permissions lets you limit who can perform searches, but not how many keywords they can use.

   B. **Incorrect:** Microsoft recommends against changing the default policy. If you do, you'll change the limits for all users, not just the ones whose limits you want changed.

    C.   **Correct:** This is the best solution because it doesn't require changes to the default policy.

    D.   **Incorrect:** You can't remove the global user-throttling policy.

3.   **Correct answer**: A

    A.   **Correct**: Raising the RechargeRate increases the speed at which the user's resource usage is credited, lowering the time they spend in a throttled state.

    B.   **Incorrect:** The CutoffBalance setting controls when the users' work is throttled, so changing it won't have any effect on the speed at which their performance returns to normal.

    C.   **Incorrect:** Raising the RechargeRate in the global policy increases the speed at which all users' resource usage is credited, not just the ones subject to the policy you defined.

    D.   **Incorrect:** This is a dangerous approach because, with no limits set, users might exceed the amount of resource usage for the workload.

Objective 4.3: Thought experiment

To meet Contoso's requirements, you need to create a mapping of a required set of permissions for each group of administrators. You need to map their job functions to existing management roles and cmdlets they provide access to. You also need to create a definition of scopes that allow administrators the ability to manage only the objects that fall within their scope of the job definition. You might also need to determine if the built-in management roles provide more, less, or just the right access to the cmdlets and parameters that the administrators need to perform their job duties effectively. Providing more access by using the built-in management roles might violate the principal of least privilege, whereas using a built-in management role that does not contain all cmdlets and parameters might hinder the administrator's ability to do their job effectively.

Start with analyzing the built-in roles and their associated cmdlets and parameters. Identify which cmdlets are required for a given job function and if there are cmdlets that are not required. Create custom roles if you need to remove cmdlets and parameters from built-in roles, as Exchange does not allow the modification of built-in roles. Create custom scopes if the inheritance of an implicit organization scope provides more access to administrators than their job function requires. Also, create custom role groups to associate custom roles and custom scopes. Add administrators to one or more role groups, as needed, to provide them with the appropriate access through RBAC.

Objective 4.3: Review

1. **Correct answer**: D

   A. **Incorrect**: You must use role assignment policy if changes need to be made by the user to their own properties.

   B. **Incorrect**: You must use role assignment policy if changes need to be made by user to their own properties.

   C. **Incorrect**: Default role assignment policy allows users to change their contact information and phone numbers. While removing the ability to change the photo meets the stated requirements, you cannot change built-in roles associated with the default policy.

   D. **Correct**: Creating a new policy with the appropriate roles and assigning it to the user mailbox meets the stated requirements.

2. **Correct answer:** A

   A. **Correct**: The regular assignment for Mailbox Import Export role isn't created by default for Organization Management role group. You must create regular assignment to the existing or new role group. Members of that role group can then use the mailbox import export cmdlets.

   B. **Incorrect**: The Export-Mailbox cmdlet does not exist in Exchange 2013, but it is a valid cmdlet for Exchange 2007 servers.

   C. **Incorrect**: The New-MailboxExportRequest cmdlet is the correct cmdlet, but administrators don't have access to the cmdlet by default.

   D. **Incorrect**: The Discovery Management role group provides the ability to perform mailbox searches. You can also export data returned by search, however, you don't have access to cmdlets that allow you to export the entire mailbox.

3. **Correct answers:** B, C, and D

   A. **Incorrect**: You cannot restrict recipient or configuration read scopes using RBAC.

   B. **Correct**: You can set the recipient scope to an OU. With the appropriate role assignments, you can allow stated functionality.

   C. **Correct**: With the exclusive scopes, you can restrict administrators from modifying objects that are within their assigned scope, but that they do not have explicit access to.

   D. **Correct**: You can achieve stated functionality by assigning two role groups with the appropriate recipient and configuration scope assigned to each.

Objective 4.4: Thought experiment

The requirement states the RPO of one hour and the RTO of two hours. The requirement also states the same RPO/RTO should be met if the primary site fails. In such a scenario, you need to deploy a solution that not only backs up data at least once an hour, but is also capable of restoring data in less than two hours. Volume Shadow Copy Service (VSS)-based backup solutions can possibly meet the stated requirements. Lagged copies might also meet the requirements based on when the failure is detected, the amount of logs that need to be replayed, and the underlying hardware capabilities. DAG can be deployed spanning multiple sites. Selected backup solution also needs to backup data from the database copy in the remote site to meet the requirement of failure at the primary site.

The most important consideration here is the RPO/RTO time requirements. The cost impact can be considerable due to solutions required for VSS backup, additional and possibly fast storage, as well as the remote site deployment of DAG members. Above all, the very short time requirements might be unrealistic from a practical standpoint and the driving factors might need to be discussed. Often, a discussion of seemingly unrealistic SLA requirements might bring the realization of cost, other impacts, and possible change to the SLA requirement for a more realistic solution.

Objective 4.4: Review

1. **Correct answers:** A, B, D, and E

   A. **Correct:** Drain connections on the load balancer to avoid distributing traffic to the server when it's under maintenance.

   B. **Correct:** Drain the hub transport to the complete delivery of pending messages and to stop receiving new connections during the draining and maintenance period.

   C. **Incorrect:** Redirecting messages to a different target server is an optimization step, but it is not a requirement.

   D. **Correct:** Run StartDagServerMaintenance.ps1 to move databases and PAM to another DAG member, and to avoid activations on the server during maintenance.

   E. **Correct:** Set ServerWideOffline to ensure all the server workloads are unavailable during maintenance.

2. **Correct answer:** A

   A. **Correct:** Lagged copies meet the stated requirements.

   B. **Incorrect:** VSS shadow copy backups can meet the time requirements, but they are not a cost-effective solution compared to lagged copies.

   C. **Incorrect:** The tape-based backup and restore solution cannot meet the stated cost requirements.

   D. **Incorrect:** The offsite synchronous database copies using a third-party solution cannot meet the stated cost requirements.

3. **Correct answers:** A and B

   A. Correct: The web.config file is replaced during CU installation and must be edited to include IMCertificateThumbprint and IMServerName values. This is required for OWA integration with Lync IM.

   B. Correct: The custom OWA logon page is replaced by CU installation and must be edited after the CU install to restore customizations.

   C. Incorrect: The OWA mailbox policy configuration is stored in Active Directory and is not replaced by the CU installation.

   D. Incorrect: Lync topology isn't affected by the CU installation and the cmdlet Enable-CsTopology does not need to be run again after the CU installation.

Index

Symbols

5xx SMTP error 259
-AuthMechanism 225
-DomainSecureEnabled 225
-ForceFullSync switch 218
/IAcceptExchangeServerLicenseTerms switch 20
/NewProvisionedServer switch 22
–OABGen $True parameter 27
/PrepareAllDomains switch 282
*-ResourcePolicy cmdlet 286
/TargetDir switch 69
"*" wildcard 236
-WorkloadManagementPolicy cmdlet 286
*-WorkloadPolicy cmdlet 286

A

ABPs. *See* Address Book Policies (ABPs)
accepted domains
   authoritative 196, 230
   configuring 229–231
   creation of 229
   defined 196
   external relay 197
   internal relay 196
AcceptMessagesOnlyFromDLMembers parameter 33
AcceptMessagesOnlyFrom parameter 33
AcceptMessagesOnlyFromSendersOrMembers
   parameter 33
Access Control Entries (ACEs) 302
access rules
   allow/block/quarantine (ABQ) process 136–145
   creating 141–142
   for users 143–145
   managing device 138–143
ACEs. *See* Access Control Entries (ACEs)

Action Reject parameter 262
Action SilentDelete parameter 262
Action Strip parameter 262
Active Directory
   deployment planning 272–274
   distribution lists and 76–77
   domain controllers 19, 273
   Edge subscription object in 209
   GC servers 272–273
   impact of Exchange on 271–284
   install path from 69
   mailbox server roles deployment 19–22
   message routing 185, 193–195
   permissions 293
   preparing for Exchange 279–282
   site link costs 195
   site topology 273
   SPF records 277–279
   split permissions 21, 299–302
   tools 20
Active Directory Domain Services (AD DS) 271
Active Directory Federated Services (AD FS) 123
Active Directory Lightweight Directory Services
   (AD LDS) 208
Active Directory Rights Management Services
   (AD RMS) 202
ActiveDirectorySplitPermissions parameter 301
Active Manager 54
ActiveSync 102–104
ActiveSyncEnabled parameter 170
AdapterEnabled parameter 276
Add-ADPermission cmdlet 76, 302
Add-AttachmentFilterEntry cmdlet 262
Add-ContentFilterPhrase cmdlet 258
Add-DatabaseAvailabilityGroupServer cmdlet 41, 70
Add-IPAllowListProvider cmdlet 254
Add-IPBlockListProvider cmdlet 254

G

H

U

About the authors

 PAUL ROBICHAUX Paul got his first computer at age 8 and quickly developed the bad habit of spending time with it instead of playing outside. Over his career, he eventually learned the value of exercise and the great outdoors, but he still spends an inordinate amount of time tinkering with computers and networks for his customers. Along the way, he's worked as a software developer, instructor, and consultant, written several books, earned his pilot's license, and started running triathlons. Paul was awarded the Microsoft Most Valuable Professional (MVP) award for Exchange for 11 years running, and in 2014 he was inducted into the Exchange Hall of Fame. As a principal architect at Summit 7 Systems, Paul focuses on Office 365, Exchange Server, and Lync.

 BHARGAV SHUKLA A structural engineer by education, Bhargav Shukla discovered his attraction to computers during his computer technology education at college. The choice was clear when he had to choose between a Masters in Civil Engineering and a Microsoft Certified Systems Engineer certification. The rest is a blur. Over the past 20 years, he has amassed experience with multiple products and platforms, but never letting his first love for Exchange fade. Ever since his Microsoft Mail days, he has been fascinated with the power of messaging and has kept up with the ever-changing world of the Exchange Server platform. He holds the prestigious Microsoft Certified Solutions Master (MCSM) certification in Exchange 2013 and is a Microsoft Most Valuable Professional (MVP). Bhargav currently works at KEMP Technologies as Director of Technology. He is also a founder of and active contributor to the Philadelphia UC User Group.